PRENTICE-HALL
FOUNDATIONS OF CATHOLIC THEOLOGY SERIES

9727

FOUNDATIONS OF CATHOLIC THEOLOGY SERIES

Gerard S. Sloyan, *Editor*

THE IMAGE OF GOD
IN CREATION

SISTER M. CHARLES BORROMEO MUCKENHIRN, CSC

Dunbarton College of the Holy Cross
Washington, D.C.

PRENTICE-HALL, INC.
Englewood Cliffs, N.J.

1963

Nihil obstat:

W. Urban Voll, OP
Censor Deputatus

Imprimatur:

✠ Patrick A. O'Boyle, DD
Archbishop of Washington

January 16, 1963

The *nihil obstat* and *imprimatur* are official
declarations that a book or pamphlet is free
of doctrinal or moral error. No implication is
contained therein that those who have granted
the *nihil obstat* and *imprimatur* agree with
the content, opinions, or statements expressed.

PRENTICE-HALL INTERNATIONAL, INC., *London*
PRENTICE-HALL OF AUSTRALIA, PTY., LTD., *Sydney*
PRENTICE-HALL OF CANADA, LTD., *Toronto*
PRENTICE-HALL FRANCE, S.A.R.L., *Paris*
PRENTICE-HALL OF JAPAN, INC., *Tokyo*
PRENTICE-HALL DE MEXICO, S.A., *Mexico City*

C

EDITOR'S NOTE

This series offers the depth and richness of the divine message of salvation proclaimed to us by Christ. The theology, or "faith seeking understanding," contained here is not on a catechetical level, nor yet on a complex, higher level; it is clear and nontechnical, but at the same time adult and thorough. It is a scholarly presentation of revelation.

These volumes do not adopt an apologetic approach. They

neither attempt to justify Catholic faith nor aim at convincing those who do not profess it of the reasonableness of believing. This series is written primarily for those who already believe, who accept the Church as the living continuation of Christ, and the Scriptures as divinely inspired.

The authors do not attempt a philosophy of God or of Christianity, but a study of the mystery of God seen through the eyes of faith. The mystery of faith will not be dispelled by the study of these books. It will remain.

Since some background in philosophy on the part of the reader is needed, and cannot in every case be presumed, there are times when philosophical terms will need to be explained. Philosophical reasoning is very much a part of speculative theology.

Although the breakdown of the series is along traditional lines, each volume is designed to emphasize the oneness of God's plan of salvation and not its different facets. Distinction is made in order to unite. What is taught in the Scriptures is stressed, so that it may be seen how men of the Bible understood the message entrusted to them. The historical aspects of doctrine as held by Christians are then treated: the testimony of the early Christian writers and the liturgy to the belief of the Church; the controversies and heresies that necessitated defense and precise formulation, and finally, the magisterial teaching in each subject area. In this way speculative theology, or the present understanding of each mystery, is not seen in isolation from the sources of faith.

Thus, the revealed Christian message is viewed as the *tradition* (in the fullest and best sense of that theological term) expressed in and through the Church over the centuries—more explicitly formulated, from age to age, and with further applications. But it is still the same saving message begun in the Old Testament and perfected in the mystery and person of Jesus Christ.

One last point is important. Although the study of theology is an exercise of intellect, it can never be exclusively this. The message of Jesus Christ is a living Word, an invitation to participate in the saving event of the redemption, starting in this world by faith and the union of grace, and culminating in heaven by vision and immediate union. This invitation demands response or living faith. The study of the Christian message through theology requires such response, for the message is not something that was heard and assented to once. It is a Word addressed to us that requires our vigorous "Yes" for a lifetime.

CONTENTS

vii

THE IMAGE OF GOD
IN CREATION

INTRODUCTION

God spoke and the universe began to exist. By his power and love he sustains it and guides it to its eternal destiny in him. The purpose of this volume is not to examine the mystery of God's creative act, but to understand more deeply its effects— the created universe in which we live. The ancients were aware of the complexity of the world and its variety. Modern man is constantly dazed by it, through his discoveries in chemistry, nuclear physics, mathematics, psychology, earth and space exploration.

God has revealed the unity of being and direction which underlies the magnitude of created reality. The Church teaches men this essential truth; without it human study can lead to confusion and atomization of knowledge. What precisely are these fundamental insights which contribute to a complete view of the meaning and destiny of the universe? The most basic one is the sense in which the entire creation, from God's point of view, is a unified reality ordered to one end, his own eternal glory. The entire created universe is somehow a great utterance of God, manifesting his goodness and beauty.

Next it is necessary to see that there is a deeply graven hierarchy of created being. This order proceeds ascendingly from material being, through man who is matter animated by spirit, to the majestic spirits who worship before God's throne and enter intimately into human destiny.

For several reasons the largest portion of this volume will be devoted to revealed truth about man. It is man whose destiny is still in balance, man on whom history bears; it is for man that the God who created him entered the human family with a redemptive purpose. Since we are human beings we are most involved personally in the ultimate meaning of this creature. God has revealed to man that he is literally central in the cosmic plan, that he has been commanded to subdue and perfect the earth and to seek a final goal in common with the angelic spirits.

There are many reasons which make particularly pertinent today a volume on creation and its rich variety of being. For the nonbeliever, who dominates large segments of our culture, the spirit world does not exist. Reality is more and more defined in terms of what is perceptible to sense knowledge, experimentation, usefulness. Angels have been relegated to the museum of myth, child's fable, touching relic of medieval simplicity. Bad as this is with regard to denying the angels of light, it obviously opens wide the field of action for the powers of evil. The latter not only exist but do the most damage when they are disbelieved in, for then they go unrecognized. The eternal destiny of good and evil men is permanently interwoven with the reality and power of good and evil spirits. The mutual working out of the eternal pattern by creatures in the two camps is the stuff of history—from God's point of view.

The almost universal disbelief in a spirit-world creates havoc among Christians with regard to the spirituality of the human soul. The more materialized a person's thought becomes, the more difficult it is for him to grasp even obliquely his own spirit with its activity of knowing and loving. Human freedom finds its intellectual bases wobbly. Commitment to a determinism of the individual by bodily drives and emotional urges becomes an increasing danger. Without an understanding of himself as spirit just as truly as he is matter, man cannot begin to understand his own nature with its intrinsic tension and potential harmonization. He tends to capitulate to the one element in himself of which he is most immediately aware.

A solid and unequivocal yet inspiring theology of man is a crying need in our times. Many seem to have despaired of any possible answer to the question of the meaning and destiny of the human family. Despite the terror and disgust that mark the modern mentality, there remains a powerful resistance to the traditional Christian wisdom about man—to the believer, an eternal wisdom. Sometimes this resistance is based on a spirit of pride and rebellion. Often, however, the Christian must admit that persons in search of ultimate values are presented with a caricature of God's revelation. How often has someone been heard to say in absolute earnestness, "But how can the fact that someone ate an apple cause war and inhumanity in the world?"

The great doctrines testified to in the first pages of the Bible must be understood and shared by believers in such a way that the relevance of these truths will stand forth in the light of God's plan of love and salvation. This volume aims, then, at a presentation of the fundamental revealed truths about created beings. Their destiny was communicated by God to the human race in his incarnate Son. It is transmitted to men through the Church until the end of time. Until Christ returns, his Church must constantly renew and revitalize her presentation of eternal truths, so that they become an authentic call to the men of every time and place. No period has needed Christ's truth more than ours; none has held richer promise for a universal humanism rooted in the truth about God and man.

Two conditions of our times make this volume extremely difficult to construct. The *first* is man's new position in the material world as a result of scientific and technological progress. The world appears to man in a guise of usefulness, a challenge to his power to understand and control it. A sense of the sacredness of things, of religious feelings of awe and wonder, has been supplanted by a profane and superficial attitude. This shift of perspective has some good results, as we shall note later, but it removes one of the traditional starting points for a religious interpretation of the phenomenal world.

The *second* condition is the renewal of intellectual vitality in the Church. She finds herself accepting courageously all that is true in any field of thought. Consequently her theologians and other scholars are deeply involved in rethinking and enlarging the human modes necessary for transmitting divine tradition. Disciplines such as archaeology, ancient literatures, depth psychology, and contemporary sociology, to mention but a few, open up vistas of insight for the whole sweep of human knowledge.

As always, each human being today finds himself facing God, and the world, and his fellow men. In achieving a relation to them, he fulfills or fails to fulfill his personal destiny. He is vaguely aware that his struggle is not just human, but is somehow involved with powers of darkness and light in an invisible world. Paradoxically, it is not possible to gain deeper insight into the contemporary situation of man without a long look at the origin of angels and men. Both, in turn, must be set into the total cosmic picture. Only then can the student place himself in historical relation to the conquest of Adam's failure that was achieved through Christ's redemptive act. Then alone can he know for certain that perfect happiness can be his forever, through life in Christ at the resurrection in the world to come. Without an understanding of Christ, human life is a resounding question. Without an understanding of Adam, Christ's historic existence is unexplainable. Together, the old Adam and Christ the new Adam explain both the source of human sorrow and the certitude of human hope.

CHAPTER ONE

THE UNIVERSE; WORD OF GOD'S CREATIVE LOVE

Man lives on the earth. Lately he has begun his search into space. A knowledge of his environment which increases daily and of his own body and soul leaves him dazed and questioning. Ultimately, scientific knowledge may help to restore man's lost sense of religious wonder in the face of a newly mysterious and expanding universe. But already God has revealed to him the basic meaning of reality, a meaning which can be grasped only in light of God's truth by the joyful acceptance of faith. Here and now, in the present moment, what does this marvelous world mean?

It means first of all that God exists and is the fullness of uncreated being. It means that his very nature is to be generous, to pour out existence on other beings. In other words, God is love. The God of Abraham, Isaac, and Jacob, the God of Jesus Christ, reveals himself from the first instant of creation as sharing, giving, loving. He gives to every being its nature, its powers, and its moment-by-moment activity. To angels and men he gives in addition the unimaginable destiny of sharing a life of happiness in the sight and possession of the all-holy God forever. God is love, and he made everything from the motive of love, if we may so speak. He draws creatures to their perfection through the appeal of love.

This chapter is the prelude to a more detailed study of the theology of angels and men. It is an attempt to see the universe as a unity before studying angels and men in detail, for before God, who alone *is,* all creation is unified in its radical unlikeness to him. Every being that is outside of God is essentially nothing. A being exists at each instant in utter dependence on the conserving power of God. From this perspective the whole of created reailty, whatever its extent and duration, is one existent Word expressive of God's creative love. "Let all the earth fear the Lord; let all who dwell in the world revere him. For he spoke and it was made; he commanded, and it stood forth. . . . The plan of the Lord stands forever; the design of his heart, through all generations." (Ps 32[33] 8f.11)[1]

THE UNIVERSE AS A WORD

What does it mean to say that the universe is a Word? The Scriptures provide an explanation and use the theme of the Word of God as one of the richest and deepest of all the unifying notions in revelation. God, boundless in his thought and power to accomplish,

---

[1] A period between verse numbers indicates that the verses cited are successive but nonconsecutive.

causes and directs everything by his living Word. God speaks, and things exist; God addresses a Word, and men heed or reject him. God's Word becomes flesh in Jesus Christ to restore the truth of a damaged world. The Scriptures and the Church are two mysterious manifestations of the living Word of God. The universe will reach its term in the Word of life or death at the final judgment. In all these senses, God's Word is always living and efficacious.

Out of these many and related uses of the theme of the Word of God, the created universe as an objectified divine utterance is an ancient Christian notion. Every creature is conceived in God's mind and called into being by him; moreover, in some way it utters him, as the artefact speaks forth the artist. Obviously creatures reflect God in two distinct ways. In creatures lower than man, there is a trace of God, a vestige, a footprint, which declares his existence and power. In various ways the subhuman world bespeaks his beauty, his intelligence and goodness. These creatures beget certitude in us that God is. But they speak to us only faintly of what God is like. They tell us nothing of his inner, personal life.

With the creatures men and angels there is not just the trace of God's power, but the created likeness of his being. For in men and angels, we have creatures who know and who love witnessing to the infinite Knower and Lover. Intelligence and free will show forth the infinite mind and the almighty will. Men and angels even when rebellious and fallen are literally images of God, capable of responsible actions. They are of course infinitely unlike him in their dependence on One who is eternal and absolutely self-sufficient.

The Word that the universe utters is a Word richly orchestrated but unmistakable. It conveys the message that God is. In the biblical perspective of creation there is no attempt to prove that God is by way of a syllogistic operation. God's existence is proclaimed by every creature, since the being of each speaks of the God who spoke it in the depths of his own majesty. Things are Words of God. Man is a Word of God; he is like God in that he can think and speak words. More and more he is coming to understand the Word of the lower creatures. The entire spirituality of the psalms is set in this cosmic dialogue between God and man on the stage of the visible world. Psalms 8, 18[19], and 103[104], are but three examples of this recurring scriptural theme.

VARIETY IN UNITY

Assuming that the entire universe is somehow a manifestation of God, how can one account for its seemingly infinite multiplicity, not to speak of the complexity introduced by sin and evil? Does the universe have a principle of unity in its functioning and destiny?

Immediately it is evident that no one creature could ever reflect God adequately. It is the complex and somehow totally grasped universe which reflects God's power and wisdom and providence. This deepest inner order is known to him alone. After revelation man knows it to the extent that his mind is illumined and informed by faith and love. God holds everything in being. He guides all creatures, but most of all free creatures, to an eternal destiny. These are truths which must be believed; they cannot be fully understood until the final day of the Lord, when all of God's magnificent plan will be made manifest.

Covenant with Noa

The story of Noa is found in Gn 6-9. It presents one of the most beautiful biblical insights into the relation between God and cosmic order. After the flood from which the just and obedient Noa and his family are saved, God makes a covenant with him. This is the covenant of God's promised faithfulness to the cosmic order of life and movement and seasons, even in the face of man's sinfulness. God restores the command given to Adam to increase and multiply and to be master of the earth. However sin has entered into the world, and this God must punish. He promises not to destroy the natural order because of sin. Rather he will preserve the universe and its functioning as the place of trial for good and evil men. The rainbow in the clouds becomes a symbol of this covenant with Noa. The universe will function in a basically orderly way as long as time goes on, not only as a sign of God's creative power, but even more as a Word of his merciful love.

Hierarchy in Creation

8   The biblical perspectives not only show forth the unity of God's creation but also manifest the sweep and variety within the pattern.

Always there is sensitivity to the beauty and power of God in the visible world. The entire range of human feeling and desire, of success and failure, is movingly present here as nowhere else in literature. And always there is the hovering awareness of the world of invisible beings who help or hinder man in his movement to God.

The great events of the Bible were recorded in Semitic cultures, where the concrete image dominated thought and sensibility. Greek thought became integrated with this Eastern thought and developed into Western Christian speculation. Gradually the concepts of matter and spirit as a duality were stressed more than the concrete imagery of the Semites as a means to delineate the order and variety in things as they are. Creaturehood was seen as existing in a threefold hierarchy. Highest of course are the pure spirits, the angels; lowest are the purely material beings. Man, the embodied spirit, the "little world," combines the two. He stands on the frontiers of two worlds, a vital part of the earthly, visible world—indeed its crown—yet possessed of a spiritual life-principle ordered to life with God. Man is central in the universe, both *de facto* by God's having made him image of God and steward of creation, and metaphysically, in the very arrangement of created being. This sort of perspective on man gives added insight into the cosmic implications of the fact that the Son of God assumes human nature.

Angels, material beings, men—these make up the created universe. Owing to the limitations of human knowledge, it is necessary to study one or the other in isolation. However, it is crucial that each of these three be kept in the total framework of one revealed pattern, for in the actuality of existence they are interwoven into the one story of human destiny and salvation. The world is man's setting, the angels are his ministers or his tempters. Man is to master the earth and his own nature, moving with the good spirits toward the eternal kingdom that will come after this earth has served its purpose. The time line of history cuts through a structured universe in which man, the microcosmos, is the joining place of material and spiritual worlds. God's call into being, and the answers given by men and angels, are the very story of the created universe.

We find this intimate union between the two orders of creation expressed beautifully in the *Exsultet* sung during the Easter Vigil, when the whole world celebrates its deliverance from evil and sin and darkness through Christ's saving death. In the time of nature's spring awakening, the angelic hosts are called upon to exult with man as he recalls his fall in Adam and his restoration as a creature even more glorious in Christ. Light from waxen candles, water, bread and wine, and the very stars of heaven, are brought into the Easter exultation. The blood of Christ, in washing man, cleanses the universe. Great mystery is here, and the Church leaves no doubt about its cosmic extension.

MAN AND THE MATERIAL WORLD

In light of this revelation it seems more necessary than ever for man to understand himself as God has made and intended him, as Christ has restored and uplifted him. It seems equally crucial that man should understand his place in the universe, for a total vision is required if he is to understand himself. The scriptural picture of man is significantly different from the pre-Christian, Greek notion of man's place in the world. The Scriptures show us man coming from the hand of God by a creative Word, as the final utterance in his production of "the world and all that is in it." Man is seen as the free king of creation, not as one caught between visible things and the whims of capricious gods and malevolent demons. Scripture reveals the existence of a spirit world, but it too is totally subject to the living God. Under God, the spirits are involved in the salvation history of man.

If a total vision of man in the universe was always a necessity, its recovery today is of the utmost urgency. The marvels of modern scientific achievement tend to reduce man in his own eyes to a plaything of powerful forces, manipulated by faceless social, economic, and political groupings. Those with power seem not to know its purpose; those without power feel helpless and meaningless. Is the vision of man to end in a prefabricated shelter underneath the earth? Do invisible, intelligent beings play some role in man's present sense of losing control of personal and planetary life, in the face of the very inventions of his own intelligence and skill?

Never has man felt so alone in the face of nature, so isolated from the fellow men to whom he is closely bound; never has he been so aware of uncontrollable forces in the depths of his own psyche. In God's providence, this tangible failure of every merely human answer to the meaning of life may be the preparation for a new readiness to turn to the living God and be illumined and saved. It is in any case more evident each day that no answer exists to the riddle of the universe except the one given by its Maker—taught to the human race in its full meaning by Jesus Christ.

REVELATION ABOUT
THE MATERIAL WORLD

What precisely has God revealed about the meaning of the material world? The remainder of this book will deal with God's revelation about angels and men. Here the question of cosmic meaning is asked in its narrowest sense, that is, as applied specifically to the terrestrial world. First of all it is important to remember that God has revealed on this subject only what it is essential for man to know, things that he could not know, or know readily, from any other source. He leaves the exploration and detailed understanding of the material world to man's research, discovery, thought, and meditation. This is the area of human science in all its ramifications. It is one of the most profound and deeply human modes of answering God's command to man to subdue and master the earth. Revealed knowledge of the world will deal precisely with those aspects which man cannot investigate and learn through his own effort. It is this truth which underlies the impossibility of conflict between revealed and natural, or human, truth. Though the perfect synthesis of the two may be difficult, slow, or even unattainable, owing to the limitations of human intelligence, both sources of truth return to one creating God.

Its Origin

In regard to the cosmos, the truths essential to know and not discoverable by man are those concerning the beginning and the end of things. By its nature the human mind questions in both directions. How and when did the world begin? How and when will it end? Neither question can be answered explicitly and certainly except by revealed truth. The God who pre-exists the world, brings it into being, guides its every instant, and will terminate it according to his eternal plan, must unlock the mystery. "In the beginning God created the heavens and the earth." From this opening sentence of the Bible, the entire story of salvation is the gradual making known of God's plan for man. The story is an *apokálypsis,* a revelation. The setting for this human existence is the world, which in its turn receives more meaning as man's destiny is clarified and fulfilled.

The Church teaches that God, who is the fullness of reality and infinitely powerful, made everything that is, material and spiritual, out of no pre-existing reality. He did this, not from eternity, but at a beginning of time. In other words the Church has always taught that the divine creative act brought into being and sustains in being all that exists outside of God himself. (Cf. D1,19,21,29,54,86,235,421,501.) The Church does not teach any doctrine on the actual age of the world nor on the stages of its development under God's sustaining power. The fact of creation from nothing stands necessarily at the head of God's revelation, for it radically separates God and works, Creator and creatures, eternally. It establishes the absolute dependence of everything on God for its being and activity. It makes a vital and constant relationship with the living God who causes the universe to be and who directs its course.

This vision dominated the cosmic awareness of Israel and separated the chosen people from all the nations surrounding them. The Psalms abound in passages like the following: "Bless the Lord, O my soul! O Lord, my God, you are great indeed! You are clothed with majesty and glory, robed in light as with a cloak. You have spread out the heavens like a tent-cloth; you have constructed your palace upon the waters. You make the clouds your chariot; you travel on the wings of the wind." (Ps 103[104],1–4) "O Lord, our Lord, how glorious is your name over all the earth! You have exalted your majesty above the heavens. . . . I behold your heavens, the work of your fingers, the moon and the stars which you set in place. . . ." (Ps 8,1)

Christianity adds the revelation of God's infinite life and love made known in Christ, the unsuspected fact that the Creator God who loves his creation with an infinite love is Father, Son and Holy Spirit. This material universe in which the Son of God lived, died, and rose is totally and constantly the product of the divine creative power. Probably the most succinct statement of this New Testament perspective which sees the creative Word in the redeeming Savior is the classic text from Saint Paul's letter to the Colossians:

He is the image of the invisible God, the firstborn of every creature. For in him were created all things in the heavens and on the earth, things visible and things invisible, whether thrones, or dominations, or principalities, or powers. All things have been created through and unto him, and he is before all creatures, and in him all things hold together. Again, he is the head of his body, the Church; he, who is the beginning, the firstborn from the dead, that in all things he may have the first place. For it has pleased God the Father that in him all his fullness should dwell, and that through him he should reconcile to himself all things, whether on the earth or in the heavens, making peace through the blood of his cross. (Col 1,15-20)

The revealed fact of creation out of nothing connotes an act of free mercy and love on God's part. It already implies a plan and direction toward a destiny. The Church teaches clearly that the universe is the providential setting for the testing and eternally valid choice of man, God's image on earth. This world derives its meaning from its relation to man. The teachings on the origin and fall of man will be interwoven with the reality of a world of here and now. But the development and understanding of the material world is left to man's free study and innate capability to penetrate. Thus the doctrine on creation, and the consequent relation of material things to man's destiny, provide the ultimate reference point for all humanly acquired knowledge about the world. A thought system or claim of discovery which contradicts strict creation as the origin of matter, or which subverts the relation between man and matter, simply cannot be true. Human science deals legitimately with the *structure*, not the ultimate origin of things.

Its Termination

Like the beginning, the end of the material world is known only to God. He tells us that the universe will be terminated by his free act just as surely as it was begun by him. The difference is that while the world came from nothing, it will *not* return to nothing. Its condition as we know it will be destroyed, and the universe will somehow share in the glorification of the human race transformed in Christ. The new heavens and the new earth of the prophets' visions become the object of the Christian's hope also. The universe created by God as setting for man's trial, damaged by man's sin as we shall see, will be renewed and transformed at the end of time. Mysterious as the mode remains, the

13

entire creation restored in Christ will praise and glorify the triune God forever.

Chapter 3 of the second epistle of Peter gives us in obscure yet moving language some glimpse of the meaning and destiny of the material world:

> Ever since the fathers went to their rest, all is as it was from the foundation of the world. They are fain to forget how, long ago, heaven stood there, and an earth which God's word had made with water for its origin, water for its frame; and those were the very means by which the world, as it then was, came to perish, overwhelmed by water. That same word keeps heaven and earth, as they now are, stored up ready to feed the fire on the day when the godless will be judged and perish. . . . The heavens will vanish in a whirlwind, the elements will be scorched up and dissolve, earth, and all earth's achievements will burn away. All so transitory; and what men you ought to be. . . . And meanwhile we have new heavens and new earth to look forward to, the dwelling place of holiness; that is what he has promised. (2 Pt 3, 4–7; 10b–13)

This beautiful text is cast in the highly imaginative style of the Jewish apocalypses. The new heavens and the new earth in this passage, as well as in the Old Testament prophets and in the Apocalypse of Saint John, are not to be taken literally. However, they do refer in some obscure way to the fact that at the end of time the termination of the universe will be intimately connected with the fulfillment of the human family in Christ. Some theologians cast light on this difficult question by relating the glorification of the universe to the glorification of man's body, which will be owing to the "radiance" of his beatified soul. In any case, the material world will arrive at its term within the pattern of God's design and under the impetus of his power. The details of this culmination must await the actual events themselves.

FINAL OVERVIEW

God alone exists by very nature and right. All else is creaturehood, receiving being and activity from him. The rich array of beings that we call the created world should be seen first as one magnificent manifestation of God's power, love, and wisdom. Only when the universe is envisioned totally under the light of God's revelation can man, the image of God, be viewed both in his cosmic environment and on the plane of salvation history. Only the latter explains fully the existence and order of created reality. The spirit-world, too, must find its relevance for man in the role that angels and devils play in the unfolding of human destiny.

From eternity the Father generates the Word, his Son, the second person of the blessed Trinity. But the Word of God which actually began time is the material universe, the created Word manifesting God's generous and merciful love. Into this universe, damaged by sin, God sends the eternal Word to speak to man as man, to address to him the words of eternal life. Christ the incarnate Word recreates what had first to be created. Only at the end of time will the material world through man's history be transformed in Christ. Then it will become what God has from the first intended it to be.

> Here is God's tabernacle pitched among men; he will dwell with them, and they will be his own people, and he will be among them, their own God. He will wipe away every tear from their eyes, and there will be no more death, or mourning, or cries of distress, no more sorrow; those old things have passed away. And he who sat on the throne said, "Behold, I make all things new." (Ap 21,3–5)

CHAPTER TWO

THE ANGELS

God's revelation spreads out before man the panorama of a universe, the noblest beings of which are invisible spirits similar to God. It is surprising to discover how much is revealed indirectly about these great spirit-beings in the telling of the story of man's salvation. The Scriptures are concerned directly with man's destiny and thus reveal the angels mainly in relation to man. However, the thought and meditation of men of faith over the centuries have synthesized much that is certain about the angels, their nature, their trial, and their consequent relation to God and men.

NATURE AND EXISTENCE OF ANGELS

It is the teaching of the Church that there exist created beings who are absolutely pure spirit having no admixture of even the most etherealized matter. (D428,1783) They are images of God in the strict sense in their total being, having only the faculties of intellect and will. It is easy to see the fittingness of their existence, granted that the created universe is a harmonious and full manifestation of God. Only spirit beings, in their place in the cosmic hierarchy, can show forth the Creator who is infinite spirit. It is equally easy to see that the spirit-world is not immediately accessible to human reason, which must start with sense impressions. For this reason there is the necessity, if angels are to be in contact with men, of their assuming an appearance of some sort which is discernible. Because of the ambiguity of such appearances, human and angelic contact short of that in the ultimate, heavenly community remains solidly based only on the teaching of faith and the life of grace which angels and men have in common.

The word "angel" is indicative of the revealed nature of the spirit-world. It comes from the Greek word for "messenger," which in turn renders a Hebrew word having the same meaning. The term denotes the purpose fulfilled by those angels whose appearance is recorded in the Scriptures. (Cf. Gn 16,7; 19,1–28; 28,12; Dn 9,21; 2 Sm 1,2–8; Is 37,36f; Ps 34[35],8; Ps 35[36],5f; Ps 91[92],11f; 2 Mc 11,1–12; Tb and Za *passim*) Although messenger is the lowest function of the pure spirits it is the one closest to men, therefore it has been extended to cover all the beings higher than man who are the image of God in their very essence and not just in their spiritual soul. As a man advances in the life of faith he grows in understanding and development of his own spiritual image of God. But he should also become more vitally aware of the presence and activity of the magnificent creatures who make up the invisible cosmos and enter intimately into human destiny.

18

What Is an Angel?

The basic teaching of the Church on the angels is that their existence is certain. (D428) It is believed that they were created before the beginning of the material world. They certainly existed before the creation of Adam and Eve, for a principal character in their drama is an evil spirit. (Cf. Ap 12,1–9; 2 Cor 11,3) The essential nature of an angel is that of an intellectual and spiritual being. They began to be at the instant of their creation, and they will continue to exist forever. Since they are not material, they have no relation to space. This also means that they have a different mode of duration than the time that man knows. The amount of "spirit-being" each angel has was determined at the instant of creation; it is thought to be equivalent to the capacity of his intelligence. The angels do not grow in knowledge. They grasp all they will know at once. They have free will, and a mysterious yet powerful control over matter. In relation to the material world, an angel is where he wills to act. He is the normal link between the infinite spirit, God, and the world of matter and men. The angel is the free messenger of God's will in the governing of the universe.

The Number and Order of the Angels

The above statements are true of every angel. Two other aspects of revelation need to be added in order to achieve a proper perspective on the spirit world. The angels exist in overwhelming multitude. "Suddenly there was with the angel a multitude of the heavenly host praising God and saying, 'Glory to God in the highest, and on earth peace among men of good will.'" (Lk 2,13f) Although the exact number is unknown, there are some principles involved which incline one toward the notion of tremendous magnitude. Each creature is a reflection of the Creator. But a pure spirit by his nature reflects God in a much higher way than all of material creation together, omitting from consideration the question of supernatural gifts. Since no one angel reflects God adequately, the more angels he creates, the more he is reflected in pure spirit beings. It is not mere number but the variety of unique types of reflection that adds more glory and majesty to God's creative power.

In this short chapter it is not possible to enlarge on the absorbing but highly speculative theology of the order among angels and their mutual interrelationships. It is certain that their prime function is to adore and worship God. The scriptural passages about heaven or the court of Yahweh always show us the angelic multitudes thronged about the throne of the living God. It is equally certain that some of the angels carry out functions regarding men. These spirits enter directly into the story of salvation. Although each angel is a unique being, Christian thought traditionally has grouped them according to the "choirs" of seraphim, cherubim, thrones, dominations, virtues, powers, principalities, archangels and angels. (Cf. Gn 3,24; Ez 10,1f; Is 6,2.6; Eph 1,21; Col 1,16; 1 Thes 4,15; Jude 8) These names do not signify classifications but remind men of the variety of angelic functions and the range of their richness of power and beauty.

In the worship service of the Church the angels are always present, as participating in the heavenly liturgy of which our sacramental worship is an earthly extension. They are explicitly invoked and mentioned often. For example in the Mass of the Roman rite the opening confession of our sinfulness is made before the heavenly hosts, especially St. Michael. The Gloria is an exultant paraphrase of the angels' song at the birth of Jesus. At the Sanctus prayer the faithful on earth join the angels in the threefold praise of God's infinite holiness as revealed to Isaia in his great vision of heaven. (6,3) After the consecration there is reference to the sacrifice being lifted up to the altar before the throne of God by the holy angel. From the exorcisms of baptism which drive out the evil one to the hymn "In Paradisum" after the Mass of burial, man is assumed by Christian faith to be in living contact with the angels of God and the devils who reject him.

The Angels and Art

While he is on earth, man will always find thinking about the angels a difficult proposition. His mind can grow in understanding of their true nature and mission, but he will necessarily use images when thinking of the angels. The history of Christian art is a reminder of the real problem involved in visual representation of the angels, both good and evil. Obviously the material symbols chosen should be in conformity with the revealed thought signified. Devils must connote evil, hatefulness, duplicity, power, intelligence—certainly not coyness or stupidity.

20

For good angels symbols of spirituality, beauty, reverence, kindness, joy and majesty are eminently fitting. Such are the attributes implied through the angels that were depicted in the early centuries, particularly in primitive mosaics, Byzantine art, and medieval and early renaissance frescoes. Artistically, the later renaissance confused and obscured the true teaching on angels. The symbols gradually degenerated to the forms of earthy infants or even tiny baby heads with little wings. It seems necessary to mention this, for psychologically man is much more influenced by the art in which he sees doctrinal truth portrayed than by the verbal formulas in which it is stated. The degeneration of the art forms in which angels were presented has done much to wipe out real conviction concerning their existence. It has totally confused their true nature and mission. Such a lack of seriousness in art with respect to the angels can bring about subtly harmful effects on man's sense of God's power and grandeur, as well as the marvelous reality of man's own soul.

TESTING OF THE ANGELS

Granted that pure spirits exist and are beings of wonder, what can we know of their destiny, their present relation to God and to the destiny of man? The teaching of the Church is that the pure spirits were, like man, created not for a merely natural end, but for the supernatural end of the direct and everlasting possession of God himself. Like man, they were created in a state of trial in which they could freely accept or reject this supernatural destiny. Those who chose God and accepted the gift of eternal life in his presence entered into the life of heaven. Those who rejected God and refused the gift of grace began the permanent state which we call hell. This is the eternal loss of God's life and presence.

Natural and Supernatural Life

These teachings of the Church on the destiny, trial, and two states of angelic being are certain in faith. Theology helps us to look more deeply at their meaning. First of all it seems necessary to clarify the notions of natural and supernatural destiny, for without such clarification the whole story of angelic and human creation is meaningless. By natural

21

is meant what belongs by right to any creature once God freely wills to create it. For example, if God wishes to create purely spiritual beings, he must give them intelligence and freedom. The supernatural, on the other hand, implies a mode of being which belongs by right only to God and is therefore *super*—beyond—the natural rights or endowments of any creature, actual or possible. Thus, the power to share in God's life, to know and love as God does, to see his essence directly and without intervening concepts or ideas, all these are strictly supernatural gifts. God owes them to no created being. Sanctifying and actual grace, the infused virtues and the gifts of the Holy Spirit, the beatific vision, are all strictly above the rights of an angel or a man.

The whole point of revelation from Adam to Christ is that man's destiny was never purely natural, that freedom and trial are intrinsic to human life precisely because this life is ordered to the divine life of freely given grace. There are scattered scriptural references which point to the trial and fall of part of the angelic world. For example,

> there was a battle in heaven; Michael and his angels battled with the dragon, and the dragon fought and his angels. And they did not prevail, neither was their place found any more in heaven. And that great dragon was cast down, the ancient serpent, he who is called the devil and Satan, who leads astray the whole world; and he was cast down to the earth and with him his angels were cast down. (Ap 12,7ff)

By analogy with man's trial, the Church has developed over the centuries a unified presentation of the supernatural situation of the spirit world. It is important here to remember that the entire creation, material and spiritual, is the effect of the one creating God. It is a universe, a unified total effect ordered by God to one final and fulfilling end, no matter how hidden this divine order may be during the unfolding of historical time.

The Angelic Trial

The theology of faith tells us that the angels were called into being by God with the fullness of their natural gifts, with sanctifying grace, with faith, hope, and charity. In other words they were living a supernatural life in the imperfect state of trial, not yet seeing God but knowing by faith and desiring by hope. We simply do not know the exact nature of the knowledge revealed to them by God, acceptance of which determined their eternal blessedness or damnation. A common theological opinion is that this knowledge may have involved the future incarnation of the Son of God, to whom in his humanity these spirits would owe adoration. Whatever the details of their trial, the fact is that some undetermined number of angels rejected God's grace. They preferred their own natural excellence of intelligence and freedom to the eternal possession of God as a supernatural gift of love, though the latter would have involved loss of neither intelligence nor freedom. There is nothing in all of revelation which shows so clearly the fundamental nature and malice of sin as this first sin in the universe, the sin of the angels. It was committed by beings of lucid knowledge and unrestrained freedom—beings whose acts are so total that they can never make an intellectual mistake or change freely willed decisions. Their sin is pride. This sin sets the creature in an attitude of refusal toward God, of hatred of the divine good precisely because it does not belong by right to the creature. In angelic sin more than anywhere else we see the depth of mystery which lies at the base of every grave sin. Why does a creature refuse God's gift of himself?

Results of Rebellion

Since we do not know the number of the angelic multitude, we do not know how many failed in their trial of freedom. The common opinion is that the number was very great but that the majority of the angels chose God and eternal life. Whatever the case, Lucifer or the "light-bearer" (that is, Venus, the morning star, a title first applied to the king of Babylon [Is 14,12]) comes to be understood as the leader of the fallen angels beginning with the third century A.D. This leader of the fallen angels has consistently been viewed in the Christian tradition as one of the highest of all by natural endowment. He was transformed by sin into Satan, "the adversary," the father of lies. He and his fellow demons keep their natural intelligence, strength of will, and spiritual power over matter. Since their fall, however, these natural gifts are fixed in hatred, perversely turned against God and all that is of God. Therefore a total vision of the created universe must always include the awareness of a spirit-world above man, composed of both magnificent angels of

23

holiness and love and great beings of darkness and hate. The very greatness of their nature makes redemption an impossibility for the evil angels. In the strictest sense they cannot repent, for their intelligence and freedom were irrevocably committed in their first clear and everlasting decision.

ANGELS IN THE COSMIC ORDER

The spirit-world exists. It exists within a context of the supernatural meaning of the entire universe. Like the human world of our experience, it is sundered by sin and evil. Human and angelic sin are closely interwoven with human and angelic holiness. This close relation is not just in the telling of the story of man, but in the living out of each day of human existence until Christ returns to establish the eternal separation between the holy and the damned. This is the City of God magnificently revealed in the sweep of the Scriptures and enlarged upon in Saint Augustine's classic work of that name. The one living God, through his incarnate Son, draws to himself forever a family of men and angels bound together by grace. He rejects forever the angels and men who freely refuse his love and mercy.

From this oneness of God's universal plan the Church helps us to see the present relation of the angels to God and to man. She draws most of her insight into these truths from the unique biblical book of the Apocalypse. The great visions described there show us the angelic throngs eternally loving and adoring the living God and the Lamb. They show also the angels carrying out missions of intervention in helping the saints on earth and in punishing sinners. The good spirits appear in two roles—fighting evil spirits and assisting God in the culmination of the universe as we know it, the inauguration of the new heavens and the new earth.

Role of the Demons

A significant characteristic of the Apocalypse is that book's vivid awareness of good and evil spirits as creatures of God—both types completely in his creative and sustaining power, both carrying out his inscru-

24

table will. The powers of angelic evil are certainly active in the world. Perhaps we are beginning to be aware of this again. But it is essential to remember that these great spirits are kept in existence by God. They can do nothing but what God permits for the ultimate good of men in this world. Evil as such cannot exist, but evil spirits and evil men do exist by their own free choice. Only revelation can embrace the horrible reality of such creatures within a larger design, in which good triumphs in the lasting sense.

The relation of the angels to God is, then, that of creatures who freely love and serve him, or freely hate and reject him. In relation to man's destiny, it is necessary to clarify many different roles of angelic activity. The first member of the spirit world to enter the human story is the evil spirit who tempted Eve. From the beginning of human history there is a link between angelic sin and the primeval fall of the human race. The sin of Adam and the sin of Eve, as we will see in greater detail, are instances of free and responsible human activity. But the pair was led by an already perverted, fallen spirit. The solidarity of sin in the universe as a whole is a mystery as incomprehensible to us as the solidarity of the human race, fallen in the sin of one man.

From the paradise of Eden to the heralding of the paradise of the second coming of Christ, the demons are unceasingly busy tempting every man. This is his time of trial. They cannot attack the life of God in God himself, but they are free to do everything possible to get man to renounce him forever through unrepented sin. It is important to clarify what the Church teaches us about this power of the evil spirits to affect man's eternal destiny. The basic principle which must not be forgotten is that the devils are creatures acting only with God's permission. Since they are spirits they can affect material things, and so can reach man through his sense and imagination. They cannot move the human will or affect it directly. Only God can touch the inmost heart of man's freedom and self-mastery. Since the human body is material, the demons can attack it (obsession), and even take over physical control of it in rare cases (possession). But these mysterious powers cannot of themselves force the consent of the will of the person involved.

Jesus Christ, creator of all the angels and their king in virtue of his glorification as incarnate victor over sin, called the evil one the prince of darkness, the prince of this world. The dark thread of the influence of evil spirits runs through the design of human history. As a Catholic one must believe in the power of the demons, but not allow a fascination with their seeming success to lead to exaggeration of angelic power, or to forgetfulness of Christ's absolute kingship of all creatures. Although it is necessary in a photographic print to have dark and light and variously shaded sections, it is the lighter sections which convey the content of the picture; so with the existence of demons. They must be present in our picture of the universe and our own lives if we are to be realistic. They may never be there as the main element. The predominant awareness of the believer must be of the goodness of all creatures, and the ultimate transformation of the great numbers in Christ unto eternal joy. This transformation is already radically achieved. It is now in process of extending itself to the boundaries of the human and material universe.

ANGELS AS HELPERS TO MEN

What can the Church tell men about the good spirits, the holy angels, those creatures who are perfect in both natural and supernatural endowment? It is refreshing to realize that the Church teaches much more about the good angels than about the demons. This is as it should be. The former have more being, more knowability. They are radiant with supernatural light and grace. They do something positive, understandable to some extent, in carrying out God's loving will for the world. This is in sharp contrast to devils who are warped, twisted, full of darkness and deviousness, who always act with ambiguity and lies.

Throughout the Scriptures holy angels appear constantly in roles through which they cooperate with God as secondary causes in the governing of the world. They are especially evident in directing the saving history of the human race. Abraham, Jacob, Moses, to mention only the greatest, are men whose lives are crucially affected by intervention of angels. God somehow shapes the vocation and mission of these men through angelic messengers. The angel Raphael dominates the story of the book of Tobia. Certainly the crown of angelic delegation is the pivotal and exquisitely told story of the mission of the angel Gabriel to Mary (patterned linguistically by Luke on the angel's message to Gideon in Jgs 6), to ask her consent to the mystery of the incarnation. Later, angels are evident in the lives of Christ and the apostles. Un-

26

questionably in general, though with varying degrees of certitude in particular instances, the angels play the role of messenger in apparitions in the life of the Church.

Guardian Angels

God has revealed another role of the angels which has been the constant and consoling teaching of the Church. This is their role as protectors and guides of men. Weakened by original and personal sin, sought by demons, each human being is aided by an angel. The exact nature of this help varies for individuals and situations. In general the Church tells us that the angel can, by acting on our senses and imagination, stimulate us to good thoughts and deeds. In particular the guardian angels protect us physically and even spiritually through warding off the attacks of evil spirits. In the Roman liturgy this aspect is particularly stressed in the feast of the Guardian Angels (October 2) with its passages from Ex 23,20–23, and Christ's own direct reference to angelic helpers. (Mt 18,10) The postcommunion prayer of the feast is very explicit: "O Lord, we have received the divine mysteries rejoicing in the feast of your holy angels. Grant that through their protection we may be always free from the attacks of the evil one, and defended against all adversity."

It is strongly probable that public persons who bear great responsibilities like leaders of nations have special angelic help. Also it seems that nations and privileged holy shrines have angels watching over them. Monasteries are considered to be particularly under angelic care because their professed work is, like that of angels, the formal praise of God.

A final function of the angels stresses the unity of God's plan for his entire creation. The angels act as our intercessors, praying for us and offering our prayers to God. "And another angel came and stood before the altar, having a golden censer; and there was given to him much incense, that he might offer it with the prayers of all the saints upon the golden altar which is before the throne. And with the prayers of the saints there went up before God from the angel's hand the smoke of the incense." (Ap 8,3f)

In the last moments of each individual's life, both the good and evil spirits are especially active. This is the moment of eternal decision.

27

After the soul has left the body, existing in the world of the spirit, in a way unnatural to it, it goes to heaven or hell in the company of angels. The soul which has left the body with God's life in it is led to purgatory or heaven by its guardian angel, who rejoices in the accomplishment of his assigned task.

Men and Angels in Heaven

The final panorama which the Church presents to us is the vision of the eternal kingdom of God, after the glorious resurrection of the dead. This kingdom will consist in the joyous brotherhood of men and angels, all living by the life of God's grace. Fra Angelico has beautifully captured this spirit of angelic and human unity in heaven in the way he paints the world to come. On green fields, scattered over with tiny blossoms, we see circle after circle of dancing figures clothed in exquisitely colored robes. The dancing circles are made of men and angels hand in hand, eternally happy together in joyful love of God and each other. The incarnate Son of God will be the king of this world of happiness. But we should never forget that the queen of the kingdom, the holiest of creatures reigning with love over men and angels, is not a spirit but a woman, Mary of Nazareth, the Mother of God. In this truth perhaps more than anywhere else in the theology of the angels do we see how interwoven is the existential situation of angels and men. It is in the human race and not in the angelic multitudes that the key to the meaning of the universe is found. The Son of God became not an angel but a man.

The main result of study of the revealed world of angelic creation should be a growing awareness of the reality of both devils and good angels, an awareness of the power, freedom, and destiny of spirit being. This can be a great help toward a less superficial way of thinking and acting. This awareness can be a powerful antidote to materialism and the overstressing of the value of the goods known through sense impressions. Most of all, knowledge of the angels should lead us to pray to and depend on the guardianship of angels, each of us finding strength and serenity in the face of physical danger through trust in our divinely appointed helper. The Christian not only hopes to arrive at the heavenly kingdom, but also to recognize as a fellow citizen the angel whose personal care has accompanied him in his journey on earth.

28

CHAPTER THREE

THE ORIGIN
OF MAN

What has God revealed concerning the mystery of man? Simply this: that God's magnificent universe centers on the fulfillment of the destiny of the human family. The unfolding of his plan for man is precisely revelation, or the salvation-history achieved in Jesus Christ. The remaining chapters of this book will present in theological order and development the great truths concerning man's origin and destiny, trying to distinguish various aspects of these truths while keeping an awareness of the total unity of divine revelation.

Preliminary Remarks

It is necessary to turn first to what God has made known about man's coming into existence, then to man's relation to God before sin. The nature of original sin and its effects on the first man and woman and on their descendants must be studied. Finally the relevance of these basic truths to the present human situation must be considered. In these chapters we will concentrate on the unchanging revealed doctrine, on certain fundamental insights which are true for all men in all ages and cultures. The subject of man is as vast as human thought. A strongly delineated presentation of the revealed truth about him is the more urgently needed as man extends the frontiers of discovery about the human race. Otherwise the natural and supernatural truths about man can be so indiscriminately mixed as to confuse both approaches to human reality.

There are two preliminary aspects of the mystery of man which must be dealt with immediately, since they permeate all theology. To forget or ignore these aspects can lead to distorted doctrines or superficial digressions.

Christ—the Fullness of Revelation

When Jesus Christ appears in human history, mankind is confronted with the perfect man, man as God planned him for all eternity. The fact that Christ came into the world, that the Son of God himself assumed a human nature in order to restore the human family, points immediately to the question of the need for restoration. This in turn raises the question of sin, separation from God, some primordial failure which looks backward to a human beginning that was other than life as man experiences it. Thus the mystery of man from God's point of view is rooted in the polarity between Adam and Christ, the old man and the new man, the first man and the last, the perfect, man. Christians know the meaning of Adam by opposition to the meaning of Christ. The intelligibility of both mysteries stands or falls mutually. This book will deal directly with the theology of the first man and his descendants. The

30

believer must hold these truths in vital relation to Christ, who alone gives meaning to Adam and his progeny.

The Church's Use of the Sources

The living Church draws her teaching about man from an elaborate use of the sources of revelation. Under the infallible guidance of the Holy Spirit she has developed, over the centuries, an articulate presentation of the mystery of man. At every moment of her passage through history, she tells her children about their eternal destiny which was lost in Adam and regained in Christ. It should occur to us to ask how the Church has come to know so much about events which took place thousands of years before Jesus appeared on earth. About these events we do not have any record of direct teaching by Christ. Where did the Church get her certain knowledge of the origin of man, paradise, man's fall and subsequent shattered existence? The Catholic answer is that God revealed these basic truths to his Church. If the Church be true, this answer is true. But a closer look at the question still leaves the inquirer wondering just how God made these truths known.

THE SOURCES OF REVEALED TRUTH
ABOUT MAN

The essential structure of the Church's way of receiving and transmitting revealed truth is unchanging. Jesus Christ's life on earth was the revelation of God in the flesh. He committed the fullness of his truth and life to his Church. Her mission is to make Christ's own mission of salvation more fully operative in men. The Church of the apostles knew that Christ had redeemed men from the effects of the sin of the first man. Saint Paul was the instrument used by God to make this relationship explicit in unequivocal terms, as we shall see later. The infant Church was from the beginning illumined by Christ's light to read the Old Testament in terms of its achieved meaning in the Savior. The story of the first man was grasped immediately by its antithesis to Christ; subsequently the idea of a polarity between the first woman and Mary was developed. The problems which we encounter in reading Genesis did not exist for the first Christians. Semitic literary forms were the context of religious thought for Jewish Christians, while the Hellenes were well aware of the epic genre and so experienced no greater difficulty. (An exception would be comprised by philosopher-types like Origen's opponent Celsus.)

There is at present a phenomenal growth in scientific study of the languages and literary forms of the Scriptures, the development of the liturgy, the translation and interpretation of the Fathers of the Church. All of these provide treasures for understanding the teaching of the Church on the origin and destiny of man as revealed by God. It seems important to keep in mind throughout the following chapters that modern studies can only contribute deeper insight into unchanging truths. This new insight frequently eliminates popular notions which stem not from revelation but from cultural and psychological sources. There is no change in doctrine, but rather in the mode in which the human mind grasps it and communicates it. Often there is a change in what was erroneously but popularly thought to be the doctrine of the Church.

How does the Church know the truth about the origin of man? She knows it in her knowledge of Jesus Christ who founded her, who helps her to understand the Scriptures, and who guides and protects her by his Spirit in her centuries-long penetration of God's living Word. She knows about Adam and Eve, their destiny, trial and fall, because she knows that these were the providential occasion for the incarnation of the Son of God. The Church alone can tell us what were the beginnings of the human family for she is the mystical body of the Son of God, his Word and truth revealed in human form.

It is good to face directly the fact that we know absolutely nothing about the original creation and ultimate meaning of man except through divine revelation. This comes to men only through the infallible teaching of the Church. Such an approach is an intellectually honest one. It clears the ground for the valid distinction between scientific study of prehistoric man and the transcendent level of study—divine revelation about man.

Official Teaching of the Church

To avoid repetition in later chapters, we will give an overview here of the sources of our knowledge of human beginnings. The revealed data

32

always keep the creation, trial, and fall of the first man inseparably united, while more detailed study necessitates looking at each aspect singly. The source closest to us of human knowledge about human origins is the teaching of the living Church in our own lifetime. This teaching re-echoes the solemn statements of the great Church councils throughout the ages. The following text from the Vatican Council, 1869–70, is typical. It is taken from Chapters 2 and 3 of the schema of the dogmatic constitution on the principal mysteries of faith:

> This is what holy mother Church believes and teaches about the origin and the nature of man as she has learned it from Scripture. God was intent on making man to his own image and likeness. That man might have dominion over the entire earth, God breathed the breath of life into the body that he formed from the dust of the earth. This was the soul, created from nothing, immaterial, incorruptible, immortal, and gifted with intelligence and free will. This rational soul is essentially different from the human body, but it is truly, of its own nature, and essentially the form of that body, so that together with the body it constitutes human nature truly and really one. (*TCT* 348)
>
> Moreover, in this beginning of the human race, the Christian faith sees a great mystery of divine goodness. Man was created in the image of God and, by his very nature, ordained to know, worship, and love God in way proper to his innate ability. But God, the supreme creator and lord of creation, whose power is not limited by the properties and laws of created nature, in his infinite goodness, willed to raise the human race, in the person of its first parent, to a sublime state superior to man's natural condition. In this state man is made partaker of the divine nature itself. And so, in addition to the gifts that perfect man's own nature, God poured out the Holy Spirit into man, so that he who is by nature a slave, might become, by the grace of holiness, a son. . . . This is the elevation of man which Catholic teachers, after the example of the holy Fathers, have correctly called a supernatural elevation. It is supernatural because it transcends both the powers and the exigency of created nature, and therefore, is not due to man's merits nor to his natural condition, but is a purely gratuitous gift of God's goodness. But man, ungrateful to his Creator and Father, freely violated God's command, and together with his descendants, fell from the supernatural state to which he had been elevated. (Cf. *TCT* 385)

Certain fundamental doctrines on the origin of man are listed in a question sent to the Biblical Commission in 1909, the purpose of which

33

was to ascertain if the truths mentioned must be held as definitely contained in the first three chapters of Genesis. As is evident from the question, certain matters other than doctrines of faith are asked about equivocally. It should be pointed out in passing that while the response of a commission is an instrument of ordinary teaching authority in the Church, infallible teaching is not in question here.

> III. In particular may one question the literal historical sense when these same chapters treat of facts that touch on fundamental points of the Christian religion? To give some examples, among others: the creation of all things accomplished by God at the beginning of time; the special creation of man; the formation of the first woman from the first man; the unity of the human race; the original happiness of our first parents in the state of justice, integrity, and immortality; the command given to man by God as a test of obedience; the transgression of the divine command at the persuasion of the devil in the form of a serpent, the degradation of our first parents from that primeval state of innocence, and the promise of a future redeemer. Response: In the negative. (D2123; cf. B. Orchard and others, *A Catholic Commentary on Holy Scripture,* Thomas Nelson and Sons, London, 1953, p. 69; *Rome and the Study of Scripture,* 6th ed., rev. and enlarged, Grail Publications, St. Meinrad, Ind., 1958, p. 119.)

In the ensuing fifty years of development of modern thought and particularly biological sciences, many detailed questions were raised regarding the exact way in which the believer was to understand the negative of 1909. The response sent by the Biblical Commission to the Cardinal of Paris in 1948 dealt specifically with the question of the historicity of the first chapters of Genesis.

> The question of the literary forms of the first eleven chapters of Genesis is far more obscure and complex [i.e. than the question of Pentateuch authorship in general, previously discussed in the letter]. These literary forms do not correspond to any of our classical categories and cannot be judged in the light of the Greco-Latin or modern literary types. It is therefore impossible to deny or to affirm their historicity as a whole without unduly applying to them norms of a literary type under which they cannot be classed. If it is agreed not to see in these chapters history in the classical and modern sense, it must be admitted also that known scientific facts do not allow a *positive* solution of all the problems which they present. . . . To declare *a priori* that these narratives do not contain history in the modern sense of the word might easily be understood to mean that they do not contain history in any sense, whereas they relate in simple and

figurative language, adapted to the understanding of mankind at a lower stage of development, the fundamental truths underlying the divine scheme of salvation, as well as a popular description of the origins of the human race and of the chosen people. (*AAS* 40 [1948], 45–48; translation from Orchard, *ibid.*, p. 75; cf. *Rome and the Study* . . . , pp. 150f.)

Two years later, in the encyclical letter *Humani Generis,* Pope Pius XII further clarified the attitude of the teaching Church toward modern scientific questions regarding the origin of man, particularly regarding the actual creation of the first man and woman and the unique status of this couple, often called monogenism. These specific doctrines will be dealt with later in the chapter, according to the present understanding of the Church as she utilizes the fruits of modern scientific and biblical scholarship.

Here it seems important to stress that the present movement of the Church is away from any attempt to mingle natural science and the Scriptures, any subtle forms of concordism. The Bible is more and more understood and interpreted for what it uniquely and eternally is, the living Word of God religious in power and purpose. The Scriptures are the record of the great salvation-history in which God has ceaselessly loved and forgiven and pursued his human creatures. To communicate this religious drama of mankind is the essential and infallible purpose of divine and human authors. The questions raised by the marvels of scientific research will be deepened and to some extent answered by scientific study. In other words, the Church is seeing more clearly than ever that there is simply nothing in the Bible about science in a scientific or even philosophic mode of affirmation.

Thus in the early chapters of Genesis, God and the sacred writer were communicating essential truths in forms not immediately evident to modern Western man but well suited to the immediate hearers and readers. However mankind began, God was the total originating cause. Man's relation to God, that is of creature before his Creator; man's relation to woman, that is, monogamous marriage—these are the truths powerfully taught in the midst of Oriental imagery and symbolism. We have tended to read the details of Genesis 1–3 somewhat with the attitude of a person who attends a controversial lecture and reacts with the sole comment that the speaker's voice was annoying.

The Church today knows the great truths about the origin of man

35

and woman as she has always known them. In the light of her divine and infallible tradition she is learning to see more accurately the precise mode in which God communicated them to the developing human family. It is not the religious truths as such but their literary expression which is being newly understood in our times. As always the Church knows that all truth is ultimately of God, no matter in what field of study it is discovered. The growth of scientific knowledge of man, though slow and as yet inconclusive regarding origins, is a great conquest of the human mind and spirit. Also, it frees the Church as infallible teacher from trying to reconcile data which do not view man from the same perspective. No scientific discoveries really deal with man from the biblical perspective. The meaning of man and the universe, how man attains God through living in love and truth, these essential verities come only from revelation. The Church teaches man, who comes from the hand of God not only at the beginning but at every instant, how to reach God. She welcomes the discoveries of science as enlargements of human knowledge, but in welcoming has profound knowledge that she alone has the words of eternal life.

Scripture Sources

Granted that the teaching of the Church is our proximate source of knowledge about the origins of man, what does the Church maintain infallibly on the question, and what does she point to as her sources of faith, her contact with God's revealing process? She shows us first the scriptural context of her faith, and then the transmission and living development of the doctrines as found in the writings which bear witness to her mission in past ages, particularly the writings of the Fathers and the sacred liturgy.

In a true sense, the Bible contains the story of man's relation to God as it unfolds from creation to Christ and even to the consummation of the universe as we know it. But for our present topic, the Church fixes in a special way on the first chapters of Genesis and on several key passages of Saint Paul's epistles. The Old Testament refers to the garden story on two other occasions (Sir 25,23; Wis 2,23f). Jesus refers to it obliquely once (Jn 8,44), while the apostolic preaching in Acts nowhere makes use of it, and Paul uses it once as an example of intellectual seduction. (2 Cor 11,3) The two chief Pauline passages concern-

36

ing man's fall are found in Romans 5 and 1 Corinthians 15. Typical are statements like the following: "As it is, Christ has risen from the dead, the firstfruits of those who have fallen asleep. For since by a man came death, by a man also comes resurrection of the dead." (1 Cor 15,20f) "For if by the offense of the one the many died, much more has the grace of God and the gift in the grace of the one man Jesus Christ, abounded unto the many." (Rom 5,15)

As always the Church interprets individual passages in the light of her divine tradition given orally by Christ. Under the rule of the analogy of faith, one part or truth is to be understood in relation to the whole of revelation. Thus, the Church knows the meaning of the first three chapters of Genesis, as she knows all of Scripture, in the light of Christ's redeeming death and resurrection. She grasps the meaning of God's creative act as illumined by the inspired passages of Saint Paul. For these reasons Catholic biblical scholars, safe under the guidance of the Church as to the substance of biblical and Catholic faith, use the discoveries of modern liguistic and literary studies to expose the truths that are contained in the highly symbolic narrative of Genesis.

The Church approaches Chapters 1–3 of this first biblical book in the spirit in which the ancient inspired writers composed them. Both of them think in terms of starting man's story where it must start, at the moment of his emergence from the creative hand of the all-powerful Lord of the universe. Both are interested in expressing somehow, in necessarily inadequate human language, the fact that man owes his total being to God's power and love. They know that man's original state in life was one of harmony with God and the world, that through man's free act of disobedience sin and disorder entered the cosmos. In other words, the opening chapters of Genesis are purely religious and truly historical (in the sense of "what happened to man," not in the modern historiographer's sense), in purpose and content. The language and literary form are the tool of the human author used by God to convey the basic truths of human existence.

The inspired Israelites who wrote Genesis 1–3 as we now have it were writing the prologue necessary to explain the presence of sin and suffering in life. They were supplying background material on the special vocation of the Israelites as the people of God from whom would come salvation, that is, the restoration of the life of harmony which preceded the primordial sin. The Church accepts this inspired "state of

37

the question" and further, witnesses to him who has come—the new Adam, founder of the new paradise which is her very self. To all the children of Adam she preaches Christ, the restorer of eternal life. He builds up his mystical body until he returns to inaugurate the everlasting form of paradise regained, the reality of the visions of the Apocalypse. Thus the Church sees as the context for her interpretation of Genesis 1–3 the entire sweep of the Bible and of human history. To try to find verbally in those ancient verses all that we know of our first parents is to misunderstand completely the way in which the Church possesses and transmits sacred Scripture.

The Fathers

The tradition of both the great Church Fathers and doctors of the early centuries witnesses to the Christian vision which sees the entire story of Adam and Eve in the light of its transformation in the story of Christ and his Church. The theme of the Church and ultimately of heaven as paradise regained is a constant, as is the notion that Christ himself is the essential paradise of union between God and man. Adam and Christ are more and more profoundly contrasted and compared. A quotation like the following from Saint Ambrose is not uncommon:

> Adam is born of the virgin earth, Christ is born of a Virgin. The former was made in the image of God, the latter is the image of God. The first was set over irrational animals, the second over all living beings. By a woman came foolishness, and by a Virgin true Wisdom. A tree brought death, life comes from the Cross. While one is deprived of his spiritual endowments and is clothed with leaves, the other, deprived of earthly goods, does not regret being clothed with a body. Adam is in the desert, Christ is likewise in the desert. (*Exp. Luc.* 4,7. Quoted in J. Daniélou, *From Shadows to Reality* [Westminster, Md.: Newman Press, 1960], p. 46)

The Liturgy

In the early Church, the sacramental rites and the preaching of the bishop were interwoven; therefore we find the same stresses in the liturgy as in the Fathers. The baptismal ceremonies in particular are totally in the symbolism of the waters of the paradise regained, the destruction of the ancient serpent and the forming of the new man—the

38

total Adam—by incorporation of new members into the body of Christ. Sin and death are conquered. Man is restored to eternal life with God in Christ.

The whole meaning of the liturgy, especially the eucharist, develops around the awareness of newness of life or redemption applied, so that it always implicitly presupposes that Adam is healed in Christ. The most ancient part of the Church year, the Easter season, from Septuagesima through the octave of the Pasch itself, opens with the reading of Genesis in the divine office. It culminates in the Holy Week drama of Christ's destruction of Adam's sin and its penalties through his own death and resurrection. In the preface of passiontide (de Sancta Cruce), the key sentence places side by side the two poles of human existence and meaning: "(God has) established the salvation of the human race in the wood of the cross, so that where death arose life might spring up, and that he who conquered by the tree might be conquered by a tree."

Christian Art

Through twenty centuries of history, the art produced by Christians has not only testified to personal belief but profoundly influenced the faith of new generations. Beginning with early catacomb art and continuing through the ages, the Eden event is the beginning of the story of Christ in masterpieces worked in fresco, stained glass, mosaic and sculpture. The contrast between Eve's conversation with the serpent and Mary's dialogue with Gabriel was never lost on the Christian people. With the decline of symbolism in art and the substitution of excessive realism, Christians have tended to isolate the New Testament events from their Old Testament antecedents. The biblical, patristic, and liturgical revivals are already beginning to show effects in more meaningful and symbolic tendencies in modern religious art. Christ presupposes Adam as redemption presupposes sin. The very mission of the Church presupposes the universal need for salvation.

THE CREATION OF MAN

We have tried to clarify *how* the Church knows the truths about the beginning of man. Our attempt has been to know better the precise   *39* angle from which she proposes these fundamental doctrines. It is necessary now to focus carefully on these truths one by one, in terms of *what* God has revealed about human origins. It is essential to start with the divinely inspired record, because it is here that God makes known truths which of their nature could not be known in any other way. The remainder of this chapter will concentrate on the act by which Adam and Eve began to be. What doctrinal truth do Christians know about God's creation of the first human couple?

In the opening chapters of Genesis there are two different accounts of the creation of the world and of man. They come from two of the three traditional sources which the inspired redactor used when he gave Genesis its present form. The two accounts are complementary, each stressing an important aspect of God's revelation in regard to man. The student should read carefully Chapters 1–3 of Genesis in full. Here we will quote only those passages most pertinent to our present discussion.

> God said, "Let us make mankind in our image and likeness; and let them have dominion over the fish of the sea, the birds of the air, the cattle, over all the wild animals and every creature that crawls on the earth." God created man in his image. In the image of God he created him. Male and female he created them. (Gn 1,26f)
> This is the story of the heavens and the earth at their creation. When the Lord God made the earth and the heavens, there was not yet any field shrub on the earth nor had the plants of the field sprung up, for the Lord God had sent no rain on the earth and there was no man to till the soil; but a mist rose from the earth and watered all the surface of the ground. Then the Lord God formed man out of the dust of the ground and breathed into his nostrils the breath of life, and man became a living being. . . . Then the Lord God said, "It is not good that the man is alone; I will make him a helper like himself." . . . The Lord God cast the man into a deep sleep and, while he slept, took one of his ribs and closed up its place with flesh. And the rib which the Lord God took from the man, he made into a woman, and brought her to him. Then the man said: "She now is bone of my bone, and flesh of my flesh; she shall be called woman, for from man she has been taken." For this reason a man leaves his father and mother, and clings to his wife, and the two become one flesh. (Gn 2,4–7.18.21–24)

40   The first of these accounts is situated within the framework of the six days of creation. It intends to convey the sense of man as the climax, the crown and master, of the material world. It also stresses powerfully the uniqueness of man as the creature not only made by God, but made like to God: "in his image." The second account stresses the immediate formation of the first man and woman from pre-existing matter, into which God pours or breathes the spirit of life. It also situates woman as the human equal of man, his helper and partner, one with him in origin and in their marriage.

The intention of God, the primary author, and of the inspired human author was to communicate to man fundamental religious truths about man himself. Where did he come from? Why is there evil? What is the true relation between man and woman? The answer to all these questions is implicitly given in the first part of Genesis. Through the ages the Church has made more explicit what is contained there. She tells us that the following truths have been revealed by God and must be held by those who claim to believe God's plan for human beings.

1) The first man and woman were brought into being totally by the creative power of God.

2) The souls of the first pair were immediately created from nothing by God and were spiritual and immortal principles of human existence.

3) The bodies of the man and the woman became human flesh at the instant of the infusion of the human immortal soul.

4) God established sexual difference ordered to monogamous marriage and thus manifested the true relation between man and woman.

5) There was at the beginning a unique couple from whom all the members of the human race descend by physical generation.

THEOLOGICAL DISCUSSION

On each of these points the Church has meditated and developed her insights over the last twenty centuries. We shall give the present state of her teaching on each of these points, leaving to more specialized works the task of spelling out the history of these doctrines through the ages.

The great theme of the revelation of God as Creator is that he alone *is,* and that all else exists by his will and power. So too man, highest among God's visible creatures, is planned by God and caused 41 by him in the totality of his being. In the creation story God is the subject of almost every sentence. He speaks and things spring into existence. He calls each creature from nothingness into being. He makes the world of angels (implicit in Gn 3,4 and 24) and the material universe. Then he makes man, king of visible creation. Man's nature is designed by God. His spirit-matter mystery is actualized by God. He is placed in the universe to show forth as no lower creature does the image of the spirit-God. Thus no matter how it is stated it is absolutely clear that man, in all he is and has, comes from God and is supported in being by him, is radically and forever "creature."

There is an intrinsic difficulty in trying to speak about the creation of man. Since man is matter and spirit, and since our whole experience of making things is a process that takes time, we have to beware of the notion that God took time to make man. As we shall see, he may have prepared for the creation of the first man over a period of time. But man began to be only in the instant in which God created a human, spiritual soul. Since the soul is immaterial, it cannot come into existence except by the direct act of God's creative power. This same power which intervened to create the souls of the first human creatures is operative throughout history at the conception of every human child. The difficulty in thinking about the specific first moment in which a man existed is that this first moment is first by God's omnipotence and not as term of a time process. Matter, whatever its condition, is not human flesh until it is animated by a human soul.

The Evolutionary Hypothesis

With the rancor of previous decades lessened, it seems possible to state with some accuracy the actual problem which the theory of evolution seems to raise in relation to Christianity's Adam. It is also possible to state the present position of the Church. First, the problem. Scientific studies, especially in anthropology and paleontology, have gradually accumulated evidence that points to some line of bodily connection between the higher types of ape and the earliest remains of human fossils. From this evidence, men in a non-religious tradition leaped to the conclusion a century ago that the first couple emerged by purely biological evolution, that is, apart from divine concurrence, from the lower animals. This position is contrary to what Christian faith holds about

42

man's origins, denying as it does man's spiritual nature and God's plan for him. It is also contrary to reason since it posits an effect beyond the power of the alleged cause.

Other thinkers, while accepting God's creative power and the spiritual nature of man's soul, accept the hypothesis of a long process of gradual biological evolution. In fact, there is no other scientific hypothesis. This would mean that for the believer God created the first man by endowing with a spiritual soul some creature whose antecedents had been subhuman.

On this point the encyclical *Humani Generis* of Pope Pius XII, dated 12 Aug., 1950, has said:

> The magisterium of the Church does not forbid that the theory of evolution concerning the origin of the human body as coming from pre-existent and living matter—for Catholic faith obliges us to hold that the human soul is immediately created by God—be investigated and discussed by experts as far as the present state of human sciences and sacred theology allows. However, this must be done so that reasons for both sides, that is, those favorable and those unfavorable to evolution, be weighed and judged with the necessary gravity, moderation, and discretion; and let all be prepared to submit to the judgment of the Church to whom Christ has given the mission of interpreting authentically the sacred Scriptures and of safeguarding the dogmas of faith. (*ASS*, 42 [2 Sept., 1950], 575f; *TCT* 365.)

It is important to note several things. The gradual evolution of the first man in his animal component is not "proven" in the strict sense —perhaps can never be—hence it may not be taught as if it were. It is, biologically speaking, a hypothesis. The way in which God made the first man is, in a sense, irrelevant to the revealed doctrine *that* he made him. Man's origin, for the Christian, was totally the result of God's power and love. It is much clearer today than it was fifty years ago that the truth or falsity of human evolution is a scientific problem. Whatever is shown to be true in the theory of evolution is harmonious with revelation. God seems to have chosen not to reveal anything on this beyond the fact that man as he is comes from God, body and soul. All else that we know we know by natural knowledge through reading the book of the universe.

Whatever may be the facts in the evolutionary question, the intimate link of man with the material universe is past doubting. He is its finest adornment, its steward who will bring it to its final earthly development. The inescapable stress on matter in a Christian theology of man is an affirmation of the goodness of material things—an answer to the Manichean temptation which runs throughout human history. The stress on matter reminds man of the sacredness of the human body. It elevates the use of sex in which man and woman dispose matter for the creation of a human soul. It is a foreshadowing of the incarnation in which God will take a human nature from the matter offered by the virginal body of Mary. Finally, the stress on matter in man's making prefigures the use of sacramental matter in his remaking in Christ.

The Church has made clear that the question of the evolution of man's body under God's directing providence is an open question for experts. What is her teaching on woman's relation to man at the dawn of human history?

Recall the fact that in the two creation narratives in Genesis, God is revealing absolutely fundamental truths. These truths are presented in two somewhat different literary forms. The first account (doubtless written second) is prosaic at this point: "male and female he created them." (Gn 1,27) The second account is highly imaginative and is cast in parable form. God makes Adam as a potter forms clay; animals parade before the lonely Adam; Eve is formed from Adam, cast into deep sleep.

The human race has been brought into existence by God's direct action. On this is founded all else in the story of man. In the second creation narrative, the concern of God through the human author is to teach about the relation of man and woman, the next understanding absolutely basic for the conduct of life. The woman is described as formed from the man precisely in order to show her equality of nature with him, her role as companion and helper, her loving dependence on him. Granted the notion of woman in the ancient world, the Genesis story is a magnificent way of teaching that woman is as much the image of God as man is. She is the wife, not the slave of man. Sex is planned by God himself, and planned for monogamous marriage. Man, the spirit-matter composite, is a couple, a man and a woman.

Without holding that the details of the Genesis story about Eve's creation are literally true (indeed, the nature of the biblical narrative suggests the opposite), the Church teaches that woman is one with man and not lower by nature in any sense. In no ancient culture was there such a lofty idea of woman, of sex and marriage, as among the Israelites in virtue of their revelation. Only with the coming of Mary was the Jewish ideal elevated higher still.

At a deeper level of meaning, there is a reason to accept the formation of Eve as the author of Genesis describes it. The tradition of the Fathers, who knew the first human couple as they knew Christ and the Church, saw in the emergence of Eve from the side of the sleeping Adam the prefiguring of the Church's coming from the side of Christ asleep on the cross. This typological reasoning is truly important. The Adam and Eve events come first historically, but in God's view they are ordered both in event and meaning to Christ and the Church. God formed Eve from Adam because he knew already that the new Eve, the Church, would come to life only from the death of the new Adam.

Names of Adam and Eve

In all human language names are important. This is particularly true in Scripture, owing to the Hebrew sensitivity to the name as somehow delineating the essence of the thing named. The Hebrew word *adam* is used throughout the first three chapters of Genesis: *the man,* or at times simply *man. Adamah* is the word for soil or dirt, ground, clay. The man is reminded of his earthly origins in his very name. He has a deep affinity with the clay from which God drew him and to which he will return because of sin. This use of *adam* as *the man* powerfully stresses the uniqueness of the first man, his containing the future of the human family in his very being. When the man wakes from sleep and sees the new creature before him, he says that she shall be called *woman* (Hebrew: *ishah*) because she was taken from *man* (Hebrew: *ish*). The derivation is popular etymology, and the assurance of philologists that the two words are unrelated does nothing to reduce the idea of likeness they connote. The English "man" and "woman" show a similar affinity and indicate, as with "bride" and "bridegroom," the closeness of the relation between the two sexes.

Only after the first sin and the meting out of punishment by God do we find the name Eve used. "The man called his wife Eve (Hebrew: *havva*) because she was the mother of all the living," an obvious reference to human generation. The usual way of speaking of "Adam and Eve" directly as proper names is much richer in meaning if the deriva-

45

tion of the names is known from the very story of the origin of *man*, who is man and woman.

Monogenism

It has been the constant teaching of the Church that there were two individuals, one single human couple, at the start. From them the entire human race is descended by physical generation. This supposition is called monogenism. It was not an area of heated controversy until comparatively recent times. With the growth of the evolutionary hypothesis and the continuing discovery of fossil and other remains all over the world, a theory called polygenism has been put forward. It maintains that the human race began in several places, at various times, and thus stems from several original human couples. It is immediately obvious that the Church would have to advert to this theory and clarify for modern understanding her own teaching on monogenism.

All biblical exegetes agree that mere examination of the text of Genesis 1–3 cannot decide the question of monogenism. The most obvious reason is that only recently has it been raised as a question; it certainly was not something the ancient author was aware of. The teaching of God's Church must guide thought on this subject. In the encyclical *Humani Generis*, Pope Pius XII spoke on monogenism in the following words:

> But as regards another conjecture, namely polygenism as it is called, the children of the Church by no means enjoy the same liberty. No Catholic can hold that after Adam there existed on this earth true men who did not take their origin through natural generation from him as from the first parent of all, or that Adam is merely a symbol for a number of first parents. For it is unintelligible how such an opinion can be squared with what the sources of revealed truth and the documents of the *magisterium* of the Church teach on original sin, which proceeds from sin actually committed by an individual Adam, and which, passed on to all by way of generation, is in everyone as his own. (*AAS*, 42 [2 Sept., 1950], 576; *TCT*)

Note that the Church's certitude in regard to a condition at the beginning of man's history is based on the certitude of the universality of Christ's redemption. Christ redeemed all those affected by original sin. But original sin is something at the roots of man—and not only in the sense of time beginnings. It is the sin committed by *the man,* the progenitor in an absolute sense. Only those descended from him are affected by his sin, and thus capable of redemption in Christ. The solidarity of the human family in redemption is rooted in the natural and physical solidarity of all men with Adam; it was his primordial fault that was the occasion for the coming of the new Adam. Monogenism alone can make this solidarity an intelligible reality, given the supposition that it is the unique way to account for the unity of the human race.

SUMMARY

In this chapter we have presented the viewpoint which the Church has always had in teaching about human origins. The man and the woman have been created by God as the climax of his calling into existence an angelic world and a material universe. The stage is set for the drama of human history in which each of us plays a part, but a part profoundly influenced by the actions of the first human couple. It becomes necessary now to see what was their actual condition of life, in order to understand the tragedy of their failure, and its victorious transformation in Christ.

CHAPTER FOUR

THE HUMAN
CONDITION
BEFORE SIN

God called into existence the angelic world and the material universe. He formed the bodies of Adam and Eve by infusing in them human souls. The first human couple stands on the earth in absolute newness as human history begins. What sort of beings were they? How were they related to God? The rest of revealed truth hangs on the correct answer to these questions. When sin destroys the primal pattern of man as God has made him, the eternal plan of salvation in Christ begins to unfold.

We must depend on the teaching of the Church for unshakable truth about the mode of existence of the first pair. The sources and development of this doctrine are much the same as those of the similar discussion offered in the last chapter. Here we will present what is common teaching in the Church, avoiding all speculation on details.

One warning seems essential before we try to understand the sinless Adam. The only experience we can have of human nature is our own nature as damaged by original sin. We cannot imagine either man's primal state or some state of human nature as it would have been if man were not destined for a supernatural goal. Therefore it is best to try to grasp the doctrines about original justice and innocence in their most intelligible and communicable form. It is futile to try to imagine "what it was like" to live in Eden. After the resurrection, at the end of time, we will experience total integrity in a much higher way than Adam. Until then, it is not pious imagining but doctrine held by faith that illumines our understanding and guides our choices.

Many things must be said about the first human couple, marvelous termination of God's creative process. In order to appreciate the variety and interrelationship of their gifts and qualities, it is helpful to study them from different aspects, hoping at the conclusion that the richness of the simultaneous presence of so many gifts will be more evident. The first man and woman must be situated in their natural place in relation to the universe. Then their supernatural ordination to God and the effects of this on their relation to the world can be studied.

MAN'S PLACE IN THE UNIVERSE

God has revealed to us that man is the crown and goal of the creation of the universe. He is its king and it exists to serve him, to be his dwelling during his time of trial.

One of the most wholesome effects of the present revival of Scripture studies among Catholics is the rediscovery of the true Judeao-Christian notion of man. For complex historical reasons, a dualistic notion of man as made up of two different and separable realities, matter and spirit, body and soul, had come to have disastrous effects on much Christian thinking. The impression was given that the two co-principles in

50

man were by nature opposed, that spirit was good and matter, while not evil in the Manichean sense, was a restraint on the perfection of spirit.

Body-soul Composite

The Church has always taught that man is one reality, body animated by spiritual soul, the two making up one substantially existing whole. This means that the human soul, directly created by God and capable of spiritual activity, immortal in its being, is made by God to be the form of a body, in other words, its life principle. It is not meant to exist in a purely spiritual state. The importance of the correct understanding of the substantial unity in man cannot be exaggerated. Man must be understood as his Creator intended him, must be properly inserted into the order of created reality before his supernatural elevation can be adequately understood. Not only is his relation to God at stake but also his relation to the cosmic kingdom.

God gives to each created being a certain nature. Everything is a certain *kind* of thing. This nature is the limitation of a creature's actual existence. In men and angels it is their nature which is elevated by grace but which remains angelic or human nature. Through revelation we know about man's created nature and its simultaneous elevation by grace. Still, nature is logically prior to supernature. Man as body-soul composite is precisely man. Even elevated by grace or transformed in glory at the end, the creature who exists and is supernaturalized at the end is a man. A firm grasp of this basic truth is crucially important for the entire theology of man, for understanding Christ the God-man, for building a sound moral theology or a vital sacramental life.

The biblical view of man's nature could be put this way: God takes the red clay of earth which is man's home, his element, and breathes into it spirit, a life somehow like God's. This being, made in the image of God, is man; the highest type of visible creature is alive by a life which is the source not only of the activities of the body, but of invisible activities like knowing and loving.

The Image of God

The glory of man is his being the image of God. This is the fundamental revelation about man given in the words by which God reveals man's creation and destiny. What does it mean to say that man is an image of God? The words give us the key to the meaning of man, but also indicate the source of his intrinsic mystery. Man stands visible in the material universe, yet he is the image of the invisible God. He has dominion over the world yet is totally ordered to its transcendent Creator.

The common understanding of the Christian tradition has been that man is the image of God because he has a spiritual and immortal soul, a principle of immaterial activities of knowing and loving. This can be said of no other material creature. The rest are not literally like God, made "to his image," although every creature is a reflection, a trace, a Word expressive of God's creative power and love. It is in the very nature of man to be like God in his inner and most truly personal activity.

It seems important to remember that for a correct notion of human nature it is necessary to move constantly between the awareness of man as body-soul composite and his literal imaging of God rooted in his spiritual soul. If the former is stressed, man can come to be viewed as merely the highest type of animal. If the latter, there is the danger of angelism, making man to be purely spiritual soul. As in every profound truth, the human mind must move about, clarify one idea by another, and avoid the tendency to oversimplify and schematize prematurely. Man in his entirety is in the image of God, fundamentally because of his spiritual soul. But his soul is the substantial form and life principle of his total being in a body. The body is both the soul's contact with reality and its instrument of expression.

The very nature God designed for man is a tension, a polarity, between opposite principles of being. An awareness of this must be central in all attempts to think about man's destiny and endowments on a supernatural level. The study and prayerful reading of the Scriptures is probably the greatest help we have in developing the whole notion of man as one existential reality structured in a deeply rooted, twofold composition. It is interesting to note that the true notion of man's body-soul unity as presented in the Bible is what makes the resurrection of the body seem so fitting and in a sense necessary for the final happiness of man. The overstress for centuries on man as a creature destined to "save his soul" has correspondingly weakened in the Christian consciousness the hope for true bodily resurrection and the idea of a cosmic renewal. For many modern Christians, human destiny has been pared down to soul-saving. Morality has dwindled to avoiding sins "of the flesh." This is but one example of the fundamental and irreplaceable importance of a correct idea of man as bodied spirit, image of God in the flesh.

Different Uses of "Image"

Adam and Eve emerged from the creative power of God as beings of flesh and blood, animated by spiritual souls which made them by their very nature images of God. It would be well to take time here to clarify the various ways in which the Church over the years has come to use the phrase "image of God." Since the several uses are related closely, the context in which the phrase is employed will always be important. There are four different realities which are called in theology "image of God." The most totally divine and elevated reality called by this name is the Son of God himself, the second person of the blessed Trinity, the Word. He is called in Scripture, particularly by Saint Paul, *imago Dei.* (Cf. 2 Cor 4,4.) "He has rescued us from the power of darkness and transferred us into the kingdom of his beloved Son, in whom we have redemption, the remission of our sins. He is the image of the invisible God, the firstborn of every creature." (Col 1,13ff) He is the perfect likeness, even to the point of being God himself. The word Image, like Word, is a proper name of the second person of the Trinity in Christian theology.

In creatures we distinguish three degrees of participation in God's being, so that in three distinct ways men and angels can be said to be made in the image of God. The most basic meaning, which we have already discussed, is that men and angels have spiritual principles of existence, sources of spiritual acts of knowing and loving. Thus a man or an angel by his very nature is like God in the sense that he can perform activities which are characteristic of spirit-being. The second manifestation of God's image in men and angels is that given by the infusion of divine grace, by which the intelligent creature is made a sharer in God's life. (Cf. 2 Cor 3,18.) He is made capable of knowing and loving God as God knows and loves himself. The final image of God is that achieved in the light of glory, by which the angelic or human intellect is elevated to know and love God directly in the beatific vision. (Cf. 1 Cor 15,49.) Granting these related meanings of the phrase "image of God," it is easy to see that this great doctrine embraces the whole meaning of men and

angels both in the natural and supernatural orders. It relates them somehow to that Image of God who is the Son, who assumes human nature
to restore the image of God in man. This is one of the most unifying and
synthetic themes in all of revelation.

THE SUPERNATURAL GIFTS OF ADAM

So far we have seen the sense in which the first man and woman
by nature, by their very place in the cosmos, stood forth as special beings
made to the image and likeness of God. Now it is necessary to penetrate
more deeply into their condition of being. For it is the constant teaching
of the Church that the first human couple was created not in a purely
natural but in a supernatural state. What this state was forms the setting
for the trial and failure of freedom which we call original sin.

Doctrinal Content of Genesis 2 and 3

The first thing to note about the paradise story, as we have observed, is that its whole intention is to convey great religious truths. The
origin of man and his place in nature is communicated forcefully in it.
Man is situated in a garden, a paradise of flowing waters, luxuriant
shrubbery, edible plants and a variety of animals. Given the burning
sun and parched earth of much of the Near East, the author uses such
imagery to connote a state of bliss, harmony, and effortless joy. Not one
but four rivers somehow flowed out of paradise. Man and the animals
are presented as friendly to each other. Man is a caretaker in this beautiful oasis, the shrubs of which grow without his effort or toil. He is a
vegetarian—a detail common to numerous ancient accounts of human
origins; carnivorous behavior is a sign of decline from the earliest pattern
of harmony. The tree of life is a frequent symbol in mythologies for a
mysterious, superior source of nourishment and continued existence.

Without question, the Genesis story teaches that man began in
some higher state of life, where peace and harmony reigned. Man and
woman were undisturbed by conflict between higher and lower desires.
God walked with Adam in the cool of the afternoon, communicated
with him as a friend. It is important to face realistically the outlook of
the Israelite author situated well into historical time (tenth to fifth cen-

54

tury B.C., depending on whether first authorship or final redaction is reckoned.) He was quite aware of sinful and rebellious human nature as it is now. He was out to explain the present disorder by first painting a picture of order and peace, so that sin could be seen vividly by the reader as the cause of evil and disharmony. It is this which is the great religious truth of Genesis 2 and 3, and not any description of the location of the place where the first man and woman were created.

Terms: Natural and Supernatural

With the fulfillment of the Mosaic covenant in the person and work of Christ, the Church teaches men much more explicitly the meaning of the paradise story. To this teaching the remainder of this chapter will be devoted. Pivotal to the discussion is the notion of the natural and supernatural elements in reality as revealed in Christ. The clarification of these terms natural and supernatural has proceeded through centuries of difficult and heated debate. Theology deals with the best way of stating a distinction on which the whole order of revelation literally stands or falls. The most fundamental and universally agreed upon aspects will be presented here. The more technical and debated areas which touch on important but secondary questions will be left for personal reading and later study.

Theologically, the words "natural" and "supernatural" stand in relation to one another. Natural is taken as meaning all the qualities and abilities which belong to a creature by its nature, by the very kind of thing it is. Supernatural in its most superficial sense denotes qualities and abilities which are above what is natural for a specific creature. Immediately we are faced with the root of much of the difficulty in discussing the supernatural. The human mind and consequently human language must use concepts drawn from natural reality as experienced through man's senses. Thus, the supernatural in any form at all is necessarily mysterious to man, for it deals with a world beyond direct experience. All the terminology he uses to describe it will necessarily be analogous.

However, there is a deeper cause of mystery in regard to the supernatural. God has revealed to man that the gifts and capacities he wills to give to spiritual beings are realities which belong by right to God alone. Thus, the supernatural order will be not above man's nature in any way at all, but above man's nature because it is proper to God's own being. In all that follows we will use the word supernatural in its most exact and limited sense. The supernatural will connote realities which are proper only to God.

Even brief reflection will show why this problem of the natural and the supernatural must be faced before any attempt is made to understand the gifts given to Adam and Eve and lost by sin. In the order of reality, the first man and woman were created with human natures elevated to the supernatural plane. It is necessary, however, to distinguish in our minds their natural and supernatural gifts. Only then can we see how the latter can be lost and the former retained. Conversely, the gaining and losing of grace after redemption necessitates the possibility of thinking about nature and supernature separately, even though the first man and woman came from God's creative power with the single reality of elevated human nature. The first man and women possessed human nature and thus fitted into the total cosmic pattern. This nature situated in its cosmic place was also filled with divine life. It was in a state of being quite other than that which human beings now experience. Though grace—divine life—was much less abundant, it existed in a nature harmonized with it. The tensions and counteractions of fallen human nature were as yet unknown. It is evident that the terms natural and supernatural as applied to then and now are indispensable for the study of man.

One other distinction is necessary before examining more closely the gifts of Adam and Eve. Since the word supernatural is limited in theological use to gifts in a creature which are proper to God, the term "preternatural" is used to describe gifts in man which are above human nature as he experiences it, but not properly divine. Sanctifying grace is strictly supernatural, a created participation in the divine nature. Bodily immortality is preternatural, above human nature in its present state, but not proper to God—infinite spirit. It will become evident that the connection between these supernatural and preternatural gifts is an area of great obscurity for the human mind, owing to many factors.

Adam's Supernatural State of Being

56   We have arrived at the center of the mystery of man's progenitor. The Church asks us to think reverently, and attempt to understand as

fully as possible the mystery of man as he came from God. He is God's image in the fullest sense, both by spiritual soul and by sanctifying grace. Adam and Eve began their existence with sanctifying grace. We know nothing of their external appearance. They may well have been pygmies of dark skin, cultural primitives. From revelation we know that they were perfect human specimens as to their powers of soul and body. Their body-soul composite natures were in a state of order and harmony and sheer enjoyment of existence which we cannot know until the resurrection.

It is essential to grasp intellectually the state of this pair in God's sight without getting trapped into trying to imagine what they looked like or where they lived. Adam and Eve began to be, and to be supernaturally alive in their whole nature. This means that God created man for a supernatural destiny, gave him the knowledge and means to obtain it, and established him in a supernatural plan and order of being from eternity. The so-called natural man is myth pure and simple. Man from the first instant of human existence is ordered to a supernatural end. No other destiny has ever awaited him.

Reflecting on this revealed truth, it is evident to us that God always planned that man should have as his goal the face to face vision of himself. This is totally and radically supernatural to man. It is above not only man's nature but also that of angels or any possible creature. Too often we forget that even though the angels are pure spirits, they are, as angels, completely undeserving of the eternal and face to face vision of the triune God. Their eternal destiny is the same as man's, personal possession of almighty God, who gives himself freely and supernaturally out of love. He can be attained only by free acts of love and desire by human or angelic spirits, both equally in need of supernatural elevation by divine grace. This is the basis for the unity and brotherhood of men and angels. The revealed meaning of the universe is supernatural, not merely natural. It will attain one end and live one life in the common life of heaven, where all created spirits, both human and angelic, will share direct vision and love of the one all-merciful God.

To see, to know, and to love God directly belongs by right to God only. Revelation, however, is still contingent upon God's eternal and free decree to destine men and angels to possess him directly forever. Granting this decision on God's part, the supernatural gifts of grace (in this life) and the light of glory (to strengthen the created intellect for the beatific vision) had to be given to men and angels. No creature can move toward a supernatural goal without supernatural means. He must be enabled to do actions which are truly his own but somehow have divine value. Here we touch the entire doctrine of free grace infused into man at the moment of justification.

The first point to be made about the condition of Adam and Eve at their creation is their ordering to a supernatural and not a merely natural destiny; this explains other gifts they possessed. It also explains why God had to reveal to them enough to constitute a free trial of their willingness to accept or reject his loving plan for them. The next chapter will study more thoroughly the nature of this trial and failure. Here we will examine the array of supernatural and preternatural gifts which Adam and Eve were endowed with upon being called into existence by God.

Man simply does not know anything about the primordial human condition except as transmitted through the Church in the light of revelation. Therefore it is essential to look at the truths about Adam from God's point of view. These truths do not need to be harmonized with any other kind of knowledge, for there is no other source of knowledge about the destiny and trial of the first man. God formed him and his helpmate, all the while aware of Christ who would not only undo the primal failure but be infinitely more perfect Man. Mary would be the first and fullest beneficiary of this redeemed status. God gave the original gifts of holiness and innocence to the first couple knowing that when they rejected them the gifts would be regained in an infinitely holier and more abundant way. Here is the heart of the mystery of God's free plan for our race, which was always a plan of redemptive love in Christ.

St. Paul prays, "Blessed be the God and Father of our Lord Jesus Christ, who has blessed us with every spiritual blessing on high in Christ. Even as he chose us in him before the foundation of the world, that we should be holy and without blemish in his sight in love. He predestined us to be adopted through Jesus Christ as his sons, according to the purpose of his will, unto the praise of the glory of his grace, with which he has favored us in his beloved Son." (Eph 1,3–6)

Granted, this is an unfathomable mystery. But it makes evident that God plans and guides all of creation to its destiny in one magnificent and infallibly realized plan. Human freedom is one of the essential elements in the achieving of the plan. How God's foreknowledge and man's freedom cooperate is unseeable to us here on earth. By faith there is certitude that the two work together.

Sanctifying Grace

The greatest gift with which God adorned Adam was unquestionably that of a created share in the divine nature. The first human pair possessed sanctifying grace and the virtues and gifts of the Holy Spirit needed to perform supernatural actions. Primary among these—we speak at all times from the viewpoint of the full Christian revelation—would have been faith, hope and charity: faith by which God enlightened them about their destiny and free trial; hope by which they were certain that by depending on God they could obtain God himself; charity by which they could love God above all else as a friend. They were in his supernatural image, capable of knowing and loving God as he knows and loves himself. Man was meant to be not just a created image of God but his son by the grace of adoption. This supernatural likeness to God made man to be, in a participated way, like the Son of God by nature, the Image of God, the Logos. This point will be important throughout the history of the Church in the reasons given for the incarnation of the second person of the Trinity. The image of God in man is restored supernaturally by the divine person who is by very being Son and Image.

Preternatural Gifts

The mystery of the state of original innocence and holiness does not end, but rather begins, with acceptance of the fact that man was created in sanctifying grace. This grace was accompanied by other, preternatural gifts which are in some sense an overflow, a redundance into the body-soul composite from the divine life in the soul. These gifts constituted the balanced, harmonious man—body completely docile to soul, soul completely ordered to God. In order to discuss this mysterious wholeness, it is necessary to single out its individual components. Integrity, or docility of body to spirit; bodily immortality; harmony between man and the material world; infused knowledge: these were gifts to be possessed by man, in the divine intention. They are just as certainly lost to man by Adam's fall, until the fulfillment of history.

These qualities were not just random benefits bestowed by a loving God. There are deep and important relationships among them. All are the effects of the harmony created in man's human nature by his supernatural harmony of relation to God by grace. The first man and woman entered the world as crown of the universe, image of God, visible link between the cosmos and its Maker. The whole creation was in harmony: lower things subject to man and man in loving subordination to God. God had created a beautifully ordered universe but disorder and rebellion followed angelic and human sin.

The grace in Adam's soul united him supernaturally to God. From this grace, in God's primal plan, the preternatural gifts flowed into his whole nature. His perfect harmony of body-spirit unity, known as the gift of integrity, affected to its roots the entire human reality, even its relation to the material world. A theological corollary of this state of integrity which some have drawn is that the man knew only enjoyment in the use of his bodily powers, suffering no pain, discomfort, fatigue or illness.

It is as important as it is difficult for us to gain any accurate awareness of the preternatural gifts of man at his creation. Human nature as we experience it is not human nature as God made it. Its origin in harmony and holiness we are sure of in faith, however. An awareness of the effects of the state of "original justice" is essential for any beginning of penetration into the marvellous humanity of Mary—the creature full of grace—and even more of Christ's human nature. Both resembled us, of course. But in essential holiness and harmony, interior peace and order, they were like man before sin.

The other great doctrinal area in which our understanding of the preternatural gifts of Adam is basic is the doctrine of the resurrection of the body. Christian faith and hope can believe with utter realism in original sin and its terrible effects because it is known with certitude that at the end of life each man in Christ will have a holiness, harmony, and glory even greater than that which filled Eden.

It is true that we understand the preternatural gifts of Adam and Eve best by negation, by adverting to the effects of sin as we experience them in human nature, and then believing that the condition we know was not that of our first parents. This negative aspect will be developed more at length in Chapters 6 and 7 after a study of original sin. Here we will enlarge just a little on what we know about the positive side of these original signs of God's creating love.

Integrity as Perfect Harmony

Integrity is the name traditionally given to the mysterious harmony which Adam enjoyed within the complexity of his composite nature. Doctrinally it is clear that the sense of strife and tension which we all experience as our very mode of existing and acting was not the condition of man at the outset. It is also certain that this integrity was a preternatural and free gift of God, but a gift very fitting in a creature elevated to a life of union with God by grace. Adam had all the rich variety of powers which we have: senses, bodily passions, intelligence and free will, but all so ordered that his spiritual knowledge and free will ruled without strain the functioning of his sensitive, bodily nature. Body and spirit were not only substantially one existing man; they worked harmoniously for common goals as ordered by his personal, free decisions.

The scriptural reference to the nakedness of Adam and Eve and their lack of shame in this circumstance is probably included by the sacred writer in order to point to the gift we call integrity (though in the ancient Near East nakedness connoted the shame of humiliation rather than the sex passion). In any case, Christian theology has associated the narrative with loss of control of the spontaneous movements of appetites, both sensitive and spiritual. The effortless directing of these desires by reason and will comprises the gift of integrity. Modern theologians stress that concupiscence, in the sense of desire, must not be conceived as evil. Rather, the effect of original sin was a loosening of the harmonious and easy control of spontaneous desire. Integrity made Adam and Eve more, not less, human and vital in their decisions and actions.

Immortality

Whatever the exact relation of the Genesis story is to the gift of integrity, the account makes clear that bodily immortality was given to man on condition of his obedience to God under a special command and trial. This sets the stage for the drama of the first sin. Here we are simply interested to note that granting man's composite nature, ultimate bodily decomposition would be natural for him. Thus the gift of a condition of deathlessness is strictly preternatural. It is intimately tied up with a free continuance in the state of supernatural life, with the possession of grace. God gives man a whole array of related and un-exacted gifts. The sign of the loss of this generous sharing in divine life will be the falling away, even unto death, of man's human life: "In Adam we all die." (1 Cor 15,22) It is unnecessary to speculate about how Adam's earthly stay would have terminated if he had not sinned. God's plan as we know it is the one and only one he decreed. The pos-sibility of bodily immortality was a certain, but a very brief, human hope.

Steward of Creation

In addition to the gifts which somehow transformed Adam's nature so that it was experientially quite different from ours, God put the first couple in a perfectly harmonious relation with each other and with the world. The medievals delighted in elaborating at length the details of life in paradise, particularly in regard to Adam's knowledge and to the condition of offspring if they had been born before sin. These specu-lations are always pious and sometimes profound. A few points seem probable.

Just as man was in harmony with God by grace and with himself by integrity, so he was established as steward of the material creation. It was meant to serve him. He would use it with work and effort, but without the fatigue and worry that accompany work after sin. Work is a challenge to human ingenuity. It becomes drudgery either because of man's outlook on work through his ignorance or inhumanity to fellow-man. Man's easy and intelligent mastery over nature is basic to the entire pattern of an ordered plan for creation, in which lower things are sub-ject to higher. The marvel of man's original state is that he did not have to fight nature to achieve a partial victory over it. Rather it served him, just as he served God.

The infused knowledge of the first human pair is pure speculation; although interesting to study, it cannot be presented as doctrine. The first couple stands before our mind's gaze, situated at the peak of the cosmic order, imaging God by nature and by grace. They are living both human and divinized lives. By God's loving gift, they are equipped for their journey to the vision of himself. The stage is set for their trial of freedom and love and service. On its outcome hinge cosmic and human destiny.

CHAPTER FIVE

THE FAILURE
OF FREEDOM

God created the universe with utter freedom and love. Only
when he had created angels and men did there exist creatures
literally made to his image, themselves capable of freedom
and love. It is this fact which stands behind the testing of men
and angels. Freedom belonged to them by their spiritual principles of existence. In addition they had been gratuitously
destined for eternal sharing in God's own life and vision. For

both reasons the creative act situates angels and men in a condition of testing, of freedom to choose their continued possession of grace. We know the results of the trial of the angels. Now we will attend to the trial of the human race in its first members.

This study is difficult for several reasons. It deals with the deepest natural mystery of man, his freedom and the possibility of evil. Added to this is the most profound supernatural mystery, God's plan that the universe should be redeemed in Christ. This plan is of the very fabric of the doctrine of original sin; conversely, original sin is incomprehensible without a knowledge of what God means to do to save us. Not the least of pedagogical difficulties is the fact that misconceptions abound in the popular understanding of original sin. In our times these wrong attitudes are so common that the sin of Adam is often treated as merely mythical or even comic. Frequently it is misrepresented as mainly connected with some sexual disorder.

It is necessary to approach the study of this great mystery with reverence. There must be docility to God's revealed truth as communicated to men through the infallible teaching of the Church. This teaching is stated in conciliar decrees, which in turn depend upon the interpretation put on the Genesis story by St. Paul in Romans 5 and 1 Corinthians 15. The faith of the Church expressed in her councils is deepened in penetration through the ever-advancing growth of scriptural and theological study in the Church.

The following typical statement is found in Ch. 3 of the schema of the dogmatic constitution on the principal mysteries of the faith prepared for the Vatican Council in 1870:

> Man, ungrateful to his Creator and Father, freely violated God's command, and together with his descendants fell from the supernatural state to which he had been elevated. He incurred the anger and the wrath of God; he lost holiness and justice for himself and for us; defiled by sin, he handed down to the entire human race not only death and corporal punishment, but sin, the death of the soul. This sin of Adam is transmitted to all his children by propagation, not by imitation; and it constitutes each man in the condition of a sinner. This is what the Church has always taught, and what the Council of Trent has defined. With the approval of the present council, we renew the decrees of the Council of Trent. (Cf. *TCT* 388.)

THE SCRIPTURE SOURCE

How has the Church arrived at these truths? As always in this area of the theology of beginnings, she has reflected, under the guidance of the Holy Spirit, on the earliest sources in the light of later sources. The classic source for the act of original sin is of course Genesis 3,1–13. What follows is the text and the present state of agreed interpretation on it:

Now the serpent was more cunning than any beast of the field which the LORD God had made. He said to the woman, "Did God say, 'You shall not eat of any tree of the garden'?" The woman answered the serpent, "Of the fruit of all the trees in the garden we may eat; but 'Of the fruit of the tree in the middle of the garden,' God said, 'you shall not eat, neither shall you touch it, lest you die.'"

But the serpent said to the woman, "No, you shall not die; for God knows that when you eat of it, your eyes will be opened and you will be like God, knowing good and evil." Now the woman saw that the tree was good for food, pleasing to the eyes, and desirable for the knowledge it would give. She took of its fruit and ate it, and also gave some to her husband and he ate. Then the eyes of both were opened and they realized that they were naked; so they sewed figleaves together and made themselves coverings. When they heard the sound of the LORD God walking in the garden in the cool of the day, the man and his wife hid themselves from the LORD God among the trees of the garden. But the LORD God called the man and said to him, "Where are you?" And he said, "I heard you in the garden, and I was afraid because I was naked; and I hid." Then he said, "Who told you that you were naked? You have eaten then of the tree of which I commanded you not to eat." The man said, "The woman you placed at my side gave me fruit from the tree and I ate." Then the LORD God said to the woman, "Why have you done this?" The woman said, "The serpent deceived me and I ate." (Gn 3,1–13)

Doctrinal Interpretation

Before attempting to understand more deeply this remarkable passage, it is important to re-read it slowly as if it were quite new, as in a sense it is. Three sentences masterfully deal with Eve's temptation. Two sentences suffice for the primal fall. Seven verses describe vividly man's awareness of the effects of sin. Only God could have inspired a

65

passage so full of divine and human wisdom, so pregnant with meaning for the entire history of man. The ancient author himself must have had a strong insight into the nature of sin in order to be such a good instrument of the Holy Spirit in describing this archetype of all sin. Modern biblical study has done much to tell us the primary literal sense of this passage. Paul's use of it, however, in deriving a theological meaning, remains in undisturbed possession as the Church's chief source of revelation on the doctrine of original sin.

It is obvious that the human author under God's impulse has written an exquisite parable, the story of man and woman and sin. It is unique in human writing because it was written to convey essential historical truths upon which is dependent God's entire plan of revelation. Without question the story as we now have it was written well into historical time, probably after the return from Babylonian exile in 538 B.C. It must not in any sense be viewed as the description of an eye-witness—an appropriate warning when one considers that many of the difficulties that persons have had with the doctrine of original sin stem from total ignorance of the literary vehicle of the revelation. Have we not all heard some remark like, "How silly to think that God would punish the whole human race because one person ate an apple?" St. Paul's swift and spare use of the typologies involved eliminates the charge of silliness. He puts the narrative on the theological plane where it belongs—where in fact the author of Genesis put it, long before Western ignorance of the biblical mode of writing created problems where there had been none.

The details of the story are cast in the symbolic idiom of the culture of the author. Both God and the human author intended that the story convey religious truths, first of all to the Israelites, and then to all believers. Primary among these truths is that the first man and woman, naturally and supernaturally blessed by God, were created in a situation which tested their free love and obedience to him. The terms of the trial were clear, and it was possible to obey them; its consequences were the most serious imaginable. The man and the woman were tempted to disobey God by a "serpent," the epitome of evil. They did so fully aware of the consequences of their action. Immediately after sin, man experienced the consequences of sin in his own nature and in his relation to God.

66

The passage is historico-parabolic in form. It must be held to contain the historical truths previously mentioned. However, the details of the story are not meant to be taken literally, lest the theological meaning which is its *raison d'être* be lost.

Role of the Evil One

There is universal agreement that the serpent who introduces evil and discord symbolizes the spirit of evil—some force, whether person or religious tradition, completely divorced from God. The pagan religion of the Canaanites which surrounded Israel used serpents in rites and symbolism; whether as phallic talismans or to convey the idea of new life by the annual shedding of skin is obscure. The author may have been influenced to chose the serpent in order to point out the evil of these pagan rites. Some commentators think this may have been the purpose in stressing so strongly the woman's role in Adam's sin, for a degraded use of woman played a large role in Semitic fertility rites. At any rate, man and woman are pictured as being tempted by more than human powers of evil. They enter into a larger and more mysterious cosmic evil which existed before human sin. The extent and interaction of cosmic evil is an area of theology which remains obscure. It must be accepted as a fact, without our forgetting that even the evil powers are creatures of the living God. They play their role only within the one plan of universal salvation.

Psychology of Sin

The exchange between the serpent and Eve, a masterpiece of psychology, is done with a rare sparseness of wording and density of thought. The serpent's question, seemingly innocuous, has a tone of mockery. It implies that Adam and Eve have been unjustly treated in not being allowed everything, the use of every tree in the garden. Eve's basic mistake is in answering at all; she shows from the outset that she is irritated. She contradicts the serpent's statement by saying that they *can* eat of every tree in the garden. Then realizing that this is an overstatement, she repeats clearly God's explicit prohibition in regard to the one special tree in its midst, the tree of the knowledge of good and evil. She knows the divine command well and the exact penalty for eating—even for touch- 67 ing the tree, as she exaggerates the point. Her pride has been nettled by the reminder that the gifts and blessings she and Adam enjoy are from God's bounty and have to be used in obedience to his mastery.

The serpent answers Eve in a classic phrase of ambiguity and deception. He contradicts God who said, "The day you eat of it, you must die." Death as the penalty for sin is meant, but death will not come to sinful man immediately. Reams have been written about the phrase, "tree of knowledge of good and evil." A common opinion is that it symbolizes the desire to know and experience every human reality apart from the moral quality of the experience. Another leading view of exegetes is that the "knowing" in question has to do (in the Semitic context) with the mysteries of human generation. This mystery is in God's province. Any attempt to rob him of it, as in the case of Promethean fire, is an exercise of *hybris,* arrogance. To beget offspring as men now do is part of the human condition, like the need to die. But in the beginning it was not so. In any event, the serpent has flatly contradicted God's veracity and goodness. And Eve has listened.

"Now the woman saw . . ." Eve begins to consider disobeying God, allowing herself to focus on the forbidden action and letting its goodness and attractiveness flow into her. The created good is set up as something just as desirable as God's command. In this sentence of v. 6, we see the appeal of every created good which has the power to win man's consent and turn him from the infinite good. The whole mystery of freedom and sin is in these few verses. Turning from a consideration of God's goodness and gifts and command, Eve is drawn by the forbidden fruit. She plucks it. The detail in the story is nonessential. The reality in the tale is primordial disobedience to God's command. Whatever occurred externally was only a sign of the interior sin of turning from God to a creature.

Immediately Eve draws Adam into her sin. When Adam disobeys, the human race has entered into its historic condition as we experience it. Original sin, the sin of Adam, the juridical head of the new race of men, is the sin with cosmic results because of Adam's place in God's plan. Actually, it was preceded by angelic sin, and by the sin of Eve.

The inspired author has communicated in a powerful way that man, constituted by God in holiness and harmony and peace, has freely caused his own suffering and death by disobeying an all-loving and generous creator.

The description of God coming to commune with Adam and find-

68

ing him and Eve hiding for shame has a poignant note of search and disappointment. This first couple, like the angels, has failed its trial of love and service. The author tellingly indicates a final quality of man, the sinner: his tendency to put the blame on another.

The story of the primal human sin is a literary masterpiece. In the light of the fullness of revelation, but only in this light, doctrinal truths emerge strongly and clearly. The details of the parable form will continue to be more fully understood through scholarly study, though perhaps there will always remain some mystery deriving from the ancient culture which engendered the story. For believers of all ages, the impact of the poetry and imagery is a great help to grasping truths which in any case defy purely conceptual presentation. Merely scientific study of the Bible does not discover the scriptural message. This message is believed on the testimony of Christ through his Church. Once the docile and loving Christian believes, he grows in perceiving the great doctrines as they are clothed in the language of the heart. God speaks well of God. And God alone speaks coherently about the creation and original catastrophe of the human race in its first couple.

THEOLOGICAL REFLECTIONS

During the centuries since Christ, theology has made more explicit the exact nature of the first human sin. It is certain that the essence of the sin was a spiritual act in the mind and will of the man. We have no idea of the external conditions under which his testing took place. It is clear that God set some specific action as forbidden, and forbidden by his free decree. In other words, whatever the details of the action, it did not concern an act morally wrong in itself. There is the recurring idea, at least implied, that the first human sin was a sin of sexual passion. While it is true that in its literary form the story reflects something of the Canaanite (and western Mesopotamian) pansexualism of religious and mythical concern, it is equally clear that the trial set by God was a test of free submission to his command and probably not in the sexual order. In the revolt of the human spirit lies its meaning and enormity, its character as the first great human decision against God.

Saint Paul says, "For just as by the disobedience of the one man the many were constituted sinners, so also by the obedience of the one the

69

many will be constituted just." (Rom 5,19) The entire Christian tradition has maintained that the first sin was one of disobedience motivated by pride. A careful reading of the Genesis story, even in its most obvious movement as story, discloses to us the notion of a trial set by God in which the pair knowingly refuses to obey him. Strictly speaking there could be only spiritual sin before the fall because of the gift of integrity, but this is another way of saying that even after the fall the so-called sins of the flesh are formally sins only when consented to by man in his spiritual powers. Adam understood his relation to God, and knew of God's willingness and desire to give man eternal life, even of the body, on condition of man's free love and obedience. The refusal to give willed submission was the primal sin.

The Mystery of Freedom

No one can think long about the act of original sin without asking two questions. Why did Adam not obey? Why, in God's plan, was the whole race tried in one man? Both questions contain a mysterious element which can never be entirely understood. We must wait until heaven for the direct vision of divine mysteries. In a sense the second question is more unanswerable than the first, for God is God. He is infinitely free and wise and loving. He acts out of the depth of his own mysterious being. The more we meditate on revealed truth, the more wonderful it is seen to be. But no amount of insight makes the truths revealed become suddenly lucid and necessary.

The question of why Adam sinned simply poses the problem of created freedom: the grandeur of the creature's capacity to achieve his goal freely, the misery of his possible failure, and the rejection of his true end. The literature of the world and thousands of years of philosophy and theology have deepened the understanding of human freedom, but also its mystery. The spiritual creature is destined for freely achieved union with God. However in each free action he somehow gathers up his whole self and chooses. He decides in favor of God above all created goods, or opts for a created good in proper relation to God, or for some creature in a preference to the infinite good. The "why" of these choices is what we mean by the word freedom. Adam was freer, owing to his gift of integrity, than a man affected as we are by original sin.

Adam chose to disobey with greater knowledge and commitment than we can ever imagine. In fact, what he really chose was his own independence of choice rather than free submission. Original sin seen in this light takes on its true dimensions of evil and rejection. Adam was created with special gifts; his spurning of God was a personal act without any mitigating circumstances.

The Cosmic Setting for Sin

It has been mentioned throughout, but it is important to point out specifically, that the angelic and human worlds are interwoven in the story of original sin. The rebellion of the created spirits had already admitted sin and evil into the universe. Man, ultimate creation of the material world, was still innocent. When he succumbed freely to the temptation to rebel, human and earthly elements in God's plan were also drawn into the shadow of conflict and into the experience of death. The main lines of total cosmic unity are revealed in relation to both the one source of things and their final restoration in Christ at the end of time. Between these two poles of created reality there is often more darkness than light in the mutual interrelationships between good and evil men, good and evil spirits. Without question they are all contributing to the final working out of one plan. Until judgment, the plan is clearly known only to God. The scandal of evil and suffering will be used by him to further the good which alone is intended by him. Hell itself will exist forever as sign of the earnestness with which God respects the free choice of his spiritual creatures.

The understanding of the nature of the act by which Adam forfeited original justice is not a merely speculative venture. To grasp even to a small degree the existential reality of the primal sin is to come face to face with the essence of the free act. Each person is on trial for eternal happiness. Each free act has eternal consequences for good or evil. As a result of the redemption and the long, slow healing of the weakness of human nature by the sacraments and charity, God gives most men time to make and modify choices. Still a personal mortal sin is as grave in regard to eternal life as Adam's sin was for him. This sense of the utter freedom of human destiny, of life as trial for eternal joy, is seen in brilliant focus whenever we think about Adam's sin. The latter stands as a sort of pattern, an archetype, of all grave sin. In fact it could probably be shown that there is a correlation between a person's awareness of the enormity of Adam's sin and the enormity of his own sins.

Only the free act by which the first man knowingly turned from God enables us to understand the source of evil, suffering, and death in the world. No other explanation safeguards God's absolute wisdom, goodness, and love. It is his respect for created free causes which moves God to allow sin and the consequences of sin. We know, moreover, that God foreknew Adam's sin, and permitted it only in order to heal its ravages by even greater love and generosity. The most deeprooted Christian response to the fact of Adam's sin is not gloom or sour despair, but the glorious *"felix culpa,"* blessed sin, of the Easter liturgy. God is glorified for permitting Adam's sin which was the occasion for the new Adam. Man was allowed to cut himself off from God, only to be taken back into even closer union with God in the person of Jesus Christ, Son of God and Son of Mary. Original sin for all its evil results has already been more than simply cancelled out by Christ. The cosmic plan has unfolded in the incarnation, the Church, the sacraments, and the ultimate transformation of the entire universe into the one, whole Christ.

CHAPTER SIX

IMMEDIATE EFFECTS OF ADAM'S SIN

Man appeared in the world as the visible crown of God's creative power. With Adam's act of deliberate disobedience the human race lost its original intimacy with God. The human condition as we know it began. This chapter will examine more closely the precise effects of original sin in the first pair, leaving for the next chapter the broader theme of the effects of their fall on their descendants. Two quite different types of effects must be noted. The first type includes the immediate penalties described as levied against the first man and woman. The second type deals with the beginning of the story of salvation, the promise of redemption, of which the fall became the historical occasion.

The Genesis story is highly anthropomorphic. Vivid language tells the results of sin:

> Then the LORD God said to the serpent: "Because you have done this, cursed are you among all animals, and among all beasts of the field; on your belly shall you crawl, dust shall you eat, all the days of your life. I will put enmity between you and the woman, between your seed and her seed; he shall crush your head, and you shall lie in wait for his heel." To the woman he said: "I will make great your distress in childbearing; in pain shall you bring forth children; for your husband shall be your longing, though he have dominion over you." And to Adam he said, "Because you have listened to your wife, and have eaten of the tree of which I commanded you not to eat; cursed be the ground because of you; in toil shall you eat of it all the days of your life; thorns and thistles shall it bring forth to you, and you shall eat the plants of the field. In the sweat of your brow you shall eat bread, till you return to the ground, since out of it you were taken; for dust you are and unto dust you shall return." And the man called his wife Eve because she was the mother of all the living.
>
> The LORD God made garments of skin for Adam and his wife and clothed them. And he said, "Indeed! the man has become like one of us, knowing good and evil! And now perhaps he will put forth his hand and take also from the tree of life and eat, and live forever." Therefore the LORD God put him out of the garden of Eden to till the ground from which he was taken. He drove out the man; and at the east of the garden of Eden he placed the Cherubim and the flaming sword, which turned every way, to guard the way to the tree of life. (Gn 3, 14–24)

EFFECTS OF SIN

All that has been said in earlier chapters about the present understanding of the literary form of Genesis 1–3, and of the undoubtedly historical character of the basic events recorded, is valid for the above verses. By way of symbolism and parable certain essential truths are communicated by God through a human author. The entire passage breathes an atmosphere of rejection, failure, shame, and loss. Even the glimmer of hope in v.15 would be only gradually enlarged throughout Old Testament history. It would become fully meaningful with the coming of Christ through Mary. The loss of God's friendship, the disappearance of the special gifts and joys of paradise, is described as total and seemingly irreparable.

Loss of Grace

The most terrible immediate effect of sin was what we should now call the loss of grace and the virtues. In other words, Adam lost his supernatural life and powers while still having as his destiny supernatural happiness with God. He was still a man, though in some mysteriously wounded way. But he was no longer supernaturally the image of God; no longer did he share God's love and friendship and life. All that he had been given had been truly his, but as free gift. It could all have been kept by free and humble gratitude and obedience to his creator and Father. God had not changed. Man's destiny had not been changed. But the first man and woman had lost beyond their power of recovery all the means of reaching God, of being united with him in joy forever.

Loss of Integrity

However, in the Genesis story it is not the loss of divine life but of human internal harmony which is most stressed. This is understandable for several reasons. The human author like any of us was more aware of his own disorder and sinfulness than of a conscious lack of divine life. In fact, the human harmony of Adam and Eve flowed by some sort of redundance from their graced souls into the total human composite. Thus the loss of grace would actually show up psychologically in the sudden awareness of nakedness as a despoiled condition. Human beings since original sin are painfully aware of suffering and death, and aware of them as evils which ought not to be. The revealed text aims to situate these human problems in the context of their cause.

Like a good teacher, the biblical author stresses what the reader can understand from his own experience. He relates human misery to sin as its cause, again safeguarding divine goodness and love.

All theologians agree that original sin resulted for Adam and Eve in immediate loss of grace and the mysterious beginnings of disharmony in the human composite. However there is great variety of opinion on the precise nature of the connection between these two effects, and understandably so. The only human nature that we know by experience is the disharmonious kind passed on by the hereditary process. In faith we hold that the humanities of Jesus and Mary are exceptions. Therefore it is necessary to posit as the human condition before sin a state of being which we do not know directly. This makes it possible to see intellectually the revealed truth that human nature as we know it is not the way God made it. It is at present as sin wounded it.

Adam's Punishment

We can elucidate this difficult area by looking carefully at the specific punishments meted out by God in the Genesis parable-history. In an obvious literary device of the biblical author, God deals out justice in inverse order from his questioning of first Adam, then Eve, then serpent. Interestingly enough, the order follows the sequence of the sinful acts. God addresses the serpent first. To both of the human beings God indicates that their future will be one of suffering, hard work, and ultimately death. Throughout vv.17–24, it is good to remember that the man, receives his name from *adamah,* soil or ground. How bitter for him to hear the reminder of his lowly origin, of the depth to which he has fallen after being raised to divine life and companionship. He must spend himself in working the ground, eat of plants which grow from it, and ultimately return to it. Even though by nature he is a creature of earth and wedded to it, it is a blow to Adam's pride to be told, "For dust you are and unto dust you shall return."

Eve's Punishment

Eve, created to be Adam's helper, has tempted him to grave sin. She will find herself subject to her husband, her whole nature drawn to him, yet suffering much through her family role, particularly in childbirth and all its consequences.

76

"I will make great your distress in childbearing;
in pain shall you bring forth children;

For your husband shall be your longing,
    though he have dominion over you." (Gn 3,16)

It should be noted that all of these specific punishments are to be interpreted sensibly and broadly. They indicate the normal and typical areas of human suffering and sorrow, without implying there are no individual exceptions. Any and all of life's miseries are pictured as coming ultimately from sin.

Cosmic Disorder

With Adam's punishment, the author introduces the awareness of cosmic disorder as somehow connected with sin, both of angels and men. The earth which had been obedient and useful to man will turn against him as he has turned against God. This theme, although obscure to us and profoundly mysterious, is a part of the total biblical picture. It finds further stress in the New Testament revelation of cosmic renewal at the end of history when all things will be restored in Christ, the new Adam. We cannot imagine any world order other than the one in which we live, where man must struggle to gain his living out of the earth, to bend matter to his mind and purpose. However, it is not good to exaggerate the element of challenge and difficulty as if it were intrinsically evil. Man would have had to work to perfect and complete the universe in any case. It is rather the effects of work, fatigue and suffering in the man who works, which are the punishment for sin. Also, indeed primarily, sin plays a great role in man's disordered appetite for acquiring the goods of this world. Material things can be for him a snare and a source of personal sin. In this sense they are "against him" in relation to his true good. As with the other preternatural gifts, we are unable to imagine the paradise state of being unless we deny all that is painful, evil and fatiguing.

The classic text referring to this mysterious connection between man's sin and redemption and the state of cosmic disorder and renewal occurs in Saint Paul's letter to the Romans. Talking about the meaning of human suffering in terms of its eternal reward if a life of suffering is lived in union with Christ, he says:

The sufferings of the present time are not worthy to be compared with the glory to come that will be revealed in us. For the eager longing of creation awaits the revelation of the sons of God. Creation was made subject to vanity—not by its own will but by reason of him who made it subject—in hope, because creation itself also will be delivered from its slavery to corruption into the freedom of the glory of the sons of God. We know that all creation groans and travails in pain until now. And not only it, but we ourselves also who have the first-fruits of the Spirit—we ourselves groan within ourselves, waiting for the adoption as sons, the redemption of our body. For in hope were we saved. (Rom 8,18–24)

The paradise harmony existed between God and man, man and woman, body and spirit in man, and between man and lower nature. It has been profoundly disturbed at every level. The entire story of revelation as of human history will be the movement to the new and better paradise in the incarnate Word of God, Jesus Christ.

Death

The most mysterious and symbolic and in a sense the worst punishment of original sin is death. There is no question that even Adam's paradise state would have terminated after a successful trial, following which he would have entered into heavenly life as body and spirit. We will never know what this state would have been like. Now, man must die, to rise again either to eternal and perfect joy or to unhappiness. We experience human nature only in a state of gradual dying, that is, movement toward final separation of body and soul. One day, we hope, we shall experience the reality of glorified human nature, the spirit filled with grace and totally possessing and beatifying the body. But death is the term of earthly life, and this death is the direct result of Adam's sin.

God himself made clear in arranging Adam's trial that bodily immortality was at stake, that disobedience would bring death as its result. God's ironic remark about Adam now knowing good and evil (Gn 3,22) perhaps meant that now Adam and Eve would know, that is, actually undergo, death, and the sufferings which are forerunners of it. At any rate death is a deeply mysterious human fact, one which cannot acquire meaning and positive value outside of God's revealed truth about the origin and destiny of man. Modern theologians are working on more profound study and insight into the event of death as separation of body and soul, and as the final and definitive moral act of each human life.

78

These considerations do much to illumine the natural ambiguity of death as a factual event. There is an essential difference in the meaning of death if men should die in Christ or outside of his life and love.

The Christian tradition sees in the notion of death not only mystery on a natural level but visible death as symbol of the supernatural death of grave sin and loss of grace. This is certainly the full meaning of the paradise story. By sin Adam and Eve die to divine life, lose grace. The very word "mortal" sin expresses this point accurately. Visible death is the most graphic sign of the cessation of divine life in the soul. Sin and death are inseparably interwoven in the revealed fabric of man's life and destiny. The free, evil act of disobedience brought supernatural death on Adam, and the penalty of natural death on him and his descendants; personal, free, evil acts bring on each man the loss of God's grace and the danger of natural death at a time when it will also mean eternal separation from God's love and light. The deeper our understanding of the revealed meaning of death as it comes from Adam, the more we will begin to penetrate the infinite mystery of Christ's redemptive death for mankind's sins; Christ cancelled this terrible penalty by undergoing it.

Many other specific areas of human suffering and weakness could be pointed out as effects of original sin. For example, man finds learning and the life of study very difficult. This is partly due to the loss of integrity, the imperfect control of the soul over senses and memory. It is also attributable to the influence of passion, prejudice, and the complexity of human motivation. Man's mind is fundamentally as sound as before original sin, yet the composite human being finds study fatiguing. It is a discipline requiring constant effort and self-mastery. Learning already acquired presents its own difficulties. It must be balanced by the moral virtues of humility and docility, and of subordination of knowledge to the eternal end of the whole man.

Expulsion from the Garden

The image in the Genesis story which perhaps most poignantly depicts the sum total of the results of original sin is the actual expulsion of the pair from the garden of Eden. From the delights of peace and harmony the first couple is driven out in sorrow and shame, never to return. Perhaps the detail about God's making garments for them was meant by the author to indicate his continuing providence and care for his creatures; in their new despoiled condition he yet cared for them. The basic tone of the passage, however, is harsh, ironic, and final. The tree of life is completely blocked off from Adam and his wife, for their right to it depends on their respecting the prohibition regarding the tree of knowledge of good and evil. They have tasted of the latter and will live with its bitter fruits. The former they will not taste until another and truer tree of life is inserted into human history, the cross of Jesus Christ.

THE PROMISE OF SALVATION

After examining the immediate, painful punishments inflicted upon the first man and woman, it is important to recognize the glimmer of hope which accompanied them out of Eden. For God's curse upon the evil one, the tempter, contains also a promise for the human family. First we will discover the most obvious, literal meaning of the passage of Genesis, ch.3, vv.14 and 15, remembering that we study it in the light of two thousand years of thought in the Church. God addresses the serpent, throughout the passage a symbol of Satan, and he curses him for his role in the sin of Adam and Eve. Totally subject to God's power as his creature, the evil spirit manifest will be humbled to the dust by the Lord. His very success as tempter will be his ultimate undoing. Like the punishments announced to the man and woman, the destruction of the serpent thunders from the wrath of the omnipotent and just God, who is also love and mercy.

These two verses are among the most important in the Old Testament. God proclaims enmity, unending hostility, between the serpent and the woman. Note that it is God himself who institutes this enmity. The woman will be on God's side again. In context, "the woman" is of course Eve, who will repent for having gone over to the adversary, even temporarily. This enmity, a continuing thing, will go on between the serpent whose offspring in a moral, collective sense, will constantly oppose the seed, that is the descendants, of the woman. There will be bitter war between the human race and forces of evil, with much wavering on the human side. Verse 15 in its minimal sense foretells the ultimate destruction of the devil by man, Eve's seed. St. Paul, in light of the Christ-event, rather arbitrarily confines the collective noun *zera* (seed) to an individual rather than to many (Gal 3,16; cf. Gn 22,18). But of course this was the rabbinic practice of interpreting Scripture by Scripture—or in this case by life. Some man will crush the serpent and in the process be injured himself.

These two verses, 14 and 15 of ch. 3 of Genesis are often called the protoevangelium, the first gospel. The reason is not far to seek. In their immediate context, they establish, on God's own directive, unending war and hatred between humanity and Satan. They also promise some future victory on the human side. Further indication of this unfolds gradually under the Old Covenant, the inspired oracles and writings of the prophets. With the redemption achieved in Christ and constantly more deeply understood in the Church, the real depths of the divine meaning of this passage are opened to us. He who crushes the devil and is bruised by him is Jesus Christ, the redeemer. The woman is the new Eve, Mary, the virgin mother of Christ. Between her and the devil there is total enmity from the first instant of her sinless conception, with which we shall deal more fully in the next chapter. The seed of the devil and the seed of Mary, her children who are the Church, are in eternal warfare until the consummation of history. At that time Satan's power will be completely removed from any effectiveness in God's cosmic renewal. Thus it is evident to the modern believer, profiting from centuries of doctrinal development, that the good news of the coming of Christ as God-man, redeemer and son of Mary, is truly though mysteriously announced by God at the very opening of human history.

From the first moments of man's life as we know it, fallen and sinful yet yearning for redemption and holiness, history is salvific history. God created man for the vision of his beauty and love. When man rejected this, God had already planned a more profound uniting of the human race to himself in his incarnate Son. So in Genesis after the expulsion from Eden, the prevalence of sin is graphically described.

The first murder, the first extravagant retributor in blood who is also a bigamist (Lamech), the folly of building tall towers to false gods, are all reported. During the lifetime of the pious Noa, the ultimate in degeneration takes place, and a wrathful God responds to this wickedness by sending destruction. With the call of Abraham in historic time, the promise of a savior is renewed and the story of the Israel of God begins. *81* The entire Old Testament is one intense yearning for redemption, for the salvation promised by God. There are ups and down of fervor and failure, with the final, terrible purification of the exile in Babylon. But the central movement of God's revelation received in loyal souls is toward the moment of promise. From the Genesis announcement of enmity and final defeat made by God himself, the Bible moves through the ages in God's mysterious and infinitely patient ways to that announcement for which the world was created: "Hail, full of grace, the Lord is with thee. Blessed art thou among women. . . . Behold thou shalt conceive in thy womb and shalt bring forth a son; and thou shalt call his name Jesus." (Lk 1,28.31)

CHAPTER SEVEN

ORIGINAL SIN IN THE DESCENDANTS OF ADAM

Each man during his lifetime is engaged in a testing of his freedom. His unique, individual acts of choice and direction into which go God's grace and his personal cooperation or refusal determine his eternal happiness or misery. But each man finds himself in a very old world, in a human race with a long history. In order to act intelligently, to appreciate truly the human condition, a man must know God's revelation concerning both the origin of the world and man, and man's relation to the cosmos. Most of all he must know the events which occurred concerning Adam and Christ. The purpose of this volume so far has been to present the fundamental teaching of the Church on the beginning of things, particularly the beginning of man. With the help of faith and theology the first crucial events of human history have been studied. In the last two chapters the view taken will not be one of the past, but rather of present, existential man. How do these ancient events affect each person living now? What does revelation tell us about their meaning for the man of the mid-twentieth century?

To answer these questions it is necessary to clarify the revealed doctrine on original sin as it exists in each man from the moment of his conception. Then, in the second part of the chapter, the unique privilege of Mary of Nazareth will be discussed. She alone of the human family has remained free of original sin from the first moment of her existence. Having seen the effects of Adam's sin on the present state of every human being, the final chapter will situate modern man in the reality of his vital and paradoxical relation to both his sinful first parent and to his new, life-giving head, Jesus Christ.

ORIGINAL SIN IN MAN NOW

Every human being is conscious of the fact of death, suffering of all kinds, evils both in nature and in the way men mistreat each other. The Christian experiences all these things but knows them as effects of a primal disaster. He undergoes his own human weakness, failures, ignorance, uncontrollable tendencies, and yet holds by faith that these are the deep-rooted effects in his being of Adam's sin. In other words, we do not need revelation to experience the flaws and evils in man and the world. Only God's gift of truth and light, however, can tell us the cause of suffering and death, can give meaning and value to the effects of sin. Few doctrines have been more consistently and forcefully affirmed throughout the centuries than the universal sharing of all men in the effects of Adam's fall.

Essence of Original Sin

What exactly is meant when it is taught that every human being (the blessed Virgin always excepted) enters the world with original sin? It means that the newly existing human being lacks original justice. He is not what man was before sin. Immediately it is clear that the only way to get an adult concept of original sin as a state of human existence is by grasping clearly the Church's teaching on the state of innocence. When a man sees that God made Adam and Eve perfect in every way, living the life of grace in body and spirit in a harmonious universe, he knows that man and not God is the source of evil, suffering, and death. Original sin is precisely the lack of original holiness. It is very important to conceive it so. Otherwise there is the danger of turning original sin into a positive stain or mark of defilement. It is a lack of something positive, namely divine grace, which ought to be in man's nature divinizing it. Man was at first in a condition, a mode of being, which properly related him to God, to his own nature, and the universe. Conversely, after sin the primal pair and each of their descendants exist in a condition, a mode of being, which situates them as cut off from God— disharmonized in themselves and in relation to the world. Original sin is not just a negation or an absence of grace. It is not having something that should be present, just as a child born with only four fingers has a privation, a lack of something which ought to be there.

It is good to recall that there has never been any such thing as a human being who was a purely natural creature. Man came from God's creative hand divinized, destined for the vision of God, and equipped to accept freely this marvelous vocation. When he voluntarily turned from God he lost his supernatural and preternatural gifts. He became thus a natural being, but supernaturally damaged, lacking the only true harmony or ordering of his being which God ever intended. With the grace of Christ's redemption, a man's personal supernatural relation to God is restored. But he moves toward his destiny challenged constantly by his supernaturally wounded nature. He must personally pass through the effects of original sin, suffering, and death. The essential difference after Christ is not that nature as we experience it is changed, but that man is given the power to redivinize his nature. Then after death and resurrection he will arrive at an ultimate situation more glorious than any that Adam could have imagined.

What then is the most accurate way to conceive of original sin in Adam's descendants? It is that each human being begins his earthly pilgrimage lacking sanctifying grace, lacking the essential means of doing any actions to attain his goal. In addition, as a result of this lack of grace which ought to be present, the inner harmony of man's body-spirit unity is disturbed. Although this disruption does not make man corrupt or evil as such, the harmonious control of all his powers and actions by intellect and free-will is impossible. It cannot be totally regained until the resurrection of the body at the end of time. Original sin is a great mystery both in its historical source, Adam, and in its present effects in man's deep disorder and manifold sufferings. Despite its mysteriousness, the doctrine of original sin is the only explanation for life as we experience it. Moreover, it prepares us for the grateful acceptance of the wonders of Christ's redemption from sin.

Human Solidarity

It is important to remember that God's revelation came to the human race over the centuries from Adam to Christ. Even the fullness of truth which appeared in the flesh in the life of the God-Man has been more deeply understood by the Church over the centuries. The doctrine of original sin as it is now defined is the result of much human thought, controversy and conciliar debate, guided by the Holy Spirit of Christ. The following section from Saint Paul's letter to the Romans is the first fully explicit Scripture reference to the universality of the sin of Adam in his descendants, not just in its effects, but as sin in the individuals concerned:

> Therefore as through one man sin entered into the world and through sin death, and thus death has passed unto all men because all have sinned—for until the Law sin was in the world, but sin is not imputed when there is no law; yet death reigned from Adam until Moses even over those who did not sin after the likeness of the transgression of Adam, who is a figure of him who has to come. But not like the offense is the gift. For if by the offense of the one the many died, much more has the grace of God and the gift in the grace of the one man Jesus Christ, abounded unto the many. Nor is the gift as it was in the case of one man's sin, for the judgment was from one man unto

condemnation, but grace is from many offenses unto justification. For if by reason of the one man's offense death reigned through the one man, much more will they who receive the abundance of the grace and of the gift of justice reign in life through the one Jesus Christ. (Rom 5,12–17)

It is obvious that the comprehension of the doctrine of original sin in man depends not only on the mystery of original holiness, as discussed above, but also on the mystery of human solidarity. This latter truth, a natural truth, is one that undergirds God's whole plan for man's salvation. It is revealed for our acceptance so that we will not miss its force. Perhaps one of the saddest effects of the weakening of human nature through sin is that this great truth of the oneness of the human family is violated daily, both as regards persons and the collectivity. Even Christians find this truth difficult to accept. They are aided in their refusal by the pressures of personal prejudice and ignorance, and by the impact of "rugged individualism" and exaggerated notions of personal autonomy. Sin has many effects in us, but perhaps the gravest is the conviction that we are many rather than one.

Adam, then, possessed his gifts of nature and grace by free endowment, but as head of the entire family. His trial was personal and social. He stood both for himself and for all his descendants. Original sin was in Adam a personal, actual sin. In consequence of it, he was affected by personal supernatural and bodily death. But he also affected the human condition of all those who would descend from him. He and Eve could pass on only the nature they possessed, and since they had destroyed their link with God, they would pass on human natures wounded and broken.

Original sin both in Adam and in each of us is the condition of existing destined for eternal life with God, but lacking grace and having a weakened nature. The difference is that in Adam the sin was personally voluntary. In us it is not personal and actual by our own will. It is a state, a sin of nature. Thus the state of original sin as existing in a newborn child is truly the state of sin. The cause of the state of sin was Adam's voluntary act; it is in no sense the child's. The doctrine on transmission of original sin depends on the fact that God, using human-family solidarity as a natural basis, decreed from eternity to test, and then after its failure restore, the human race through two representative men. Each of the men acts in history, with a universal effectiveness that is limited to them alone. Adam lost grace for all men. Christ regained it for all. Both function as cosmic causes, one for ruin, the other for restoration.

Transmission Through Propagation

The mystery of original holiness in Adam, his supernatural destiny and the mysterious unity which would bind him and all his descendants for better or worse, make it easier to see what is meant by saying that original sin is transmitted by human generation. Sometimes persons think that this means that the use of sex is oriented to sin; a not unrelated mentality tends to think that the act of original sin had something to do with the use of sex. While it is true that many of the Fathers had the former idea, notably Augustine, it has never been the doctrine of the Church. The true meaning of the doctrine of the transmission of original sin is much deeper than the mere supposition of uncontrolled passion in the act of generation.

When two come together and the woman conceives, God creates an immortal soul. A new human being begins to exist. Since Adam's sin the human being at conception has human nature, but owing to Adam's rejection of original holiness lacks the grace which God wants him to have. Thus, when a child is conceived and born it enters the world in a state of being that we call original sin. The child is not connected with God by a share in God's life. To say that original sin is transmitted through the generative process is the same as saying that, in the present order of things, human nature is deprived of divine life and is in need of personal assimilation of Christ's redemptive grace. Human nature as it is and is passed on is not the way God created it, but the way Adam's sin despoiled it.

Personal Sin

It is important to add, in the interest of realism, that the human situation as it is today is affected not only by the state of sin in which every human being since Adam has been born; in addition each person adds to human evil and suffering by freely committed personal sins, both mortal and venial. The wounded nature with which each person starts life explains the basic cause of evil and death. But freely committed actual sins are at the root of much specific suffering. At the present moment of history, there is a horrible solidarity in sin through which each of us bears some responsibility for evil in the world. We begin our lives in original sin. Even when this is radically taken away by Christ's grace, we add personal responsibility to the total of human suffering and sin. Though this volume does not discuss it at length, we must always recall that it is the solidarity in Adam and sin which makes each man capable of receiving redemption in Christ. Thus the principle of human solidarity which explains evil and death is the very one God used in the incarnation to enable his Son to transform the whole human family.

Summary

The Church teaches us infallibly that, except for Mary, every human being by generation receives a human nature which lacks supernatural grace. It is disordered in its body-spirit existential mode of being. This is the state of original sin. If the lack is remedied through the infusion of Christ's grace, there still remains disorder in the nature and in its relation to the universe. These two fundamental tensions can be progressively lessened but never totally conquered until the day of Christ's triumph at the end.

The doctrine of original sin in all men at birth can never be proven but must be accepted as a revealed mystery. It is obscure to our minds, partly as a result of the effects of sin. In addition, certain types of persons find it an affront to their freedom and personal self-determination to hold that an act done hundreds of thousands of years ago influences the fabric of each person from the beginning of his existence. To take this attitude, or at least not to see through its specious reasoning, is to forget that only God has absolute rights. He made man, and destined him for union with himself. Although men are free they are free under God and within the pattern he has laid out for them. Whenever a person begins to feel that it is unjust to have all men suffer for Adam's fault, he should recall that we are all saved and made capable of eternal happiness solely through the redeeming death of another unique Man. As is usually true of revealed doctrines, they cannot ultimately be understood in isolation, but must be looked upon within the context of God's plan for man and the world in his Christ.

MARY'S PRESERVATION FROM
ORIGINAL SIN

The entire human family fell from God's favor in the person of Adam as the representative head of the race, but was restored in a much higher way in Christ. Where then does the blessed Virgin fit into God's scheme of things? Did she not escape the universal blight of original sin? Here it is necessary to limit what is said to the doctrine on our Lady which touches her preservation from original sin and its consequences. Actually this is less easy than it seemed to be formerly, for during the last hundred years there has been an increasing growth in the theology of Mary, often given the name Mariology as a special part of soteriology or theology of salvation. More and more scholars are presenting in a unified way the truths about Mary which have gradually been made specific in the Church through meditation and study, and crystallized in papal definitions. Just as Christ is the living God-man about whom all Christianity revolves, so all the specific aspects of Mariology delineate more beautifully the mystery of the woman who is God's most sublime creature (the humanity of his Son excepted) and the uniquely holy member of the race of men.

The following remarks touch only on the dogmas of the immaculate conception and the assumption of our Lady, one of which tells us of Mary's preservation from original sin, the other of her preservation from the corruption of death. Two things must be kept in mind. First, the most fundamental dogma about Mary is her motherhood of Christ the Son of God, therefore "divine motherhood." This and this alone situates her forever in God's plan in her essential and utterly induplicable role. The two dogmas which we will discuss deal with God's revealed truth about the personal holiness of the human mother of Jesus Christ. They affect directly Mary's personal relation to God. Her divine motherhood deals directly with her role in regard to the entire human family, and even with the cosmic plan. She is in antitype the woman of the protoevangelium, whose seed will crush the evil one forever.

The second thing to keep in mind is that there should not be an artificial separation between Mary's universal role and her personal holiness. Although we will deal directly only with the latter, it is ob-

90

vious and becoming more so, that the patristic development of the ancient theme of Mary as the new Eve points to her holiness as one of the great signs of Christ's victory over evil. Neither Christ nor Mary can be understood or approached outside of their existential meaning and mission in the divine plan for the universe. At times, because of the limitations of human knowledge, it is necessary to study one aspect or another. But each part must be seen in relation to the whole of revelation.

The Immaculate Conception

Leaving to more specialized works the theological sources of the doctrine, we can nonetheless arrive at a comprehension of the dogma of the immaculate conception relative to our study of original sin. First, note the clear and careful definition of Pope Pius IX: "We declare, pronounce and define: the doctrine that maintains that the most blessed Virgin Mary in the first instant of her conception, by a unique grace and privilege of the omnipotent God and in consideration of the merits of Christ Jesus the Savior of the human race, was preserved free from all stain of original sin, is a doctrine revealed by God and therefore must be firmly and constantly held by all the faithful." (*Ineffabilis Deus*, Dec. 8, 1854; D1641, *TCT* 510) This solemn definition capped centuries of gradual clarification as to the holiness of Mary, a truth taught and held from the beginning of the Church. Now that the doctrine is defined and there is so much writing and commentary on it, it is perhaps hard to understand the slowness of arrival at the clearly stated dogma.

In fairness to our earlier brothers in the faith, it should be pointed out that for various reasons many learned theologians could not see how a definition of the immaculate conception of Mary would not compromise the universality of the redeeming power of Christ. The concept which removed this obstacle is the one found in the definition and in the collect for this feast, December 8. It is the concept of preservative redemption. In other words, Mary is seen as much more perfectly redeemed, much more totally affected by the power of Christ's passion, than others. For her only did he make human existence and supernatural life coincide at the first instant of conception. What is clear to us now, and was not clear to many Christians previously, is that Mary owes infinitely more to Christ's redemption than any one of us. Far from detracting from Christ,

91

she stands in the universe as the most perfect result of the paschal mystery. Christ suffered and died and rose, we may say, chiefly to merit the holiness of his mother. Obviously, there is no time element from God's point of view. That Mary pre-existed Christ is not an issue, for all those saved under the Law were given grace through the foreseen merits of Christ. But what is now clear is that there is no necessity of a certain time of existing as human but in the state of original sin, in order to be redeemed. This would attach to the notion of redemption the notion of "buying back" which necessitates the actual state of sin first. Preservative redemption is still redemption, but much more of a gift, much more a sign of the infinite power of the Redeemer.

Thus the dogma of the immaculate conception has been seen since its pronouncement as powerfully vindicating the totality of Christ's redemptive power. She who was to be his mother would exist always as holy and beloved of God. In her, not even for a second could the ancient enemy of the human race claim any dominion. She is the new Eve and even the new paradise. In her the new Adam will be formed. She appears from the first moment as the woman in total opposition to the evil one. In her he can find no complicity. Granting the doctrine of the immaculate conception, our Lady is seen as far greater than the first Eve in every way, for Mary is not only holy from the beginning, she is filled with a grace that complements her vocation. In her, God's grace and the more abundant grace won by Christ's death fills her entire being.

It seems important to note that the dogma of the immaculate conception tells us that Mary was preserved free from every stain of original sin. Reflection on this statement in the light of the essence of original sin in Adam's descendants results in some interesting conclusions. Our Lady had in her soul from the first instant sanctifying grace and all the virtues and the gifts of the Holy Spirit. This is evident. But if she was in no way even for an instant affected by original sin, then she did not have a wounded nature, did not undergo the punishments which are the effects of original sin. What does this mean?

Mary had a harmony of body and soul, of spirit transforming matter, essentially like Adam's before sin. She underwent no rebellion of lower appetites; she had an inner lucidity, peace and control beyond our imagining. However, imagining is exactly what is not helpful here. Christ 92 and our Lady had real human natures, natures fundamentally like the ones we have. Thus the traditional teaching is that they freely took on and experienced some of the effects of original sin, those that would further human redemption. They endured fatigue, hunger and thirst, suffering and death. Christ certainly died; Mary may have died, as we shall see. But neither of the two had an intrinsic disorder, ignorance, or imperfections in his body-soul being.

Mary's Assumption

The doctrine contained in the definition of our Lady's conception in her mother's womb underlies all her other prerogatives and privileges. Her absolute sinlessness, her perpetual virginity, make clear the perfection of her redemption by Christ. They show how totally she belongs to God by free cooperation with her unique vocation. But of all her personal graces, the doctrine of her bodily assumption must have special place. It not only complements the depth of truth in the immaculate conception but should also powerfully influence true devotion to Mary in the Christian life.

In 1950 Pope Pius XII defined Mary's bodily assumption into heaven in these moving words:

> We therefore, after humbly and repeatedly praying to God, and calling upon the light of the Spirit of Truth, for the glory of almighty God, who has shown great and particular love for the Virgin Mary, for the honor of his son, the king of immortal ages and the conqueror of sin and death, for the increase of the glory of his great mother, for the joy and exultation of the whole Church, by the authority of our Lord Jesus Christ, of the blessed Apostles Peter and Paul, and by Our own authority, do pronounce, declare and define as a divinely revealed dogma: The Immaculate Mother of God, Mary every Virgin, after her life on earth, was assumed, body and soul, to the glory of heaven. ("Munificentissimus Deus," 1 Nov., 1950, *AAS*, 42 [4 Nov., 1950], 753-71)

Here we find solemnly taught Mary's preservation—not from original sin, but from its most obvious effect and punishment as seen both in the garden of paradise and daily life: "You shall die the death"; "You are dust and to dust you shall return." This did not apply to Mary, for, not having been subjected to original sin, she was not to be subject to the corruption of death. Note that the definition of the fact that Mary is now in heaven body and soul does not define that she died in the sense in which we mean the word. We know for certain the essential truth that when her life on earth had reached its term she was taken by God to be with her risen Son forever. Precisely how her life terminated, whether her body and soul were separated briefly and then reunited, or whether she was simply transformed into a heavenly, glorified mode of being is not dealt with in the solemn definition. The dogma of the assumption tells us with certitude only about the state of our Lady's being since she left the earth. It leaves open the question as to whether she died or not. The dogma of the assumption is not a dogma of our Lady's resurrection. This would presuppose that she died.

In terms of the limited perspective of this book much light is shed indirectly on the doctrine of original sin by the two doctrines of the immaculate conception and the assumption regarding our Lady. Original sin is our beginning mode of being human at all. Our human lives will end their earthly term in death and corruption. In Mary the entire human race can look to the member of the human family conceived as are all men, but from the start of her existence filled with God's life and love. The most perfect result of the redemption preexists the Redeemer as if to remind us of God's infinite wisdom and power. Our Lady exists now with her Redeemer Son to encourage our hope of final body-soul glorification in heaven where each man can be forever a praise of Christ's saving death. She gave him his human nature by means of which he would redeem the human family. She manifests throughout history the goal and destiny of man already most perfectly realized in her, the virgin Queen of the universe.

PERSPECTIVES FOR A CHRISTIAN ANTHROPOLOGY

Theology is a humanly ordered presentation of divine truths made known to mankind by God. Order always means seeing relationships between parts, and between parts and the whole. This volume has aimed at consideration of the basic revealed truths about the origin and meaning of man, the angels, and the material universe. This has necessitated separate approaches to the revelation about the cosmos, about the angels, and much more at length, about the creation and fall of man. By now some order should be apparent; it is impossible, however, to deduce from divinely revealed mysteries the kind of clarity that is humanly satisfying. All that this chapter aims to do is focus what has been said so far on the question of the contemporary meaning of man in the light of God's truth.

The theme which best synthesizes revealed truth about man and situates him centrally in the total sweep of reality is the theme of the image of God discussed in Ch. 4. This final chapter will point out the unity of God's plan in terms of the image of God in creation. Some specifically modern difficulties which can be integrated into the Christian vision will be indicated. Finally, a few suggestions will be made on the Christian life as lived from the point of view of the restoration of the image of God in man.

THE DIVINE PERSPECTIVE

The believer who wants to live by his faith attempts to view reality as God sees it. God is infinite in knowledge and freedom and power. The universe which he made preexists in the divine mind and will. Once the world was created and man began to live and think, he could learn endlessly from creatures because they are concretized realities expressing the divine intelligence. But man can never by discovery and study and human teaching arrive at the answer to the ultimate questions of origin and end, meaning and direction. Man without belief in God's revelation is a voice hopelessly repeating the same eternal questions. What is man? Where is he going? Why do evil and suffering exist? Can man attain happiness? One of the frightening aspects of contemporary culture is that in some ways the questions are asked more probingly and honestly than ever before. But for many persons, the Christian answer is rejected before it has been fairly heard.

Our contribution here will be to indicate the fundamental attitude with which a believer must approach the contemporary scene. Specific areas of thought and action such as science, politics, and literature each present difficult questions of their own which must be gradually worked out by specialists in those fields. But unless there is a view from above, a personal grasp of the sweep and vision of God's revealed plan for man as he exists in the universe, the secondary areas become hopelessly complex or even relegated to a purely natural level of reference. Each man must find his understanding of reality in the source of all being, who has poured out his revelation of meaning for every person to share.

Unity of God's Plan

The most fundamental truth on which to base a contemporary Christian awareness is the one cosmic plan, designed by God from eternity and consummated in Jesus Christ.

> Blessed be the God and Father of our Lord Jesus Christ, who has blessed us with every spiritual blessing on high in Christ. Even as he chose us in him before the foundation of the world, that we should be holy and without blemish in his sight of love. He predestined us to be adopted through Jesus Christ as his sons, according to the purpose of his will, unto the praise of the glory of his grace, with which he has favored us in his beloved Son. . . . This his good pleasure he purposed in him to be dispensed in the fullness of the times: to reestablish all things in Christ, both those in the heavens and those on the earth. (Eph 1,3–6.10)

Even in its most obvious and literal meaning this text from Saint Paul tells us that there is one plan for the entire universe and that it is centered in Christ. The depths of meaning and light in this classic passage are infinite. But for our use here, the passage unequivocally gives the believer the essential point of view from which he must see all reality.

From the first instant of creation to the last moment of time, which ushers in the eternal kingdom of the world to come, all of reality is held in existence by a loving God. Everything is guided within the pattern of one divine plan. The lower creation is ordered to man. Man, as we have seen at length, was ordered to perfect happiness in the sharing of God's own life. In the sinless Adam the material world was in harmony with man; the entire human family was on trial with its father and head. Sin entered the human family in this representative head and so sullied man in himself and in his cosmic role. Under the light of revelation, we know that this primordial solidarity which issued in cosmic disaster was eternally foreseen and permitted by God, as ordered to the infinitely greater restoration of solidarity achieved in the incarnation and redemptive sacrifice of God in the flesh, Jesus Christ. The new head of the

97

human family that has been restored to sonship of God builds up his mystical body through the very mystery of solidarity which without him seems unjust and embittering.

Holding firmly to the revealed unity of the plan of God for creation does not at all mean by-passing the mystery of evil and suffering which so fills the consciousness of modern man. Divine faith in Christ does not even mean saying that we know the meaning of suffering. It will remain, until the end, a blindness and scandal to the mind and heart of man which is ordered to knowing truth and desiring good. But with Christ, suffering is unquestionably given value and lifted out of the category of absolute evil. The Christ to whom St. Paul witnessed, the Christ the Church preaches, is Christ crucified. The plan of God is achieved existentially in and through terrible suffering. The glorified Christ who now guides the universe to its fulfillment in himself is the firstborn from the dead. Revelation as we grasp it now accepts all reality as we experience it in daily life. It tells us that somehow it has all been transfigured through the earthly life and death of Christ. The effects of sin are with us until the resurrection. But the fact that Christ underwent them has changed suffering and death from evils to possible occasions of supernatural growth and life.

The Image of God Theme

At this point it should be easier to see how the Image of God theme synthesizes revelation. In its very broadest sense the entire complex of beings existing outside of God is a likeness, a trace, a Word that utters God somehow by making visible his wisdom and power. This cosmic Word finds its own unity and natural ordering in man, the king of creation, because he is literally made to the image of God. The first man and woman from the first moment of their existence had not just a natural likeness to God but a share in the divine life by grace and faith and charity. They knew God and creation through humanly acquired knowledge and by participating in God's own life and knowledge. With the angelic spirits man was to live forever in God's eternal happiness. Man was to bring the creation into himself by knowledge and love, and give himself to God as a true and beatified image of God. The plan of God always embraced the mystery of freedom and sin and redemption in Christ. Through the incarnation and its extension in the Church, the divine Word who is the Image of the Father will perfect the image of God forever in the human race.

Tensions and Obscurities

Belief in the oneness of God's cosmic plan in Christ must always include, no matter what intellectual difficulty it entails, the fact that reality is structured with tensions and polarities. Their interplay is the reality of life as it moves toward its final goal. Here we can only indicate some of these necessary tensions so as to avoid the simplistic attitude which would eliminate one or other pole of stress and interaction. Man himself is a battlefield on which matter and spirit are engaged. Whatever the mysterious original harmony was like in Adam, it has given way to disharmony until the resurrection. Man's only hope of peace and salvation lies in Christ's grace, which radically heals the rift between matter and spirit but leaves a residue for struggle that goes on until death. Man's composite nature as bodied spirit is a mystery. It remains so in the very consciousness each person has of his own being.

The most radical and eternal polarity exists between the creator and the creature, the latter finding all his meaning in existing in a living relationship to the divine wisdom and power and love. Added to this natural mystery is the *de facto* plan of God by which men and angels were always ordered to a supernatural destiny, therefore to a supernatural life and mode of existence. Much of contemporary theological thought is concentrated in this area of relation between the natural and supernatural orders of being. It is a very difficult subject to discuss, particularly because our language and concepts come from *natural* knowledge and experience. There is always the danger of reducing the supernatural to something not merely spiritual but in a sense owed to man. The entire theology of man is tied up with the fact that he has never been merely natural in his destiny or existential mode of being. Thus the concept of the natural when applied to man is hard to use accurately. To treat man as merely natural is completely to misunderstand him from the start. To treat him as solely supernatural is to cut him off from all his earthly but essential roots.

Perhaps the most intellectually painful polarity which must be held within the one plan of God is that entailed in the mystery of created freedom. Good and evil men do exist. Good and evil spirits exist. At every moment a created free being still on trial is capable of failure, of free and knowing refusal. God himself announces the eternal enmity between the serpent and the seed of the woman. In other words, the oneness of God's infallible plan is an object of faith. It is not apparent to us, and we should not expect it to be. Until the final judgment when God's design will be manifested openly, the polarities and tensions will seem more evident than the underlying unity. Herein lies the merit of believing, despite appearances to the contrary. The whole of revelation, from the call of Abraham to the visions of the Apocalypse, tells us that God's ways are *not* men's ways. To believe means to know and trust and love when the evidence is lacking. "Blessed are they that have not seen and believe," Christ himself said. A Christian theology of man can be a theology of history only in the sense of certitude about basic orientation and ultimate meaning. We cannot yield to the temptation to judge earthly events in the light of their eternal signification. Sin and evil do succeed temporarily. Faith is necessarily obscure and rests on God's infallible truth, not on evidence accessible to men.

MODES OF CONTEMPORARY AWARENESS

In order to be a modern Christian it is as important to sympathize with the contemporary world as it is to believe in God's eternal truths. It is a truism to say that the mid-twentieth century is a time of great reevaluation in human life and thought. Those who refuse to face the obvious need for vigorous thought and action are really escaping from the things they see but are afraid to acknowledge. The believer knows that God's truth is valid for every age and every human person. However, each historical period provides unique helps and hindrances when its children elect to live by faith. Of all the qualities of our time which could be considered, only three will be mentioned. The remarks made are merely suggestions for further thought, to stimulate the reader to his own synthesis of Christ and our times.

New Awareness of the Universe

Once man entered into the atomic and space eras, he found himself faced with the question of the meaning and value of man in a way quite new and crushing. Even with the normal ups and downs of life, there had been previously, especially in the nineteenth century, a sense of life as moving in a direction of necessary progress. Man gradually came to control his environment and destiny more and more. Now he is faced with the new knowledge not only of his own terrifying power through technology and science, but of his diminishing physical importance in an inconceivably large and in some sense expanding universe. Each day human beings are confronted with the news of a new nuclear war threat, exploration of space, population explosion. It is natural that they ask certain questions. Where is it all going? Is man just a highly developed cosmic accident on a tiny planet? The questions may not be ignored; they must be thought through in the light of divine faith. The contemporary Christian is a member of the Church which is herself affected by all of modern life. Not complacent answers but genuine concern for truth will enable him to broaden the Christian realities so as to include all that is true in the modern world.

Doctrines like the unity of God's cosmic plan, the ultimate fulfillment of the universe in mankind's transformation in Christ, the universality of the Church's mission, and the polarity of good and evil in life—all these give modern man bases on which to build an honest thought structure concerning the terrible realities with which he finds himself surrounded. This he must do in love. An individualistic notion of salvation, an ethereal and noncosmic attitude toward Christ's place in the universe, a sectarian approach to the Church, a nonresurrection notion of man's ultimate destiny—these have not sufficed as answers to the problems of modern man for several decades. The very fact that they are still taught and that some persons try to wall up their existence in them is a sobering thought. The Christian can be contemporary. But the process is painful and personal. Some give up the faith in order to appear modern. It is just as dangerous to deny the modern world in order to appear to have faith.

Awareness of Man's Inner Split

Another facet of modern awareness is completely different from the one previously mentioned. One senses an almost agonized awareness of the interior split within the human person. Just as space exploration makes man feel that he is vanishing in the visible cosmos, so the growth of exploration of the human psyche creates in one a sense that his personality is vanishing beneath the surface of some dark inner swamp. Man feels, ironically, that he is losing control of the outer world—just when he has gained the greatest technical control he has ever had; he also fears that he is losing control of his interior life of choice and destiny, knowledge and love and communion. What do we find in serious contemporary literature, drama and art if not powerful expressions of man's questioning and fright? Is he merely flesh, or prisoned spirit, or total absurdity?

Here again the truths of faith provide no easy answer. Rather they supply deeper facts and realities from which man can begin to rebuild the image of himself. What is contemporary literature if not a powerful presentation of human nature as it experiences itself, when it knows neither the fact of Adam's sin and its effects, nor the fact of Christ's redemption and its effects? The existentialist anguish is a cry of wounded nature that does not know its real wound. A vital rethinking of the doctrine of original sin gives to modern man the reasons for his anguish. Christ in the totality of his existence and mission gives the means not of escaping from suffering, but of perfect happiness attained forever through suffering. Man is still the image of God. Even in darkness he reaches out for the only answer that can satisfy him.

Desire for Authenticity

In addition to fears which press on him from outside and from within, contemporary man feels a great and inarticulate desire for honesty and directness, for truth that is relevant and has an authentic ring. Hence he automatically rejects Christian truths when they are only pious platitudes spoken too easily, answers given before the earnest question has been fully formulated. It is increasingly evident that the modern person is not mainly interested in isolated dogmas and specific moral principles. Much more he seeks the total meaning of life and reality. "Where is it all going?" "What's the use of anything?" His total sense of loss can be answered only by a total sense of meaning. Not that the Christian vision of God's plan for the entire universe finally achieved in Christ is easy to present or grasp. It is anything but that. Neither does it clear away the day-to-day obscurities and sufferings. It does however present God's answer on a truly cosmic scale, and it presents it in terms of a person, Christ, to be believed in and loved. Schemes of human utopias have no appeal today, unless powerfully attached like communism to primitive drives and passions. Only a divine answer can embrace all that is and still leave the problems and inadequacies of a created order. Christ is the answer to the universal search of man because he experienced the search, and can transfigure it while respecting it.

The nature and meaning of Adam and Eve and their sin, of Christ's infinite redeeming love, of the terminus of human history in a glorious eternity, are truths which fundamentally answer modern man's needs. This will not be so if he should insist on holding on to his problems just because they are his own. There is something sad and disturbing in the fact that millions of Christians can live side by side with millions of despairing fellowmen and have no truth or meaning of life that they are able to share convincingly with them. Is it any wonder that unbelievers think men of faith do not have the answers? Is the modern Christian aware of the message he carries in his heart? It often seems not.

THE IMAGE RESTORED IN CHRISTIAN LIFE

Once the theology of man's original holiness and original sin as profoundly affecting him as image of God has been conceded, the whole of Christian life can be viewed as a progress of healing and restoration in Christ. At birth, the human being is separated from God because he lacks sanctifying grace which ought to be present. His nature, even if physically perfect, is in some mysterious way wounded and ordered to disharmony and dissolution. With the infusion of grace into the soul, the human being is again restored to supernatural sonship of God. He is again a supernatural image of God capable of knowing and loving God in a divine way. This restored sonship comes to him by incorporation in Christ the incarnate Word, Image, Son of God. Thus the day to day growth in perfection of the person will be a progress in closer and closer likeness to Christ.

Christian moral teaching is at last emerging from too long an emphasis upon the negative, the mere avoidance of sin. It is beginning to present again the Christian life as growth from minimal restored image of God in the soul by grace to more perfect likeness to Christ through free and deliberate choice. Man's natural likeness to God through his mind and will is elevated to divine activity through faith and charity. He becomes more and more like God by living in and acting like Christ. The Church, the body of Christ, witnesses in a visible way proportionate to the holiness of its members to its character as incarnate Image of the God-man. The life of prayer, chiefly the liturgy, apostolic and missionary undertakings, all spring from this awareness of the reality of the Christian's inner renewal and transformation through grace which restores the divine image lost to man by Adam's sin.

The contemporary renewal in the Church with its elements of biblical renewal and vital assimilation of psychology and history in particular, orients the focus of modern Christian life toward the future. The crucified Christ is the new Adam who is now also the glorified Lord of history. He will bring the universe to its culmination and usher in the kingdom of eternal peace and justice and love. Christians are "the people of God on the march." They are the leaven of history, not withdrawn from its flow, but giving it eternal value in their own lives and in their apostolic sharing. One can only move, of course, toward the future in the present, by some awareness of a past out of which one comes. It is impossible to fix one's gaze and effort on perfect redemption to come unless there is knowledge about original sin and the need for redemption. Perhaps this is one of the deepest reasons for the sense of fixation on evil that we get from much modern literature and art. Man's present condition and inherent weakness, if endlessly stared at, become increasingly difficult to explain. Only revealed knowledge of man's original state and its loss, and of his future destiny in Christ, can throw light on his cosmic place and his irreversible direction now.

It might be well to mention here that the present resurgence in the Church is helping to deepen again the understanding of the phenomenon of religious life which has always attracted some of her members. The religious is a Christian who stands visibly as a sign of total acceptance of the doctrine of original sin and of final glorification in Christ. The whole structure of religious life has its meaning in a direct attack on the wounds of human nature through vows of poverty, chastity and obedience. This negative and purifying role is informed with total love of Christ, the end to which all Christians move. The religious simply makes the ultimate end, the final conquest of sin, his immediate point of striving with all his vital powers. Thus religious life is always a sign in the Church, not by numbers but by holiness. It is a constant witness to the ultimates of origin and end for every human being. Priesthood and lay states are likewise signs of holiness in the Church. Indeed, the increased awareness of the dignity of the latter has resulted in some temporary obscuration of the precise meaning of the virginal or celibate life, a problem to which Pope Pius XII addressed himself in the encyclical letter *Sacra Virginitas* of 1954. For that reason it is spoken of here.

CONCLUSION

Throughout this book we have meditated on the mystery and meaning of man as made known to us through God's revelation transmitted through the Church. To do this we have situated man in the total cosmic plan of God, and have concentrated on the pivotal events which occurred at the beginning of human history. Doctrinal clarity and living faith in regard to Adam are the essential starting point for any understanding of man as he actually is in the real order of things. However, it has also been evident that any exact knowledge of Adam's sin and its effects is impossible without entering into the Church's understanding of the Adam-Christ typology. Each is intelligible only in function of the other. In a sense there is no more powerful example of God's love and mercy for men. Man is not asked to face the horror of sin until he knows its conqueror.

The order and content of this book is existentially present in magnificent fashion in the Church's paschal liturgy. Most especially is it to be found in the Easter Vigil, and concentrated in a blaze of light in the "Exsultet" sung in blessing over the Easter candle. "O the marvel of your goodness toward us! O incomprehensible strength of love which sacrifices a son to redeem a slave! O blessed sin which has obtained for us so great a redeemer." No Christian prayer states more movingly and poetically the fact of sin and redemption, and the infinitely excelling power of the latter. Suffering and death become the means of happiness and life, through being experienced by the new Adam who is by right life and peace and love.

Man, by nature made in God's image, was always destined to super- *105* natural glory in the incarnate Image of God, Jesus Christ his Son. But from the beginning "man" is man and woman, the human couple. As Christian man moves through history he situates himself in battle with the powers of evil but illumined by the truth about man and woman. At the origins stand Adam and Eve tempted by the serpent. Central to history and the source of his supernatural life and actions is Christ —the new Adam, who stands with Mary—the new Eve. He also fought the serpent, but was victorious. Through a woman, moreover, came this victory. Ahead of man, calling him on, is the Christ of the Apocalypse. The woman clothed with the sun is there too, Church and mother in one, still fighting the dragon in the life battles of her earthly members; but the ultimate certitude is victory forever. Already the Man has brought the human family back to both God's kingdom and life through the woman. The meaning of man is radiantly manifest in them. The mission of the Church and of each of her members is to make man's meaning and mystery visible and desirable in the obscurity and pain of earthly life. For this, the only adequate means are personal faith and love and holiness, by which men and women show forth the image of God restored in them by life in Christ, through Mary.

Selected Readings

CHAPTER ONE

Daniélou, Jean, *Holy Pagans of the Old Testament* (Baltimore: Helicon, 1957), "Noe," pp. 69-86.

Henry, A. M., *God and His Creation* (Notre Dame, Ind.: Fides Publishers Association, 1955).

Pieper, Josef, *The Silence of Saint Thomas* (New York: Pantheon, 1957).

Vriezen, T., *An Outline of Old Testament Theology* (Wageningen, Holland: Veenman, 1960), pp. 199-231, 343-73.

CHAPTER TWO

Corte, Nicolas, *Who Is the Devil?* (New York: Hawthorn, 1958).

Daniélou, Jean, *The Angels and Their Mission* (Westminster, Md.: Newman, 1956).

Bruno de Jésus-Marie (ed.), *Satan* (New York: Sheed and Ward, 1952).

Heidt, W. G., *Angelology of the Old Testament* (Washington, D.C.: The Catholic University of America Press, 1949).

Régamey, Pie-Raymond, *What Is an Angel?* (New York: Hawthorn, 1960).

CHAPTER THREE

Rahner, Karl, *Theological Investigations* (Baltimore: Helicon, 1961), Vol. I, "Theological Reflexions on Monogenism," pp. 229-96.

Corte, Nicolas, *The Origins of Man* (New York: Hawthorn, 1958).

Hauret, Charles, *Beginnings: Genesis and Modern Science* (Dubuque, Iowa: Priory Press, 1955).

Ong, Walter, *Darwin's Vision and Christian Perspectives* (New York: Macmillan, 1960).

Hunt, Ignatius, *Understanding the Bible* (New York: Sheed and Ward, 1962).

de Fraine, Jean, *The Bible and the Origin of Man* (New York: Desclée, 1962).

CHAPTER FOUR

Rahner, Karl, *Theological Investigations* (Baltimore: Helicon, 1961), Vol. I, "Concerning the Relationship between Nature and Grace," pp. 297-317, and "Some Implications of the Scholastic Concept of Uncreated Grace," pp. 319-46.

Scheeben, Matthias Josef, *The Mysteries of Christianity* (St. Louis: B. Herder, 1951), "The Mystery of God in the Original Creation," pp. 201-42.

Vawter, Bruce, *A Path Through Genesis* (New York: Sheed and Ward, 1956), pp. 31-110.

CHAPTER FIVE

Petit, François, *The Problem of Evil* (New York: Hawthorn, 1959).

Rondet, Henri, *Theology of Sin* (Notre Dame, Ind.: Fides Publishers Association, 1960).

Scheeben, Matthias Josef, *The Mysteries of Christianity* (St. Louis: B. Herder, 1951), "The Mystery of Sin," pp. 243-312.

CHAPTER SIX

Bolt, David, *Adam* (New York: John Day Company, 1961).

Hunt, Ignatius, *The Book of Genesis with Commentary* in "Paulist Bible Pamphlet Series" (New York: Paulist Press, 1961).

CHAPTER SEVEN

Henry, A. M., *Man and His Happiness* (Notre Dame, Ind.: Fides Publishers Association, 1956), Ch. 5.

Rahner, Karl, *On the Theology of Death* (New York: Herder and Herder, 1961).

CHAPTER EIGHT

Guardini, Romano, *Freedom, Grace and Destiny* (New York: Pantheon, 1960).

Mouroux, Jean, *The Meaning of Man* (New York: Sheed and Ward, 1948).

Troquer, René, *What Is Man?* (New York: Hawthorn, 1961).

ABBREVIATIONS

The Books of the Old and New Testaments

Genesis	Gn	Canticle of Canticles	Ct
Exodus	Ex	Wisdom	Wis
Leviticus	Lv	Sirach (Ecclesiasticus)	Sir
Numbers	Nm	Isaia	Is
Deuteronomy	Dt	Jeremia	Jer
Joshua	Jos	Lamentations	Lam
Judges	Jgs	Baruch	Bar
Ruth	Ru	Ezechiel	Ez
1 Samuel (1 Kings)	1 Sm	Daniel	Dn
2 Samuel (2 Kings)	2 Sm	Osea	Os
1 Kings (3 Kings)	1 Kgs	Joel	Jl
2 Kings (4 Kings)	2 Kgs	Amos	Am
1 Chronicles (Paralipomenon)	1 Chr	Abdia	Abd
2 Chronicles (Paralipomenon)	2 Chr	Jona	Jon
Ezra	Ez	Michea	Mi
Nehemia (2 Ezra)	Neh	Nahum	Na
Tobia	Tb	Habacuc	Hb
Judith	Jdt	Sophonia	So
Esther	Est	Aggai	Ag
Job	Jb	Zacharia	Za
Psalms	Ps(s)	Malachia	Mal
Proverbs	Prv	1 Machabees	1 Mc
Coheleth (Ecclesiastes)	Coh	2 Machabees	2 Mc

In the enumeration of the Psalms, the first number follows the Vulgate, the number within brackets, the Hebrew text.

St. Matthew	Mt	1 Timothy	1 Tim
St. Mark	Mk	2 Timothy	2 Tim
St. Luke	Lk	Titus	Ti
St. John	Jn	Philemon	Phlm
Acts of the Apostles	Ac	Hebrews	Heb
Romans	Rom	St. James	Jas
1 Corinthians	1 Cor	1 St. Peter	1 Pt
2 Corinthians	2 Cor	2 St. Peter	2 Pt
Galatians	Gal	1 St. John	1 Jn
Ephesians	Eph	2 St. John	2 Jn
Philippians	Phil	3 St. John	3 Jn
Colossians	Col	St. Jude	Jude
1 Thessalonians	1 Thes	Apocalypse	Ap
2 Thessalonians	2 Thes		

Apocrypha and Qumrân Material

Henoch	Hen	Testament of the	
Jubilees	Jub	Twelve Patriarchs	Test
Psalms of Solomon	Ps Sol	Manual of Discipline	MD

Other Source Material

Acta Apostolicae Sedis
    [Acts of the Apostolic See]   *AAS*
Ancient Christian Writers,
    ed. J. Quasten and others   *ACW*
Acta Sanctae Sedis
    [Acts of the Holy See]   *ASS*
Codex Iuris Canonici
    [Code of Canon Law]   *CIC*
Denzinger-Bannwart, *Enchiridion
Symbolorum*, 30th ed. [Handbook
of the Creeds]   D
Patrologia, series graeca,
    ed. J. P. Migne   *PG*
Sacrorum Conciliorum nova
    . . . Collectio   *Mansi*

Patrologia, series latina,
    ed. J. P. Migne   *PL*
Summa contra Gentes
    S. Thomae Aquinatis   *S.C.G.*
Quatuor Libri Sententiarum
    Petri Lombardi [Four Books
of Opinions]   *Sent.*
Summa Theologiae
    S. Thomae Aquinatis   *S.Th.*
Supplementum tertiae partis Summae
    Theologiae (Ottawa ed. 1941)
    Suppl.
The Church Teaches,
    ed. J. Clarkson and others   *TCT*

INDEX

Bridges
NOT WALLS

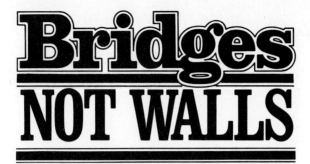

NOT WALLS

A Book About Interpersonal Communication

Second Edition

Edited by

JOHN STEWART

University of Washington

ADDISON-WESLEY PUBLISHING COMPANY

Reading, Massachusetts
Menlo Park, California • London • Amsterdam • Don Mills,
Ontario • Sydney

This book is in the
ADDISON-WESLEY SERIES IN SPEECH COMMUNICATION

Consulting Editor
Frederick W. Haberman

Selections from *I Touch The Earth, The Earth Touches Me*, copyright © 1972 by Hugh Prather. Reprinted by permission of Doubleday & Company, Inc.

Photographs of Rollo May and Erich Fromm by Jill Krementz.

ISBN 0-201-07227-0
EFGHIJ-HA-79

for Kris

Books and Men

Imagine yourself in a situation where you are alone, wholly alone on earth, and you are offered one of the two, books or men. I often hear men prizing their solitude, but that is only because there are still men somewhere on earth, even though in the far distance. I knew nothing of books when I came forth from the womb of my mother, and I shall die without books, with another human hand in my own. I do, indeed, close my door at times and surrender myself to a book, but only because I can open the door again and see a human being looking at me.

MARTIN BUBER

PREFACE
TO THE
SECOND EDITION

I started working on the second edition of *Bridges Not Walls* for a couple of reasons; the most important was that I could no longer say that the first edition represented the best articles, talks, and essays about interpersonal communication that I know of. About a thousand feedback sheets from readers of the first edition indicated clearly which articles were working and which weren't. In addition, since that book went to press in 1972, I've discovered a number of new essays that do a better job of saying some important things than was done by some selections in the first edition.

Although my motivation for doing this edition is different from my original reason for doing the book, much of the rest of my point of view remains the same. My heroes are still persons like Martin Buber, Abraham Maslow, Rollo May, and Carl Rogers. I believe even more strongly now in the potential of this approach to teaching and learning about human communication, and if the proliferation of new interpersonal communication texts and courses is any indication, so do many other persons.

I still want to emphasize that this book *about* interpersonal communication cannot substitute for the real thing—for direct, caring contact between vital human beings in the concrete, everyday world. That's why I've again begun with Buber's comment about "Books and Men" and ended with Prather's words about the world of ideas and the world of persons.

As before, I owe a great deal to others. The authors and publishers of material reprinted here have been very cooperative. I'm especially pleased that Hugh Prather agreed again to let me use materials from two of his books, *Notes to Myself* (Lafayette, Calif.: Real People Press, 1970) and *I Touch The Earth, The Earth Touches Me* (New York: Doubleday, 1972). His writing was one of the most-liked parts of the first edition, and I suspect the same thing will happen again. I also owe a special thanks to Dennis Wilson for his photography. Because Dennis is sensitive to the ideas in the book, he is able to create visual images that really "work" well.

I am also greatful to student and faculty reviewers and to the persons I'm lucky enough to contact regularly: students who are continually helping me grow, like Lyall Crawford and Barbara Keely; colleagues like Steve Stephenson,

Gary D'Angelo, Jody Nyquist, and Tom Nilsen, who both support me and challenge my ideas; and important friends like Helen and Sam Felton, Willy Clark, and Jim and Molly Booth. My closest friend, student, and teacher—Allen Clark—died suddenly while I was working on this book, so our relationship can't grow much more. I think he understood, though, both my love and my gratitude. My most important living relationships—with Kris, Marcia and Lisa, my parents and sister, and John Campbell—are still the central reasons for and the ultimate tests of this perspective.

In other words, I continue to be convinced of the difficulty and necessity of interpersonal communicating and excited by the challenge of working toward achieving it. I hope that some or all of that excitement can rub off on you.

Seattle, Washington   J.R.S.
November 1976

CONTENTS

—Connecting thoughts by Hugh Prather—from *Notes to Myself* and *I Touch the Earth, The Earth Touches Me*

INTRODUCTION

BRIDGES NOT WALLS

Writing about interpersonal communication, especially in a context like this one, is extremely difficult, primarily because it's almost impossible to practice what you preach. I could simply think of you as "reader" or "student" and of myself as "author," "editor," or "teacher" and then proceed to "tell you what I want you to know." But the result of that kind of thinking would be a lot closer to superficial role-relating than to interpersonal communication.

The reason such an attitude wouldn't work is that although I am obviously writing this, I am *not* simply "author," "editor," or "teacher," and you are not just "reader" or "student." Each of us is a unique person. My name is John Stewart, I've been teaching college for about nine years, and I like almost everything about my job. I also like to sail on salt water, to watch what sunsets do to mountains, to smell the wet freshness of Pacific Northwest winters, to feel the exhilaration of making it up a steep hill on my bike or down a moguled hill on my skis, to hug friends. I don't like phony smiles, smog, pretentious academicians, rules that are vaguely stated but rigidly enforced, lies, or cooked zucchini. I was raised in a small town in Washington state, went to school there and in Tacoma, Evanston, and Los Angeles, and am currently sharing a house—with John Campbell, a friend who teaches in the same department I do—located on the side of a hill with a beautiful view of Mt. Rainier and Lake Washington. At this point in my life—I just turned 35—I'm acutely aware of how everything changes, of how much different my today is from my yesterday, last year, and five years ago. Especially relationships are changing. For instance, unlike when I began teaching college, students seldom see me any more as "almost one of them." I don't look or act young enough for that. Senior faculty also view me as less of a "kid." I've also noticed that since two years ago when a marriage I entered too young was dissolved, relationships with my family, colleagues, and friends have changed. One reason is that they now see me as "single," which to some means "shameful" or "out of place" and to others "available" or "attractive." During the same time, my daughters Marcia and Lisa have moved from childhood into the turbulence of adolescence while our relationships with each other have had some violent ups and downs and have now settled into a firmer maturity. Over the past year and a half I've also discovered with a woman named Kris how exciting and difficult it is to establish and maintain an intimate relationship that's secure without being static and that's responsive to each partner's uniqueness.

As I reread the introduction to the first edition of this book, which I wrote in 1972, those changes really jump out at me, but I also see the things that haven't changed. I'm still affected by each of the jobs I've had—as floral delivery person, janitor, warehouse worker, tire salesperson, fork lift driver, swimming pool manager, and college teacher. I still feel the influence of people who contacted me in special ways—my first "real boss," Marc Burdick; important teachers, such as Alice Atkinson, Robert Harris, Katherine Kemp, Peter Ristuben, and Walter Fisher; and many special friends. I also sense the presence of an unchanging central me, a core self that's never static but that's securely anchored in the values, understandings, strengths, and weaknesses that make me uniquely me.

If I were just "writer" or "author," I could also conceal the fact that I am as excited about doing this second edition of *Bridges* as I was about doing the first, and for the same reason—I get to share some ideas and feelings about interpersonal communication that have helped me grow. I was also apprehensive about the first edition because I wasn't sure you would allow me to talk to you this way, instead of in the safe, sterile third person of most "educational materials," but I no longer worry about that; not only did most readers allow it, many of them wrote to tell me they appreciated and liked it, and I feel good about that.

The role-restricted attitudes I mentioned will also get in the way of our communicating, because *you* are not simply "reader" or "student." Where were you born and raised, and what effects has it had on you? Are you reading this book because you want to or because somebody told you to? If your reading is related to a college course, how do you expect the course to turn out? Challenging? Boring? Threatening? Useful? Exciting? Inhibiting? How do you generally feel about required texts? About administrative regulations? About going to school? What groups have you chosen to join? A sorority or fraternity? YAF? BSU? NOW? GLF? An honor society? MECHA? Young Life? Nichiren Soshu? What other important choices have you made recently? To move? Change majors? End a relationship? Quit work? Make a new commitment?

I'm not trying to say that you have to pry into the intimate details of somebody's life before you can communicate with him or her. But I am trying to say that interpersonal communication happens between *persons*, not between roles or masks or stereotypes. Interpersonal communication can happen between you and me only when each of us recognizes and shares some of what makes us human beings *and* is aware of some of what makes the other person too.

It's going to be very difficult to make that happen between you and me. I can continue to share with you some of my personness, but I don't really know whether what I share is what you need to become aware of some of who I am. And I end up right now knowing nothing about what makes you a person—nothing about your choices, your feelings, your individuality. All that is why *writing* about interpersonal communication is sometimes frustrating for me; interpersonal communication can be discussed in print, but it can't really happen here.

More can happen, though, than what usually happens with a "textbook." The relationship can be closer to interpersonal quality communication than what it often is. I will work toward that by continuing to share some of what I'm actually thinking and feeling. I hope you'll be willing to share yourself by becoming honestly involved enough in this book to see clearly which of the ideas are worthwhile for you and which are not. I also hope you'll be able to share yourself with other persons reading this book, so they can benefit from your insights and you can benefit from theirs. Finally, I hope you'll share some of your thoughts with me. I'd appreciate it if you'd write some comments on the feedback sheet at the end of the book and send it to me. It will be a little awkward and not at all as immediate as interpersonal communication usually is, but at least I'll get to know you a little better. It would probably work best to wait until you read most or all of the book, but use your own judgment. Fill it out now if you want to. I'll send you my responses to your comments as soon as I can.

So far I've tried to say that for me, interpersonal communication differs from noninterpersonal communication in that it's a meeting *between* (inter) *persons*. That means that for interpersonal communication to happen, each participant has to be willing and able to share some of what makes him or her a person and to be aware of some of what makes the other a person. That willingness and ability will happen, it seems to me, only when the people involved: (1) are familiar with the basic ingredients of the human communication process, (2) can accurately and sensitively tune in to themselves and others, (3) recognize how sharing self and others works through disclosing, asserting, and empathic listening, and (4) can put the whole complex of attitudes and skills together in a human synthesis that works for them.

That's why I've organized this book as I have. The first chapter explores some of what it means to say that interpersonal communication is a meeting between persons. I feel strongly that it's crucially important to get your head around both those terms—"meeting" and "persons"—so I've talked about them in some detail in Chapter 1, and I've included three other articles that speak to some of the same ideas in different ways. The second and third chapters complete the outline of the basic ingredients of human communication. Chapter 2 discusses verbal cues—how words can help people understand you and help bring people together. In Chapter 3, several authors talk about how nonverbal cues work in human communication, how we send emotional messages nonverbally, and specifically how tone of voice, body talk, and touch affect our relationships with others.

In Part II the focus shifts from communication in general to one of its key elements, perception. How you see yourself and how you see the people you're in contact with significantly affects your communication. The three articles in Chapter 4 discuss the first of those processes, self-perception. Chapter 4 is put together on the assumption that if you're going to make some of your personness available to somebody else, it'd be a good idea to first reflect on who you are. The next step is to reflect on how you perceive others. That topic is treated in Chapter 5. The essays there explain how our perception of people differs in important ways from our perception of objects. They also illustrate how some complex and confounding communication problems can often arise from inaccurate and twisted perceptions that we have of others.

Part III moves another step, from perception to the communication behaviors that grow out of who and how you perceive. Chapter 6 explores how self-perception is manifested in the communication behavior of self-disclosure and how that behavior can affect your ability to contact others as persons. Then the readings in Chapter 7 address some questions that interpersonal communication classes often overlook: "What about negative feelings?" "What do I do when I'm angry?" and "How can I communicate interpersonally when I feel like I'm getting shoved around?" The readings there demonstrate that interpersonal communication attitudes and skills don't just apply to situations in which everybody feels good and loves everybody else. Sharing your self with others can include sticking to ideas you believe in; it doesn't have to mean giving in to others just to keep the peace. The final chapter in Part III focuses on empathic listening, the communication behaviors that can come from full and accurate perception of the other person. In Chapter 8 two essays and a short story emphasize how much this kind of listening can contribute to effective interpersonal communication.

In the final part of the book I've collected four statements, each of which integrates, synthesizes, pulls together the ideas in the other readings. Each author in Part IV is a central figure in the development of the ideas in this book—you'll find their names scattered throughout the writings in other chapters. Each is also a different kind of pioneer or central figure. Carl Rogers is a well-known humanistic psychotherapist who has been an important figure in the human potential movement. Erich Fromm has been called a social prophet; he brings a sociological perspective to some of the same ideas as he talks about love as an important part of society and culture. Rollo May is another psychologist and psychotherapist, but he brings a unique blend of Christian training and existential philosophy to his writing about interpersonal relationships in our society. Finally, Martin Buber is a Jewish philosopher and the person who is most responsible for originally explaining the basic ideas everyone else in this book develops.

Around and in between the readings, I've put three things: before each piece there are some introductory comments which pinpoint what I think are the key ideas that appear there. At the end of each reading I've included some "probes," questions intended to provoke your thinking, especially your thinking about how the ideas in that reading relate (1) to your own life experiences, and (2) to ideas in the other readings. I've also included 21 of Hugh Prather's comments as connecting thoughts. As you may have already discovered by reading his books, *Notes to Myself* and *I Touch The Earth The Earth Touches Me*, Hugh is uniquely able to capture in a few lines insights that it takes most of us pages to explain.

So that's what's coming. I hope it'll be helpful *and* fun.

I

INTRODUCTION TO INTERPERSONAL COMMUNICATION: THE BASIC INGREDIENTS

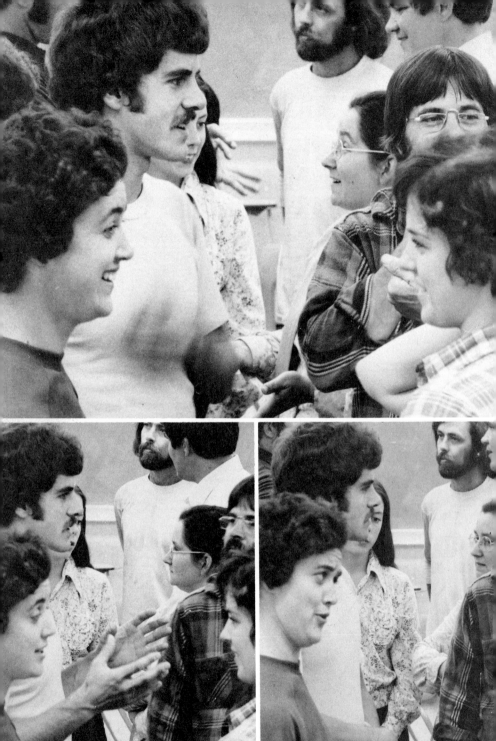

1

A RELATIONAL POINT OF VIEW

*Perceptions are not of things
but of relationships. Nothing,
including me, exists by itself—
this is an illusion of words.
I <u>am</u> a relationship, ever-changing.*

HUGH PRATHER

One of the most exciting courses I took during my first year of college was Introduction to Philosophy. Part of the appeal was the teacher; he knew his stuff, and
he loved to teach it. But, as I discovered a few years later, I also enjoyed the
course because the pattern of thinking reflected in the materials we read and the
discussions we had was a comfortable pattern for me; it seemed as though I
usually thought that way myself. As I continued through college, I supplemented
my speech communication courses with other work in philosophy, and the topics I
talk about in this article reflect that dual interest.

Philosophy, as I understand it, involves the systematic critique of presuppositions. That can be a stuffy, seemingly irrelevant process. But frequently it's really
exciting and important because it's the philosopher who says, "Hold it! Before you
go off to spin a complicated web of explanations about human communication, or
the history of culture, or the operation of political systems, or whatever, try to get
clear about some basic things: when you're talking about human communication,
what are you assuming, for example, about one person's ability really to know
what another person is saying, or about whether part of being a person is wanting
to get in contact with others?" "If each human perceives the world in his or her
own way," the philosopher might say, "then I can only communicate with my perception of you; I can never really get in touch with you. All I can do, when it
comes right down to it, is communicate with myself."

Those kinds of basic topics are important to me. I know that many potentially
exciting conversations have been squelched by someone's dogmatic insistence that
everybody "define the terms." But I also know that a great deal of fuzziness can
be cleared up when a conversation starts with some shared understandings about
what's being discussed.

In this essay I describe my understanding of the topic of this book—interpersonal communication. I talk mostly about the two parts of the word "interpersonal"—"persons" and "inter," or "between." In the process I try to clarify what it
means to talk about and to help create communication between persons. All of the
topics in this essay look pretty simple on the surface. But there's more to them
than first meets the eye, and I believe that your understanding of these topics will
greatly affect your understanding of all the rest of the book.

INTERPERSONAL COMMUNICATION—
A MEETING BETWEEN PERSONS

John Stewart

As I said a few pages back, there is an important difference between interpersonal and noninterpersonal communication, and I'm convinced that the first
step toward learning to communicate interpersonally is understanding what
that difference is. I think the distinguishing feature of interpersonal communica-

tion is that it's a meeting *between* (inter) *persons*. That definition looks pretty simple and obvious. But the two main terms in it—"persons" and "between"— are keys to understanding just about everything this book is about. In fact, I believe that until you get clear about what those terms mean in this context, the best you can hope to get from this book is a vague awareness of the nature of communication or maybe some zingy communication gimmicks. But if you really understand the meaning of a "meeting between persons," you will be able to understand this approach to communication well enough to integrate it into all of your contacts with others—at school; in your apartment, dorm, or house; with your family; on the job; wherever.

PERSONS

Let me start with the "persons" part. It seems to me that you and I tend to relate with others in two ways: we treat them and are treated by them as objects or as persons.[1] I don't mean that there is a sharp dichotomy; sometimes we treat others and are treated by them more like people than like objects, and some-times it's the other way around. But "personifying" and "objectifying" seem to be two ends of the continuum that describes how we relate with others. Com-munication with bank tellers, receptionists, registration clerks, and most other institutional representatives tend to be objectifying, and much of the time that's completely expected and legitimate; in fact it's impossible to do anything else. Communication with family members, lovers, and spouses tends at least part of the time to be personifying. One central theme of this book is that although all our communicating cannot be personifying (i.e., it cannot be all interpersonal quality communication), *more of it could be*. If it were, things would be greatly improved both for us and for the people we communicate with.

In order to move in that direction, it's important to recognize what we mean by the common terms "objects" and "persons." For me, four characteris-tics distinguish these two terms. The first difference between them is that each person is unique, but each object isn't. Although a microscopic examination of the pencil I'm writing with right now might reveal some nicks, coloration, or erasure contours that are different from any other pencils, for all practical pur-poses this pencil is the same as any other No. 2 pencil. The same can be said for all the other objects around me now—my typewriter, chair, lamp, paperweight, pocket calculator, etc. There might be microscopic distinctions, but for all practical purposes this typewriter is interchangeable with others of the same model, and so are the other objects here.

Persons aren't that way. We can be treated as if we're interchangeable parts, but for *many* practical purposes it's important to be in touch with each person's uniqueness. Each of us is unique in a couple of ways. I remember hearing a geneticist say that given the complexity of each individual's makeup of genes and chromosomes, the probability of two persons having identical genetic materials was one in ten to the ten-thousandth power. That's less than one chance in a billion trillion!* In other words, each of us is virtually a genetic one-of-a-kind. But even if we weren't—even if persons had the same biological raw material—each would still be unique because each would experience the world differently. After you get through with this chapter, ask a friend who's also read it how he or she is experiencing this book, or this paragraph, or this sentence. Superficially your experiences may be similar, but if you probe them even a little, it will be clear that they're unique. There's only one you.

A second difference between objects and persons is that objects can only react, but persons can both act and react. An object obviously can't initiate movement on its own; my typewriter can't choose to start typing, this pencil can't choose to start writing. Automatic pilots, photoelectric switches, and thermostats sometimes seem to "operate on their own" or "turn themselves off and on," but they too are dependent on actions initiated outside them. The pilot has to be programmed; the thermostat reacts to the temperature, which reacts to the sun rays, which react to the earth's rotation, etc. Similarly, a ball can only react to the force of a foot that kicks it, and if you're good enough at physics calculations, you can pretty much pinpoint how far and where it will go, based on weight, velocity, the shape of your shoe, atmospheric conditions, etc.

But you can't very accurately predict what will happen if you kick your roommate, your teacher, or the grocery clerk. The reason you can't is that when persons are involved, human choice intervenes between cause and effect, stimulus and response. If you tap my knee, you may cause a reflex jerk, but the behavior that accompanies my reflex might be anything from giggles to a lawsuit, and there is no way that you can predict for sure which it will be. Like objects, persons sometimes react, but we can also *choose, decide, act.*

The importance of choice is a key point of several approaches to studying persons that go under the general heading "existential." You've probably heard that term before in reference to plays, novels, philosophy, or psychology. One of the existentialists' main insights is that persons are subjects not objects. Part of what they mean is that human subjects, like grammatical subjects, "define themselves through their own activities while objects are defined by the activities of subjects; subjects modify [choose]; objects are modified [get chosen upon]."² Nobody argues that humans are *completely* free to choose to do anything they want to. I can't fly, return to my childhood, or run faster than a speeding bullet. But my future is not determined by my past or present, and neither is yours. We can choose to respond to conditions that confront us.

That freedom and power to choose is a uniquely human characteristic. Objects don't have it and, so far as we know for sure, neither do most animals. The

---

*The "one chance in . . ." number is so large—ten followed by ten thousand zeroes—that we have no name for it.

more we're in touch with it, the more human we are. When I feel like, "I *had* to shout back; he was making me look silly!" or "I just *couldn't* say anything!" or "Sure I *withdrew*, but she made me—she was always on my back about something!" I'm out of touch with part of what it means to be a person. Persons can act, not just react; persons can choose. And interpersonal communication is in part communication that maximizes our ability to do those uniquely personlike things.

Communicating interpersonally also means keeping in mind a third distinction between objects and persons: objects are completely measurable, but persons aren't. Even extremely complex objects, such as giant computers, well-equipped automobiles, and 50-story buildings, can be completely described in space-and-time terms. That's what blueprints do; they record all the measurements necessary to recreate the object—length, width, height, velocity, amperage, voltage, specific gravity, circumference, hardness, etc. Although it's difficult to measure some things directly—the velocity of a photon, the duration of an explosion—no object has any parts that are unmeasurable, in theory at least.

The same can't be said for persons. Even if I accurately identify your height, weight, temperature, specific gravity, velocity, and electric potential, I will not have exhaustively accounted for the person who's you. Some philosophers, theologians, and people on the street have been saying this for years. But recently even those who demand a strictly scientific description of persons have also begun to recognize this characteristic. Behavioral psychologists, for example, include in their model of person the notion of a "black box," an unmeasurable, uniquely human something that is continuously affecting human behavior and that escapes all the rigorously scientific measurement that can be applied to it. Less scientifically inclined people call this unmeasurable "black box" the human "spirit," "soul," "psyche," or "personality." But whatever you call it, the point is, it's there.

The clearest manifestations of this unmeasurable part of us are those phenomena we call "emotions" or "feelings." Although we can measure things related to feelings—brainwaves, sweaty palms, heart rate, paper-and-pencil responses—what the measurements record is a long way from the feelings themselves. "Pulse 110, respiration 72, Likert rating 5.39, palmar conductivity .036 ohms" might be accurate, but it doesn't quite capture all of what's going on in me when I greet somebody I love.

Another thing, these unmeasurable emotions or feelings can't be turned off or on at will; they're always part of what we are experiencing. Contemporary educators pretty much agree now that it's unrealistic to try to focus a class exclusively on the "intellectual," "objective" aspect of some subject matter, because people are always thinking *and* feeling. As one writer put it, "it should be apparent that there is no intellectual learning without some sort of feeling, and there are no feelings without the mind's being somehow involved."[3] Sometimes what we are experiencing is more thinking than feeling and sometimes vice-versa, but neither function is ever entirely missing. We're always feeling something, or perhaps more accurately "feeling somehow."

In short, there is more to persons than just what's observable and measurable. Although the human "black box" or "spirit" and human "feelings" are concretely *real* in the sense that we are experiencing them all the time, those elements of us cannot be exhaustively accounted for in space-and-time terms. Communication that is responsive to those unmeasurable, uniquely human parts is more interpersonal than communication that isn't.

A fourth distinction between objects and persons is that persons are inherently of value and objects aren't. This distinction is not recognized by all human cultures, but most modern societies operate in part on this assumption. For most persons in most cultures, an object may or may not be valuable, depending on what it does, but a person is prized just because he or she is a person. In contemporary Western culture this idea is often traced back to the eighteenth-century German philosopher Immanual Kant, who grounded his ethics in the principle that an object could be treated as a means to an end, but that persons, because of their intrinsic value, should never be treated as the means to achieve some end, but should always be treated as an end in themselves.[4] As you will see in later chapters, most of the authors represented in this book either implicitly accept or explicitly make this point. It's not that everything a person does is good just because he or she is a person. Humans are obviously capable of thoughtless, inconsiderate, selfish, and even brutal acts. Newspapers, television, and our own life experiences make that abundantly clear. And nobody is suggesting that we ought to value or even to accept getting knifed, malicious gossip, lying, or other forms of interpersonal violence.

But there is a difference between condoning or accepting behavior and affirming the inherent value of the human person. Barry Stevens says it nicely:

> What really makes my stomach turn over is this picture of love, love, and love, and I love everything about you and never say no. . . .
>   When my child bites another child, I do not love that. But when he explains, "he tore my lei and I bit him, and he bit me, and (with angry tears) we each had only one bite before the teacher made us stop!" I have a deep feeling for him, and love him.[5]

That's the central point. You cannot value all human behavior positively, but you can value each human positively. That's another way we distinguish between things and people. To give your communication an interpersonal quality, it's important to keep that distinction in mind.

To sum up, when I say that interpersonal communication is different from noninterpersonal communication because interpersonal communication happens *between persons*, the word "persons" means more than just "thinking quadriped" or "the animal who laughs." Persons are different from objects in four special ways, and it's impossible to communicate with them as persons unless you keep those four differences in mind. (1) Each person is a unique, non-interchangeable part of the communication context. (2) Persons are choosers who are free to act, not just react to the conditions they're in. (3) A person is more than just an amalgamation of observable, measurable elements; he or she is always experiencing feelings or emotions. (4) Persons are of value just because they are persons; that doesn't mean you should condone or support everything anyone *does*, but rather that you can be open to accepting the other as a person, to respecting his or her humanness.

The first step toward communicating interpersonally, then, is to relate with others in ways that affirm their "personness." That means doing several things, and each chapter that follows is about one or more of those things. For example, it means looking for the uniqueness in each person (Chapter 5) instead of being satisfied with what makes this person "just like every other _____ (jock, company man, sorority sally, farm kid, etc.)." It also means remembering that even in a conflict situation, both you and the other person are *choosing* to feel as you do, so you both need to own your feelings, to be responsible for them (Chapter 7). Sharing some of your feelings (Chapter 6) and listening to the feelings of others (Chapter 8) are also important. The key is to be aware of your own and the other's personness and to communicate in ways that manifest, that demonstrate your awareness. That's the central point. You can't value all human behavior positively, but you can value each human positively. That's another way we distinguish between things and people. To help make your communication interpersonal quality communication, it's important to keep that distinction in mind.

BETWEEN

When I say that interpersonal communication is communication between persons, the word "between" also has some special meaning. Just as your ability to communicate interpersonally is affected by your recognition of what it is to be a *person*, it will also be affected by your recognition of what it means to say that communication occurs *between* persons. There are several practical reasons why it's important to develop your ability to see the betweenness, or relational nature, of human communication. For example, until you do, it's hard to keep from getting mad at the person who criticizes you or to keep from feeling defensive whenever you're being evaluated or controlled. Until you see the betweenness, it's also hard to keep track of the complex, continually changing myriad of things that affect your communication with a person you are close to. Without a relational perspective it's also difficult to stay in the here and now and not to let the past determine what's going on in the present. In fact, all the communication behaviors discussed in later chapters—touch, tone of voice, self-disclosure, self-assertion, empathic listening, etc.—make real sense only when you see them relationally, as part of what's going on *between* persons.

The problem is, most people don't actually see communicating that way. If you were to ask the person on the street what communication means, he or she would probably say something like "getting your ideas across" or "making yourself understood." That's a common view of the communication process, a view that's operating every time someone says, "How did you screw that up? I *told* you what to do!" or "I'm sure they understood; I *explained* it three times." In those cases the conception that is operating is that communication is something *I do*. From this point of view, communication doesn't occur "between," but rather "in" the communicator. When things don't work out, it's because I didn't communicate well or because you didn't, the company didn't, the supervisor didn't, or whatever. From this point of view, in other words, communication is an *action*, something determined entirely by the communicator's choices. As the diagram below indicates, this point of view says that communication is like giving or getting an innoculation; ideas and feelings are prepackaged in a mental and physical syringe and then forced under pressure in a straight line into the receiver.

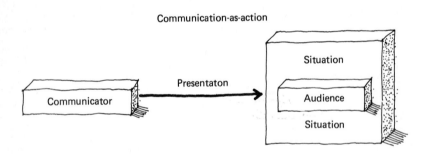

Communication-as-action

If you think about it for a minute, it becomes pretty clear why that view is inaccurate. When you see communication as just an action, you're ignoring feedback, something that's present whenever people communicate. Even on the phone, we make noises to indicate we're listening to a long comment or story. If you doubt the importance of that feedback, try being completely silent and see how soon the person on the other end asks, "Are you still there?"

The model of communication as action is also oversimplified in another way. It suggests that when you speak, there can be "an audience"; that is, a group of persons who are homogenous—whose backgrounds, thoughts, feelings, and attitudes toward the topic and communicator are more similar than different. It also implies that the communicator's identity is not greatly affected by what goes into, or goes on during, the communication experience. In other words, it implies that regardless of any changes in the situation, the communicator is always "teacher" and never "learner," always "boss" and never "friend," for example.

The point is, the common view that communication is an *action*, something one person *does* to somebody else, is drastically oversimplified. All of our communication behavior is affected by not only our own expectations, needs, attitudes, and goals, but also the responses we are getting from the other person involved. So it's more accurate to view communication as an *interaction*, as a process of *mutual* or *reciprocal* influence.

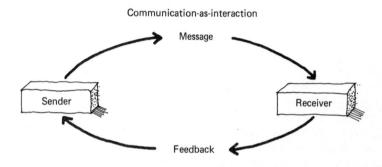

Communication-as-interaction

The interactional point of view can account for quite a bit of complexity. Communicologist David Berlo, for example, includes in an interaction the expectations, hypotheses, or guesses that you sometimes make about how the person will respond.[6] This point of view emphasizes that communication involves not just action, but rather action and reaction; not just stimulus, but also stimulus and response. According to this perspective, a "good" communicator not only skillfully prepares and delivers messages, but also watches for significant reactions to his or her communication. The study of human communication becomes a study of how people "talk" and how they "respond."

Although the interactional viewpoint is an improvement over communication-as-action, it still has some weaknesses. The most serious one, it seems to me, is that although it's not as oversimplified as the action view, the interactional view still distorts human communication by treating it as a series of causes and effects, stimuli and responses. For example, think about the last time you had a conversation with someone you know. What was the stimulus that caused you to greet the other person? His or her greeting? His or her look? Your expectations about the other's eagerness to talk with you? Was your greeting a response, or was it a stimulus to his or her next utterance? Or was it both? What caused you to say what you said? What the other person said? What you thought the other's words *meant*? What you *felt* because of those words? What you felt because of *how* the other person said what she or he said? What you felt because of how the other *looked* when speaking? Are you able to distinguish clearly between the stimuli and responses in that conversation or between the actions, the hypotheses about the reactions, and the reactions?

George Kelly, a fairly well-known psychologist, reports that he has "pretty well given up trying to figure out" the relationship between stimuli and responses. He writes, "some of my friends have tried to explain to me that the world is filled with 'S's' and 'R's' and it is unrealistic of me to refuse to recognize them. But before they have talked themselves out they become pretty vague about which is which."[7]

What I'm saying is that it's more accurate to see communication as an inter-action than to see it as just an action one person performs. But if you stick to an interactional view, you will still miss an important part of what it means to say that communication occurs *between* persons, and the part you will miss is the one part that makes the most difference, the part that can make interpersonal quality communication happen.

Over the last seven years I found that helping students see this "part," help-ing them see communication from this relational point of view, is one of the most important and most difficult things I do as a teacher. In my own life I'm also continually reminded of how important it is to see communication rela-tionally—every time I try to explain a concept in class, discuss a disagreement over a grade, negotiate a weekend with Marcia and Lisa, divide housekeeping responsibilities with my roommate, or work through an argument with some-one I love. Every time my communication is really important, in other words, I rediscover how necessary it is to view what's happening relationally, to see that it's occurring *between* persons. Since this perspective is so vital, I want to talk about it in different ways, using three different terms: *transaction, relationship,* and *spiritual child.*

Transaction

One way to say what I mean is to use the term *transaction* and to contrast it with the *action* and *interaction* points of view.* As I said, if you see communi-cation as an *action*, you're likely to be most concerned with each individual's performance. But human communication is much more than just independent message-sending. If you view communication as an interaction, you'll begin to see *some* of this "much more." The most obvious additional element you will see is feedback—how one's communication behavior is in part a response to the

---

*John Dewey and Arthur Bentley originally made this three-part distinction in their book *Knowing and the Known* (Boston: Beacon Press, 1949).

other person's, how human communication continually involves mutual and reciprocal influences.

It is important to see beyond performance to feedback, but there is another element that you will still miss if you stick within the interactional perspective. That element is this: *Every time persons communicate, they are continually offering definitions of themselves and responding to definitions of the other(s) which they perceive.* That process goes on all the time. Your clothes are part of your "this is how I define myself" message, just as mine are. Your tone of voice also reveals how you define yourself in relation to the situation and the person you're talking with. Recall in your mind's ear the sound of your voice when you're talking with a young person whom you define yourself as superior to. Contrast that with you tone of voice when you see yourself as an inferior talking with your supervisor or your parent. Touch, distance, eye contact, and choice of words all contribute to self-definition too. Look at the ways I've defined myself in relation to you in this book—the words I have chosen, the examples I have used, and so on. I have also assumed how you're defining yourself, and part of what I'm doing is responding to your self-definition. *And I could not not do these things.* This process of self-definition and response to the definition of the other is going on whenever people communicate.

Recently the term "transaction" has been introduced to talk about this process. When it's used this way, it means more than it does in the phrase "business transaction."[8] A dictionary of psychological terms defines a transaction as "a psychological event in which all parts or aspects of the concrete event derive their existence and nature from active participation in the event."[9] In other words, a transaction is an event in which *who we are* (our "existence and nature") emerges out of the event itself. Human communication is that kind of event. Human communication is transactional. Whenever humans communicate, part of what's going on is that each is defining himself or herself in relation to the other persons involved. That is, each is sending messages about his or her "existence and nature" and interpreting and responding to messages about the "existence and nature" of the other people involved.

Obviously this defining process has some limits. I am male, 35, and brown-eyed, and I can't define myself as female, 10, and blue-eyed. But I *can* offer a definition of myself that says I see myself as more masculine—or more feminine—than you and as in some sense younger or older than you. Then it's up to you to respond to the definition of self I offer. You may accept it, partly accept it, or reject it altogether. The point is, at a given moment, neither of us can change our identity absolutely, but we do change in relation to each other.

To review, then, you can see human communication as an action if you want to, but if you do you will miss a lot of what's happening. You can look at human communication as an interaction too, but you will still miss an important part of what's going on. The part you will miss is the ongoing process of self-definition-and-response-to-definition-of-other, and you won't see that clearly until you recognize that communication is a transaction, an event defined by that very process. All human communication is transactional. We're always engaged in the definition-and-response-to-definition process. Sometimes we see our communication as transactional and sometimes we don't. I'm convinced that when we don't, it's a whole lot harder to help interpersonal quality communication happen.

The main reason is that when you see communication as an action, you aren't focusing on what's going on *between* the persons involved. All you're seeing is one person's choices, one person's behavior. When you see communication as an interaction, you still aren't seeing what's *between* person A and person B. You see each person functioning something like a sophisticated billiard ball—reacting to forces from the other billiard balls, the table surface, cue stick, pads, etc. From an interactional point of view, one's actions are affected by the others, but *who one is* doesn't change.

When you adopt a transactional point of view, though, you can't help but look at what's *between* the persons involved. If you focus your attention on just person A, for example, you realize that since person A is who he or she is only in relation to person B, you have to look immediately at what's happening *between* them. The same goes for person B. Since *who the persons are*—their "existence and nature"—emerges out of their meeting with each other, you can't help but focus on the meeting itself rather than on the individual meeters.

Relationship

I want to shift vocabularies now and make the same point in slightly different terms. As I mentioned above, some psychologists have fairly recently adopted the term "transaction" to talk about what happens between persons. Another term—"relationship"—has been used for a longer time by philosophers to talk about a similar thing.

Philosophers, as you probably know, are interested in answering the most basic possible questions. One of those most basic questions is, "What is there?" A philosopher addressing that question is not asking, "What is there in this room?" or "What is there on this page?" but rather "What is there *generally*?" That is, "What is the most basic, most fundamental reality?" In the history of the Western world—from the fifth century B.C., when those famous Greeks, such as Aristotle and Plato, were active, to the present—philosophers have offered three different responses to that most basic question, "What is there?"

One response has been to say that the most fundamental realities are *ideas*; this philosophy is called idealism or more accurately ideaism. From this point of view the stones, trees, and metals we see around us are not the world's most basic constituents. Nor are the elements on chemistry's periodic table. The ideaist argues that since all of the elements in the universe fit together in such a complex but complementary and workable way, there must be some intent, purpose, or mind "behind" them. That mind is obviously a more basic reality than the physical objects it controls. So the answer to the question, "What's the fundamental nature of reality?" is "mind" or "ideas." As one philosopher puts it:

> . . . whatever is ultimately real in the universe is such stuff as ideas are made of rather than such stuff as stones and metals are made of. That is, if we are looking for the substance of things, the ultimate being which explains all other beings, we shall find it to be mental in nature—the thinker and his thought, the will and its doings, the self and its self-expression. And whatever appears initially to be other than this, independent of it all or hostile to it, as matter [rocks, metals, etc.] or force or space and time, will be found to depend on the mind for its very existence.[10]

As you probably recognize, most religions were originally based on this perspective, on some form of ideaism. But ideaism is also more than theology; it's a kind of pure philosophy that in the Western world is usually traced back to the Greek philosopher Plato.

Plato's student and teaching assistant, Aristotle, is usually considered to be the father of the second response to the "What is real?" question. Aristotle's approach, called *realism*, begins from the conviction that the most basic realities are the things, the objects, we sense all around us. The realist argues that it's a waste of time and energy to look beyond the obvious. The floor under me is obviously "really" there; there is "really" a tree outside my window; and so on. The world presents itself to us in all kinds of identifiable forms, and there is no reason to assume that there is something "more real" than the objects we can see, hear, smell, taste, and touch. Our main goal, according to the realist, should be to catalogue this objective reality in as many systems as it takes—tables of chemical elements, biological classifications of genera and species, legal systems, political systems, etc.—and to study them as objectively as possible, that is, with a minimum amount of human interference. According to realists, in other words, the most basic reality is not "the thinker [human or divine] and his thought," but rather things, objects, the "sense-able" furniture of the world.

It's only a slight overgeneralization to say that up until the start of this century, the history of Western philosophy has been the history of the struggle between various forms of ideaism and various forms of realism. Today many thoughtful persons believe strongly in one or the other of those points of view. But in the early twentieth century, a third approach was introduced, an approach that has greatly influenced today's history, psychology, theology, sociology, literature, art, and communication by introducing an alternative, *relational* perspective.

The name of the new approach is phenomenology, or as it often appears, *existential phenomenology*. Its perspective is relational because the phenomenologist argues that the answer to the question "What is real?" is neither "subjective ideas" nor "objective things," but rather the relationship between subject and object, mind and thing, person and world. The phenomenologist argues that neither the ideaist nor the realist view of the world explains things adequately. Trees and rocks and floors are much too real to be dismissed as constructs of somebody's mind, so the ideaist view doesn't work. On the other hand, there is no way that I can get out from behind my mind and my awareness to get in touch directly with those same trees, rocks, and floors. Even the scientist cannot remove *all* human elements from a measurement or observation; total objectivity is impossible.[11] So the realist's insistence on objective observation and objective classification also creates serious problems. The answer seems to lie, both figuratively and literally, *between* those viewpoints.

Here's part of how the phenomenologist gets to this relational position: If I start out, the phenomenologist says, like the Renaissance philosopher Descartes did, questioning everything that *appears* to be real, I end up just where Descartes did, being unable to doubt that I am doubting. In other words, I might be able to question, for theoretical purposes anyway, whether the floor under me is really solid, or that God exists, or that the sun will rise tomorrow, or virtually *anything*. But I can't question the fact that I am doing all that questioning. When I get to the point where I can't doubt that I am doubting, I am forced to recognize that consciousness, awareness, or thinking (of which doubting is one form) is the primary, indubitable reality, the one reality I can't question. That's what Descartes concluded: *"Cogito ergo sum."* Loosely translated, that means, "I can question or doubt everything but the fact that I'm doing all that questioning, so since I *can't* doubt that fact, it's the most basic fact."

But the phenomenologist insists that we need to go beyond Descartes. Phenomenologists argue that we also need to notice that thinking never occurs without something being thought about; there's *always* an object of my awareness or consciousness—something I'm aware *of*. I'm never just aware; I'm always aware of something—aware of the sun shining on this paper, aware of the sound and feel of my stomach rumbling, aware of my fear of heights, or whatever. So Descartes was only partly right. It isn't just my questioning that's the most basic fact; it's my questioning and what I question, or my doubting and what I doubt, or my consciousness and what I'm conscious of. *Together.*

The way the phenomenologist puts this point is to say that consciousness or awareness is inherently *intentional*, or directed toward an object. So if you say (1) that awareness or consciousness is the most basic thing there is, and (2) that awareness is always, by its very nature, directed toward some object of awareness, you are saying that both awareness *and* the something I'm aware of, both consciousness *and* its objects, are always there. Or more accurately, you're saying that the *relationship*, or meeting, between awareness and what I'm aware of is always there. That's another way of saying that the most basic, fundamental datum of reality is the *relationship between* mind and matter, consciousness and thing, subject and object, person and world.

Although the explanation of this point of view is heavy going in spots, it's crucially important to understand it clearly. As I've already indicated, our inability—or unwillingness—to see communication relationally has the most impact when we're in the middle of a conflict. When you're really arguing with somebody, it *seems* obvious that he or she is making you mad, that the argument is the other person's fault, that you're right about important points and the other person is wrong. But all those conclusions that *seem* so obvious come from seeing what's happening not as a *relationship*, but as a cause-effect stimulus-response thing. For example, as Chapter 7 points out, nobody *makes* you feel angry; your anger emerges in the relationship, and it's primarily *your* choice to feel angry. Similarly, you won't get anywhere trying to figure out whose "fault" an argument is. You'll probably get something like this: "I clam up because you keep nagging me; it's your fault!" "But I only nag you because you won't say anything; it's your fault!" Neither person is "right" or "wrong"; the conflict emerges in the relationship, and so long as you're looking at just one side, you'll stay stuck in the blaming game, and the communication won't improve much.

Spiritual Child

Let me briefly put this point one more way, and then we'll go on to something else. I was discussing this transactional, relationship idea with John Keltner about a year ago; John is an interpersonal communication teacher at Oregon State University who wrote the first widely used interpersonal speech communication textbook. He said that the idea reminded him of an interesting concept that he and Loraine Halfen, a communication counselor in Denver, had talked about. John and Loraine suggested that it's easier to see human communication transactionally or relationally if you think in terms of a "spiritual child" that is the inevitable offspring of every human meeting.

In other words, whenever you encounter someone, the two of you together create a spiritual child—*your relationship*. Unlike the creation of physical children, there are no contraceptives available for spiritual children; when two people meet, they always create a relationship of some sort. Also unlike physical children, the spiritual child lives as long as at least one person lives. If two persons once have a relationship, their relationship endures, even though years and continents may separate them. The spiritual child can change drastically, but it can't be killed. That's one of the reasons why it's so hard to deal with the break-up of a long-term, intimate relationship. Since the spiritual child won't die, the relationship won't cease to exist, and each person has to learn to live with a radically, maybe even tragically, changed "child."

There are some similarities, though, between a physical and a spiritual child. For example, if the child is born in a meeting characterized by manipulation, deceit, and exploitation, it will be deformed and ugly. If it's raised in that same atmosphere, it will never be healthy. Often it can be nurtured back to health, but it takes a heavy commitment from both parents, the best possible outside help, and time. On the other hand, if it's born and raised in an open, caring atmosphere, it will grow healthy and strong. As John puts it, "properly nourished, honestly and lovingly cared for, this new essence created by two persons in a dyadic relationship can be a glorious being."[12]

I hope that the spiritual child metaphor is useful for you. What it does for me is to give me another way to look at the relationship, the transaction, what's between the persons. As a child, you are neither of your parents, but the result of their meeting, their contact. Similarly, the spiritual child who is born whenever two persons communicate is an entity that emerges *between* them.

SUMMARY

All of that is what I mean when I say that interpersonal communication is communication that occurs *between persons*. All three key words—"meeting," "between," and "persons"—carry a lot of meaning in that statement. But if you keep in mind what it is to be a person and what's meant by a "meeting between," you can come up with a pretty straightforward definition of interpersonal communication:

> Interpersonal communication is the kind or quality of transaction, relationship, or spiritual child that happens when two or more humans are willing and able to meet as persons by making available or sharing some of their personness—their uniqueness, active choosing, emotions and value—and by being sensitive to or aware of some of the other's personness. Or more briefly, interpersonal communication is the transaction that happens when communicators are willing and able to share some of their own personness and to be aware of the personness of the other(s).

As I've already said, this book is organized around that definition, and each chapter further explains and gives examples of one aspect of interpersonal quality communication. Part I (Chapters 1–3) explores the basic ingredients—the transactional point of view, the function of words, and the working of nonverbal cues. Part II (Chapters 4 and 5) deals with being aware of personness—yours and the other's. In Part III (Chapters 6–8), the first two chapters deal with sharing yourself through disclosing and being assertive, and Chapter 8 explores empathic listening, a process that involves both being aware and sharing. Part IV (Chapters 9–12) includes essays by four people who have been able to put all of these ideas together.

I hope the ideas and suggestions here work for you. They make a real difference to me!

NOTES

1. Gary D'Angelo and I make some of these same points in Chapter 1 of *Together: Communicating Interpersonally* (Reading, Mass.: Addison-Wesley, 1975). We wrote that chapter more than two years ago, though, and as you'll see if you read both this version and that one, my thinking has changed some since then.

2. Ervin Singer, *Key Concepts in Psychotherapy*, 2d ed. (New York: Basic Books, 1970), p. 17.

3. George Isaac Brown, *Human Teaching for Human Learning: An Introduction to Confluent Education* (New York: Viking Press, 1971), p. 4.

4. Obviously, this principle is also central to the Judaeo-Christian tradition, which has strongly influenced the ethics of the Western world.

5. Carl R. Rogers and Barry Stevens, *Person to Person: The Problem of Being Human* (New York: Simon & Schuster/Pocket Books, 1971), p. 104.

6. David Berlo, "Interaction: The Goal of Interpersonal Communication," in *The Process of Communication* (New York: Holt, Rinehart and Winston, 1960), pp. 106–131.

7. George A. Kelly, "The Autobiography of a Theory," *Clinical Psychology and Personality: The Selected Papers of George Kelly*, ed. Brendan Maher (New York: Wiley, 1969), p. 47.

8. This is also different from what's meant by "transactional analysis."

9. Horace B. English and Ava Chompney English, *A Comprehensive Dictionary of Psychological and Psychoanalytical Terms* (New York: Longmans, Green, 1958), p. 561.

10. William Ernest Hocking, *Types of Philosophy*, 3rd ed. (New York: Scribner, 1959), p. 152.

11. Theodore Roszak makes this point persuasively and clearly in a chapter called "The Myth of Objective Consciousness" in his book *The Making of a Counter Culture* (Garden City, N.Y.: Doubleday, 1966), pp. 203–238.

12. John Keltner, "The Third Being in Dyadic Communication," unpublished paper, 1974, p. 6.

In this brief talk, Dr. William Pemberton, a clinical psychologist in Mill Valley, California, explains in his own terms the relational perspective or point of view I just talked about.

I like the way he emphasizes how our basic, unstated assumptions affect just about everything we do. I also think that his taste-of-the-chemical example is a good way to illustrate what it means to say that a transaction is an event that goes on *between* people. The taste, in other words, is neither "in", the paper nor "in" the person, but is a "transaction," a "relationship," a "spiritual child."

THE TRANSACTIONIST ASSUMPTION
William Pemberton

In the past few years I have been studying the dynamics of human insult, and I find that much of human insult comes when one person questions, doubts, or criticizes the assumptive knowledge of another person. For instance, if you believe in God, and someone asks you why, or doubts the value of your belief, or is openly critical of such a belief, how do you react? Or, if someone asks you if you believe in free enterprise, in the democratic process, or more controversial issues, such as desegregation, the test ban treaty, interrupting the conceptual process by other than natural means, how quickly may you be insulted!

One of the useful bits of information about human nervous systems is that one's assumptive knowledge (which we call secondary nature) is indistinguishable from primary nature (our sensory and apperceptive processes) in determining the nature of reality.

Let me discuss now three different ways of talking about an experience; or, I might say, three different assumptions we can make about the nature of reality: the absolutistic, the relativistic, and the transactional. These represent roughly three stages of man's growing sophistication about the nature of himself and his cosmos. They could represent beliefs about reality that we might classify as prescience, early science, and modern science, respectively. For purpose of demonstration, I sometimes distribute to my lecture groups bits of paper which have been dipped in phenyl-thio-carbamide, a harmless chemical which tastes bitter to approximately seventy per cent of the participants, but tasteless to the remaining thirty per cent. The papers are prepared by dipping a sheet of typing

This is an abridgment of an article originally appearing in ETC under the title "Semantics and Communication." Reprinted from ETC, Vol. 23, No. 3 by permission of the International Society for General Semantics.

paper into the solution, drying it, and cutting it up. The result is that each person gets, comparatively speaking, the same amount of the substance. I then make a statement of fact about this event: "There is no taste in the paper," which is valid for me. Then I ask what is the thinking of the group, and get such responses as "You're wrong," "You've a different paper," "You're crazy," "Your taste buds are faulty," and the like. The accumulated scientific information: whether or not you taste the paper is determined by your inherited genes. The insult patterns started, however, are mostly because of the *assumptions* about the event; for instance, one being that if we are having the same experience we must be reacting in the same way "or else someone must be wrong" (or deficient, or what not).

Let us look again at the three different assumptions that predominate man's thinking on this kind of event—whether it is through taste, sight, hearing, or other sensory modalities.

- The assumption of the "absolutistic" person is that "the taste is in the paper" (i.e., qualities are in things).

- The assumption of the "relativistic" person is that "the taste is in me" (i.e., qualities are in me; for instance, color is determined by the cones in my eyes); some taste it, some do not, "so who cares?"

- The assumption of the "transactionist" is that there is a transaction going on between what's in the paper and what's going on in me. Some people react to the transaction in one way, some in another. All I can talk factually about is *my* reaction to the transaction, and then make inferences or inquire about yours.

With this assumption of modern science, based upon our knowledge about human nervous systems, I am neither defensive about my reactions nor critical of yours. We may react alike, or differently, and thus learn from one another. We can learn what we have in common, and respect each other as to the ways that we are different.

In a similar way, we can talk about not only the similarities and differences in primary reactions, but also differences in feeling, in judgments, in standards, values, qualities, morals, meanings, which are based upon our individual and cultural collections, our secondary nature. This holds as well for our beliefs. If we find someone who has a belief or assumption about the nature of the cosmos which is different from our own, whether monotheistic, polytheistic, atheistic, pantheistic, or agnostic, the reaction is change from one of insult to one of interest, inquiry, and sharing.

An important reminder for some people is the fact that once I understand that your reality and mine may be different (by reality meaning the way we look at things, feel about or value them, think about them) it *does not* destroy *my* reality, my values, my preferences; but it *does* make possible a respect for *your* reality. When my behavior becomes influenced by this modern assumption about the nature of reality, something in the manner of reciprocity begins to develop, simply because of the diminishing of insult, and the natural concern of homo sapiens for the survival of his own species. And please note: those who operate by the assumption of modern science respect the coexistence of those with other assumptions, while searching for still other assumptions more meaningful, more applicable to mankind. And while searching for these new assumptions, a self-revising process is going on.

My contention is that until we understand the assumptive level of human knowledge, until we learn something about the nature of nervous systems, and the evaluative process, the best that we can do is learn to be tolerant of others who have different assumptive knowledge. This usually means putting up with others until they learn how things "really are," and until they are "more like us," which is, of course, the right way to be. (This is, of course, a series of assertions that is based on obsolete, absolutistic assumptions.)

Once understood, and once applied, modern assumptions can clarify such diverse subjects as: morality, law, education, ethics, politics, or religion. They can increase the potential of organizational structures from the simple to the complex. They can ease relationships within the family, or within the family of nations. They can operate more effectively on the job, in the home, within, between or among the multiple institutions of man.

A key to diminishing man's inhumanity to man (the same key to improving communication as I see it) thus lies in the direction of the dissemination of knowledge about human evaluation, how brains establish and maintain reality; how assumptive knowledge may act as barrier to effective communication, whereas knowledge *about* assumptive knowledge can open the gates to deeper understanding and can increase our capacity to be human beings.

PROBES

Would you say that your assumptions are generally "absolutistic," "relativistic," or "transactional"?

Do you think that Pemberton is saying anything more than the old cliche, "Try to see things from the other's point of view"? What?

In this paper Kenneth Boulding develops the relational or transactional assumption that Dr. Pemberton outlined.

Like Pemberton, Boulding believes that the answer to the question, "What is there?" is *"relationships."* But Boulding's word for "relationships" is *image.* In Boulding's terms the relationships are between me and my view of space, me and my view of time, me and my field of personal relations, and so on, and all of those sets of relationships go together to make up my *image.* In other words, Boulding says that our reality is not made up of objective "facts" or subjective "ideas," but of our image, which is the relationship between us and things, i.e., our whole subjective view of the objective world. Our image affects everything we do.

As Boulding explains, communication is the process of two or more images getting in contact, and the meaning of any communication is, for each of us, the change which is produced in our image. Boulding notes that when a message "hits" any image, it can add to it, reorganize it, introduce doubt into it, or change it in a revolutionary way. He also points out that the "facts" we often communicate about are actually what are commonly called "values." They are, in other words, a manifestation of our image.

INTRODUCTION TO *THE IMAGE*
Kenneth Boulding

As I sit at my desk, I know where I am. I see before me a window; beyond that some trees; beyond that the red roofs of the campus of Stanford University; beyond them the trees and the roof tops which mark the town of Palo Alto; beyond them the bare golden hills of the Hamilton Range. I know, however, more than I see. Behind me, although I am not looking in that direction, I know there is a window, and beyond that the little campus of the Center for the Advanced Study in the Behavioral Sciences; beyond that the Coast Range; beyond that the Pacific Ocean. Looking ahead of me again, I know that beyond the mountains that close my present horizon, there is a broad valley; beyond that a still higher range of mountains; beyond that other mountains, range upon range, until we come to the Rockies; beyond that the Great Plains and the Mississippi; beyond that the Alleghenies; beyond that the eastern seaboard; beyond that the Atlantic Ocean; beyond that is Europe; beyond that is Asia. I know, furthermore, that if I go far enough I will come back to where I am now.

In other words, I have a picture of the earth as round. I visualize it as a globe. I am a little hazy on some of the details. I am not quite sure, for instance, whether Tanganyika is north or south of Nyasaland. I probably could not draw a very good map of Indonesia, but I have a fair idea where everything is located on the face of this globe. Looking further, I visualize the globe as a small speck circling around a bright star which is the sun, in the company of many other similar specks, the planets. Looking still further, I see our star the sun as a member of millions upon millions of others in the Galaxy. Looking still further, I visualize the Galaxy as one of millions upon millions of others in the universe.

I am not only located in space, I am located in time. I know that I came to California about a year ago, and I am leaving it in about three weeks. I know that I have lived in a number of different places at different times. I know that about ten years ago a great war came to an end, that about forty years ago another great war came to an end. Certain dates are meaningful: 1776, 1620, 1066. I have a picture in my mind of the formation of the earth, of the long history of geological time, of the brief history of man. The great civilizations pass before my mental screen. Many of the images are vague, but Greece follows Crete, Rome follows Assyria.

I am not only located in space and time, I am located in a field of personal relations. I not only know where and when I am, I know to some extent who I am. I am a professor at a great state university. This means that in September I shall go into a classroom and expect to find some students in it and begin to talk to them, and nobody will be surprised. I expect, what is perhaps even more agreeable, that regular salary checks will arrive from the university. I expect that when I open my mouth on certain occasions people will listen. I know, furthermore, that I am a husband and a father, that there are people who will respond to me affectionately and to whom I will respond in like manner. I know, also, that I have friends, that there are houses here, there, and everywhere into which I may go and I will be welcomed and recognized and received as a guest. I belong to many societies. There are places into which I go, and it will be recognized that I am expected to behave in a certain manner. I may sit down to worship, I may make a speech, I may listen to a concert, I may do all sorts of things.

I am not only located in space and in time and in personal relationships, I am also located in the world of nature, in a world of how things operate. I know that when I get into my car there are some things I must do to start it; some things I must do to back out of the parking lot; some things I must do to drive home. I know that if I jump off a high place I will probably hurt myself. I know that there are some things that would probably not be good for me to eat or to drink. I know certain precautions that are advisable to take to maintain good health. I know that if I lean too far backward in my chair as I sit here at my desk, I will probably fall over. I live, in other words, in a world of reasonably stable relationships, a world of "ifs" and "thens," of "if I do this, then that will happen."

Finally, I am located in the midst of a world of subtle intimations and emotions. I am sometimes elated, sometimes a little depressed, sometimes happy, sometimes sad, sometimes inspired, sometimes pedantic. I am open to subtle intimations of a presence beyond the world of space and time and sense.

What I have been talking about is knowledge. Knowledge, perhaps, is not a good word for this. Perhaps one would rather say my *Image* of the world. Knowledge has an implication of validity, of truth. What I am talking about is what I believe to be true; my subjective knowledge. It is this Image that largely governs my behavior. In about an hour I shall rise, leave my office, go to a car, drive down to my home, play with the children, have supper, perhaps read a book, go to bed. I can predict this behavior with a fair degree of accuracy because of the knowledge which I have: the knowledge that I have a home not far away, to which I am accustomed to go. The prediction, of course, may not be fulfilled. There may be an earthquake, I may have an accident with the car on the way home, I may get home to find that my family has been suddenly called away. A hundred and one things may happen. As each event occurs, however, it alters my knowledge structure or my image. And as it alters my image, I behave accordingly. *The first proposition of this work, therefore, is that behavior depends on the image.*

What, however, determines the image? This is the central question of this work. It is not a question which can be answered by it. Nevertheless, such answers as I shall give will be quite fundamental to the understanding of how both life and society really operate. One thing is clear. The image is built up as a result of all past experience of the possessor of the image. Part of the image is the history of the image itself. At one stage the image, I suppose, consists of little else than an undifferentiated blur and movement. From the moment of birth if not before, there is a constant stream of messages entering the organism from the senses. At first, these may merely be undifferentiated lights and noises. As the child grows, however, they gradually become distinguished into people and objects. He begins to perceive himself as an object in the midst of a world of objects. The conscious image has begun. In infancy the world is a house and, perhaps, a few streets or a park. As the child grows his image of the world expands. He sees himself in a town, a country, on a planet. He finds himself in an increasingly complex web of personal relationships. Every time a message reaches him his image is likely to be changed in some degree by it, and as his image is changed his behavior patterns will be changed likewise.

We must distinguish carefully between the image and the messages that reach it. The messages consist of *information* in the sense that they are structured experiences. *The meaning of a message is the change which it produces in the image.*

When a message hits an image one of three things can happen. In the first place, the image may remain unaffected. If we think of the image as a rather loose structure, something like a molecule, we may imagine that the message is going straight through without hitting it. The great majority of messages is of this kind. I am receiving messages all the time, for instance, from my eyes and my ears as I sit at my desk, but these messages are ignored by me. There is, for instance, a noise of carpenters working. I know, however, that a building is being built nearby and the fact that I now hear this noise does not add to this image. Indeed, I do not hear the noise at all if I am not listening for it, as I have become so accustomed to it. If the noise stops, however, I notice it. This information changes my image of the universe. I realize that it is now five o'clock, and it is time for me to go home. The message has called my attention, as it were, to my position in time, and I have re-evaluated this position. This is the second possible effect or impact of a message on an image. It may change the image in some rather regular and well-defined way that might be described as simple addition. Suppose, for instance, to revert to an earlier illustration, I look at an atlas and find out exactly the relation of Nyasaland to Tanganyika. I will have added to my knowledge, or my image; I will not, however, have very fundamentally revised it. I still picture the world much as I had pictured it before. Something that was a little vague before is now clearer.

There is, however, a third type of change of the image which might be described as a revolutionary change. Sometimes a message hits some sort of nucleus or supporting structure in the image, and the whole thing changes in a quite radical way. A spectacular instance of such a change is conversion. A man, for instance, may think himself a pretty good fellow and then may hear a preacher who convinces him that, in fact, his life is worthless and shallow, as he is at present living it. The words of the preacher cause a radical reformulation of the man's image of himself in the world, and his behavior changes accordingly. The psychologist may say, of course, that these changes are smaller than they appear, that there is a great mass of the unconscious which does not change, and that the relatively small change in behavior which so often follows intellectual conversion is a testimony to this fact. Nevertheless, the phenomenon of reorganization of the image is an important one, and it occurs to all of us and in ways that are much less spectacular than conversion.

The sudden and dramatic nature of these reorganizations is perhaps a result of the fact that our image is in itself resistant to change. When it receives messages which conflict with it, its first impulse is to reject them as in some sense untrue. Suppose, for instance, that somebody tells us something which is inconsistent with our picture of a certain person. Our first impulse is to reject the proffered information as false. As we continue to receive messages which contradict our image, however, we begin to have doubts, and then one day we receive a message which overthrows our previous image and we revise it completely. The person, for instance, whom we saw as a trusted friend is now seen to be a hypocrite and a deceiver. . . .

One should perhaps add a fourth possible impact of the messages on the image. The image has a certain dimension, or quality, of certainty or uncertainty, probability or improbability, clarity or vagueness. Our image of the world is not uniformly certain, uniformly probable, or uniformly clear. Messages, therefore, may have the effect not only of adding to or of reorganizing the image. They may also have the effect of clarifying it, that is, of making something which previously was regarded as less certain more certain, or something which was previously seen in a vague way, clearer.

Messages may also have the contrary effect. They may introduce doubt or uncertainty into the image. For instance, the noise of carpenters has just stopped, but my watch tells me it is about four-thirty. This has thrown a certain amount of confusion into my mental image. I was under the impression that the carpenters stopped work at five o'clock. Here is a message which contradicts that impression. What am I to believe? Unfortunately, there are two possible ways of integrating the message into my image. I can believe that I was mistaken in thinking that the carpenters left work at five o'clock and that in fact their day ends at four-thirty. Or, I can believe that my watch is wrong. Either of these two modifications of my image gives meaning to the message. I shall not know for certain which is the right one, however, until I have an opportunity of comparing my watch with a timepiece or with some other source of time which I regard as being more reliable.

The impact of messages on the certainty of the image is of great importance in the interpretation of human behavior. Images of the future must be held with a degree of uncertainty, and as time passes and as the images become closer to the present, the messages that we receive inevitably modify them, both as to content and as to certainty.

The subjective knowledge structure or image of any individual or organization consists not only of images of "fact" but also images of "value." We shall subject the concept of a "fact" to severe scrutiny in the course of the discussion. In the meantime, however, it is clear that there is a certain difference between the image which I have of physical objects in space and time and the valuations which I put on these objects or on the events which concern them. It is clear that there is a certain difference between, shall we say, my image of Stanford University existing at a certain point in space and time, and my image of the value of Stanford University. If I say "Stanford University is in California," this is rather different from the statement "Stanford University is a good university, or is a better university than X, or a worse university than Y." The latter statements concern my image of values, and although I shall argue that the process by which we obtain an image of values is not very different from the process whereby we obtain an image of fact, there is clearly a certain difference between them.

The image of value is concerned with the *rating* of the various parts of our image of the world, according to some scale of betterness or worseness. We, all of us, possess one or more of these scales. It is what the economists call a welfare function. It does not extend over the whole universe. We do not now, for instance, generally regard Jupiter as a better planet than Saturn. Over that part of the Universe which is closest to ourselves, however, we all erect these scales of valuation. Moreover, we change these scales of valuation in response to messages received much as we change our image of the world around us. It is almost certain that most people possess not merely one scale of valuation but many scales for different purposes. For instance, we may say A is better than B for me but worse for the country, or it is better for the country but worse for the world at large. The notion of a hierarchy of scales is very important in determining the effect of messages on the scales themselves.

One of the most important propositions of this theory is that the value scales of any individual or organization are perhaps the most important single element determining the effect of the messages it receives on its image of the world. If a message is perceived that is neither good nor bad it may have little or no effect on the image. If it is perceived as bad or hostile to the image which is held, there will be resistance to accepting it. This resistance is not usually infinite. An often-repeated message or a message which comes with unusual force or authority is able to penetrate the resistance and will be able to alter the image. A devout Moslem, for instance, whose whole life has been built around the observance of the precepts of the Koran will resist rigorously any message which tends to throw doubt on the authority of his sacred work. The resistance may take the form of simply ignoring the message, or it may take the form of emotive response: anger, hostility, indignation. In the same way, a "devout" psychologist will resist strongly any evidence presented in favor of extrasensory perception, because to accept it would overthrow his whole image of the universe. If the resistances are very strong, it may take very strong, or often repeated messages to penetrate them, and when they are penetrated, the effect is a realignment or reorganization of the whole knowledge structure.

On the other hand, messages which are favorable to the existing image of the world are received easily and even though they may make minor modifications of the knowledge structure, there will not be any fundamental reorganization. Such messages either will make no impact on the knowledge structure or their impact will be one of rather simple addition or accretion. Such messages may also have the effect of increasing the stability, that is to say, the resistance to unfavorable messages, which the knowledge structure or image possesses. . . .

Even at the level of simple or supposedly simple sense perception we are increasingly discovering that the message which comes through the senses is itself mediated through a value system. We do not perceive our sense data raw; they are mediated through a highly learned process of interpretation and acceptance. When an object apparently increases in size on the retina of the eye, we interpret this not as an increase in size but as movement. Indeed, we only get along in the world because we consistently and persistently disbelieve the plain evidence of our senses. The stick in water is not bent; the movie is not a succession of still pictures; and so on.

What this means is that for any individual organism or organization, there are no such things as "facts." There are only messages filtered through a changeable value system. This statement may sound rather startling. It is inherent, however, in the view which I have been propounding. This does not mean, however, that the image of the world possessed by an individual is a purely private matter or that all knowledge is simply subjective knowledge, in the sense in which I have used the word. Part of our image of the world is the belief that this image is shared by other people like ourselves who also are part of our image of the world. In common daily intercourse we all behave as if we possess roughly the same image of the world. If a group of people are in a room together, their behavior clearly shows that they all think they are in the same room. It is this shared image which is "public" knowledge as opposed to "private" knowledge. It follows, however, from the argument above that if a group of people are to share the same image of the world, or to put it more exactly, if the various images of the world which they have are to be roughly identical, and if this group of people are exposed to much the same set of messages in building up images of the world, the value systems of all individuals must be approximately the same.

The problem is made still more complicated by the fact that a group of individuals does not merely share messages which come to them from "nature." They also initiate and receive messages themselves. This is the characteristic which distinguishes man from the lower organisms—the art of conversation or discourse. The human organism is capable not only of having an image of the world, but of talking about it. This is the extraordinary gift of language. A group of dogs in a pack pursuing a stray cat clearly share an image of the world in the sense that each is aware to some degree of the situation, which they are all in, and is likewise aware of his neighbors. When the chase is over, however, they do not, as far as we know, sit around and talk about it and say, "Wasn't that a fine chase?" or, "Isn't it too bad the cat got away?" or even, "Next time you ought to go that way and I'll go this way and we can corner it." It is discourse or conversation which makes the human image public in a way that the image of no lower animal can possibly be. The term "universes of discourse" has been used to describe the growth and development of common images in conversation and linguistic intercourse. There are, of course, many such universes of discourse, and although it is a little awkward to speak of many universes, the term is well enough accepted so that we may let it stay.

Where there is no universe of discourse, where the image possessed by the organism is purely private and cannot be communicated to anyone else, we say that the person is mad (to use a somewhat old-fashioned term). It must not be forgotten, however, that the discourse must be received as well as given, and that whether it is received or not depends upon the value system of the recipient. This means that insanity is defined differently from one culture to another because of these differences in value systems and that the schizophrenic of one culture may well be the shaman or the prophet of another.

Up to now I have sidestepped and I will continue to sidestep the great philosophical arguments of epistemology. I have talked about the image. I have maintained that images can be public as well as private, but I have not discussed the question as to whether images are *true* and how we know whether they are true. Most epistemological systems seek some philosopher's stone by which statements may be tested in order to determine their "truth," that is, their correspondence to outside reality. I do not claim to have any such philosopher's stone, not even the touchstone of science. I have, of course, a great respect for science and scientific method—for careful observation, for planned experience, for the testing of hypotheses and for as much objectivity as semirational beings like ourselves can hope to achieve. In my theoretical system, however, the scientific method merely stands as one among many of the methods whereby images change and develop. The development of images is part of the culture or the subculture in which they are developed, and it depends upon all the elements of that culture or subculture. Science is a subculture among subcultures. It can claim to be useful. It may claim rather more dubiously to be good. It cannot claim to give validity.

In summation, then, my theory might well be called an organic theory of knowledge. Its most fundamental proposition is that knowledge is what somebody or something knows, and that without a knower, knowledge is an absurdity. Moreover, I argue that the growth of knowledge is the growth of an "organic" structure....We do not have to conceive of the knowledge structure as a physico-chemical structure in order to use it in our theoretical construct. It can be inferred from the behavior of the organism just as we constantly infer the images of the world which are possessed by those around us from the messages which they transmit to us. When I say that knowledge is an organic structure, I mean that it follows principles of growth and development similar to those with which we are familiar in complex organizations and organisms. In every organism or organization there are both internal and external factors affecting growth. Growth takes place through a kind of metabolism. Even in the case of knowledge structures, we have a certain intake and output of messages. In the knowledge structure, however, there are important violations of the laws of conservation. The accumulation of knowledge is not merely the difference between messages taken in and messages given out. It is not like a reservoir; it is rather an organization which grows through an active internal organizing principle much as the gene is a principle or entity organizing the growth of bodily structures. The gene, even in the physico-chemical sense, may be thought of as an inward teacher imposing its own form and "will" on the less formed matter around it. In the growth of images, also, we may suppose similar models. Knowledge grows also because of inward teachers as well as outward messages. As every good teacher knows, the business of teaching is not that of penetrating the student's defenses with the violence or loudness of the teacher's messages. It is, rather, that of co-operating with the student's own inward teacher whereby the student's image may grow in conformity with that of his outward teacher. The existence of public knowledge depends, therefore, on certain basic similarities among men. It is literally because we are of one "blood," that is, genetic constitution, that we are able to communicate with each other . . . .

PROBES

How do you respond when Boulding says that for any individual there are no such things as separately existing "facts," but only "messages filtered through a changeable value system"? Do you agree with him, or do you believe that things like "two plus two equals four" or "the sun is hot" are facts? If Boulding is right, does communication become easier or harder for you?

Can you think of a time when a message affected your image in a revolutionary way? What happened? Can you see how, after that event, your reorganized image affected everything you experienced?

In this essay Dean Barnlund, a speech communication teacher in San Francisco, outlines an approach to communication based on the transactional, or relational, perspective introduced and explained by Pemberton, Boulding, and me. Barnlund uses still another set of terms for the same basic idea. He calls the communication-as-action point of view "message-centered" and the relational, transactional view "meaning-centered."

Barnlund shows how theories that are not meaning-centered can't adequately explain human communication, a process he describes as being complex, circular,

irreversible, unrepeatable, and involving the total personality of all of the participants. He also explains that a meaning-centered philosophy focuses on "the state
of mind, the assumptive world and the needs of the listener or observer." At the
end of this piece, Barnlund talks about some of the ethical implications of this
viewpoint.

Persons in my classes have often been able to use this message-cen-
tered/meaning/centered distinction to summarize and clarify the whole action-
interaction-transaction analysis I talked about before. If you view human communication as a process of message-creating, message-sending, and message-receiv-
ing, you're looking at it as an action or interaction. Only when you see how our
communicating is a process of *meaning*-sharing do you begin to view it
transactionally, or relationally.

TOWARD A MEANING-CENTERED
PHILOSOPHY OF COMMUNICATION

Dean C. Barnlund

...To be acceptable, a philosophy of communication should fulfill the
following criteria: (1) It should provide a satisfactory explanation of the aim of
communication. (2) It should provide a technically adequate description of the
process of communication. (3) It should provide a moral standard that will protect and promote that healthiest communicative behavior. Once this process is
defined and its nature exposed, the way should be clear for facing the practical
decisions involved in giving effective instruction.

AIM OF COMMUNICATION

We begin by asking why men communicate? What human need does it, or
should it, satisfy? While there is almost universal agreement that communication is tied to the manipulation of symbols, there is widespread disagreement as
to what constitutes effectiveness in this endeavor. A brief review of some abortive explanations of communication is essential because, in spite of repeated
criticism, these conceptions continue to influence current training in speech.

One of these theories is that the aim of communication is to transmit
information. Success hinges on mastery of the facts, effective arrangement of
materials and strength of expression. It is a message-centered philosophy of
communication. And it is largely amoral. Critical standards for determining the

This is an abridgment of an article originally appearing in the *Journal of Communication*, Vol. 12
(1962), pp. 197–211, reprinted by permission of the *Journal of Communication* and the author.

effectiveness of communication, as in the critical evaluation of literature, are internal; they are found within the message itself. When a writer or speaker or critic asks, "Was it well said?" he is usually viewing communication as a mode of expression. The training in communication that follows from this premise and perspective is destined to be truncated and unrealistic. Talk is not a guarantee of communication. Facts and ideas are not shared because they are articulated loudly or even well. Messages do not influence automatically because of being broadcast on the mass media. The inadequacy of this approach lies in its neglect of the listener as terminus of the communicative act, in its failure to provide an explanation of how meaning arises through communication and in its disregard for all but public and continuous discourse.

A second theory is that the aim of communication is to transfer ideas from one person to another. Here the listener is admitted as part of the communicative situation. The focus, however, in research and training, is upon the message formulator. Effectiveness in communication is thought to turn not only on the content and phrasing of the message, but on the intelligence and credibility of the source. Relatively little attention is paid to the listener other than to note that messages should be adapted to his interests. It ends by becoming a speaker-centered philosophy. Communicative events are explained largely in terms of the experiential milieu that shaped the mind of the speaker and find expression in his messages.

As an explanation of communication it, too, fails in several important respects. First, the listener tends to be regarded as a passive object, rather than an active force in communication. Unfortunately, it is not that simple to deposit ideas in another mind. Teachers of great intelligence and high purpose often find their lessons disregarded or misapplied. Messages flowing through an industrial complex are not received undistorted like images in a hall of mirrors. Second, this approach also fails to provide a satisfactory theory of meaning, and of how messages from highly credible sources can provoke so many and such contradictory meanings. Finally, it is too parochial. It neglects man's communication with himself—an area that is fast becoming one of the most vital in communication research—and it fails to account for the fact that communication is as often a matter of hiding or protecting what is in men's minds as it is a matter of revealing their thoughts and intentions.

Neither of these schools of thought, of course, omits the constituent elements in communication altogether. It is, rather, a question of emphasis. Questions of emphasis, however, are not irrelevant or inconsequential in establishing a productive orientation for a discipline. The pedagogical consequences of both of these approaches is to place a disproportionate emphasis on the source and message elements in communication. Both schools of thought tend, also, to minimize or overlook completely, the interactive and dynamic nature of the communicative process.

Communication, as I conceive it, is a word that describes the process of creating a meaning. Two words in this sentence are critical. They are "create" and "meaning." Messages may be generated from the outside—by a speaker, a television screen, a scolding parent—but meanings are generated from within. This position parallels that of Bervo when he writes, "Communication does not consist of the transmission of meaning. Meanings are not transmitted, nor transferable. Only messages are transmittable, and meanings are not in the message, they are in the message-user."[1] Communication is man's attempt to cope with his experience, his current mood, his emerging needs. For every person it is a unique act of creation involving dissimilar materials. But it is, within broad limits, assumed to be predictable or there could be no theory of communication.

The second, and more troublesome word, is "meaning." Meaning is not apparent in the ordinary flow of sensation. We are born into, and inhabit a world without "meaning." That life becomes intelligible to us—full of beauty or ugliness, hope or despair—is because it is assigned that significance by the experiencing being. As Karl Britton put it, "A world without minds is a world without structure, without relations, without facts."[2] Sensations do not come to us, sorted and labeled, as if we were visitors in a vast, but ordered, museum. Each of us, instead, is his own curator. We learn to look with a selective eye, to classify, to assign significance.

Communication arises out of the need to reduce uncertainty, to act effectively, to defend or strengthen the ego. On some occasions words are used to ward off anxiety. On other occasions they are means of evolving more deeply satisfying ways of expressing ourselves. *The aim of communication is to increase the number and consistency of our meanings within the limits set by patterns of evaluation that have proven successful in the past, our emerging needs and drives, and the demands of the physical and social setting of the moment.* Communication ceases when meanings are adequate; it is initiated as soon as new meanings are required. However, since man is a homeostatic, rather than static, organism, it is impossible for him to discover any permanently satisfying way of relating all his needs; each temporary adjustment is both relieving and disturbing, leading to successively novel ways of relating himself to his environment.

. . . Communication, in this sense, may occur while a man waits alone outside a hospital operating room, or watches the New York skyline disappear at dusk. It can take place in the privacy of his study as he introspects about some internal doubt, or contemplates the fading images of a frightening dream. When man discovers meaning in nature, or in insight in his own reflections, he is a communication system unto himself. Festinger refers to this as "consummatory communication." The creation of meanings, however, also goes on in countless social situations where men talk with those who share or dispute their purposes. Messages are exchanged in the hope of altering the attitudes or actions of those around us. This can be characterized as "instrumental communication," as long as we remember that these two purposes are not mutually exclusive.

What I am describing is a meaning-centered philosophy of communication. It admits that meaning in the sender, and the words of the messages are important, but regards as most critical the state of mind, the assumptive world and the needs of the listener or observer. The impact of any message from "See me after class" to "What's good for General Motors is good for the country" is determined by the physical, personal and social context, the most critical ingredient of which is the mind of the interpreter. Communication, so defined, does not require a speaker, a message, or a listener, in the restricted sense in which these terms are used in the field of speech. All may be combined in a single person, and often are.

A theory that leaves out man's communication with himself, his communication with the world about him and a large proportion of his interactions with his fellowman, is not a theory of communication at all, but a theory of speechmaking. Indeed, it seems applicable to speechmaking only in the most formal and restricted sense of that word. There is little in the traditional view of speech that is helpful in the analysis of conversation, interviewing, conflict negotiations, or in the diagnosis of the whole span of communicative disorders and breakdowns that are receiving so much attention currently. Upon so limited a view of communication it is unlikely that there can develop theories of sufficient scope and stature to command the respect of other disciplines or of the larger public that ultimately decides our role in the solution of man's problems. The field of speech seems to be fast approaching what the airlines call a "checkpoint" where one loses the freedom to choose between alternative flight plans, between a limited interest in speechmaking and a broad concern with the total communicative behavior of man. By defining communication operationally, by examining a wider range of communicative acts, the way might be prepared for making the startling theoretical advances that have, so far, not characterized our field.

THE COMMUNICATION PROCESS

A satisfactory philosophy should also provide a starting point for the technical analysis of communication. One way of accomplishing this is to ask what characteristics would have to be built into a scientific model that would represent, at the same time and equally well, the entire spectrum from intrapersonal to mass communication. It should not be a model that is mechanically or structurally faithful, but one that is symbolically and functionally similar. Space is too limited here to more than suggest a few of the principles that would have to be reflected in such a model.

1. Communication is not a thing, it is a process. Sender, message and receiver do not remain constant throughout an act of communication. To treat these as static entities, as they often are in our research, is questionable when applied to the most extreme form of continuous discourse, is misleading when used to analyze the episodic verbal exchanges that characterize face-to-face communication, and is totally useless in probing man's communication with himself. Changes in any of these forces, and few forces remain constant very long, reverberate throughout the entire system. Students of communication are not dissecting a cadaver, but are probing the pulsing evolution of meaning in a living organism.

2. Communication is not linear, it is circular. There are many situations in life where a simple, linear, causal analysis is useful. One thing leads to another. A, then B, then C. I push over the first domino and the rest, in turn, topple over. But this sort of thinking is not very helpful, though quite appealing in its simplicity, in studying communication. There is not first a sender, then a message and finally an interpreter. There is, instead, what Henderson calls "mutual dependence" or what I have termed "interdependent functionalism." The words "sender" and "receiver" no longer name the elements in a communicative act, but indicate the point of view of the critic at the moment.

3. Communication is complex. Someone once said that whenever there is communication there are at least six "people" involved: The person you think yourself to be; the man your partner thinks you are; the person you believe your partner thinks you are; plus the three equivalent "persons" at the other end of the circuit. If, with as few as four constants, mathematicians must cope with approximately fifty possible relations, then we, in studying communication, where an even greater number of variables is concerned, ought to expound with considerable humility. In this age of Freudian and non-Freudian analysts, of information theory specialists, of structural linguists, and so on, we are just beginning to unravel the mysteries of this terribly involved, and therefore fascinating, puzzle.

4. Communication is irreversible and unrepeatable. The distinction being suggested here is between systems that are deterministic and mechanical, and those that are spontaneous and evolutionary. One can start a motor, beat a rug, or return a book. But you cannot start a man thinking, beat your son, or return a compliment with the same consequences. The words of a teacher, even when faithfully repeated, do not produce the same effect, but may lead to new insight, increased tension, or complete boredom. A moment of indifference or interest, a disarming or tangential remark, leave indelible traces.

5. Communication involves the total personality. Despite all efforts to divide body and mind, reason and emotion, thought and action, meanings continue to be generated by the whole organism. This is not to say that some messages do

not produce greater or lesser dissonance, or shallower or deeper effects on the personality; it is only to hold that eventually every fact, conclusion, guilt, or enthusiasm must somehow be accommodated by the entire personality. The deeper the involvement produced by any communication, the sooner and more pervasive its effects upon behavior.

Research or instruction that disregards these characteristics of the communicative act would appear both unsound and of dubious value.

THE MORAL DIMENSION

The perennial and legitimate concern with ethics in the field of speech arises out of the inherent moral aspect of every interpersonal communication. As was noted earlier, the aim of communication is to transform chaotic sense impressions into some sort of coherent, intelligible and useful relationship. When men do this privately, either in confronting nature or in assessing their own impulses, they are free to invent whatever meaning they can. But when men encounter each other, a moral issue invades every exchange because the manipulation of symbols always involves a purpose that is external to, and in some degree manipulative of, the interpreter of the message. The complexity of communication makes it difficult to know in advance, and with certainty, the impact of any bundle of words upon the receiver of them. The irreversibility of communication means that whatever meaning is provoked by a message cannot be annulled. A teacher may erase a blackboard, a colleague apologize, or an employer change his mind, but there is no way of erasing the effect of a threatening ultimatum, a bitter remark, or a crushing personal evaluation.

Meaning, in my opinion, is a private preserve and trespassers always run a risk. To speak of personal integrity at all is to acknowledge this. Any exchange of words is an invasion of the privacy of the listener which is aimed at preventing, restricting, or stimulating the cultivation of meaning. Briefly, three types of interference may be distinguished. First, there are messages whose intent is to coerce. Meaning is controlled by choosing symbols that so threaten the interpreter that he becomes capable of, and blind to, alternative meanings; second, there are messages of an exploitative sort in which words are arranged to filter the information, narrow the choices, obscure the consequences, so that only one meaning becomes attractive or appropriate; third, there is facilitative communication in which words are used to inform, to enlarge perspective, to deepen sensitivity, to remove external threat, to encourage independence of meaning. The values of the listener are, in the first case, ignored, in the second, subverted, in the third respected. While some qualification of this principle is needed, it appears that only facilitative communication is entirely consistent with the protection and improvement of man's symbolic experience. Unless a teacher is aware of these possibilities and appreciates the differences in these kinds of communication, it is unlikely that he will communicate responsibly in the classroom. . . .

Alfred North Whitehead once said that any discipline deserving a place in the curriculum must have a philosophy, a method and a technique. The statement is undoubtedly true, but somewhat incomplete if philosophy, method and technique exist as isolated units of instruction. Too often what results is that the technical and moral aspects remain separate, lacking any vital connection in the classroom, and more importantly, in the personality of the student. The result is schizophrenic communication. Men learn to blot out all but technical considerations when communicating in a coercive or prejudicial way, but turn around and attack someone else's communication on moral grounds when it proves technically superior to their own. It is this sort of inconsistency that fosters pathological communication and pathological personalities.

Integrative instruction in communication encourages the student to work out better meanings concerning his own communication with himself and his fellowmen. By "better" I refer to meanings that permit more consistency in his personality between what he assumes, what he sees, and what he does. By "better" I refer to meanings that will increase his openness, curiosity and flexibility. By "better" I refer to meanings that will make him more independent, and more confident of his own judgment. . . .

REFERENCES

1. David Berlo, *The Process of Communication* (New York: Holt, Rinehart and Winston, 1960), p. 175.

2. Karl Britton, *Communication: A Philosophical Study of Language* (New York: Harcourt, Brace, 1939), p. 206.

PROBES

How do you respond when Barnlund defines communication as "the process of creating a meaning"? Does that describe what you're doing when you communicate?

How do you see Barnlund's discussion of meaning relating to Boulding's idea that the meaning of a message is the change it produces in the image?

What are some examples from your own experience of the irreversibility and unrepeatability of communication?

Do you agree with Barnlund that communication has a "moral dimension"? How so?

The difference between talking "at" and talking "with" is the difference between touching, and touching and being touched.

HUGH PRATHER

2

VERBAL CODES

The basic ingredients, or raw materials, of human communication are usually divided into two large categories—verbal codes and nonverbal codes. As Knapp mentions in the next chapter, there are some problems with that division; it's sort of a "words" and "other" categorization. But the division is made because those two ingredients tend to work differently; they perform somewhat different communicative functions.

I say "tend to" and "somewhat" because the differences between the ways words and nonwords work are often differences of degree. Words generally carry most of the information load in human communication. You use words to describe, explain, outline, detail, compare and contrast, etc. Nonverbal codes, on the other hand, generally indicate a lot about how each person defines himself or herself, what the feeling or emotional content is, etc.

It's important, though, to develop an awareness of both codes. Consequently, the purpose of the next two selections is to introduce how words work in communication; the three articles in Chapter 3 will do the same for nonverbal codes.

Gary D'Angelo and I wrote this next selection to make several points. The first point is that the study of verbal language is complex and has been going on for a long time. The second is that words don't do just one thing; in fact, they work in at least six different ways: to refer to or stand for something else, to perform an action, to evoke emotion, to affect the way you perceive things and people, and to bring people together. We also mention how the English language makes it difficult to talk about ongoing processes, a phenomenon you might have noticed as you read the attempts in Chapter 1 to talk about the ongoing processes of communicative transactions and relationships. We also note the subtle sexism that's present in much of our language. But the final function of language is the one that relates most clearly to our interest in *interpersonal* communication. Words, as we suggest there, can bring people together.

WORDS AND HOW THEY "WORK"
John Stewart and Gary D'Angelo

All communication contexts include nonverbal cues, and most contexts consist of *both* verbal and nonverbal cues. Occasionally, verbal and nonverbal cues "work" in similar ways. For example, the traffic sign

serves the same purpose as the words "NO LEFT TURN." But it's important to remember that in most human communication situations, these two kinds of cues "work" in significantly different ways. In other words, when humans are communicating, a word just doesn't do the same thing as a sign; vocabulary choice doesn't affect the situation or the persons involved the same way that tone of voice or facial expression does. Words are good for some things and almost worthless for others. Nonverbal cues are sometimes the most important part of human communication, and sometimes they're almost irrelevant. . . .

VERBAL CUES

Verbal cues are words. That seems easy enough; everybody knows what a word is, right? Well, yes and no. Scholars have been studying language since about 400 B.C., when an ancient named Panini wrote a lengthy commentary on the *Vedas*, the sacred books of India. In the nineteenth century, researchers, such as Wilhelm von Humboldt and Ferdinand de Saussure, made important advances in linguistics, and the twentieth century's leading linguist, MIT's Noam Chomsky, has become almost as famous as Daniel Berrigan. But these scholars have not yet agreed on the defining characteristics of the basic unit of their study, the *word*.

From John Stewart and Gary D'Angelo, *Together: Communicating Interpersonally* (Reading, Mass.: Addison-Wesley, 1975), pp. 38–44. Reprinted by permission.

There are several problems involved. For example, if you define language as what people write, then you can define a word as a group of letters set off by space. But linguists generally agree that written language is only a reflection of what people say, that the *spoken* word is primary. And that creates difficulties. Would you say that your "Howareya!?" to somebody you meet on the street is one *spoken* word or three? Is "loves" a different word from "love," or are they two forms of the same word? How about "lover" or "loving"? Is "bazoo" a word? The letters fit together, and some English-speaking people use it when they talk, but it doesn't seem to be in any English dictionary. What about the "words" Don Martin creates? Is "shklork" a word? "Thak"? "Shtonk"? How about "Gish Goosh"?

© 1971 by Don Martin and E.C. Publications. Reprinted courtesy of the artists, Don Martin and Dick DeBartolo.

Obviously, we aren't going to be able to answer a question that's stumped linguists for over 2000 years. For our purposes it'll be good enough to avoid the problem by agreeing that things like "cat," "mainsail," and "empathy" are words and that things like

†*?%&,   and

are not. That approach won't handle the borderline cases, but they're fairly uncommon, anyway. The main point we want to make is that studying words is not as simple as it might at first appear to be.

Not only is it next to impossible to define exactly what you're studying, it's also difficult to identify all the ways in which words function in human communication. It's often assumed that all words are names for things, that they always *refer to* or *stand for*, in one way or another, the things they name. You've probably heard that before—the word "dog" refers to a certain kind of four-legged animal, "tree" to a certain kind of botanical life, and "rock" to a hard, stony object *or* to a repetitive movement made by a certain kind of chair, *or* to a type of music, *or*.....Well, *sometimes* words function by referring to "things in the world," but not always. Words work in several other important ways, too.

Sometimes, for example, you use words not to talk about things, but to *perform an action*. The words, "I do" or "I will" in a marriage ceremony do not refer to anything; they make up part of the act of getting married. "I christen thee" at a ship launching works the same way as does "I promise" or "I'll bet you...." When you make a serious bet or an important bargain with somebody, the words you use to seal the agreement don't refer to objects or events or even states of mind. They constitute, for example, the act of betting itself. When you sing in the shower or curse your smashed finger, these words are also functioning as actions; they don't "stand for" or "refer to" actions. Cursing *is* a part of being angry; singing *is* part of being happy, romantic, melancholy, or whatever. In short, *performing actions* is one of the things we often use words for without realizing that we're doing it.

Words can also work by *evoking emotion*. It's always been intriguing for me (John) to notice how a bunch of black marks on a page can make me angry, excited, or even weepy. I've been reading J.R.R. Tolkein's books recently—all about the magic ring and the inhabitants of Middle Earth, including Bilbo and Frodo the Hobbits, Gandalf, the wizard, the Orcs, Nazguls, Balrogs, Elves, and so on. Several times I've become so involved with the lives of these fantasy crea-tures that I've neglected to go to bed. At exciting parts I notice my heart rate in-creases, I breathe quicker, my body tenses—it's just as if something was "really" happening. And words are doing it. Just words. No pictures even!

Language also works to *affect the way you perceive things and people*. In Chapter 7 we'll be talking about how your perception affects your communicat-ing. When you get there you might keep in mind the idea that you perceive what you do partly because of the words you know how to use. Linguists disagree on how words affect perception—and how *much*—but most language scholars agree that the existence of many words for "horse" in Arabic, for "snow" in Eskimo, and for "yam" in the language of the Trobrand Islanders is tied to how these people perceive horses, snow, and yams. This point of view is often called "linguistic determinism" or "the Sapir-Whorf hypothesis" and has been sum-marized by the anthropologist Benjamin Lee Whorf.

> . . .the background linguistic system (in other words the grammar) of each lan-guage is not merely a reproducing instrument for voicing ideas but rather is itself the shaper of ideas, the program and guide for the individual's mental activity, for his analysis of impressions. . . .We dissect nature along lines laid down by our na-tive language.[1]

We've discovered that our native language, which we're using to write this book, is sometimes limiting us in frustrating ways. English, unlike some other languages, maintains clear distinctions between subjects and predicates, causes and effects, beginnings and ends. The word system of the Navaho doesn't do that. According to Harry Hoijer, Navaho speakers characteristically talk in terms of processes—uncaused, ongoing, incomplete, dynamic movings. The word Navahos use for "wagon," for example, translates roughly as "wood rolls about hooplike."[2] As Hoijer explains, the Navaho words that we would trans-late "He begins to carry a stone" mean not that the actor produces an action, but that the person is simply linked with a given round object and with an already existing, continuous movement of all round objects in the universe.[3] The English language is significantly different from that. It requires you to talk in terms of present, past, future, cause and effect, beginning and end. But some things English speakers would like to discuss just can't be expressed in these terms. We would like to be able to talk more clearly about the ever-changing, processslike, ongoing nature of communication and about the betweenness of the quality of communication we're calling "interpersonal." But the English language makes it difficult to do that, as you'll probably notice when you read through parts of this book.

You might also notice that we've had some trouble with the male orienta-tion of standard American English. Our language includes an incredible number of terms which subtly, but effectively, limit our perception of women. For example, in our culture we use the male pronoun "his" or "him" to make a general or universal reference to people;[4] a married man tends to talk about "his" wife; and professional limitations are suggested by job titles such as "salesman," "foreman," "fireman," "policeman," "chairman of the board," and "metermaid." As Aileen Hernandez, past president of the National Organization of Women, has noted:

> There's a "housewife" but no "househusband"; there's a "housemother" but no "housefather"; there's a "kitchenmaid" but no "kitchenman"; unmarried women cross the threshold from "bachelor girl" to "spinster" to "old maid," but unmarried men are "bachelors" forever.[5]

Much of the sexism of American English may seem trivial and unimportant. But when all the subtle terms and uses are put together, they significantly affect the way we perceive female persons.

The same thing happens to other groups. Ossie Davis's essay "The English Language Is My Enemy"[6] details the way our meanings for the words "black" and "white" affect our perceptions of black and white persons. Similarly, language terms and uses also severely limit the ways in which people perceive Asians, Chicanos, Native Americans, and other racial and ethnic minorities.

A fifth way words function is to *reduce uncertainty*.... Words can reduce your uncertainty by limiting the possible conclusions you can draw about something or someone. When you see a large, rectangular, green and white freeway sign in the distance, you know that it could possibly indicate scores of different things, including an approaching exit, a lane change, or the mileage to the next large town. When you get close enough to read the first word, the number of possibilities is reduced significantly, and when you can read all of the words your original uncertainty about the sign is reduced even more. The goal of sign writers is to use words that reduce your uncertainty to nearly zero. They try to avoid ambiguously worded signs

> SAN FRANCISCO TRUCKS PROCEED
> RIGHT LANE MERGE LEFT
> ONE MILE

in favor of those whose meaning is unmistakable, as shown on the next page.

> ### LAST EXIT BEFORE
> ### TOLL BRIDGE

When a friend you're used to seeing every day suddenly disappears for several days, you know that the absence could indicate many different things—your friend might be ill, in trouble, angry at something you've done, tired of being around you, upset about something, cramming for an exam, moving, or a dozen other things. Your uncertainty about why your friend is absent can be reduced only when the person explains verbally—in speaking or writing—that "I took a few days off to go home and collect my thoughts."

The guessing game "Twenty Questions" is based on the ability of language to reduce uncertainty. The point of the game is for one person to guess the identity of an object which another person is thinking about. The questioner can ask no more than 20 questions, the "yes" or "no" answers to which should enable her or him to narrow the range of possible objects to the one the other person has in mind. It's often fun to see how 18 or 19 well-chosen questions can lead to something as unlikely as "the left front wheel of that bus" or "the statue on top of the bank building."

Not all words do function to reduce uncertainty, but the point we want to make here is that they *can*. They can categorize, point, specify, distinguish, and clarify much more efficiently than can nonverbal cues and that's one reason why they're so important for interpersonal communication.

The final function of words that we want to mention here is kind of difficult to explain. Words, especially spoken words, can work to *bring people together*. (Of course, words can also help create enemies, but they don't have to.) Martin Buber describes the unifying function of words this way:

> The importance of the spoken word, I think, is grounded in the fact that it does not want to remain with the speaker. It reaches out toward a hearer, it lays hold of him, it even makes the hearer into a speaker, if perhaps only a soundless one.[7]

This is the sense in which words are truly *symbolic*. In Greek the word "symbolic" is made up of "bolos," which means "to throw," and "sym," which means "with" or "together." One meaning of "symbolic," then, is "throw togetherness," or *"unifying."* And words can work that way. Think of the times you've found a friend just by listening to somebody talk—in person, on the radio or television, or in a book. His or her words helped bring you together. The words we use on these pages can bring us closer together with you, too.

They can help bridge the gap between us. Again, we know that they *don't* always work that way, but they *can*, just as your words can help you move closer to others.

Words, in short, are a flexible and richly varied part of many communication contexts. They can *refer* the persons involved to nonverbal things or events. Sometimes, we use words to *perform actions.* Words can also *evoke emotion*, and the language you're able to use even *affects the way you perceive.* Words can *reduce uncertainty* and, perhaps most importantly for us, words can *unify* persons, can bring humans together.

REFERENCES

1. John B. Carroll, ed., *Language Thought and Reality: Selected Writings of Benjamin Lee Whorf* (New York: Wiley, 1956), pp. 212–213.

2. Harry Hoijer, "Cultural Implications of Some Navaho Linguistic Categories," *Language*, **XXVII** (1951): 117.

3. *Ibid.*, p. 119.

4. "One Small Step for Genkind," *New York Times Magazine*, April 16, 1972.

5. Aileen Hernandez, "The Preening of America," *Star News*, Pasadena, Calif., 1971 New Year's edition, cited in Haig A. Bosmajicin, "The Language of Sexism," *ETC: A Review of General Semantics*, **XXIX** (September 1972): 307.

6. Ossie Davis, "The English Language Is My Enemy," *Language in America*, ed. Neil Postman, Charles Weingartnen, and Terence P. Moran (New York: Pegasus, 1969), pp. 73–82.

7. Martin Buber, "The Word That Is Spoken," *The Knowledge of Man*, ed. Maurice Friedman, trans. Maurice Friedman and Ronald Gregor Smith (New York: Harper & Row, 1965), p. 112.

PROBES

How do words function most often in your communication experience? To refer or stand for? To perform an action? Evoke emotion? Affect perception? Reduce uncertainty? Bring people together?

Without jumping forward to the next chapter, can you identify some ways that the *nonverbal* parts of communication affect how the *verbal* parts function?

Do you agree that the English language promotes sexism? Why or why not?

What's your most recent experience when *words* (not touch, tone of voice, or other nonverbal cues) made it possible for you to make contact with another person?

> *If I want to talk to someone and I am stuck for something to say, one of the simplest ways for me to get started is to state honestly what I am experiencing: "I want very much to talk to you but no words are coming."*
>
> HUGH PRATHER

In this article Gerard Egan explores in some depth the ability of language to "bring people together." This selection is longer than many others in this book, but Egan uses the space to make several interesting and useful points.

He is writing about how language works in a contract sensitivity laboratory, a special group situation in which people sign a contract committing themselves to work for a set period of time on specific interpersonal communication skills. Egan begins by citing behavioral scientists, philosophers, novelists, and playwrights who have emphasized the *power* language has. (You will note that Egan is fond of citing sources; I hope you can see that as part of his uniqueness, his personhood, and not let it get in the way of listening to what he is saying to you.) Even though language is potentially powerful, though, Egan notes that there are several problems that face the members and the facilitator of a contract group. One set of problems relates to the language people use there. I believe that these same language problems affect most groups studying interpersonal communication—including the class you're probably in now.

A key difficulty is the tendency for people to stick with what Egan calls "exsanguinated" language, language with all the life and most of the person taken out of it. "Commercial speech," "cliché talk," and "anti-logos," are other kinds of language that *prevent* people from coming together.

Egan argues that in order for interpersonal communication to happen, people need to use the kind of language he calls *logos*. Logos is the translation of your *self* into language; it's based on your ability to "hand yourself over to others" via your words. Logos isn't always eloquent or smoothly fluent, but when it is genuine, it accurately reflects some of the person behind it.

Poiesis, says Egan, is a special form of logos. Poiesis is logos with a strong and pure emotional content. As he puts it, we tend to deal with emotions by suppressing them or by foisting them on to others. Poiesis is an alternative to both those approaches, a way of using language to *express* emotions—even hostile and negative ones—and yet to promote contact with the other person. It isn't easy to have poiesis in our culture; people don't generally expect you to express your emotions honestly. But if we could use more of this kind of language, Egan suggests, we could experience more intrapersonal *and* interpersonal growth.

Again, this article is a little lengthy and Egan sometimes writes rather impersonally. But I hope you will listen past those obstacles for the good ideas that are here.

THE ELEMENTS OF HUMAN DIALOGUE: PATHOS, LOGOS, POIESIS

Gerard Egan

LOGOS: MAN'S TRANSLATION OF HIMSELF INTO LANGUAGE

As Wiener and Mehrabian (1968) note,

> Anyone who listens carefully to the way people say things quickly learns that the particular words a speaker uses to describe an event or experience can be a rich source of information about his feelings and attitudes. The bases for making these kinds of inferences are not usually explicit, although members of a communication group appear to respond regularly to these subtle variations in word usage[1]. . . .

What follows is a brief indication of the aspects of language that might be profitably considered and experimented with in a sensitivity laboratory. The laboratory experience is an opportunity for the participants to examine man as one who speaks by subjecting their own verbal interactions to the scrutiny of the group.

The Problems and Potential of Language

Problems There are various ways in which people underuse or abuse language in interpersonal situations and many reasons why they do so. Some language problems stem directly from, and reflect varying degrees of, psychopathology. Bettelheim discusses children who have surrendered the use of language because of parental disapproval, their mutism being an indication that they have given up any hope of influencing their world. This surrender of speech closes a vicious circle:

> Once the child has even stopped communicating with others, his self becomes impoverished the more so the longer his mutism lasts, and the more so the longer his personality remains underdeveloped at the time of the onset of withdrawal.
> If this [mutism] happens before he has fully learned to manipulate symbolic forms, before the age of three or four, then the child also fails to develop the higher intellectual processes.[2]

Erikson discovered that one of the outcomes of traumatic war experiences was a distrust and devaluation of language. Meerloo found neurosis manifested in language-use disturbances: "The insecure neurotic shrinks from free word-play; he tries to manipulate words mechanically, like machinery. He fears the adventure of communication."[3] Ruesch sees the origin of communication problems in parents' inability to adapt themselves to the maturation level of their children. . . . If parents do not adapt their language to the developmental stage of their children, while at the same time offering encouragement to improve verbal-language proficiency, then communication disturbances may arise in their children.[4]

Language problems arise from and reflect not only psychopathology in the strict sense; they reflect also the psychopathology of the average. Many normal men fear the communication process because of more or less normal fears of involving themselves deeply with others. They neither pour themselves into their language in interpersonal situations nor expect others to do so. Language must remain on a safe level. They habitually put filters between what they really think and feel and what they say. This results in exsanguinated or muddied, but safe, communication. Some men engage in language that is overly precise—they ask too much of language—while others engage in language that is too vague—that is, they ask too little of language. Both extremes are usually defensive measures, ways of keeping interpersonal contacts at acceptable levels of intensity. Some men are victims of poor education in language. They have lived in families or in societies that are afraid of open communication, with the result that patterns of language are not available to them to express what they would like to express. . . .

In societies that subtly discourage or limit conversational freedom and deeper interpersonal contact through language, some men abandon language (at least in a relative sense) either because it is useless as an instrument of deep human communication or because the patterns of language allowed are identified with the establishment that is being rejected. In the case of the present [youth] culture, this flight from language involves both (1) the creation of an argot reflecting a break from the values of society seen as useless or oppressive, while emphasizing the values of the subculture and (2) an often irresponsible immersion in the *pathos* dimensions of living. A counter language evolves, and a counter *pathos* society is established, parallel to or outside the confines of the society being rejected.

Potentialities Despite the problems involved in using exsanguinated language and communication, language is still one of the most dramatic ways in which man differs from other animals. Stout sees language as an instrument by means of which man examines the world around him. If he is afraid of this world, his language will be anemic and feeble, but if he loves the world and is challenged by it, his language will be strong and searching.[5] To adapt a phrase from Wittgenstein, the limits of a person's language are the limits of his world. Cioran sees silence as unbearable and says he would find it easier to renounce bread than speech. He claims that one cannot withdraw one's confidence from words "without setting one's foot in the abyss."[6] Language exposes, reveals both individuals and societies: "Words, at least in traditional societies, often express far more than feelings or ideas. The way words are used—in tales, riddles, proverbs, and typical modes of address and conversation—can reveal a great deal about the structure and values of a society."[7]

Novelists and writers frequently have, if not deeper insights, at least more striking, distinctive, and challenging insights into the nature and force of human language than do behavioral scientists. Writers continually try to enlarge the possibilities of language. D.H. Lawrence, Virginia Woolf, and James Joyce never hesitated to experiment with verbal symbols that would most fully convey what they experienced. As Burgess notes: "Language, of its very nature, resists tautology; it wants to launch out, risk lies, say the thing which is not."[8]

Brian Friel's entire play *Philadelphia Here I Come* is based on the distinction between what the leading character really thinks, feels, and would like to say and what he actually says. In the play, there are two levels of conversation—the vague, hesitant, compliant, failed bravado of the son about to leave his father in Ireland to seek a new way of life in the United States, and the vigorous speech of the son's "inner core" (played by a separate character). The pity of it all is that, although the audience is electrified by what the "inner man" says, it knows that his speech really dies (and in a sense the son dies with it) because it is never spoken. The man who chains his language chains himself. . . .

The purpose of what is said here is not to apotheosize language, for . . . language is sometimes a sensitive instrument and sometimes a clumsy tool of communication. But when a man enlarges the possibilities of his language, he enlarges his own possibilities. The laboratory gives him the opportunity to extend the range of language in order to contact himself and others at deeper levels. In the safety of the laboratory, he can run risks in his use of language that he could not take in everyday life. The following discussion of language might serve as a basis for experimentation.

Different Kinds of Language

In keeping with the consideration of language from [an] interactional point of view, the following distinctions—again, despite the fact that they are somewhat abstractive—might give direction to the discussion that follows.

Logos *Logos*, in the strict or restricted sense, refers to man's ability to translate his real self into language. *Logos* is language filled with the person who is speaking, and therefore refers to his ability to use speech to express his identity. It also refers to the use man makes of speech in order to establish some kind of growthful interpersonal contact. Negatively, it is the refusal to use speech merely to fill interactional space and time or as a smoke screen or shield behind which to hide.

Just as there are different kinds of truly human contact and various degrees or levels of such contact, so there are different kinds of *logos*. If a man talks meaningfully about his political or religious beliefs, this is *logos*. *Logos* need not be self-disclosure in the sense discussed in Chapter 6, but, in that it is meaningful speech, it will always provide some insight into the identity of the speaker. Meaningful speech with an intimate friend will be on a different level from meaningful speech with one's fellow workers. The special ability to allow one's language to express not only one's thoughts but also the feelings and the emotions that surround these thoughts is a special kind of *logos* called *poiesis*. *Poiesis* will be treated separately.

Logos must be clearly differentiated from the ability to speak fluently and elegantly, for both fluency and elegance are at times used to camouflage, rather than reveal, one's identity.... *Logos* here means translating oneself, or handing oneself over to others, through the medium of speech, whatever the esthetic value of the language used.

Logos implies a respect for language as a form of communication and contact. It implies dialogue, and...for certain contemporary existentialist thinkers, authentic existence *is* communication, life *is* dialogue. Dialogue is certainly the life of the contract group. That is why the group member, by contract, is expected to examine his use of speech. If he is to develop new ways of being present to the members of the group, he must discover new ways of speaking and perhaps develop a new respect for language.

Dialogue, in the sense in which it is used here, is opposed to "game" communication. Dialogue is game-free, or at least an attempt to make communication game-free. Rapoport and Wiener, both of whom have made significant contributions to the mathematical theory of games, caution against the use of game theory as a basis for human communication. Rapoport finds dialogue with the "strategist" impossible, for the basic question in the strategist's mind is: In a conflict, how can I gain an advantage over my opponent? Rapoport thinks that the much more basically human question is: If I can gain an advantage over another, *what sort of person* will I become? The "cybernetic" man is basically monological, not dialogical, and for him, communication is intimately wedded to control—the control of the other.[9]

Berne uses "game" in a somewhat different sense. The "games people play" are ways of avoiding intimacy in human relationships. The game prevents dialogue. Berne goes so far as to say that the most that one can expect in a psychotherapeutic group is the discovery and analysis of the games played there. Real intimacy, he says, is almost never found in such group situations.[10] It is the contention of this book that the members of a contract interpersonal-growth group can establish dialogue, can free themselves, to a great extent, from a game approach to one another, and can establish not just the social imitation of intimacy that Berne speaks of, but real human intimacy.

Commercial speech "Commercial speech" refers to the language of the marketplace, the use of language in the commercial transactions of men. Such language is lean, utilitarian, pragmatic; it deals with objects rather than persons, for it is a medium of exchange rather than of interpersonal contact. Much of such language today is left to computers. It would be of no interest to us here were it not for the fact that there are people who use commercial speech as their principal mode of speech in interpersonal transactions. They see people as objects to be manipulated, rather than persons to be contacted, and this is reflected in the quality of their speech.

If speech is principally commercial, then, as McLuhan suggests, it can be dispensed with: "Electric technology does not need words any more than the digital computer needs numbers.[11] However, . . . speech defines man. It is just strange that he makes such poor use of it in his effort to humanize himself.

Cliché talk "Cliché talk" refers to anemic language, talk for the sake of talk, conversation without depth, language that neither makes contact with the other nor reveals the identity of the speaker (except negatively, in the sense that he is revealed as one who does not want to make contact or does not want to be known). Cliché talk fosters ritualistic, rather than fully human, contact ("Do you think that it is really going to rain?"—"The way they're playing, they'll be in first place by the first of September!"). Cliché talk fills interactional space and time without adding meaning, for it is superficial and comes without reflection. Perhaps it is the person who is overcommitted to maintenance functions, a person who is either unaware (because he lacks the requisite social intelligence) or afraid of possibilities for further interpersonal growth, whose speech will be predominantly cliché talk.

People usually listen politely to cliché talk, especially when it is pseudo-*logos*—that is, dressed up or doctored to sound important:

When a conversation fails to capture the spontaneous involvement of an individual who is obliged to participate in it, he is likely to contrive an appearance of being involved. This he must do to save the feelings of the other participants and their good opinion of him, regardless of his motives for wanting to effect this saving.[12]

If the needs of the listener are such that he is willing to put up with the boredom of cliché talk in order to enjoy the safety that is found in ritual, then the circle is complete and the field is wide open for such conversation.

One of the most common forms of cliché talk in our culture (and perhaps this is a transcultural phenomenon) is "griping," a more or less superficial communication of dissatisfaction with persons, institutions, or things outside oneself. It is one of the few verbal expressions of feeling allowed in public, and it is probably allowed because it is a ritual and most rituals are safe. The trouble with chronic griping is that it is a fixative. . . . A person's verbalizations to himself and others often stand in the way of change: "Forces outside me control me"; "I can do nothing to change."

Cliché talk is just words, while *logos* always connotes human contact. Some people speak endlessly about themselves and say nothing (if they were really disclosing themselves, others would not find it boring). They say nothing about themselves because they have no real feeling for themselves—they are deficient in the *pathos* dimension of life—and could hardly be expected to relate what they do not experience. Such people simply are not using speech as a mode of contact. For them, speech is . . . monologue rather than dialogue.

Anti-logos When language is actually used to destroy growthful interpersonal contact rather than to foster it, then it is *anti-logos*. There are a number of forms of speech that are really violations, rather than uses, of language. For instance, in the heat of anger, language can be used as a weapon, a tool of destruction rather than an instrument of growthful encounter. When a married couple stand shouting at each other (often saying things they do not really mean), language becomes completely swallowed up in emotion; it loses its identity as language. At such times it has more in common with a sledgehammer than with speech. Lying, too, can be a form of *anti-logos*, for deception cannot be the basis of growthful interpersonal contact. The speech of the psychopath, for example, is frequently, if not continually, *anti-logos*, for he uses speech to create situations, to manipulate others rather than to engage in growthful encounters with them. Finally, the language of the psychotic, while it might have its own peculiar logic (and without discounting the possibility that a psychosis may be a desperate form of revolt against a sick family or society), is frequently *anti-logos*. The psychotic, at least at times, appears to use language to drive others away. He fears human contact so deeply that he reverses the function of language, making it a barrier instead of a bridge. . . .

Most men engage in all four kinds of speech at one time or another. They not only use commercial speech in strictly commercial transactions, but also allow it to slip occasionally into interpersonal encounters. Indeed, life without some cliché talk would be intolerably intense for most men. It is a question, however, of proportion, and most men need to find ways of increasing the amount of *logos* (in the restricted sense) in their lives. . . .

Language and Self-Identity

One of the messages of G.B. Shaw's *Pygmalion* is that, in some fashion, language makes the person. Not only do differences in the use of language reflect class differences in society, but language actually helps create and maintain the differences in values that separate one class from another. For instance, a person from a lower class might speak quite freely about sexual matters and do so in public, while a member of an upper class might not feel free to speak about sexuality at all. Language, then, is an instrument of reinforcement regarding the different approaches to sexuality that exist in the two classes. What is true with respect to social identity is also true in the area of self-identity. . . . Language not only reveals a person's identity, who he is, but in some way it makes him the person he is. The literary dictum, *Le style c'est l'homme même*, can also be applied to a person's style of speaking: *La parole c'est l'homme même*. If a person's language is weak, insipid, cliché-ridden, and consistently ritualistic in social situations, this says much about the person's ability *and* willingness to relate both to himself and to others. Language not only reflects his encapsulation but becomes one of the instruments of his self-imprisonment.

Erikson sees the relationship between language and self-identity as developing early in the maturational process:

> . . . A child. . . learning to speak. . . is acquiring one of the prime functions supporting a sense of individual autonomy and one of the prime techniques for expanding the radius of give-and-take. . . . Speech. . . defines him as one responded to by those around him with changed diction and attention. . . A spoken word is a pact: there is an irrevocably committing aspect to an utterance remembered by others. . . . The child may come to develop, in use of voice and word, a particular combination of whining or singing, judging or arguing, as part of a new element of the future identity, namely, the element "one who speaks and is spoken to in such-and-such a way. . . .[13]

Erikson also discusses the case of a man who wanted to bury his past, to break with certain aspects of his self-identity. One of the things he did was to pursue graduate studies in a foreign language. Erikson suggests that this new language, in terms of a new career, a new medium of expression, and a new culture, may well have offered his client an opportunity to establish a different self-picture.

It is hypothesized, then, that language reveals certain dimensions of a person's life style and also creates and serves to maintain certain patterns of living and interacting. Ryle, for instance, suggests that personality differences exist between those who use dispositional verbs such as *believe, wonder, suppose,* and *aspire*, which signify ability, tendency, and proneness-to, and those who deal principally in modal verbs such as *does, can,* and *must.* The person who constantly *believes, wonders,* and *supposes* is seen to be differently oriented toward reality from the person who disposes of reality in terms of what *does, can,* or *must* happen.

Identity crises, too, are reflected in the use of language. The adolescent, who, according to Erikson, goes through a kind of natural period of identity diffusion and a moratorium in which society allows him to experiment with a number of different roles, speaks the specialized language of his subculture. Language becomes one of the ways in which he declares that he is not just an appendage of parents, church, school, and society in general, but a person in his own right.

The training group, then, is a laboratory in which the participants have the opportunity to reflect on the implications of the propositions: "My language is me," and "In some way I use language to make myself what I am." It is an opportunity to examine the ways in which they use *logos*, commercial speech, cliché talk, and *anti-logos* to fashion a communication life style.

POIESIS: WORDS MADE FLESH

When *pathos** finds expression in human language, when *logos* is suffused with human feeling and emotion, a new term is needed to describe the communication that takes place. The term used here is *poiesis*, which comes from the Greek verb meaning "to do, to make." The English word "poetry" comes from the same stem. When meaning and feeling become artfully one in language, the result is poetry. In human dialogue, when words are meaningfully filled with human emotion, when feelings and emotions find creative expression in human language, the result is *poiesis.* . . . *Poiesis* is word made flesh in human dialogue.

Men seem to feel safer when they compartmentalize their experiences. Feelings are all right, and language is all right, but they are to be kept apart, if possible. Lynch recognizes in movies a similar movement—that is, toward immediate, private, and wordless experience. He deplores such a movement: "Words and ideas have been given a hard time; they have been pushed into a polarized state, devoid of contact with images and things. They need to be allowed to reenter the world and re-establish their relation to things and their own power as a human art."[14] Meaningless words and unverbalized feelings both sin against

---

*Pathos refers to all the elements, passive and active, that constitute the experience of feeling and emotion.

human communication. Lynch suggests that even brutal language is better than either emasculated words or silences that hide hate and bitterness:

> . . . The words in *Who's Afraid of Virginia Woolf* are, on the surface, ordinary human words that say something. On the second level they turn out to be words describing games being played at, unrealities, fictions. On the third and final take they have inflexibly human rules behind them and are the only forms of salvation and *contact*, cruel though they might be, between George and Martha. [emphasis added][15]

Language, then, can be strong medicine, if it is made strong by becoming the vehicle of the speaker's experience. . . .

Failed poiesis: action divorced from language While perhaps the primary failure to achieve *poiesis* consists in an inability or a refusal to include emotion in verbal expression, there is also another, even more dramatic, form of failed *poiesis*. It involves what Bloch calls "an inability to substitute and utilize language for action and activity."[16] When a married couple stand screaming at each other, a kind of communication through action is taking place, but the use of language is really incidental to the whole process. This dumping of raw emotion on each other is an action or an activity devoid of both *logos* and *poiesis*. But if a marriage begins primarily on the level of *pathos* so that, although each experiences the other, neither is capable of translating that experience into language, and if the marriage continues principally on the level of *pathos*, with commercial speech alone used in the necessary transactions between partners, then trouble is almost unavoidable. The couple turns up in some marital-counseling situation, and it is discovered that their problem is, predictably, a lack of communication. From the beginning, their feelings toward each other have been strong and turbulent, but strength and turbulence do not imply depth. They have never really questioned their feelings. They eschew *logos*: they never speak meaningfully about their core, their values, their goals, the interlaced meanings of all the phases of their lives. *Pathos*, therefore, is not modified, stimulated, and matured by effective *logos*. There has never been any "need" for words. When ephemeral feeling dies away, however, and the inevitable problems of living together arise, communication fails because it has never really been a part of the relationship. The *pathos* level on which the relationship has been based is not sufficient to handle the problems. When undiscussed problems mount too high, irresponsible *pathos* runs wild, with words becoming the lackeys of feeling. Then the conversation that does exist is nothing but a caricature of communication. The sooner a couple realize the potential of human language and make mature verbal interactional systems part of their relationship, the better prepared will they be to handle problems that arise, and, more important, the greater will be their potential for interpersonal growth.

The Expression of Emotion

In human affairs there seem to be two highly prevalent, though probably not growthful, ways of handling strong feeling—both positive and negative feeling. Actually, both are ways of avoiding, rather than handling, emotion in transactional situations.

The suppression of feeling The safest way of handling strong feeling is to suppress it. Perhaps "conceal" is a more accurate word than "suppress," for hidden emotion does make itself felt under a number of disguises. For instance, if a person suppresses or conceals his anger, it frequently comes out in a number of deceitful ways, such as coolness, unavailability, snide remarks, obstructionism, and other subtle forms of revenge. Feeling has not really been suppressed; rather, it has been translated into a number of nongrowthful activities that are difficult to deal with precisely because of their underground character.

Riecken describes a work camp in which, because of the philosophy and religious convictions of the members, the prevailing atmosphere was one of friendly and gentle interactions. Since the members disapproved of all kinds of aggression, both physical and verbal, a problem arose with respect to the handling of the minor antagonisms that arose daily and tended to interfere with the work to be done. Meetings were held, but problems were discussed in a most abstract and intellectualized way. Because of the failure to institute real emotional communication, the antagonisms persisted, much to the dissatisfaction of everyone. But an intellectual approach to a nonintellective situation was bound to fail.[17]

Acting out The second way of handling strong feeling is to foist it on the other. Pent-up anler is allowed to explode, or pent-up affection is allowed to overwhelm the other. Such solutions are rationalized as forms of honesty, but, strangely enough, such honesty seldom results in growthful encounter. Acting out does satisfy immediate instinctual needs, but seldom serves the process of communication. Some people pride themselves on "blowing up" and getting it "out of their systems," claiming that this is more honest than concealment and the subtle leakage of negative feeling that ensues. This may well be true, but such pride should be tempered by the knowledge that there is a more human way.

Poiesis in responsible encounter Let us suppose that once George has been angered by John, he says something like this: "John, I am really angry with you. I could try to swallow my anger or I could blow up, but I don't think that either of these would solve anything, because I think that in a way my anger is really *our* problem, yours and mine, and I'd like to talk it out with you. How about it?" Such a tack (especially if the stylized way in which it is presented here is overlooked for the moment) is rarely employed, for it demands too much honesty and one runs the risk either of refusal or of disquieting discoveries about oneself. It also demands dealing with feelings instead of relinquishing them in one way or another. George remains angry, but now his anger becomes a point of possible contact instead of just an abrasive force. Sometimes a person has to choose between the pain of talking out another's hostility toward him and the discomfort of being the victim of a dozen covert expressions of hostility so rationalized that it is impossible to get at them.

The responsible expression of hostility as a form of poiesis Contract-group members are in no way discouraged from expressing anger or hostility, but they are asked to do so in as constructive a way as possible. . . . The mere expression of negative feelings is not the issue; it is rather *how* they are expressed. Negative feelings, too, are part of the human condition and are experienced by the intelligent and well-adjusted. The hypothesis here is that the intelligent and well-adjusted, when they do express negative feelings, would tend to do so in a positive way—that is, through some form of *poiesis*. . . .

The meanings of hostility Hostility frequently expresses more than raw "againstness." Especially in group interaction, it can mean many things. (1) It may be a way of expressing one's individuality or showing strength in the group. This use of hostility, however, is relatively immature and usually characterizes only the earlier sessions of the life of the group. Real strength and individuality can be displayed in [other] ways. (2) For the person who feels threatened by the interaction of the group, hostility may be a defensive maneuver rather than a form of attack. (3) Planned hostility may be used as a dynamite technique to stimulate action during a boring session. (4) Hostility can also have a more subtle and constructive meaning: it may be an attempt to achieve some kind of interpersonal contact or intimacy. A number of authors. . . have suggested (and some have conducted research that supports the hypothesis) that identification tends to follow aggression. For instance, Slater states: "It is for this reason that aggression leads to identification: in fantasy the attack is a freeing of the desirable attributes from the hateful shell that prevents their acquisition."[18] It would take rather ingenious empirical investigation to determine whether this is true, but it does seem to be a fact that sometimes after two people storm at each other, they tend to draw closer together. Perhaps the direct route to intimacy is too difficult, and the turmoil of the indirect route is all that is available. . . .

The Problems and Potentialities of Poiesis

One of the problems of *poiesis* is that it is an anti-manipulative and anti-"game" form of communication in a manipulative and game-prone culture. Even therapy does not escape verbal manipulation, for...the communication of therapeutic influence is a function of the therapist's verbal behavior....The patient learns the rote that the therapist expects of him through verbal conditioning. And yet the hypothesis under which this book is being written is that the less manipulation there is in human interaction, the more growthful will the interaction be.

A second problem is that it is doubtful that our present culture is ready for a sharp rise in the amount of *poiesis* in interpersonal relating. The character Jerry in Albee's *The Zoo Story* is somewhat disconcerting to the average reader, for people are not accustomed to dealing verbally with reality on the level that he deals with it. Jerry is resented both because he feels too much and because he translates what he feels into language. Therefore, even those who are responsibly and intelligently "poetic" in their encounters must expect to experience a certain amount of rejection from those who cannot tolerate intimacy.

And yet, as Lynd sees it, men have a moral obligation to become artists in communication. This is difficult, for schisms within man, according to Maslow—for instance, splits within the personality due to the inward battle between impulse and control—cause splits in his communication: "To the extent that we are split, our expression and communications are split, partial, one-sided," but, on the other hand, to the extent that we are integrated and whole, our communications are "complete, unique, idiosyncratic, alive, and creative."[19] The split between feeling and verbal language reflects the schizoid nature of the average man. His task is to overcome this split, because, if Lynd is right, too much will be lost if he does not:

> It may be asked why, since the language of intimacy will always be to a large extent a language of gesture, facial expression, and touch, it should be important to enlarge the possibilities of verbal language for such communication. For at least three reasons: 1. Lack of a verbal means of communication of certain experiences may sometimes lead to atrophy or lack of awareness of the experiences themselves. 2. Ranges of mutual exploration may be cut off and unnecessary misunderstandings may arise if there is a feeling that words should not be used or an unwillingness to search for words to use as one medium of communication. 3. The creation of symbols in language is a characteristically human ability that can bring unconscious creative forces into relation with conscious effort, subject into relation with object, can give form to hitherto unknown things and hence make possible the apprehension of new truth.[20]

Such integration of words and feeling is perhaps both a cause and a reflection of the general integration of the individual. If the participants of a contract laboratory come away with a deeper respect for honest emotion, honest language, and honest attempts to integrate the two, then the laboratory has been successful.

REFERENCES

1. M. Wiener and A. Mehrabian, *Language Within Language: Immediacy, A Channel in Verbal Communication* (New York: Appleton-Century-Crofts, 1968), p. 1.

2. B. Bettelheim, *The Empty Fortress* (New York: Collier-Macmillan, 1967), pp. 56, 57.

3. J. Meerloo, *The Rape of the Mind* (Cleveland: World, 1956), p. 87.

4. J. Ruesch, *Disturbed Communication* (New York: Norton, 1957).

5. G.F. Stout, *Analytic Psychology*, Vol. 2 (New York: Macmillan, 1902).

6. E.M. Ciorcan, *The Temptation to Exist*, trans. R. Howard (Chicago: Quadrangle, 1968).

7. R.D. Abrahams, "Public Drama and Common Values in Two Caribbean Islands," *Trans-action* 5 (1968): 62.

8. A. Burgess, "The Future of Anglo-American," *Harper's* **236** (1968): 53–56.

9. A. Rapoport, *Strategy and Conscience* (New York: Harper & Row, 1964).

10. E. Berne, *Principles of Group Treatment* (New York: Oxford University Press, 1966).

11. M. McLuhan, *Understanding Media: The Extensions of Man* (New York: McGraw-Hill, 1964), p. 80.

12. E. Goffman, *Interaction Ritual: Essays on Face-To-Face Behavior* (Garden City, N.Y.: Anchor Books, 1967), p. 126.

13. E.H. Erikson, "The Problem of Ego Identity," *Journal of the American Psychoanalytic Association* **4** (1956): 115.

14. W.F. Lynch, "Counterrevolution in the Movies," *Commonweal* **87** (1967): 79.

15. *Ibid.*, p. 83.

16. H.S. Bloch, "An Open-Ended Crisis-Oriented Group for the Poor Who Are Sick," *Archives of General Psychiatry* **18** (1968): 178.

17. H. Riecken, "Some Problems of Consensus Development," *Rural Sociology* **17** (1952): 245–252.

18. P.E. Slater, *Microism: Structural, Psychological, and Religious Evolution in Groups* (New York: Wiley, 1966), p. 146.

19. A.H. Maslow, "Synanon and Eupsychia," *Journal of Humanistic Psychology* **7** (1967): 197.

20. H.M. Lynd, *On Shame and the Search for Identity* (New York: Science Editions, 1958), pp. 249–250.

PROBES

Can you recall some specific opportunities you've recently had to put more life—more of *you*—into your language? Were you able to do that? What happened?

How well do you feel that your language makes you "present to" others? What can you do to improve that part of your communicating?

Do you agree with Egan that your language reveals your self-identity? How so?

Under the heading "Failed Poiesis," Egan discusses a marriage relationship based on emotion without communication. Whether or not you've been married, have you experienced a relationship like that? Or are you experiencing one now with a man or a woman friend, spouse, family member, or lover? Can you see how you could put more poiesis, more logos, in your talking with that person?

Do you agree that verbal expressions of hostility can be what Egan calls poiesis?

3

NONVERBAL CODES

If I ignore the emotional plea and respond only to the words, I will not be communicating with you, there will not be a flow of understanding between us, I will not be feeling you and so I will be frustrated and you will be also. The heart of any conversation is the demand being made on my emotions. If I feel frustrated, that is a good sign I am avoiding the emotions you are trying to communicate—I have not paused long enough to ask, "What do you really want from me?"

HUGH PRATHER

Did you ever stop to think how your communication is affected by breath and body odors? Furniture placement and window location? Dilation of the pupils of your and other people's eyes? Angle of pelvic tilt or thrust? Cigarettes butts visible? Audibility of breathing? It's not always obvious, but we are affected by the meanings we give these and a multitude of other nonverbal cues. Some nonverbal cues are more obvious—tone of voice, rate of speaking, amount and type of gesture, proximity, facial expression, touch, and so on. But whether they're obvious or subtle, nonverbal cues strongly affect communication. In fact, as Knapp indicates, researchers agree that about 65 percent of social meaning of most human communication events is carried by nonverbal cues. Sixty-five percent! If you want to promote interpersonal quality communication, it is obviously crucially important to become aware of what nonverbal cues are and how they work.

This chapter moves toward that end by presenting an overview of nonverbal cues, an investigation of one important function of nonverbal communica-tion—the expression of emotions—and two articles dealing with specific types of nonverbal cues—one that explores body talk and tone of voice and one that dis-cusses touch. The purpose of this first article is, frankly, to increase your aware-ness of how many types of nonverbal cues there are and how many different ways they function in our day-to-day contact. If you count both main and subcategories, Knapp identifies 19 types of nonverbal cues, each of which can operate in six different ways. That adds up to a mind-boggling set of possible combinations, more than anybody could keep absolute track of.

The point, though, is not to snow you with categories, but to emphasize that what we do nonverbally and how we do it makes a difference in our communicat-ing. People sensitive to nonverbal cues are much more able to listen effectively and empathically, to distinguish appropriate from inappropriate self-disclosure, to reduce others' defensiveness, to provide meaningful support, and to handle con-flict interpersonally. So the sensitivity you can pick up from this article and the information and skills available in the next three selections can help you apply much of what is in the rest of the book.

NONVERBAL COMMUNICATION: BASIC PERSPECTIVES
Mark L. Knapp

Those of us who keep our eyes open can read volumes into what we see going on around us.

—E. HALL

Herr von Osten purchased a horse in Berlin, Germany in 1900. When von Osten began training his horse, Hans, to count by tapping his front hoof, he had no idea that Hans was soon to become one of the most celebrated horses in history. Hans was a rapid learner and soon progressed from counting to addition, multiplication, division, subtraction, and eventually the solution of problems involving factors and fractions. As if this were not enough, von Osten exhibited Hans to public audiences where he counted the number in the audience or simply the number of people wearing eye glasses. Still responding only with taps, Hans could tell time, use a calendar, display an ability to recall musical pitch, and perform numerous other seemingly fantastic feats. After von Osten taught Hans an alphabet which could be coded into hoofbeats, the horse could answer virtually any question—oral or written. It seemed that Hans, a common horse, had complete comprehension of the German language, the ability to produce the equivalent of words and numerals, and an intelligence beyond that of many human beings.

Even without the promotion of Madison Avenue, the word spread quickly and soon Hans was known throughout the world. He was soon dubbed "Clever Hans." Because of the obviously profound implications for several scientific fields and because some skeptics thought there was a "gimmick" involved, an investigating committee was established to decide, once and for all, whether there was any deceit involved in Hans' performances. Professors of psychology, physiology, the director of the Berlin Zoological Garden, a director of a circus, veterinarians, and cavalry officers were appointed to this commission of horse experts. An experiment with Hans from which von Osten was absent demonstrated no change in the apparent intelligence of Hans. This was sufficient proof for the commission to announce there was no trickery involved.

The appointment of a second commission was the beginning of the end for Clever Hans. Von Osten was asked to whisper a number into the horse's left ear while another experimenter whispered a number into the horse's right ear. Hans was told to add the two numbers—an answer none of the onlookers, von Osten, or the experimenter knew. Hans failed. And with further tests he continued to fail. The experimenter, Pfungst, discovered on further experimentation that Hans could only answer a question if someone in his visual field knew the answer.[1] When Hans was given the question, the onlookers assumed an expectant posture and increased their body tension. When Hans reached the correct number of taps, the onlookers would relax and make a slight movement of the head—which was Hans' cue to stop tapping.

The story of Clever Hans is frequently used in discussions concerning the capacity of an animal to learn verbal language. It also seems well suited to an introduction to the field of nonverbal communication. Hans' cleverness was not in his ability to verbalize or understand verbal commands, but in his ability to respond to almost imperceptible and unconscious movements on the part of those surrounding him. It is not unlike that perceptiveness or sensitivity to nonverbal cues exhibited by a Clever Carl, Charles, Frank, or Harold when picking up a girl, closing a business deal, giving an intelligent and industrious image to a professor, knowing when to leave a party, and in a multitude of other common situations. This [chapter] is written for the purpose of expanding the reader's conscious awareness of the numerous nonverbal stimuli confronting him in his everyday dialogue with his fellow man. . . . First, however, it is necessary to develop a few basic perspectives. . . .

PERSPECTIVES ON DEFINING NONVERBAL COMMUNICATION

Conceptually, the term *nonverbal* is subject to a variety of interpretations—just like the term *communication*. The basic issue seems to be whether the events traditionally studied under the heading *nonverbal* are literally *non* verbal. Ray Birdwhistell, a pioneer in nonverbal research, is reported to have said that studying *nonverbal* communication is like studying *noncardiac* physiology. His point is well taken. It is not easy to dissect human interaction and make one diagnosis which concerns only verbal behavior and another which concerns only nonverbal behavior. The verbal dimension is so intimately woven and so subtly represented in so much of what we have previously labeled *non*verbal that the term does not always adequately describe the behavior under study. Some of the most noteworthy scholars associated with nonverbal study refuse to segregate words from gestures and, hence, work under the broader terms *communication* or face-to-face *interaction*.

While many researchers recognize this theoretical and conceptual problem with the term *nonverbal*, their research proceeds. Most of this research is based on the premise that if words are not spoken or written, they become nonverbal in nature. Also included in the term *nonverbal* under this definition are all those nuances which surround words—e.g., tone of voice or type of print. This is frequently called paralanguage. In their early classic, *Nonverbal Communication: Notes on the Visual Perception of Human Relations*, Ruesch and Kees took essentially this point of view. But, in addition, the authors outlined what they considered to be the primary elements in the study of nonverbal communication. This classification system has been highly influential in providing a basis for most of the work done in this field to date.

> In broad terms, nonverbal forms of codification fall into three distinct categories:
>
> *Sign Language* includes all those forms of codification in which words, numbers, and punctuation signs have been supplanted by gestures; these vary from the "monosyllabic" gesture of the hitchhiker to such complete systems as the language of the deaf.
>
> *Action Language* embraces all movements that are not used exclusively as signals. Such acts as walking and drinking, for example, have a dual function: on one hand they serve personal needs, and on the other they constitute statements to those who may perceive them.
>
> *Object Language* comprises all intentional and nonintentional display of material things, such as implements, machines, art objects, architectural structures, and—last but not least—the human body and whatever clothes or covers it. The embodiment of letters as they occur in books and on signs has a material substance, and this aspect of words also has to be considered as object language.[2]

Another way of defining a field of study is to examine the work that has been done to see if any common directions have been followed. As previously mentioned, one common trend is the assumption that nonverbal communication encompasses those events in which words are not spoken or written. Other recurring trends are exemplified by the following classification system which represents a definition of the field of nonverbal human communication as evidenced in the writing and research available.

Nonverbal Dimensions of Human Communication

I. Body motion or kinesic behavior Body motion, or kinesic behavior, typically includes gestures, movements of the body, limbs, hands, head, feet and legs, facial expressions (smiles), eye behavior (blinking, direction and length of gaze, and pupil dilation) and posture. The furrow of the brow, the slump of a shoulder and the tilt of a head—all are within the purview of kinesics. Obviously, there are different types of nonverbal behavior just as there are different types of verbal behavior. Some nonverbal cues are very specific, some more general; some intended to communicate, some expressive only; some provide information about emotions, others carry information about personality traits or attitudes. In an effort to sort through the relatively unknown world of nonverbal behavior, Ekman and Friesen[3] developed a system for classifying nonverbal behavioral acts. These categories include:

A. Emblems. These are nonverbal acts which have a direct verbal translation or dictionary definition—usually consisting of a word or two or a phrase. There is high agreement among members of a culture or subculture on the verbal definition. The gestures used to represent "A-OK" or "Peace" are examples of emblems for a large part of our culture. Toffler notes in his bestseller, *Future Shock*, that some emblems which were perceived as semi-obscene are now becoming more respectable with changing sexual values. He uses the example of the upraised finger—designating "up yours." Emblems are frequently used when verbal channels are blocked (or fail) and are usually used to communicate. The sign language of the deaf, nonverbal gestures used by television production personnel, signals used by two underwater swimmers, or motions made by two people who are too far apart to make audible signals practical—all these are emblems. Our own awareness of emblem usage is about the same as our awareness of word choice.

B. Illustrators. These are nonverbal acts which are directly tied to, or accompany, speech—serving to illustrate what is being said verbally. These may be movements which accent or emphasize a word or phrase; movements which sketch a path of thought; movements pointing to present objects; movements depicting a spatial relationship; or movements which depict a bodily action. Illustrators seem to be within our awareness, but not as explicitly as emblems. They are used intentionally to help communicate, but not as deliberately as emblems. They are probably learned by watching others.

C. Affect displays. These are simply facial configurations which display affective states. They can repeat, augment, contradict, or be unrelated to, verbal affective statements. Once the display has occurred, there is usually a high degree of awareness, but it can occur without any awareness. Often, affect displays are not intended to communicate, but they can be intentional.

D. Regulators. These are nonverbal acts which maintain and regulate the back and forth nature of speaking and listening between two or more interactants. They tell the speaker to continue, repeat, elaborate, hurry up, become more interesting, give the other a chance to talk, etc. They consist mainly of head nods and eye movements, and there seem to be class and cultural differences in usage—improper usage connoting rudeness. These acts are not tied to specific spoken behavior. They seem to be on the periphery of our awareness and are generally difficult to inhibit. They are like overlearned habits and are almost involuntary, but we are very much aware of these signals sent by others. Probably the most familiar regulator is the head nod—the equivalent of the verbal mm-hmm.

E. Adaptors. These nonverbal behaviors are perhaps the most difficult to define and involve the most speculation. They are labeled adaptors because they are thought to develop in childhood as adaptive efforts to satisfy needs, perform actions, manage emotions, develop social contacts, or perform a host of other functions. They are not really coded; they are fragments of actual aggressive, sexual or intimate behavior and often reveal personal orientations or characteristics covered by verbal messages. Leg movements can often be adaptors, showing residues of kicking aggression, sexual invitation, or flight. Many of the restless movements of the hands and feet which have typically been considered indicators of anxiety may be residues of adaptors necessary for flight from the interaction. Adaptors are possibly triggered by verbal behavior in a given situation which is associated with conditions occurring when the adaptive habit was first learned. We are typically unaware of adaptors.

II. Physical characteristics Whereas the previous section was concerned with movement and motion, this category covers things which remain relatively unchanged during the period of interaction. They are influential nonverbal cues which are not movement-bound. Included are such things as: physique or body shape, general attractiveness, body or breath odors, height, weight, hair, and skin color or tone.

III. Touching behavior For some, kinesic study includes touch behavior; for others, however, actual physical contact constitutes a separate class of events. Some researchers are concerned with touching behavior as an important factor in the child's early development; some are concerned with adult touching behavior. Subcategories may include: stroking, hitting, greetings and farewells, holding, guiding another's movements, and other, more specific instances.

IV. Paralanguage Simply put, paralanguage deals with how something is said and not what is said. It deals with the range of nonverbal vocal cues surrounding common speech behavior. Trager felt paralanguage had the following components:[4]

A. Voice qualities. This includes such things as pitch range, pitch control, rhythm control, tempo, articulation control, resonance, glottis control, and vocal lip control.

B. Vocalizations.
>   1. *Vocal characterizers.* This includes such things as laughing, crying, sighing, yawning, belching, swallowing, heavily marked inhaling or exhaling, coughing, clearing of the throat, hiccupping, moaning, groaning, whining, yelling, whispering, sneezing, snoring, stretching, etc.
>
>   2. *Vocal qualifiers.* This includes intensity (overloud to oversoft), pitch height (overhigh to overlow), and extent (extreme drawl to extreme clipping).
>
>   3. *Vocal segregates.* These are such things as "uh-huh," "um," "uh," "ah," and variants thereof.

Related work on such topics as silent pauses (beyond junctures), intruding sounds, speech errors, and latency would probably be included in this category.

V. Proxemics Proxemics is generally considered to be the study of man's use and perception of his social and personal space. Under this heading, we find a body of work called small group ecology which concerns itself with how people use and respond to spatial relationships in formal and informal group settings. Such studies deal with seating arrangements, and spatial arrangements as related to leadership, communication flow, and the task at hand. The influence of architectural features on residential living units and even on communities is also of concern to those who study man's proxemic behavior. On an even broader level, some attention has been given to spatial relationships in crowds and densely populated situations. Man's personal space orientation is sometimes studied in the context of conversational distance—and how it varies according to sex, status, roles, cultural orientation, etc. The term "territoriality" is also frequently used in the study of proxemics to denote the human tendency to stake out personal territory—or untouchable space—much as wild animals and birds do.

VI. Artifacts Artifacts include the manipulation of objects in contact with the interacting persons which may act as nonverbal stimuli. These artifacts include: perfume, clothes, lipstick, eyeglasses, wigs and other hairpieces, false eyelashes, eyeliners, and the whole repertoire of falsies and "beauty" aids.

VII. Environmental factors Up to this point we have been concerned with the appearance and behavior of the persons involved in communicating. This category concerns those elements which impinge on the human relationship, but which are not directly a part of it. Environmental factors include the furniture, architectural style, interior decorating, lighting conditions, smells, colors, temperature, additional noises or music, etc. within which the interaction occurs. Variations in arrangements, materials, shapes, or surfaces of objects in the interacting environment can be extremely influential on the outcome of an interpersonal relationship. This category also includes what might be called traces of action. For instance, as you observe cigarette butts, orange peels, and waste paper left by the person you will soon interact with, you are forming an impression which will eventually influence your meeting.

PERSPECTIVES ON NONVERBAL COMMUNICATION IN THE TOTAL COMMUNICATION PROCESS

We are constantly being warned against presenting material out of context. This chapter deals almost exclusively with nonverbal communication and there is a danger that the reader may forget that nonverbal communication cannot be studied in isolation from the total communication process. Verbal and nonverbal communication should be treated as a total and inseparable unit. Birdwhistell makes this point when he says:

> My own research has led me to the point that I am no longer willing to call either linguistic or kinesic systems *communication* systems. All of the emerging data seem to me to support the contention that linguistics and kinesics are *infra*-communicational systems. Only in their interrelationship with each other and with comparable systems from other sensory modalities is the emergent communication system achieved.[5]

Argyle flatly states, "Some of the most important findings in the field of social interaction are about the ways that verbal interaction needs the support of nonverbal communications."[6] What are some of the ways in which verbal and nonverbal systems interrelate? How do nonverbal behaviors support verbal behaviors?[7]

Repeating. Nonverbal communication can simply repeat what was said verbally. For instance, if you told a person he had to go north to find a newspaper stand and then pointed in the proper direction, this would be considered repetition.

Contradicting. Nonverbal behavior can contradict verbal behavior. A classic example is the parent who yells to his child in an angry voice, "Of course I love you!" Or the person who is about to make a public speech whose hands and knees tremble, beads of perspiration form around his brow and he not so confidently states, "I'm not nervous." It has been said that when we receive contradictory messages on the verbal and nonverbal level, we are more likely to trust and believe in the nonverbal message.[8] It is assumed that nonverbal signals are more spontaneous, harder to fake, and less apt to be manipulated. It is probably more accurate to say, however, that some nonverbal behaviors are more spontaneous and harder to fake than others—and that some people are more proficient than others at nonverbal deception. With two contradictory cues—both of which are nonverbal—again we predictably place our reliance on the cues we consider harder to fake. Interestingly, young children seem to give less credence to certain nonverbal cues than do adults when confronted with conflicting verbal and nonverbal messages.[9] Conflicting messages in which the speaker smiled while making a critical statement were interpreted more negatively by children than adults. This was particularly true when the speaker was a woman. Shapiro's work casts a further shadow on the "reliance on nonverbal cues in contradictory situations" theory.[10] Shapiro found student judges to be extremely consistent in their reliance on either linguistic or facial cues when asked to select the affect being communicated from a list of incongruent faces and written messages. This suggests that through experience, some people rely more heavily on the verbal message while others rely on the nonverbal. Although one source of our preferences for verbal or nonverbal cues may be learned experiences, others believe there may also be an even more basic genesis—such as right-left brain dominance.

Substituting. Nonverbal behavior can substitute for verbal messages. When the dejected and downtrodden executive (or janitor) walks into his house after work, his facial expression substitutes for the statement, "I've had a rotten day." With a little practice, wives soon learn to identify a wide range of these sub-stitute nonverbal displays—all the way from "It's been a fantastic, great day!" to "Oh, God, am I miserable!" She does not need to ask for verbal confirmation of her perception. Sometimes, when substitute nonverbal behavior fails, the communicator resorts back to the verbal level. Consider the woman who wants her date to stop "making out" with her. She may stiffen, stare straight ahead, act unresponsive and cool. If the suitor still comes on heavy, she is apt to say something like, "Look Larry, please don't ruin a nice friendship...etc."

Complementing. Nonverbal behavior can modify, or elaborate on, verbal messages. A student may reflect an attitude of embarrassment when talking to his professor about his poor performance in class assignments. Further, nonver-bal behavior may reflect changes in the relationship between the student and the professor. When a student's slow, quiet verbalizations and relaxed posture change—when posture stiffens and the emotional level of the verbalized state-ments increases—this may signal changes in the overall relationship between the interactants. Complementary functions of nonverbal communication serve to signal one's attitudes and intentions toward another person.

Accenting. Nonverbal behavior may accent parts of the verbal message much as underlining written words, or *italicizing* them, serves to emphasize them. Movements of the head and hands are frequently used to accent the verbal message. When a father scolds his son about staying out too late at night, he may accent a particular phrase with a firm grip on the son's shoulder and an accompanying frown on his face. In some instances, one set of nonverbal cues can accent other nonverbal cues. Ekman, for instance, found that emotions are primarily exhibited by facial expressions, but that the body carries the most accurate indicators regarding the *level* of arousal.[11]

Relating and regulating. Nonverbal communication is also used to regulate the communicative flow between the interactants. Some have labeled this a rela-tional function. A head nod, eye movement, or shift in position—any one of these, or combination of them, may signal the other person to continue to speak or to stop speaking because you want to say something. Speakers generally rely on this feedback to determine how their utterances are being received—or whether the other person is even paying attention.

The future of research in human communication will also require an analy-sis of verbal and nonverbal behavior as an inseparable unit. Some efforts in this direction have already been made. Harrison[12] and Buehler and Richmond[13] have outlined basic frameworks for the analysis of verbal and nonverbal behavior in two person settings. Reece and Whitman,[14] among others, are trying to isolate the verbal and nonverbal components which convey interpersonal "warmth." Exline[15] is trying to relate eye behavior to various kinds of verbal material. Agulera[16] found touch gestures by nurses changed the nature of their verbal interaction with patients. Goldman-Eisler[17] is studying the predictability of verbal content following pauses of various types and lengths.

Birdwhistell feels that the whole system of body motion is comparable to spoken language. He reports the existence of kinemes and various types of kinemorphs which combine to form higher level syntactic structures. These kinesic units are comparable to the phoneme, morpheme, and other syntactic units used to analyze spoken language. He even goes so far as to state that a well-trained "linguistic-kinesiologist" should be able to tell what movements a man is making simply by listening to his voice. In like manner, he claims to be able to tell what language the late New York Mayor, Fiorello LaGuardia, was speaking simply by watching his gestures. LaGuardia spoke Italian, Yiddish, and English.

PERSPECTIVES ON THE PREVALENCE AND IMPORTANCE OF NONVERBAL COMMUNICATION

The importance of nonverbal communication would be undeniable if sheer quantity were the only measure. Birdwhistell, generally agreed to be a noted authority on nonverbal behavior, makes some rather astounding estimates of the amount of nonverbal communication taking place. He estimates that the average person actually speaks words for a total of only 10 to 11 minutes daily—the standard spoken sentence taking only about 2.5 seconds. He goes on to say that in a normal two person conversation, the verbal components carry less than 35% of the social meaning of the situation; more than 65% is carried on the nonverbal band.

Another way of looking at the quantity of nonverbal messages is to note the various systems man uses to communicate. Hall outlines ten separate kinds of human activity which he calls "primary message systems."[18] He suggests that only one involves language. Ruesch and Kees discuss at least seven different systems—personal appearance and dress, gestures or deliberate movements, random action, traces of action, vocal sounds, spoken words, and written words. Only two of the seven involve words.[19]

It is not my purpose here to argue the importance of the various human message systems, but to put the nonverbal world in perspective. It is safe to say that the study of human communication has for too long ignored a significant part of the process....

REFERENCES

1. O. Pfungst, *Clever Hans, The Horse of Mr. Von Osten* (New York: Holt, Rinehart and Winston, 1911).

2. J. Ruesch and W. Kees, *Nonverbal Communication: Notes on the Visual Perception of Human Relations* (Berkeley: University of California Press, 1956), p. 189.

3. P. Ekman and W. V. Friesen, "The Repertoire of Nonverbal Behavior: Categories, Origins, Usage, and Coding," *Semiotica* 1 (1969): 49–98.

4. G. L. Trager, "Paralanguage: A First Approximation," *Studies in Linguistics* 13 (1958): 1–12.

5. R. L. Birdwhistell, "Some Body Motion Elements Accompanying Spoken American English," in *Communication: Concepts and Perspectives,* ed. L. Thayer (Washington, D.C.: Spartan Books, 1967): 71.

6. M. Argyle, *Social Interaction* (New York: Atherton Press, 1969): 70–71.

7. Cf. P. Ekman, "Communication through Nonverbal Behavior: A Source of Information about an Interpersonal Relationship," in *Affect, Cognition and Personality,* ed. S. S. Tomkins and C. E. Izard (New York: Springer, 1965).

8. Some evidence to support this notion is found in: E. Tabor, "Decoding of Consistent and Inconsistent Attitudes in Communication" (Ph.D. diss., Illinois Institute of Technology, 1970).

9. D. E. Bugental, J. W. Kaswan, L. R. Love and M. N. Fox, "Child Versus Adult Perception of Evaluative Messages in Verbal, Vocal, and Visual Channels," *Developmental Psychology* 2 (1970): 367–75.

10. J. G. Shapiro, "Responsivity to Facial and Linguistic Cues," *Journal of Communication* 18 (1968): 11–17.

11. P. Ekman, "Body Position, Facial Expression and Verbal Behavior During Interviews," *Journal of Abnormal and Social Psychology* 68 (1964): 295–301. Also: P. Ekman and W. V. Friesen, "Head and Body Cues in the Judgement of Emotion: A Reformulation," *Perceptual and Motor Skills* 24 (1967): 711–24.

12. R. Harrison, "Verbal-Nonverbal Interaction Analysis: The Substructure of an Interview" (Paper presented to the Association for Education in Journalism, Berkeley, Calif., August 1969).

13. R. E. Buehler and J. F. Richmond, "Interpersonal Communication Behavior Analysis: A Research Method," *Journal of Communication* 13 (1963): 146–55.

14. M. Reece and R. Whitman, "Expressive Movements, Warmth, and Verbal Reinforcement," *Journal of Abnormal and Social Psychology* 64 (1962): 234–36.

15. R. V. Exline, *et al.,* "Visual Interaction in Relation to Machiavellianism and an Unethical Act," *American Psychologist* 16 (19y1): 396. Also, see R. V. Exline, D. Gray and D. Schuette, "Visual Behavior in a Dyad as Affected by Interview Content and Sex of Respondent," *Journal of Personality and Social Psychology* 1 (1965): 201–9.

16. D. C. Agulera, "Relationship Between Physical Contact and Verbal Interaction Between Nurses and Patients," *Journal of Psychiatric Nursing and Mental Health Services* 5 (1967): 5–21.

17. F. Goldman-Eisler, *Psycholinguistics: Experiments in Spontaneous Speech* (New York: Academic Press, 1968).
18. E. T. Hall, *The Silent Language* (Garden City, N.Y.: Doubleday, 1959).
19. Ruesch and Kees, *Nonverbal Communication.*

PROBES

Egan said in Chapter 2 that our language reveals our self-identity. Can you see how our nonverbal cues reveal our self-identity too?

For example, what conclusions about you do you think other people draw from the way you move? What does the quality of your voice say about you?

For many persons, touch communicates messages only of greeting, hostility, or sex. Is that true for you?

Are you surprised about the importance of nonverbal communication? How might the information about the 65%–35% breakdown affect your communicating?

In this article from the magazine *Psychology Today,* a teacher from Salt Lake City discusses some conclusions he has come to after studying the nonverbal communication of 50 couples 18 to 24. He makes several points that seem to me to be worth thinking about.

First, he suggests that the "good vibes" and "bad vibes" most people notice in their communication are probably responses to nonverbal cues. We communicate very well nonverbally, and we pick up a great deal of what others are "saying" nonverbally to us.

He also found that the emotional temperature or climate of a marriage relationship is pretty accurately indicated by the nonverbal cues the man and woman display—how much they touch themselves as opposed to each other, how close they sit, what they do with their eyes, etc.

Beier suggests three additional conclusions that make me think more about my nonverbal communication. The first is that we tend to use our nonverbal communication to "pull" corresponding verbal and nonverbal behavior from others. In other words, we nonverbally communicate that we need or want support, that we want to share happiness, etc. Moreover, most people, Beier's study suggests, are unaware of what their nonverbal communication is saying to others. Some people *think* they're nonverbally communicating anger, fear, indifference, seductiveness, happiness, and sadness, for example, but people viewing films of these moods see only anger or only seductiveness. "Everyone," Beier summarizes, "appears to send out misinformation." Finally, Beier speculates that what others get from our nonverbal cues is often an indication of what we "unconsciously" want to say. He suggests that nonverbal cues often indicate accurately some of what's below our level of awareness, so other people pick up what we're "really thinking."

NONVERBAL COMMUNICATION: HOW WE SEND EMOTIONAL MESSAGES

Ernst G. Beier

People are forever saying one thing and meaning another. A husband says to his wife, "I love you." According to the dictionary, the man is expressing his affection. He cherishes his wife. He is attracted to her. His life is bound to hers. There are times when she excites him sexually and other times when he would risk his life to protect her. The wife replies coldly, "Go to hell!" and stamps out of the room, slamming the door behind her.

Absurd? Let me add a few details to this imaginary scene.

The man has just returned home at nine p.m. for the 50th night in a row. He smells like a brewery and looks sullen. He sits down without a word, crosses his legs tightly, and starts reading the paper. His wife asks him how his day went. He answers with a grunt.

She says, "I want a divorce." He says, "Where's dinner?" She says, "I'm serious. I've had enough of you. I treat you well and you treat me like a servant. I don't *like* you any more."

The man looks up from his distractions. There's a look of incomprehension on his face. He needs his wife. He's obviously afraid now. He doesn't want her to leave.

"Give me one reason why I shouldn't walk out of here tonight," she demands.

Perspiration has appeared on his upper lip. He starts to say something but lights a cigarette instead. He avoids her stare, and his eyes dart around the room as if searching for an answer. Then he clears his throat and says with a grin, "I love you."

THE ELOQUENCE OF ACTION

Dialogues like this one—exaggerated and even comic as it may seem—take place all the time. The man's actions spoke louder than his words. He was communicating with his face and posture, with his intonation and choice of words, with the way he placed himself in the room. The lexical meaning of "I love you" amounted to a stupid joke in the context of his evident lack of interest.

From *Psychology Today*, October 1974, pp. 53–56. Copyright © 1974 Ziff-Davis Publishing Company. Reprinted by permission of Psychology Today Magazine.

And yet there is another level to this scene. When confronted with his wife's anger, the man sits up and listens. He communicates his fear of losing her as accurately as he communicated his distaste.

What are we to make of this man's style of communication? We may think of him as unattractive, neurotic, confused, weak, childish; but we wouldn't say that he had much trouble communicating his feelings. He was communicating perfectly. First he communicated indifference, and later he communicated panic. His messages were discordant yet full of meaning. We can assume, moreover (since this is an imaginary scene), that his words of love had often paid off in the past. They are sweet words, and he himself probably believed them. It couldn't be helped that the discrepancy between one of his messages and all the others seemed so blatant that his wife finally decided to believe his behavior alone.

I have been investigating nonverbal communication for several years, both clinically and experimentally. I am interested in some of the same human behaviors that Robert Rosenthal and his colleagues described [see "The Language Without Words," PT, September 1974]. But whereas Rosenthal measured the sensitivity of many different receivers to one standardized sequence of nonverbal cues, I am more concerned with the *senders* of emotional information. Specifically, I would like to know how married couples communicate well-being or unease to each other. I also want to elucidate some of those common human transactions in which one person sends another person a clear emotional message of which the sender is unaware but which is nevertheless intended.

VIBES—GOOD AND BAD

Not long ago, the word "vibrations" entered American slang. "Vibes" are feelings that one person arouses in another by supposedly unobservable means. According to popular usage, one person sends vibes and others get them. The term is a metaphor for the communication of emotion. In another sense, vibes are more than a simple message; they're an emotional climate, and like any emotional climate, particularly those evoked by first impressions, they tend to be categorized by receivers as beneficial or dangerous.

It is plausible that vibes may result from certain kinds of nonverbal communication. If so, then the communication of well-being, security, affection and similar feelings would cause good vibes, while messages of hostility, insecurity and anxiety would cause bad vibes. In any case, whether you think of the word "vibes" as a term with definite behavioral correlates or simply as a suggestive metaphor, the fact remains that a person can create beneficial and/or dangerous emotional environments through body movements and tones of voice.

Daniel P. Sternberg and I conducted an experiment with 50 newlywed couples in an attempt to learn if they used body language to communicate cues of marital conflict and harmony. Our newlyweds were all between the ages of 18 and 24 and had been married only a few weeks. We gave each couple a questionnaire designed to tell us how much conflict there was in their marriage. Many of them, it turned out, were already experiencing serious problems. We also interviewed the couples and asked them to take turns telling about themselves, about their expectations and disappointments, and about various other aspects of their short lives together. Meanwhile, we videotaped each.couple in order to record their nonverbal behavior.

LOOK AT THE EYES

Once we had assessed the relative closeness, stability and harmony of each couple's relationship, we ran the videotapes for several trained judges of nonverbal behavior, who rated each couple purely on the basis of nonverbal interactions. The judges were looking specifically for eye contact, laughing, talking, touching (of the self or of the spouse), and also for the way they held their arms and legs, either open or closed.

It became clear when we analyzed the data that nonverbal cues express a person's feelings very accurately. The happy couples would sit closer together, look more frequently into each other's eyes, would touch each other more often than themselves, and would talk more to their spouses. The happier couples, in short, were able to create for each other a more comfortable and supportive bodily environment.

The couples who were experiencing the most conflict sent out more distant vibrations. They tended to cross their arms and legs, had less eye contact, and touched themselves more frequently than they touched each other.

We further analyzed the data by dividing all the couples into four groups: (1) those who were equally dissatisfied with the relationship; (2) those where the husband had more complaints; (3) those where the wife had more complaints; and (4) those where both had a minimum of complaints. When we measured the emotional climates that these four types created, we found, as expected, that the couples who had the most serious conflicts were also communicating the most distance. The second most serious conflict group was the one in which the woman complained more than the man.

To have a dissatisfied woman apparently makes a couple far unhappier than the presence of a dissatisfied male, at least as can be measured by distance values obtained through nonverbal communication.

A follow-up study, conducted nine months latern indicated that the style of being together which marriage partners initiate seems to maintain itself over time. Those couples who had great dissatisfaction with each other remained dissatisfied; those who lived in reasonable peace with each other managed to preserve that peace, possibly because they consistently communicated harmony without the use of words.

We made another interesting discovery in comparing the complaint scores of husbands and wives. The husbands as a group maintained their complaint score at a medium level, while females increased their complaint scores as the marriage went on. We concluded from this observation that women typically expect a great deal from marriage but don't get much, whereas males typically expect little in the first place and are therefore not let down.

WE MAKE OUR OWN ENVIRONMENTS

The study of newlyweds lends support to the common intuition that people can, and do, communicate by means of moods. These moods, when received, are more than bits of information; for no matter how perceptive and cool-headed someone may be, he or she is still liable to be influenced by the communication of someone else's emotional expression. Most of us are probably aware of this already. We know that our own moods somehow bounce off and make demands of those around us, especially people who are very close to us. Communication by moods can be quite simple, as when laughter sets off a similar laughter in everyone. Or, it can be complex and of great importance to the nature of human relationships. When we send out listening or caring cues that allow people to feel deeply understood, then people respond quite differently than if we had sent out cues that are seen to be controlling. By using such cues, consciously and unconsciously, we determine to a large extent the human world around us, and we are more responsible for the reactions we obtain from other people than we dare realize. This situation may add credence to the old moral that says we should look carefully at our own behavior before complaining about the behavior of those we live with.

I ran into some striking examples of just how people restrict their emotional environments during a recent experiment involving some of our newlyweds. My students and I were trying to learn more about the nature of emotional expressions, particularly about the frequent discordance between intended expressions and those that are actually—but unconsciously—portrayed.

ANGRY, ANGRY, ANGRY

We asked several people to act out six different moods on videotape. The moods were anger, fear, seductivity, indifference, happiness and sadness. Then we let our subjects review their portrayals and eliminate any that they felt were unrepresentative. The chosen portrayals, in other words, were emotionally authentic in the eyes of their creators.

When we played these videotapes to large audiences to discover if they could decode the moods intended, we found that most senders were able to project accurately only two of the six moods. The particular moods, of course, varied from sender to sender, but in general we were surprised to learn that everyone appears to send out misinformation. Their portrayals often failed to represent their intentions. This finding lent strength to the hypothesis that the discordance between our emotional expressions and our intentions may represent conflicting impulses. It is possible, admittedly, that our audiences were unusually poor judges of nonverbal behavior; our senders, moreover, may have been better actors in less artificial settings. But at least we found evidence for the notion that there are many people whose emotional intentions and self-images are out of harmony with their actual behavior.

I shall never forget two examples of this discordance. One girl, who tried like everyone else to appear angry, fearful, seductive, indifferent, happy and sad—and who subsequently edited her own performances for authenticity—appeared to her judges as angry in every case. Imagine what a difficult world she must have lived in. No matter where she set the thermostat of her emotional climate, everyone else always felt it as sweltering hot. Another girl in our experiment demonstrated a similar one-dimensionality; only in her case, whatever else she thought she was doing, she invariably impressed her judges as seductive. Even when she wanted to be angry, men whistled at her.

COMPROMISE BEHAVIORS

The whole question of how people encode and decode emotional signals is extremely complex, and we're fortunate that many psychologists today are investigating nonverbal communication. Yet despite the complexity of emotional expressions, the principle of discordance seems to persist. We may say, for example, that we want another person to like us, and we absolutely believe what we say; yet we send out information, through facial expressions, posture, tone of voice, and many other cues, that we don't like that person. Perhaps we made an error in communication, or perhaps the other person misinterpreted our meaning. A simpler explanation, particularly if such discordant behavior persists, is that we really wanted to communicate two different feelings at the same time. And so we compromised. We maintained the self-image of a person who wants to show liking, but at the same time we managed to communicate *dis*like, without feeling responsible. The transmission of discordant cues is a way of having our cake and eating it.

Such behavior is common among intimates. Without a doubt, some of the newlyweds who sat with their legs and arms together, touching themselves but rarely touching their spouse, had often spoken words of love and closeness, aloud and to themselves. Meanwhile they kept their distance without really knowing it and also told their spouse to stay away. The man who told his wife, "I love you," although he probably meant something of substance, did not support his statement with his body. The obvious discordance in these cases, although imperfectly understood by the actors, paid off in definite advantages. Or at least they were supposed to pay off; there are times, inevitably, when such compromise behaviors become transparent, and the motivations behind them are recognized as confused and destructive.

I accept Freud's proposition that many of our acts spring from hidden desires. What I have tried to do is find evidence for this notion in the contradictions between one's intentions and one's actual behavior. We can measure nonverbal cues, therefore, as expressions of unconscious motivations. The evidence, I think, suggests that we often create our own problems by stimulating the world around us without knowing what we're doing. Our nonverbal behavior often serves ends that are obscure to nearly everyone, especially to ourselves.

PROBES

Do you agree that "vibes" are the result of nonverbal communication?

Do you agree with Beier that we tend to use our nonverbal communication to "pull" verbal and nonverbal behavior from others?

How much misinformation are you sending out nonverbally?

Do you nonverbally infect others with your moods?

This team of two students, two teachers, and an electronics engineer has designed a sound-film-and-paper-and-pencil-test to indicate how sensitive people are to two kinds of wordless communication—tone of voice and movements of the face and body. The team members originally got interested in developing this test when they studied student-teacher communication and found that tone of voice "told" students a great deal about how a teacher felt about them and what he or she expected of them.

After having hundreds of people of all ages and occupations complete their test—which they call the Profile of Nonverbal Sensitivity, or PONS—they have come to several intriguing conclusions. One is that we need very little nonverbal information to make interpretations about what people mean. Some people can accurately interpret a cue after seeing it for only 1/24th or 1/12th of a second! Another conclusion is that females are generally better at detecting nonverbal cues than males are. The authors offer several explanations for that outcome, including the suggestion that "perhaps motherhood requires nonverbal skills," and the alternative, because females tend to be oppressed in this society, they *have* to learn to read nonverbal cues well in order to survive comfortably.

Results of giving the test indicate pretty clearly that nonverbal sensitivity is not tied to IQ or grade-point average. People whom the test identifies as nonverbally sensitive, however, do report different friendship patterns from those who don't do as well on the PONS. Those who score well indicate that they have fewer friends but that their relationships are warmer, more honest, and more satisfying. Some people who score very high also report problems caused by their "supersensitivity"; they sometimes feel as though they know *too* much about others.

It goes without saying that the results reported here are far from "the final word" on tone of voice and body talk, but this essay does offer some interesting ideas about how we communicate nonverbally.

BODY TALK AND TONE OF VOICE: THE LANGUAGE WITHOUT WORDS

Robert Rosenthal, Dane Archer, M. Robin DiMatteo,
Judith Hall Koivumaki, and Peter L. Rogers

Communication that doesn't involve words probably makes up a large part of whatever meaning flows between one person and another. Consider the richness of sounds and sights; think of how much information we gain from the senses of smell and touch. There are obviously other modes of communication than plain speech.

We've developed a test called the Profile of Nonverbal Sensitivity (PONS) which measures a person's ability to understand two kinds of wordless communication—tones of voice and movements of the face and body. These two don't constitute a person's entire nonverbal repertory, but they're a good start. Most of us, after all, would probably agree that certain intonations, together with certain facial expressions and bodily movements, are the clearest part of a person's message aside from the words themselves.

THE PROBLEM OF EXPECTANCY

Scientists of diverse backgrounds have taken up the study of nonverbal communication, but our own work grew out of our interest in the effects of one person's expectations on the performance of another. Years ago, we learned that something as simple as a friendly smile from a psychologist administering a test could raise his subject's score [see "Self-Fulfilling Prophecy," PT, September 1968]. The effects of expectancy soon appeared to be not only a methodological

From *Psychology Today*, September 1974, pp. 64–68. Copyright © 1974 Ziff-Davis Publishing Company. Reprinted by permission of Psychology Today Magazine.

problem for behavioral scientists but a phenomenon worth studying for its own interest and possible utility. Schoolteachers are an example of people who use the expectancy effect all the time—for good or ill and whether they know it or not—because students respond to their teachers' wordless expectations, divulged through such subtle means as tone of voice [see "The Pygmalion Effect Lives," PT, September 1973]. We were dealing, in other words, with an area of human behavior that has important consequences both in the lab and in daily life.

Much of the early research on interpersonal expectation suggested strongly that some kind of nonverbal communication was the medium through which one person's feelings and ideas were transmitted to another. Moreover, there seemed to be differences among experimenters and teachers (and everyone else for that matter) in the clarity and effectiveness of their "sending" and "receiving" powers. These findings raised specific questions. What kinds of senders, for example, influence particular receivers most effectively? An answer to this question would apply not only to the analysis of expectation but to many other interpersonal transactions.

"EXPRESSING JEALOUS ANGER"

The Profile of Nonverbal Sensitivity Test promises to increase our understanding of nonverbal behavior in several ways. The test consists of a 45-minute film which presents the viewer with a series of scenes such as facial expressions or a few spoken phrases that are audible as sounds and tones but not as words. Some of the scenes are both seen and heard. After each scene, a test-taker chooses the appropriate situational label from two labels offered on a standardized form. For example, the movie may show a woman's face for two seconds; she looks upset; she's saying something that sounds important, but the words aren't clear. Then the scene disappears.

The test-taker can mark one of two characterizations: "expressing jealous anger" or "talking about one's divorce." Or, the two situational labels might be "leaving on a trip" and "expressing deep affection"; or "asking for forgiveness" and "helping a customer." There is only one correct answer for each scene. The point of the test is to find out which individuals and categories of people do well on the test and which do poorly. Eventually we hope to know why.

THE CHANNELS OF PERCEPTION

The PONS uses only sight and sound, but it uses them in 11 different ways. Some of these 11 "channels" of nonverbal communication are pure while others are mixed. The three pure *video* channels are face only, body only (neck to knees), and face plus body. There is no sound in these channels. The two pure *audio* channels are called "electronically content-filtered" and "randomized-spliced." These names refer to two methods of making the verbal messages incomprehensible. Our content-filtering technique, developed by Peter L. Rogers, removes certain critical frequencies from the voice so that it sounds muffled, as though coming from inside a closet. Randomized-splicing is a simple technique developed by Klaus Scherer: audio tape is cut into small pieces, rearranged randomly and then spliced back together. This randomized-splicing leaves unchanged what content-filtering alters, namely the pitch and loudness; but it also loses what content-filtering preserves—sequence and rhythm.

Besides the five pure channels just mentioned, the PONS also tests sensitivity to six mixed channels, which are audio-visual combinations of the pure channels. A person's scores on the 11-channel test are represented as a line on a graph; this is his profile of nonverbal sensitivity. By now we've collected thousands of such profiles.

Judy Koivumaki portrayed the various situations for us. Altogether, there are 20 situations, but the final film represents each of them 11 times, using the 11 different channels, for a total of 220 scenes. Our sender acted out each situation spontaneously, in interaction with another person just off camera. She performed three different takes of each situation, and a panel of judges who knew her, including the portrayer herself and her husband, rated each recording for authenticity.

QUICK CUES

We learned one crucial thing about nonverbal sensitivity even before sending the PONS test out into the world. In its original length, each scene lasted about five and a half seconds. But we discovered during preliminary trials that test-takers were much too accurate. So we cut each scene to two seconds. At this speed, the PONS test began to distinguish between good and poor nonverbal receivers.

Although the regular PONS test now uses scenes that last two seconds, we wondered how far we could decrease exposure time before driving test scores down to the level of chance. We developed the "Fast PONS" to answer this question. Several experiments with the Fast PONS show that some people understand nonverbal expressions—at least of the face and body, the only two channels used—even when exposure time drops to a fraction of a second. In fact, we often found scores better than chance when we reduced exposure time down to *one-24th of a second*, the time it takes to show a single frame of film. One frame by itself isn't even a motion picture. Nonverbal communication can be amazingly quick and subtle.

As expected, accuracy on the Fast PONS usually rose with exposure time, from one-24th to three-24ths, to nine-24ths, to 27-24ths of a second. The greatest leap in accuracy came between one-24th and three-24ths, or from one still photo to a fast scene in motion. We don't know yet whether increased exposure time or the presence of motion is responsible for this improvement.

One of the most intriguing revelations of the Fast PONS is that accuracy improves with increased exposure time only for the easier and more obvious scenes, whereas accuracy worsens for the more difficult scenes. (We classified scenes as obvious or obscure on the basis of scores on the full PONS.) Just why it should be that the longer one looks, the less one understands, is something of a mystery. Perhaps for easy items, additional exposure provides "supporting" or consistent information, while for difficult items additional information is merely confusing and inconsistent. A related possibility is that easy items can be nicely apprehended in an intuitive, nonanalytic manner and are then further clarified by the cognitive processing of further information. Difficult items, on the other hand, which may also be intuitively apprehended, could *lose* their clarity as a result of more detailed analysis.

THE SUBTLER SEX

Results of the Fast PONS—interesting as they are—seem meager compared to results of the full PONS test, which we have given to more than 130 groups of people over the past several years. These sample groups represented both sexes, many ages, many nationalities and ethnic groups, many levels of education, different degrees of mental health, and many occupations. In short, all kinds of people have taken the PONS test, and after analyzing their profiles we know a lot more about nonverbal sensitivity than we knew three years ago.

The PONS has corroborated the popular opinion (and some previous experimental evidence) that females are better than males at detecting nonverbal cues. Females of all ages, from third grade through adult, showed a small but reliable advantage over males. Out of 98 sample groups in which two or more of each sex participated, the females in 81 groups got higher total scores. We also examined male versus female performance on each of our 11 channels of nonverbal receiving skill; and again the correlation between performance and sex was strong.

It's worth noting that this difference between the sexes narrowed significantly, and even reversed itself, among men in occupations, or training for occupations, that we considered to require "nurturant," artistic, or expressive behavior. Actors, artists, interior and industrial designers, psychiatrists, clinical psychologists and the staff of mental hospitals, college students in visual-studies courses, and schoolteachers—among such people the men tended to score "like women." We don't know yet whether this results from self-selection, screening or training.

We realized immediately that the superior scores of women might have re-sulted from the fact that our sender was a woman. But subsequent research argues strongly against this interpretation. On an audio test identical to the audio portions of the full PONS test, but using a male sender instead of a female, women still showed greater sensitivity to nonverbal cues.

Other analyses indicate that females perform particularly well compared to males when body cues are included in the nonverbal stimuli. It's hard to know just why. Perhaps women identify with another woman's body. Or perhaps males become sexually distracted by the sight of a woman's body and thus miss the intended message. A video test with a male sender might solve the problem.

NECESSARY SKILLS

So far we haven't discovered the earliest age at which females become more sensitive than males. Our third-grade girls were already better than boys, and we haven't tested anyone younger. Someday we'll develop a test we can use with very young children; only then will we learn when girls gain the advantage. We may, of course, discover that girls are more sensitive from birth.

There are several possible explanations for why women are more sensitive. Perhaps motherhood requires nonverbal skills. Such skills might be part of their genetic make-up, selected during the course of evolution. On the other hand, if the traditional requirements of motherhood are somehow learned rather than inborn, then nonverbal sensitivity could be one of these learned abilities, acquired at a very early age and in many cultures. Our own research suggests that mothers of children just learning how to talk are particularly accurate at deciphering content-filtered speech, which, after all, sounds a bit like the speech of children who are learning how to talk.

One purely social explanation would derive from the premise that women are socially oppressed. If women, as well as other oppressed groups, must "read" the expressions of others with great accuracy in order to advance or even survive, then they could become nonverbally sensitive at an early age. Some commonplace support for this hypothesis is the stereotype of the designing or conniving woman who can engineer social situations to her advantage and manipulate her spouse so that she can get her way while he thinks he's getting his. When one is powerless, one must be subtle.

AGE AND PERSONALITY

We have given the PONS test to people of various ages. Until college age, at least, younger people seem less sensitive to nonverbal messages than older people. Our working explanations for this are that young people have simply had less access than adults to the languages of tone and movement, and that children's verbal and test-taking skills are less developed.

The youngest children proved to be relatively poor at reading *facial* cues. When we finally develop a test that we can use with very young children, we may account for this phenomenon. Perhaps the small stature of young children doesn't allow them much access to the faces of adults.

Differences in nonverbal sensitivity according to occupation, sex and age suggested to us that the PONS might also discriminate among personalities. We therefore conducted several studies, using standard personality tests, to see what correlations we could find.

One multidimensional test indicated that high scorers on the PONS test tended to function better, socially and intellectually, than low scorers. Another test, which measures styles of leadership, showed that task-oriented workers performed better on the PONS than "people-oriented" workers. The significance of this finding isn't totally clear, but perhaps it means that task-oriented personalities develop their nonverbal sensitivity in order to increase the efficiency of whatever communication they have with fellow workers.

Still another test, designed to distinguish autocratic schoolteachers from democratic ones, suggested that the democratic teachers were more sensitive to nonverbal cues. It's hard to say which came first—whether sensitivity to children's feelings encouraged democratic values, or democratic values allowed such sensitivity to develop.

We delved into another area of personal behavior when we asked people in several test-taking groups to evaluate their relationships with others. In general, both males and females who performed well on the PONS test tended to report fewer friends but to report warmer, more honest, and more satisfying same-sex relationships than those who got lower PONS scores.

The matter of friendship became more complicated, however, when we compared scores on the Fast PONS with the test-takers' evaluations of their interpersonal relations. Those who were most accurate at high speeds told us that they had less satisfactory interpersonal relationships than those who weren't so accurate. This finding seems to confirm another stereotype: that of the super-sensitive person who "knows too much" about others. To use the language of Erving Goffman, high-speed accuracy permits access to those backstage regions that are best kept from the audience.

GOOD JUDGES OF PEOPLE

In our search for a definition of nonverbal sensitivity, we have related our findings to several measures of cognitive ability, such as IQ and scholastic aptitude, as well as to some less familiar measures. We wanted to learn, among other things, whether a person's nonverbal profile was a reflection of general intelligence, or if it represented a trait in its own right. As for IQ, most of our studies pointed to only a slight relationship; the same was true of scholastic aptitude. Nonverbal sensitivity, in other words, appears to be relatively independent of general intelligence or test-taking ability. Nor could we find much of a correlation between PONS and the grades of students in high school and college.

On two other tests, however, we discovered a distinct relationship between nonverbal sensitivity and the sort of "intelligence" that makes someone a good judge of people. One of these tests measures cognitive complexity. Those who perform well on it are presumably more capable than others of processing a rich variety of information about their own behavior and that of other people, and then coming up with complex but integrated explanations. Such individuals, we found, also perform well on the PONS test.

Similarly, we found positive correlations between high PONS scores and high scores on a test that measures a person's ability to predict events in another person's life. This interesting test, designed by Charles Dailey, offers the test-taker one event after another from some actual person's case history. The test-taker, meanwhile, plays the role of prophet or realistic novelist and tries to intuit what the character will do and think next, choosing from a number of suggested alternatives. People who are nonverbally sensitive seem to do quite well at this exercise in human wisdom.

STRANGERS LOOK, FRIENDS LISTEN

During the years that we have worked with the PONS test, we have learned dozens of other things about differences in nonverbal sensitivity besides what we have described here. Psychiatric patients and alcoholics, for example, tend to run into trouble on the PONS whenever a scene presents them with too much information; they get higher scores on pure-channel items than on mixed channel, and perform better on audio than video.

We've also found that practice tends to improve a person's score. People who took the test more than once got much better scores the second time around. In another experiment examining the effects of practice, we gave the PONS test to a group of people who all knew the young woman in the film. Surprisingly, their total scores were no better than the scores of a group of strangers. This experiment has suggested various fresh lines of research; for a detailed analysis of each group's performance revealed that male strangers performed better than female strangers, and that friends scored higher on pure audio while strangers scored higher (relatively speaking) on pure video.

When we learn more about such differences, we shall begin to trace the process whereby some people understand others without the need for words.

PROBES

Do you think you "read" nonverbal communication as rapidly as the information here suggests that you do?

Why do *you* think women scored higher than men on PONS?

Do you see yourself as nonverbally sensitive? If so, do you find yourself behaving as the people reported here did—having few relationships but having unusually warm, honest, and satisfying ones?

Have you ever felt that you knew too much about others? What did you do?

Almost every person who wrote to me about the first edition of *Bridges* identified this brief talk as one of their favorites. It doesn't need much introduction, so I'll just underline a few of what I think are the key ideas.

One is that despite the very real human need to touch, a need "proved" by scientific research and, more importantly, *felt* by each of us, our repertoire of touching behaviors is pitifully small. As Mike Young puts it, "so far as a language of touch is concerned, we have condemned ourselves to a sort of pig-latin where, if we touch at all, our meaning must always be veiled."

A second point is that one reason touch is so powerful is that it's almost impossible to lie using this nonverbal cue. Consequently, communicating via touch is usually very risky.

I also think Mike is onto something when he suggest that one reason why our culture is so hung up on and fouled up about sex is that we've burdened that one act of communication with *all* of our needs for touch. Since the courtship-intercourse situation is virtually our only allowable intimacy, that situation has to meet almost *all* of our needs for touch. No wonder intimate relationships often crumble under the pressure.

THE HUMAN TOUCH: WHO NEEDS IT?
Michael G. Young

Every human being needs to touch and be touched. Each of us has thoughts and feelings so deep and personal that words will simply not bear their weight. And yet, we long to communicate them, to share them with another. Our most

This is a sermon given at the Palo Alto Unitarian Church, Palo Alto, California, on November 28, 1965, by Rev. Young, minister of the Unitarian Society of Los Angeles–West, Los Angeles, California. Reprinted by permission of Rev. Young.

intense joy is amplified and given permanence by being shared. Our deepest fears and anxieties are made endurable and manageable by being shared. But they can only be truly shared in their full depth and significance when they are shared in the totality of who we are. They cry out for touch.

We need to touch. Perhaps in our artificial technologized culture we need the closeness and intimacy of touch more than ever. Our Western culture has achieved such a level of cerebration, of the worship of intellect and intellectualizing, that we are terrified of touch.

We have so hidden from ourselves those deep feelings about which we cannot intellectualize that their sheer pressure inside of us terrifies us. We are taught almost from birth that man's glory is his intellect and his emotions are fetters from which he needs to be freed. Emotions are to be risen above, avoided, denied, escaped. One of the greatest unlearned lessons of history is that emotional and intellectual freedom is to be found not in freedom from feelings, but in being freed for them. Indeed, I have come to the conclusion that what differentiates man from the beasts is not his mental skill, for all his superiority in that. What sets man apart most profoundly is the depth and complexity of his capacity for emotion.

We need to share ourselves with each other as surely as we need to breathe. But just as surely, that sharing cannot be accomplished on a merely verbal level. What we need to communicate is more primal, more basic, than language.

You have perhaps heard of the nursery babies who die without the human touch, who need only to be played with, handled and cuddled to survive. Recent experiments with baby monkeys, even, indicate that without the physical intimacy or mothering they do not develop properly. Those completely starved of touch, die.

Research in the teaching of reading indicates that not only is verbal facility—the ability to use words—not our primary mode of communication, but children who do not crawl, and touch, and handle things, almost invariably have difficulty with language. The thought and word are not our primary mode of communication, we are primarily animals who touch! Our deepest thoughts and feelings can only be communicated by touch—by physical intimacy.

When your child comes to you, frightened and hurt, *TELL* him you care, *TELL* him you love him, *TELL* him you are sorry. Then *TOUCH* him. Take him in your arms and cuddle him. Then he will believe you. Then he will know you care.

But to whom can you go when you are frightened or hurt? With whom can you share those deepest feelings, which can only be shared by touching?

We adults have limited touch to three areas. We allow the handshake and such similar symbolic but safe, gestures. We may touch in sexual intercourse. And we may touch in hostility, where one feeling—anger—protects us from the others that might burst out. That is just about it! So far as a language of touch is concerned, we have condemned ourselves to a sort of pig-latin where, if we touch at all, our meaning must always be veiled.

Let us examine these three areas of touch open to us.

A handshake is a ritualized caress. It is a symbolic reestablishment of communication. As a gesture of friendship, no symbol could be as powerful as that of touch. For there is power in touch. It demands and communicates a dimension of commitment and trust unlike any other form of communication. I may talk to you and remain hidden from you. But, if we touch, I am vulnerable. I may reveal more of myself to you than I can trust you with. There is a feeling of control in verbal discourse that is absent with physical intimacy. Sham and pretense is much more difficult.

This is precisely why we are wary of touching. It is a terribly risk-filled form of human relatedness. The more so because we need it so much and are starved for it. We are well aware that if the power of touch is loosed, those feelings that we keep carefully bottled up inside may come spilling out. Touch has the power to burst the floodgates of our damned-up emotional lives.

And we are right! Touch is dangerous. It is not by accident that we use the same word—feeling— to refer to emotion and to touching. They are that closely related.

So, when we meet again after a period of separation, we shake hands. We need to reestablish contact, to be together again. But touch is dangerous. So, we keep it off, out there. The handshake becomes at the same time a caress and a fending off, a contact and a buffer. We need to touch, but we are afraid of its power and the trust it demands.

The second area of touch we allow ourselves—sexual intimacy—is really our only area of open intimacy. In bed, preferably with a member of the opposite sex and properly only one who is a legal mate, we finally allow ourselves to touch. There we may speak, as only touch can, of who we are and how we feel.

That, the courtship-intercourse situation, is virtually our only allowable intimacy. And so we fill that one allowable intimacy with all of our needs to touch. We thrust all sorts of totally inappropriate feelings into that relationship. That one act must bear the weight of all our needs to communicate what cannot be said! Is it any wonder our culture is obsessed with sex, and yet plagued with problems and frustrations about it?

Is it any wonder our teen-agers, like their parents, are hung up on sex? The only vocabulary of feeling we have given them is that of seduction. In any given parked car with young people necking, there is involved *FAR LESS* sex than the need to be close to another—to speak in touch the anxiety, the joy, the affirmation and the uncertainty of being alive; to give and to receive the comfort and security of being together that *CANNOT* be said.

There is, in back of our so-called sexual revolution, more than simply new attitudes towards sex. There is rather a groping for a new vocabulary of feeling.

The major problem in that revolution is not the threat of sexual license. The major problem is our culturally inherited inability to distinguish the need for and expression of sex, from the rest of our deepest feelings—the inability to distinguish physical intimacy from seduction.

The final area where we allow ourselves to touch is that of overt hostility. It is seen in contact sports; both those in which we engage and those we watch, touching vicariously. It is seen in the disciplining of children. It is seen in the various outbursts of physical violence, even in much antisocial behavior.

The need to touch can be expressed in hostility while minimizing the risk of the floodgates bursting. The expression of strong hostility keeps the other feelings from being revealed. There is more love present, but hidden, in most of our acts of anger than we are often aware of. And, tragically, many a child is only able to get physical intimacy from his parents by misbehaving.

The consequent emotional confusion, misunderstanding, and apparent irrationality that clutter our lives are quite understandable in light of our starvation for touch. This unfortunate state of affairs even infects that one intimacy we allow ourselves. Misplaced and misused hostility is often responsible for our hang-ups in our sexual adjustment.

To whom can you go when you are frightened, or hurt, or just need to be WITH someone? To whom can you go for the human touch?

To a handshake?

To a fight?

Or, to bed?

We are alone with our deepest feelings, and we long to share them. But we have cut ourselves off from this most profound means of communication. We have invested too much stock in talk and we are in danger of bankruptcy. No one is hung up for lack of an argument—philosophical, theological, or scientific. NO ONE!

If we would minister as a church to the terrors and hurts of the world; if we would care, the only way caring can be heard; if we would be whole again, and bring wholeness to those we love; we must, perhaps, become as little children, and learn again the human touch.

PROBES

Do you agree with what Mike Young says here? What do you think can be done to permit more tactile communicating?

Do you think your most intimate relationship would be stronger if it didn't have to meet all of your needs to touch and be touched? Would you be willing to let your partner fulfill some of his or her needs by, for example, hugging, holding hands with, and being touched by others? Or is the thought of that happening too risky to permit?

It is not necessary to always think words. Words often keep me from acting in a fully intuitive way. Fears, indecision, and frustration feed on words. Without words they usually stop. When I am trying to figure out how I should relate to someone, especially a stranger, if I will stop thinking words, and listen to the situation, and just be open, I find I act in a more appropriate, more spontaneous, often original, sometimes even courageous way. Words are at times good for looking back, but they are confining when I need to act in the present.

HUGH PRATHER

II

PERCEIVING SELF AND OTHERS

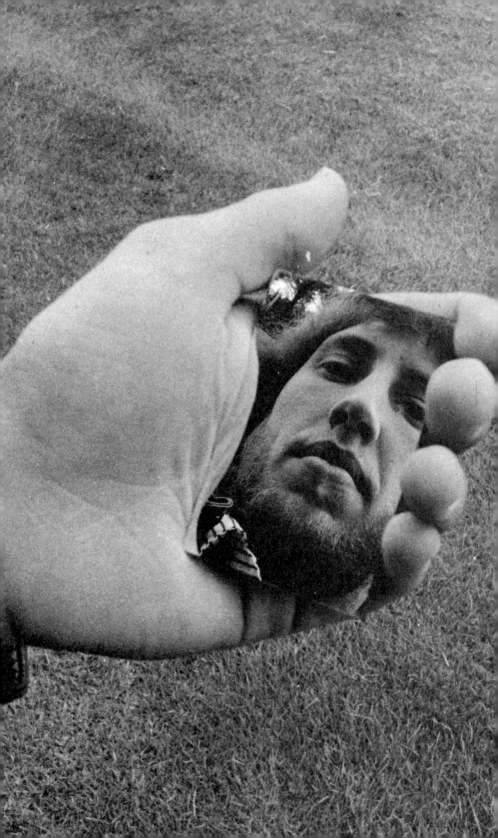

4

SELF-PERCEPTION

At first I thought that to "be myself" meant simply to act the way I feel. I would ask myself a question such as, "What do I want to say to this person?" and very often the answer was surprisingly negative. It seemed that when I looked inside, the negative feelings were the ones I noticed first. Possibly I noticed them because of their social unusualness; possibly they stood out because acting negatively was what I feared. But I soon found that behind most negative feelings were deeper, more positive feelings—if I held still long enough to look. The more I attempted to "be me" the more "me's" I found there were. I now see that "being me" means acknowledging all that I feel at the moment, and then taking responsibility for my actions by consciously choosing which level of my feelings I am going to respond to.

HUGH PRATHER

If Earl Kelley is able to put into practice what he describes here, he is the kind of educational administrator I would like to have charge of the school my daughters, Marcia and Lisa, attend.

Although this article is a little longer than some of the others, I include it because it makes so many important points. One is that each of our selves is unique, is continually growing, and grows most in relationships with others. Another is that unfortunately, many people do not like their selves and as a result, experience problems communicating.

Kelley offers three suggestions here for enhancing your view of yourself: (1) Recognize that your self is a living organism whose "food" is perceptions, especially perceptions of how others see you. Perceptions are affected by the kind of "selective screen" you have, and the screen is made up of values *you* establish or values forced on you by *others*. (2) Intrinsic values—the ones you establish—are much more satisfying, and they grow best in "facilitative relationships" with others. Facilitating relationships are characterized by openness, respect, cooperation, and real feelings of involvement and confirmation. (3) Finally, there is a flexible checklist of characteristics of the self who has been well fed by facilitating relationships. This person generally thinks well of himself or herself and thinks well of others, is aware that he or she is continually growing and changing, appreciates the usefulness of mistakes, values relationships with others, lives within his or her own value system, and is creative.

All of that is not meant to be an unrealistic prescription for personal perfection; it's just an outline of how we "get" our selves, how our communication contact affects both the selves we are becoming and the selves we help others become.

THE FULLY FUNCTIONING SELF

Earl C. Kelley

In a discussion of the self, it will perhaps be helpful to attempt to say as well as we can what it is we are trying to discuss. This is done at the risk of using the conversation stopper, "Let's define it." Many a fine discussion has ended at this point.

The self consists, in part at least, of the accumulated experiential background, or backlog, of the individual. It is what has been built, since his life be-

From *Perceiving, Behaving, Becoming: A New Focus for Education*, 1962 Yearbook. Washington, D.C.: Association for Supervision and Curriculum Development, 1962, pp. 9–20. Reprinted with permission of the Association for Supervision and Curriculum Development. Copyright © 1962 by the Association for Supervision and Curriculum Development.

gan, through unique experience and unique purpose, on the individual's unique biological structure. The self is therefore unique to the individual.

This self is built almost entirely, if not entirely, in relationship to others. While the newborn babe has the equipment for the development of the self, there is ample evidence to show that nothing resembling a self can be built in the absence of others. Having a cortex is not enough; there must be continuous interchange between the individual and others. Language, for example, would not be possible without social relationships. Thus, it is seen that man is necessarily a social being.

The self has to be achieved; it is not given. All that is given is the equipment and at least the minimal (mother and child) social environment. Since the self is achieved through social contact, it has to be understood in terms of others. "Self and other" is not a duality, because they go so together that separation is quite impossible.

The self consists of an organization of accumulated experience over a whole lifetime. It is easy to see, therefore, that a great deal of the self has been relegated to the unconscious, or has been "forgotten." This does not mean that these early experiences have been lost. It merely means that they cannot readily be brought into consciousness. We must recognize the fact that the unconscious part of the self functions, for weal or woe, depending on the quality of the experiences.

It is intended here, however, to deal with the conscious self. The unconscious self (not a separation but a continuum) is difficult to deal with for the very reason that it is below the level of consciousness. We want here to look especially at how the individual sees himself. This is indeed the critical point, because it is what the person *sees* that is enabling or disabling. The crucial matter is not so much what you are, but what you think you are. And all of this is always in relationship to others.

The fully functioning personality (self) needs to have certain characteristics. Here, perhaps, is as good a place as any to discuss word trouble. We live in a moving, changing, becoming-but-never-arriving world, yet our language was built by people who believed this to be a static world. I have often spoken of the adequate self, but "adequate" will not do, because it is static. In fact, "inadequate" is a more useful word than "adequate." If there were a word that combines "aspiring-becoming," it would come close to our needs. I have chosen "fully functioning," which I think I learned from Carl Rogers, as the best I can do. This expression at least implies movement.

In order for a person to be fully functioning, when he looks at his self, as he must, he must see that it is enough—enough to perform the task at hand. He must see in his experiential background some history of success. He needs to see process, the building and becoming nature of himself. This being so, he will see that today has no meaning in the absence of yesterdays and tomorrows. In fact, there could be no today except for both yesterday and tomorrow. He must like what he sees, at least well enough for it to be operational.

MANY PEOPLE DO NOT LIKE THEIR SELVES

Unfortunately, many people in the world today suffer from inadequate concepts of self, which naturally lead to mistaken notions of others. Perhaps everybody is afflicted thus to some degree. There may be some rare spirits who are not, but they are few indeed.

We see evidence of this all around us. We see people ridden by unreasonable fears. The fearful person looks at his self and sees that it is not sufficient to meet what he fears. Middle-aged graduate students are afraid to stick their necks out. They are afraid to write; they suffer from stage fright. The question uppermost in their minds is, "What will people think?" Their selves are veritable skeletons in their closets, and if one has a skeleton in his closet, it is best not to do anything except to keep quiet. Any move may reveal it. So they try to sit tight so that they may not be revealed to others. This is a great loss to others—to mankind—for new paths are forbidding and exploration is fraught with terrors.

This is Crippling

An inadequate concept of self, so common in our culture, is crippling to the individual. Our psychological selves may become crippled in much the same way as our physical selves may be crippled by disease or by an accident. They are the same, in effect, because each limits what we can do. When we see ourselves as inadequate, we lose our "can-ness." There becomes less and less that we can do.

Perhaps it is unfortunate that we cannot see the psychological self in the same way that we see the physical self. Our hearts go out to the physical cripple—we do not enter him in a foot race—but we expect the psychological cripple to step lively and meet all of the vicissitudes of life as though he were whole. Both kinds of cripples need therapy, though of different sorts. Many benefit by therapy, though all do not.

How Do We Get That Way?

Now we come to the question, "How do we get that way?" We get that way in the same way that a physical cripple does—by the lives we lead. Of course there are some cases of congenital defect, but if these were the only cripples we had, we would be fortunate indeed.

The newborn babe has enormous potential for health, but this health has to be built out of his experience with others. It has to be achieved, and it has to be achieved in relationship to others. The health potential then lies strictly in the quality of the people around him, since the infant, for many years to come, has, himself, no control over whom he will associate with.

Damage to the self, so disabling to so many of us, comes from the fact that we grow up in an authoritarian culture. While it is true that this is a democracy in governmental form, we have not achieved democracy in the home, the school, or the church. The fact that we have a democratically chosen president or governor has no effect upon the developing child. He is built by the people close to him, and he does not elect them. The people close to him, having themselves been crippled, know no better than to continue the process.

The evils of authoritarianism are more extensive than is ordinarily understood. It is easy to see on a grand scale, as when a Hitler gains power. We all abhor a Hitler, but we seem to think that tyranny in small doses or on a small scale is somehow good. All in all, it appears that small tyrants do more harm than grand ones. The small tyrant operates on the growing edge of the personality of the young.

The trouble with the tyrant is basically that he does not have any faith in anyone except himself. He gets that way by living with people who never had any faith in him. Of course he does not really have any faith in himself either, but he has longed for and striven for a position of power over others weaker than himself. Getting his concept of others from his concept of himself, he believes that nothing worthwhile will happen unless he forces it to happen.

Lack of faith in others—the feeling that one has to see to it that others, who are perverse by nature, do what they should—starts a chain reaction of evils, one piled upon another. The burden one bears when he feels that he must watch others and coerce them must be unbearable. And so it turns out to be, for the tyrant deprives himself of others, and grows in the direction of more loneliness and hostility.

From this we can see what happens to the newborn babe as he faces the tyrant. Of course, the tyrant loves his baby in such manner as he is able to love. But he still regards the infant as a "thing," naturally in need of correction. One might think that the very young would not know the difference. But there are ample data to show that even in the first few days after birth, the child knows the difference between being loved and being viewed as in need of coercion. He knows whether the parent is doing things *with* him or *to* him. And the personality at that stage must be tender.

After five or six years of the authoritarian home, the child goes to school. The school is a place inhabited by adults, and too often these adults hold adult concepts of what a child ought to be. These concepts are unverified by the study of children. Here he meets preconceived standards, grade levels, and all of the other paraphernalia of the adult-centered school. If he does not measure up to these standards, then obviously he is perverse and in need of coercion. The fact that these standards are not derived from the child, that there is nothing about them in the Bible, that they arise and reside only in the minds of adults, bothers the adults not at all. Thus, coercion and criticism become the daily fare, while the deviations in behavior brought about by the uniqueness of the personality are stopped. Conformity is the way to the good life, and the best way to conform is to withdraw. One cannot be unique and extend himself and still conform. His uniqueness will show. Shells look a great deal alike, and so if one crawls into his shell, his differences will not be so apparent.

In our authoritarian culture, many forces converge upon the young individual which have the effect of making him think less of himself. The church is one of these forces. The concept of guilt, with its imaginary burden of sin, cannot help one to think well of himself. Of course one can acquire these damaging concepts without getting them at church. But those who have salvation to dispense hold a powerful weapon. When one is made to feel unworthy, he is crippled in some degree, because he cannot do what he otherwise might.

There is a distinction here between the effects of religion and the effects of the church as often administered. It is not religion per se which makes one think ill of himself. It is the representatives of religion who use authoritarian methods to gain their ends. Likewise schooling or education can be expanding in their nature. It is that the representatives of the school—teachers and administrators—often have their own ends to be served, not those of their learners. They act from their own fears, which cause them to dampen and delimit the expanding personalities of their young, thus defeating the very purpose for their being.

Nor is it intended here to deny the need for standards. A fully functioning personality cannot operate without standards. Such standards are the basis for aspiration, the basis for the hope for tomorrow. But it is doubtful that extrinsic, materialistic standards can be successfully applied. Standards have to be the product of values held, and of the life that has been led. The better the quality of the life that has been experienced, the better the values held and the standards which result from these values. Standards will be unique—not the same for everyone—even as the experience from which they are derived has been unique. They will be in terms of other human beings.

BASIS FOR HEALTHY GROWTH

The dynamic which changes a speck of protoplasm into a fully functioning human being is growth. The questions, then, are: What does he grow on? What are the environmental conditions which feed him?

We need to consider that in growing up one is developing both his physical structure and his psychological structure. We are most familiar with the physical structure and are apt to think of that as growth. We know what the body needs to develop and that lack of development will result in physical crippling. We can identify the diseases of malnutrition and know that a man will not become truly a man in the best sense without an adequate supply of the required stuff of physical growth.

All of the time that the physical body is being developed, so also is the psychological self. The physical body fortunately stops growing after about 20 years. The psychological self, however, continues to grow throughout life. As the physical body has its own unique food requirements, so does the psychological self. This is a different kind of stuff, however, with a different point of intake. We feed the psychological self through the perceptive process. This is what comes into consciousness when stimuli from the environment impinge on the organism. It is the stuff of growth for the personality, and builds attitudes, habits, and knowledge. The perceptive stuff of growth provides the experiential background from which we operate. This controls what we do with the body. The quality of the perceptive stuff of growth therefore determines the quality of the behavior of the individual.

It is necessary here to make clear the fact that the physical body and the psychological self do not constitute a duality, even though it is necessary to speak of them one at a time. The organism is unitary in its operation. There is no body apart from personality, no psychological self without a body to inhabit. What affects one affects all. But that does not prevent speaking of a part. Although we know that hand and foot, attitude, emotion, and habit are all one, we still can talk of the hand as having certain characteristics while the foot has others. Speaking of parts does not deny the unitary nature of the individual.

WE SELECT WHAT WE WILL PERCEIVE

Since in this paper we are primarily concerned with the development of the fully functioning self, we will discuss what feeds the self and how it is fed. As we have noted, perception is the stuff of growth for the psychological self. The perceptive process is the only avenue by which the self can be fed. Recent understandings as to the nature of this process have enabled us to see more clearly than before how the self is built.

One of the most revealing facts about perception is that it is *selective*. We do not see everything in our surroundings. There are thousands of coincidences in the situation in which we find ourselves at any point of time. To perceive them all would cause pandemonium. We therefore *choose* that which the self feeds upon. The direction of the growth of the self depends upon those choices.

The choices seem to be on the basis of experience and unique purpose. We all have a background of experience upon which perception is in part based. We cannot see that which we have no experience to see. But experience is not enough to account for what happens, for there are many objects in our surroundings with which we have had experience, but which we do not perceive.

The additional element which appears to determine perceptive intake is purpose. There is ample evidence now to show that all living tissue is purposive, and, of course, in man this purpose is partly, but only partly, on the conscious level. In perception, purpose operates automatically most of the time. And so, just as we do not eat everything, our psychological selves are particular as to what they feed on. What they take in has to suit their purposes, and has to fit onto their past experiences.

ENHANCEMENT AND DEFENSE

The self "looks out" upon the surrounding scene largely in terms of its own enhancement or defense. It tends to extend in the direction of that which promises to make it better off. It withdraws from that which seems likely to endanger it. This is largely true throughout life and entirely true in the early stages when the self is being established—when "self" and "other" first come into being. Altruism is a highly sophisticated concept, and, if it is achieved at all, it comes late. It is the result of great understanding of the self-other interdependency.

THE SELF NEEDS BOUNDARIES

If the self is going to reach out toward facilitating factors and withdraw from endangering ones, it has to have something to reach out from, something to hide behind. It helps to understand this if we assume that the self has to have boundaries in much the same sense that the physical self has to have a skin. The self has certain things that it will let in, others that it will keep out. The boundaries are not, of course, physical—to be seen—but neither is the self. A physical concept, however, helps us to comprehend it. So if we can imagine a physical shell, or armor, necessary for the confinement of the self, we then can imagine how it functions.

Some kind of boundary—a selective screen—is therefore essential to the maintenance of the self. We could not manage the affairs of living without something of this kind. It follows that the nature of the environment, whether it is seen to be facilitating or endangering, will determine the permeability of this screen. That is, the more facilitating the environment, the less need for protection. The more endangering the environment, the greater need for protection. Thus, under adverse conditions, the screen develops into a shell, so that very little is admitted. When this process is continued over a long period of time, that which enabled us to be selective in our perception becomes almost impermeable.

Boundaries then become barriers. Protection becomes isolation. The self becomes a prisoner in its own fort. We have all seen persons off whom words or ideas seemed to bounce. They have built their barriers against other people so strong that they have become inaccessible. Since fear feeds on itself, especially when a person is in isolation, it has a tendency to extend itself beyond the people who are endangering, to include all people.

When the fearful person withdraws within his psychological shell, communication is shut off. It is just as difficult for such a person to give as it is for him to receive. The self then is denied that which it feeds on. The psychological self feeds on ideas, which come from other people. Without the stuff of growth, the self becomes less adequate, and the whole person loses its ability to do, to venture, to create. The individual comes to see himself as impoverished, but he is not able to do much about it by himself.

THE LIFE GOOD TO LIVE

Such a person, however, by having enhancing relationships with others, can break down some of the barriers which separate him from others. By good experiences, he can become less fearful and more open. This process, too, feeds on itself, and confidence can be built by the quality of his experience with others. Confidence opens the barriers so that the perceptive stuff of growth can again be received. He has to learn not to see others as threats, but as assets. Of course, this will not happen unless others cease to act toward him as threats. The parent or teacher who depends upon threats or other techniques of fear will not be able to open the self of one who is in his power.

Fortunate indeed, and not too common in this authoritarian culture, is the person who has had the opportunity to grow up with people whom he can see as facilitating. Most of us have to build our shell against others, and if we are to have fully functioning selves, we have to have experiences which will open these shells.

For the development of a fully functioning self, a person needs to have opportunity to live the life good to live. This life, or his world, needs to be populated by people whom he can view as facilitating. It is almost entirely a matter of people, not things. Facilitating people can be poor in material things. In fact, some of the happiest and most open people are found in poor material circumstances. The most closed and fearful people, the most authoritarian people, may be surfeited by the material goods of the earth. While this is no plea for poverty and privation, it seems that the very possession of great quantities of material goods is apt by its very nature to make the holder fearful that he will lose his goods to others. Vague fear always causes the personality to close up and to become less accessible.

The life good to live does not depend upon the material status of the person. It depends upon the quality of the people around him. He needs people who are open, so that he can feel their quality. He needs people who respect him as a person from the very beginning. It is paradoxical that many parents love their young, but do not respect them. Parents and teachers often say that the child is, of course, too young to be able to make any decisions for himself. It is true that the newborn infant cannot make decisions. But the babe can feel the difference between being held in respect and being regarded as though he had no personality. Respect for the budding self brings it out. Disrespect starts the process of closing up, which in some of our older children and adults is often so complete.

The life good to live is a cooperative one. No child is too young to sense whether or not he lives in a cooperative relation with the people around him. The reason that cooperation is so important is that the cooperative atmosphere is one of involvement. The growing self must feel that it is involved, that it is really part of what is going on, that in some degree it is helping shape its own destiny, together with the destiny of all. Perhaps there is no one quality more important for the developing self than this feeling of involvement in what is taking place. This is what gives a person a "reason to be." The lack of consultation and involvement is the cause of the continuing war between parents and their children, between teachers and learners, between teachers and administrators, employers and employees, ad infinitum. When the person is a part of something, then he becomes responsible.

Whenever the cooperative life is proposed, the authoritarians say, "Oh yes, you want children (or workers or teachers) to do just as they please!" This is a gross misunderstanding of the cooperative way of life, and the shell on such people is so thick that we are baffled in our efforts to reach them. The fact is that in the cooperative life there is much less freedom "to do just as they please" than there is under the surveillance of the autocrat. For the obligation is owed, and the responsibility is felt, to ourselves and to those who facilitate us. The obligation is with us 24 hours a day, rather than just when the autocrat is looking. We do not neglect or sabotage our own projects. This happens to the other's project, particularly if he has met us with threat or fear.

The cooperative life, where everyone from his beginning receives the respect due to a person, and, as he is able, becomes involved in and responsible for what goes on, is not an easy life. The obligation is continuous and pressing.

But the difficulties of such a life are inherent in the living, and they cause the self to extend and stretch and grow. These difficulties have quite the opposite effect from those thought up by and inflicted on us by someone else. The latter, not having meaning to the person, cause him to withdraw and begin to calculate how he can protect himself.

THE FULLY FUNCTIONING PERSON

What is a person with a fully functioning self like? This can be answered only in terms of his behavior. Conclusions can be drawn from this behavior. The temptation here is to vest this person, like Rose Aylmer, with "every virtue, every grace." Rather than simply listing virtues, there are some characteristics not necessarily cherished in our culture, which such a person would logically have. From what has been stated here, it might be inferred that nobody has escaped with a fully functioning self. And it seems to be likely that very few survive home, church, and school without damage to the self.

Yet, there are a good many people who, through contact with facilitating persons, have been reopened and whose selves function well. To argue otherwise would be to deny the potential for change and improvement on which life itself depends. In fact, it can be considered that no one can experience elation who has never known despair; no one can be courageous without having known fear. So the human personality is not doomed to endure its present state, but can be brought into flower by enhancing experiences. As Karen Horney has said, "My own belief is that man has the capacity as well as the desire to develop his potentialities and become a decent human being, and that these deteriorate if his relationship to others and hence to himself is, and continues to be, disturbed. I believe that man can change and keep on changing as long as he lives."[1]

The fully functioning personality thinks well of himself. He looks at himself and likes what he sees well enough so that he can accept it. This is essential to doing, "to can-ness." He does not see himself as able to do anything and everything, but he sees himself as able in terms of his experience. He feels he can do what is reasonable to expect on the basis of his experience.

Those who do not like what they see when they look at themselves are the fearful ones—not just afraid of present danger, but taking a fearful view of everything in general. Fear renders them helpless, and this leads to alienation from others and hostility toward others, thus shutting themselves off from the stuff they feed upon. The harmful ramifications of not accepting self are endless, because one attitude leads to another.

He thinks well of others. This comes about automatically because of the one-ness of the self-other relationship. It is doubtful that there can be a self except in relation to others, and to accept one implies the acceptance of the other. The acceptance of others opens a whole world with which to relate. It is the opposite of the hostility which results from non-acceptance of self.

He therefore sees his stake in others. He sees that other people are the stuff out of which he is built. He has a selfish interest then in the quality of those around him and has responsibility in some degree for that quality. The whole matter of selfishness and altruism disappears when he realizes that self and other are interdependent—that we are indeed our brother's keeper, and he is ours. Coming into the awareness of mutual need modifies human behavior. He comes to see other people as opportunities, not for exploitation, but for the building of self. He becomes a loving person, so that he can get closer to the real source of his power.

He sees himself as a part of a world in movement—in process of becoming. This follows from the whole notion of self and others and the acceptance that they can feed off each other and hence can improve. When one looks outward rather than inward, the idea of change—in self, in others, in things—becomes apparent. The acceptance of change as a universal phenomenon brings about modifications of personality. The person who accepts change and expects it behaves differently from the person who seeks to get everything organized so that it will be fixed from now on. He will not search for the firm foundation on which he can stand for the rest of his life. He will realize that the only thing he knows for sure about the future is that tomorrow will be different from today and that he can anticipate this difference with hopeful expectation.

Optimism is the natural outcome of an accepting view of self and hence of others. Such a person is a doer, a mobile person, one who relates himself in an active way with others. Such activity would be meaningless unless the person had hopes for improvement. As has been stated, today has no meaning except in relation to an expected tomorrow. This is the basis for hope, without which no one can thrive. Improvement is that which enhances and enriches self and others. Neither can be enhanced by itself.

The fully functioning personality, having accepted the ongoing nature of life and the dynamic of change, *sees the value of mistakes.* He knows he will be treading new paths at all times, and that, therefore, he cannot always be right. Rigid personalities suffer much from their need to be always right. The fully functioning personality will not only see that mistakes are inevitable in constantly breaking new ground, but will come to realize that these unprofitable paths show the way to better ones. Thus, a mistake, which no one would make if he could foresee it, can be profitable. In fact, much of what we know that is workable comes from trying that which is not. In our culture, it seems that most of our moral code is based on the values of rigid people who cannot bear to be wrong, and so, making a mistake is almost a sin. The effective person cannot afford to have his spirit of adventure thus hampered. He knows that the only way to find out is to go forward and to profit from experience—to make experience an asset.

The fully functioning self, seeing the importance of people, *develops and holds human values*. There is no one, of course, who does not come to hold values. Values come about through the life one lives, which determines what one comes to care about. The better the life, the better the values accumulated. The one who sees human beings as essential to his own enhancement develops values related to the welfare of people. Holding these values in a world which most people consider to be static, he encounters problems in meeting static mores. He is, therefore, on the creative edge of the generally accepted mores or morals. Values in terms of what is good for all people are continuously in conflict with materialistic values held by the majority.

He knows no other way to live except in keeping with his values. He has no need continuously to shift behavior, depending upon the kind of people nearest him. He has no need for subterfuge or deceit, because he is motivated by the value of facilitating self and others. While treading new paths is fraught with risk, he does not have to engage in a continuous guessing game to make his behavior match new people and also be consistent with what he has done before. A fully functioning person, holding human values, does not have to ask himself constantly what it was he said last week.

We are tempted to call this courage and integrity. This is another way of saying that one has what it takes to live as life really exists and to do it all in one piece. Can we call it courage when there is no alternative?

Since life is ever-moving and ever-becoming, *the fully functioning person is cast in a creative role*. But more than simply accepting this role, he sees creation going on all around him. He sees that creation is not something which occurred long ago and is finished, but that it is now going on and that he is part of it. He sees the evil of the static personality because it seeks to stop the process of creation to which we owe our world and our being. He exults in being a part of this great process and in having an opportunity to facilitate it. Life to him means discovery and adventure, flourishing because it is in tune with the universe.

REFERENCE

1. Karen Horney, *Our Inner Conflict* (New York: Norton, 1945), p. 19.

PROBES

How do you see Kelley's ideas fitting with what Boulding said in Chapter 1 about our "images"?

How do Kelley's comments about choice relate to what I said in Chapter 1 about humans being choosers?

When is it easiest for you not to like your self? Is your language, as Egan suggests in Chapter 2, affected by your view of your self? What other ways does your view of your self affect your communicating?

What kind of "selective screen" do you have? What conditions or pressures make your screen develop into a shell?

When are you best able to function as a "facilitating person"? Who functions that way for you?

Which characteristics that Kelley mentioned at the end of the article are most difficult for you to achieve?

The paradox of progress is that I grow each time I realize that I can only be where I am.

HUGH PRATHER

These are excerpts from a report of a survey completed by 62,000 readers of *Psychology Today* magazine. The survey asked people about their body image, how that relates to their self-image, and how the combination affects and is affected by their contacts with others. I include this article because body image is a part of self-image, and self-image greatly affects our communicating. More specifically, body image seems to be one of those not-to-be-talked-about, myth-shrouded factors that affects our communicating more than it needs to. In other words, although we may protest that body image is irrelevant to our communicating, we're actually much more affected by it than we need to be.

This survey indicates that most people are more satisfied with their bodies than advertisers often lead us to believe. Both men and women tend to be dissatisfied with their teeth, many women worry about the size of their hips, and many men are concerned about their spare tire. But there does not seem to be an overwhelming percentage of people convinced that they are sexually impotent or socially inept because they don't fit the thin, beautiful, young, and sexy American stereotype.

The survey also shows, however, that our body image, like other parts of our self-image, is affected by our contacts with others. Childhood teasing, for example, has lasting effects on self-image. Whether we're seen as a fat or a thin child seems to be especially important.

There is also a positive correlation between body image and self-esteem. People who feel good about their appearance tend to feel good about themselves and tend to have satisfying communication experiences.

This article agrees that after a relationship is established, factors other than appearance are most important. But when we *initiate* relationships, body image tends to make a real difference.

THE HAPPY AMERICAN BODY: A SURVEY REPORT

Ellen Berscheid, Elaine Walster, and George Bohrnstedt

"No one is free who is a slave to the body," wrote Seneca some 1,900 years ago. Judging from the advertisements, products, and best sellers that deluge us daily, we are a nation of slaves. We are obsessed with being thin, beautiful, young, and sexy, and we will go to extraordinary lengths to approach those ideals.

In the July 1972 issue of *Psychology Today*, we offered readers the opportunity to express their thoughts and feelings about the body. The topic was timely and the response overwhelming: more than 62,000 readers returned the 109-item "Body Image" questionnaire. But they were divided and ambivalent on the matter of how important attractiveness and physical looks are—or should be.

A good number of people wrote letters to protest a "whole survey" on the body. Some said that appearance is a superficial matter, not worthy of undue discussion: "Perhaps if I thought I were ugly or beautiful I would spend more attention on my appearance," wrote one woman. "But as it is, this is a topic of little concern for myself. There are just many more important matters in my life." Nevertheless, she filled out the whole questionnaire.

Another woman summarized the views of many: "There's a lot more to me than my looks. I know I'm attractive, but I don't want to be attractive to someone only because of physical appearance. That would be ghastly."

By contrast, other respondents acknowledged, some reluctantly, the importance of one's appearance. "Your questionnaire made me feel as though I have floated through life ignoring my body. You have made me dissect myself and realize that I do think it's important. Now I must learn to connect my body with the rest of myself." "The questionnaire was extremely thought-provoking," seconded an older woman. "My long-held belief that our bodies are unimportant was shattered." One honest soul confessed, with some shame, that "I discriminate against beautiful people, probably out of jealously, and tend to label them shallow and egotistical."

BEAUTY AND THE BODY

The purpose of our survey was to determine just how important bodies are to our attitudes, to self-esteem, to experiences with the same and the opposite sex. We wondered, in short, whether beauty is only skin deep, or whether it plays a lasting and important role in a person's life and self-concept. A woman who considers herself beautiful recounted her whole life story to us, "to show how *very* important surface looks have been in my life. Society places such a premium on being attractive. It counts. I may be vain. I realize beauty is only surface. But I enjoy having it, and take care of it."

Our concept of body image, which differs from some other psychological approaches, refers to one's *satisfaction* with his or her body. We measured body image with a list of 25 body parts and characteristics; for each one, the respondents indicated their satisfaction or dissatisfaction on a six-point answer scale. For example, in addition to satisfaction with "overall body appearance" and "overall facial appearance," respondents rated their hair, eyes, mouth, voice, complexion, extremities, torso, sex organs, height and weight.

We assumed that respondents would have a high level of dissatisfaction with their bodies, since our society places so much emphasis on physical appearance. Further, we assumed that women would be more dissatisfied with their bodies than men, since appearance is reputedly more important for women in attracting a mate, in feeling feminine, in having high self-esteem.

Our assumptions were logical, perhaps, but they turned out to be wrong. Only seven percent of the women and four percent of the men in our sample said that they were quite or extremely dissatisfied with their overall body appearance. And only 16 percent of the women and 11 percent of the men said they were even "slightly" dissatisfied.

On the other hand, only about half are quite or extremely *satisfied*: 45 percent of the women and 55 percent of the men. Women, then, did lag behind men in having a positive body image, as we suspected. And women were slightly more likely than men to agree that *physical attractiveness is very important in day-to-day social interaction for most persons* (32 percent to 29 percent).

ONE'S FACE IS ONE'S FORTUNE

The same was true for ratings of overall facial attractiveness. Almost everyone was happy with his or her face; only 11 percent of the women and eight percent of the men expressed any dissatisfaction.

Either our respondents are an unusually good-looking lot, or people worry less than advertisers assume about how they look. We know from extensive research that people do judge others on the basis of physical attractiveness; nevertheless, our respondents are apparently unconcerned about such judgments. One woman pointed out the difficulty of interpreting such questionnaires: "I am 'quite satisfied' with myself, as I indicated. But does this mean that I am very good looking and know it—or could it mean that I'm sick of so much emphasis on physical appearances and that I just don't give a damn about a trivial thing like being 'pretty'? In my case, it is the latter." Both alternatives are possible, of course: but the important thing is that so many respondents are so satisfied.

The respondents were not uniformly delighted with specific aspects of their faces, however. Both men and women are unhappiest with their teeth—almost one third were dissatisfied; one fourth complained about their complexions; and one in five did not like their noses.

Given the American preoccupation with sex and sexual performance, we expected that women would complain about the size of their breasts, while men would worry about the size of their penises. Sex researchers and psychotherapists have observed for years that patients are unduly worried about size of their sex organs, and barroom folklore has added to people's anxieties.

We received several letters from women who worried that their breasts were too small or too big.

"Mine are much too small, and the first thousand bucks I get, they're going to get bigger. When your very first gynecologist says to you, out of the blue, 'Do you feel unfeminine because of your small breasts, dear?' you begin to think they're a bit on the small side."

"I'm basically satisfied with my large breasts (32D)...but since I started going braless two years ago, I find that my breasts attract undue and undesired attention and add to my feelings of self-consciousness."

"In my 22 years I'd never met a man who wasn't foaming at the mouth over big boobs. Not until I met my husband did I realize that even a girl with small breasts can be considered sexy and attractive."

But such letters were the exception to the rule. Only one female respondent in four is dissatisfied with her breasts, and only nine percent are very dissatisfied. And to our considerable surprise, only 15 percent of the men worry about the size of their penises; barely six percent are very dissatisfied.

Apparently, popular discussion has overemphasized the concern that men and women have about the size and appearance of sex organs, or, again, we drew an unusually satisfied group. Possibly, the respondents were denying their concern, but we think this interpretation less likely because of the anonymity of the questionnaires. ("I've admitted a lot of things to you that I don't even admit to myself," confided one reader.) We are encouraged that the percent of adults who might suffer low self-esteem on these grounds is lower than many have assumed....

To say that most of the respondents are satisfied with their overall appearance is not to say that they are happy with all aspects of their bodies. The great concern that society places on a trim figure, especially for females, is reflected in their answers.

Table 1

Satisfaction and Dissatisfaction With Body Parts

	Quite or extremely dissatisfied		Any dissatisfaction		Any satisfaction		Quite or extremely satisfied	
	Female	Male	Female	Male	Female	Male	Female	Male
Overall body appearance	7%	4%	23%	15%	77%	85%	45%	55%
Face Overall facial attractiveness	3	2	11	8	89	92	61	61
Hair	6	6	19	20	81	80	53	58
Eyes	1	1	6	7	94	93	80	81
Ears	2	1	7	5	93	95	83	82
Nose	5	2	23	16	77	84	55	64
Mouth	2	1	7	6	93	94	73	75
Teeth	11	10	30	28	70	72	50	46
Voice	3	3	18	15	82	85	55	58
Chin	4	3	13	11	87	89	67	69
Complexion	8	7	28	22	72	78	48	58
Extremities Shoulders	2	3	13	11	87	89	68	67
Arms	5	2	16	13	84	87	62	62
Hands	5	1	19	8	81	92	60	75
Feet	6	3	20	11	80	89	57	70
Mid torso Size of abdomen	19	11	50	36	50	64	29	42
Buttocks (seat)	17	6	43	20	57	80	37	56
Hips (upper thighs)	22	3	49	12	51	88	32	64
Legs and ankles	8	4	25	11	75	89	52	69
Height, weight and tone Height	3	3	13	13	87	87	72	67
Weight	21	10	48	35	52	65	31	43
General muscle tone or development	9	7	30	25	70	75	38	45

Almost half of the women and about one third of the men said they are un-happy with their weight, and twice as many women as men are *very* dissatisfied (21 percent to 10 percent). Perhaps because excess weight tends to settle in the mid-torso area—abdomen, buttocks, hips and thighs—people who were unhappy about their weight were also unhappy about these particular body parts. Women may not be worrying about the size of their breasts, but they are worrying about the size of their *hips*—49 percent are dissatisfied. Men may not be worrying about penis size, but some 36 percent fret over that spare-tire problem. Among all respondents, those who are happy with their weight are also more satisfied with their bodies.

We also expected to find widespread dissatisfaction with height—with men wanting to be tall and women afraid of being too tall. Not so. Only 13 percent of both sexes expressed any discontent with their height, and actual height was not related to body satisfaction.

THE BODY AND THE SELF

Body image is part of a larger self-concept, which includes identities based on marriage, job, friendships and other roles. The self concept, wrote theorist Charles Horton Cooley, develops out of the reflected appraisals others have of us. People respond not only to what we say and do, but also to our appearance—clothes, grooming, physical attributes. We form opinions of our abilities, emotional states, and attractiveness largely from the feedback we get from others. Often their reactions are indirect, but we rarely misunderstand them.

Gregory Stone, a colleague at the University of Minnesota, has studied the role of appearance in social transactions. He asserts that just as people often rehearse the words they will say prior to a new situation, so they rehearse the presentation of their physical selves—they will check themselves out in a mirror, seeking assurance from a quick self-appraisal.

The preadolescent years are critical in the development of the self-concept generally, and of one's body image in particular. Children can be painfully honest and painfully cruel to one of their number who is too fat, too freckled, too skinny, too odd. "When I was a child, I wished for long, straight, black hair. Mine was extremely curly-frizzy and blonde. I hated it then—no shine, no control, no doing what the other kids did with their hair," wrote one woman.

Table 2

Percent of Respondents with Below-Average
Body Image Teased as Children

	Never	Sometimes	Frequently
Women	25	31	37
Men	15	26	27

We expected that a person who got such taunts as a child would incorporate them into a negative body image that might last for years. We asked readers whether their peers had made fun of them or rejected them for any aspect of their appearance when they were children. And we asked them to rate their attractiveness as children relative to that of their peers. It seems that childhood teasing has a lasting effect. People who were teased as children and who felt homely are less satisfied with their bodies as adults.

Our own experiences indicated that boys are much more likely to be the initiators and recipients of such taunts than girls, and we were right. The relationship between having been made fun of as a child and later body image was stronger for males than for females. Apparently being overweight was the main reason for ridicule. "The horror of being 14 and standing in front of that mirror and seeing the skinny person crying in the disguise of a fat boy, was the first time I saw the realities of life," wrote one young man. "I realized that no one, absolutely no one, would ever love me, a fat slob. The next month I lost 30 pounds." But for men there was also a relationship between childhood taunts and present dissatisfaction with their faces, indicating that their weight was not the only thing that bothered some of them as boys.

One reader aptly pointed out that we did not ask about the effects of parents on their children's body image. "My mother had a few pet names for me such as 'prune face,' and 'garbage disposal,' " she wrote. "These comments had more of an influence on me than anything my peers had to say."

GOOD LOOKS AND SELF-ESTEEM

In their studies of body image done in the 1950s, Paul Secord and Sidney Jourard found that college students who had negative body images also tended to have low self-esteem. Our survey gave us the opportunity to test this relationship on a more diverse group of people. . . .

We found that for both sexes, body image is strongly related to self-esteem. Only 11 percent of those with a below-average body image (compared to 50 percent of those with an above-average body image) had an above-average level of self-esteem. We also looked at the links between satisfaction with various parts of the body and self-esteem, and found that, for both sexes, the face makes the difference. People who are satisfied with their faces are more self-confident.

For males, the body part that had the second strongest impact on self-esteem is the chest; for females, the second most important factor was the mid-torso area, reflecting their worry about weight. Satisfaction with sex organs or torso was not significantly related to self-esteem for men or women. This provides further evidence that the importance of penis size and breast size is exaggerated in this society; our respondents paid little attention to size of sex organs. A woman's self-esteem relates to her feeling pretty and slim; a man's self-esteem relates to being handsome and having a muscular chest.

Most psychologists have overlooked the connection between body image and self-esteem. Obviously, body image is only one component of self-esteem; a person's assessment of his or her abilities and other attributes is equally important. Some respondents felt that other sources of self-esteem can supersede the relevance of body image; looks don't matter, runs this view, since I'm bright/talented/charming or whatever.

Of course, one trouble with survey findings is that we cannot determine cause and effect. A positive body image may increase a person's self-esteem, or basic self-esteem may lead a person to feel good about his or her body. Our readers themselves disagreed on what causes what:

"Body image is so important. If I had been plain instead of pretty I would be a much weaker and sadder person."

"I rather like my body, imperfect though it is. My body gets more and more pleasing as I grow more self-assured and begin to like myself more."

"My own opinion of my physical faults doesn't seem to matter. Especially as I get older. I could be clubfooted and cross-eyed but that wouldn't matter cuz there's *me* inside . . ."

Or it may be that the groundwork for *both* positive body image and high self-esteem is set early in life. "I have a childhood bank of positive responses to draw on," said one happy woman. "Probably it is because I was little and cute and jolly and bright in my youth that I'm able to ignore it now."

Table 3

In comparison with "average person," respondent feels more:	Body image is:		
	Above average	Average	Below average
Likeable	69	54	40
Intelligent	86	75	69
Assertive	60	45	30

Self-esteem—the general feeling that one is competent and confident—spills over into other areas of personality. Respondents who have above average positive body images also consider themselves to be more likeable, assertive, conscientious and even more intelligent than the "average person." For example, of those who rate their body images as above average, 69 percent also indicate that they're more likeable than the average person, compared to 40 percent of those who rate their body images below average.

People who are happy with their bodies may actually be more assertive and likeable than those who have negative body images. Or they *think* they are. One young man explained that in the last year his body image has changed very much for the better, as a result of his personal development: "I've gone from considering myself some sort of asshole to believing that I'm a charismatic individual nearly impossible to dislike...I have more friends than I know what to do with."

SEX AND THE BODY

Some respondents may have chosen to deny, for themselves, the importance of body image in contributing to self-esteem and happy sex lives, but they are wrong when it comes to most people. Positive body image was strongly related to sexual satisfaction. Men and women who like their bodies have had more sexual partners, have more sexual activity, and enjoy sex more than those who have negative body images.

People who are dissatisfied with their bodies also tend to find it "difficult to relate well to persons of the opposite sex," and to agree that *one or more of my body features probably makes me a poor sex partner* (although one respondent amended: "if you would have asked me *which* body feature, I would have answered, 'My mind' ").

Most surprising to us was that men who are dissatisfied with their bodies also tend to feel uncomfortable around other men. Body image and discomfort with the same sex were not so strongly linked for women. This finding completely contradicts the stereotype, which says that women are always comparing themselves physically to other women and worrying about the results. Instead it turns out that men are the worriers. We hypothesize that men try to gain power and enhance their status in relation to other men in literally a physical way. Men may need to feel that they look big and powerful in order to impress other men; perhaps women rely upon clothes and style rather than upon body attributes to compare themselves to other women.

Contrary to the *Playboy* ideal of the single man as carefree, sexy, and free-wheeling, bachelors in this sample tended to be more dissatisfied with their bodies than married men did. There was no difference between single and married women. Apparently unmarried males are concerned about sexual performance: the lower their body-image score, the more they felt that some body feature makes them poor sexual partners, and the more dissatisfied they were about penis size and shape.

We don't really know why this finding should be so, except that sexual performance is more of a worry to single men than to married men or women. Perhaps they are single precisely because they are apprehensive about sex and their bodies, and thereby avoid intimate relationships with women; perhaps the current life-style of the single man fosters such apprenhension. Women, by contrast, are permitted, indeed *supposed* to await male initiative.

BEAUTY, THE BODY, AND SOUL

George Bernard Shaw once noted that "beauty is all very well, but who ever looks at it when it has been in the house three days?" The answer is, almost everybody. Our respondents strongly agreed that physical attractiveness is important in getting along with others, in acquiring mates, in having good sex lives, in feeling satisfied with themselves. Good looks were important to respondents from small towns and large cities, to people who have traveled widely and those who have stayed home, to people who deal constantly with strangers and those who work with friends.

Personality and self-esteem do not rest exclusively on satisfaction with one's body, but neither is the body an irrelevant shell in which the soul happens to live. We treat beautiful people differently from the way we treat homely ones, and denying this truth will not make a person's looks less important.

PROBES

How do you view your body? Is your view of your body similar to the majority of views reported here?

Are you in touch with the way your body image affects your communication—for example, your ways of initiating relationships, responding to others, communicating your sexuality?

Is body image part of the image Boulding discussed in Chapter 1? Or is it an entirely different thing?

What relationships do you see between this discussion of body image and the comments about nonverbal communication in Chapter 3? More specifically, how do you see body image affecting proxemics? How does your body image affect the way you communicate via touch?

Some of the ways that I have kept myself out of touch with my body:

Consulting a clock to see if I have had enough sleep.

Trying to recall how much I have eaten in order to know how much I want to eat now.

Putting on glasses when my eyes hurt (instead of resting them).

Using aspirin and antacids.

Wearing loose clothes so that I won't feel the objectional contours of my body.

Putting thick soles and heels between me and the ground.

Breathing through my mouth (which has no sense of smell).

Using strong chemicals to prevent my body from perspiring and having its natural odor.

Never brushing up against a stranger in a crowd.

Holding myself back from touching people when I talk to them.

Not looking at the parts of another person's body that I want to look at.

HUGH PRATHER

Psychologist Carl Rogers has influenced many of the persons who have written selections in this book. I highly recommend that you read at least one of his books—for example, *On Becoming a Person, Person to Person: The Process of Becoming Human,* or *Freedom to Learn.*

This article is not an analysis of self or a report of findings about it. Instead, it's a thoughtful comment by one individual about what's important to him. I especially resonate with the way he talks about the importance of "permitting" himself to understand another person and "opening channels whereby others can communicate their feelings, their private perceptual world, to me." I have also found it to be true for me, as it is for Rogers, that things work better when I avoid my tendency to "rush in to fix things." And I'm struck by the accuracy of the apparent paradox: "What is most personal is most general."

It seems to me that the attitudes and qualities Rogers is talking about here are those that enhance interpersonal communication. By getting to know which ones you cannot yet completely accept or achieve, you can get a clearer picture of what aspects of your own interpersonal communication could be improved.

SOME SIGNIFICANT LEARNINGS

Carl R. Rogers

I would like to make it very plain that these are learnings which have significance for *me*. I do not know whether they would hold true for you. I have no desire to present them as a guide for anyone else. Yet I have found that when another person has been willing to tell me something of his inner directions this has been of value to me, if only in sharpening my realization that my directions are different. So it is in that spirit that I offer the learnings which follow. In each case I believe they became a part of my actions and inner convictions long before I realized them consciously. They are certainly scattered learnings, and incomplete. I can only say that they are and have been very important to me. I continually learn and relearn them. I frequently fail to act in terms of them, but later I wish that I had. Frequently I fail to see a new situation as one in which some of these learnings might apply.

They are not fixed. They keep changing. Some seem to be acquiring a strong emphasis, others are perhaps less important to me than at one time, but they are all, to me, significant.

I will introduce each learning with a phrase or sentence which gives something of its personal meaning. Then I will elaborate on it a bit. There is not much organization to what follows except that the first learnings have to do mostly with relationships to others. There follow some that fall in the realm of personal values and convictions.

I might start off these several statements of significant learnings with a negative item. *In my relationships with persons I have found that it does not*

From *On Becoming A Person: A Therapist's View of Psychotherapy*, by Carl R. Rogers, pp. 15–27. Copyright © 1970 by Houghton Mifflin Company. Reprinted by permission of Houghton Mifflin Co. and Constable Publishers (London).

help, in the long run, to act as though I were something that I am not. It does not help to act calm and pleasant when actually I am angry and critical. It does not help to act as though I know the answers when I do not. It does not help to act as though I were a loving person if actually, at the moment, I am hostile. It does not help for me to act as though I were full of assurance, if actually I am frightened and unsure. Even on a very simple level I have found that this statement seems to hold. It does not help for me to act as though I were well when I feel ill.

What I am saying here, put in another way, is that I have not found it to be helpful or effective in my relationships with other people to try to maintain a façade; to act in one way on the surface when I am experiencing something quite different underneath. It does not, I believe, make me helpful in my attempts to build up constructive relationships with other individuals. I would want to make it clear that while I feel I have learned this to be true, I have by no means adequately profited from it. In fact, it seems to me that most of the mistakes I make in personal relationships, most of the times in which I fail to be of help to other individuals, can be accounted for in terms of the fact that I have, for some defensive reason, behaved in one way at a surface level, while in reality my feelings run in a contrary direction.

A second learning might be stated as follows—*I find I am more effective when I can listen acceptantly to myself, and can be myself.* I feel that over the years I have learned to become more adequate in listening to *myself;* so that I know, somewhat more adequately than I used to, what I am feeling at any given moment—to be able to realize I *am* angry, or that I *do* feel rejecting toward this person; or that I feel very full of warmth and affection for this individual; or that I am bored and uninterested in what is going on; or that I am eager to understand this individual or that I am anxious and fearful in my relationship to this person. All of these diverse attitudes are feelings which I think I can listen to in myself. One way of putting this is that I feel I have become more adequate in letting myself *be* what I *am.* It becomes easier for me to accept myself as a decidedly imperfect person, who by no means functions at all times in the way in which I would like to function.

This must seem to some like a very strange direction in which to move. It seems to me to have value because the curious paradox is that when I accept myself as I am, then I change. I believe that I have learned this from my clients as well as within my own experience—that we cannot change, we cannot move away from what we are, until we thoroughly *accept* what we are. Then change seems to come about almost unnoticed.

Another result which seems to grow out of being myself is that relationships then become real. Real relationships have an exciting way of being vital and meaningful. If I can accept the fact that I am annoyed at or bored by this client or this student, then I am also much more likely to be able to accept his feelings in response. I can also accept the changed experience and the changed feelings which are then likely to occur in me and in him. Real relationships tend to change rather than to remain static.

So I find it effective to let myself be what I am in my attitudes; to know when I have reached my limit of endurance or of tolerance, and to accept that as a fact; to know when I desire to mold or manipulate people, and to accept that as a fact in myself. I would like to be as acceptant of these feelings as of feelings of warmth, interest, permissiveness, kindness, understanding, which are also a very real part of me. It is when I do accept all these attitudes as a fact, as a part of me, that my relationship with the other person then becomes what it is, and is able to grow and change more readily.

I come now to a central learning which has had a great deal of significance for me. I can state this learning as follows: *I have found it of enormous value when I can permit myself to understand another person.* The way in which I have worded this statement may seem strange to you. Is it necessary to *permit* oneself to understand another? I think that it is. Our first reaction to most of the statements which we hear from other people is an immediate evaluation, or judgment, rather than an understanding of it. When someone expresses some feeling or attitude or belief, our tendency is, almost immediately, to feel "That's right"; or "That's stupid"; "That's abnormal"; "That's unreasonable"; "That's incorrect"; "That's not nice." Very rarely do we permit ourselves to *understand* precisely what the meaning of his statement is to him. I believe this is because understanding is risky. If I let myself really understand another person, I might be changed by that understanding. And we all fear change. So as I say, it is not an easy thing to permit oneself to understand an individual, to enter thoroughly and completely and empathically into his frame of reference. It is also a rare thing.

To understand is enriching in a double way. I find, when I am working with clients in distress, that to understand the bizarre world of a psychotic individual, or to understand and sense the attitudes of a person who feels that life is too tragic to bear, or to understand a man who feels that he is a worthless and inferior individual—each of these understandings somehow enriches me. I learn from these experiences in ways that change me, that make me a different and, I think, a more responsive person. Even more important, perhaps, is the fact that my understanding of these individuals permits them to change. It permits them to accept their own fears and bizarre thoughts and tragic feelings and discouragements, as well as their moments of courage and kindness and love and sensitivity. And it is their experience as well as mine that when someone fully understands those feelings, this enables them to accept those feelings in themselves. Then they find both the feelings and themselves changing. Whether it is understanding a woman who feels that very literally she has a hook in her head by which others lead her about, or understanding a man who feels that no one is as lonely, no one is as separated from others as he, I find these understandings to be of value to me. But also, and even more importantly, to be understood has a very positive value to these individuals.

Here is another learning which has had importance for me. *I have found it enriching to open channels whereby others can communicate their feelings, their private perceptual worlds, to me.* Because understanding is rewarding, I would like to reduce the barriers between others and me, so that they can, if they wish, reveal themselves more fully.

In the therapeutic relationship there are a number of ways by which I can make it easier for the client to communicate himself. I can by my own attitudes create a safety in the relationship which makes such communication more possible. A sensitiveness of understanding which sees him as he is to himself, and accepts him as having those perceptions and feelings, helps too.

But as a teacher also I have found that I am enriched when I can open channels through which others can share themselves with me. So I try, often not too successfully, to create a climate in the classroom where feelings can be expressed, where people can differ—with each other and with the instructor. I have also frequently asked for "reaction sheets" from students—in which they can express themselves individually and personally regarding the course. They can tell of the way it is or is not meeting their needs, they can express their feelings regarding the instructor, or can tell of the personal difficulties they are having in relation to the course. These reaction sheets have no relation whatsoever to their grade. Sometimes the same sessions of a course are experienced in diametrically opposite ways. One student says, "My feeling is one of indefinable revulsion with the tone of this class." Another, a foreign student, speaking of the same week of the same course says, "Our class follows the best, fruitful and scientific way of learning. But for people who have been taught for a long, long time, as we have, by the lecture type, authoritative method, this new procedure is ununderstandable. People like us are conditioned to hear the instructor, to keep passively our notes and memorize his reading assignments for the exams. There is no need to say that it takes a long time for people to get rid of their habits regardless of whether or not their habits are sterile, infertile, and barren." To open myself to these sharply different feelings has been a deeply rewarding thing.

I have found the same thing true in groups where I am the administrator, or perceived as the leader. I wish to reduce the need for fear or defensiveness, so that people can communicate their feelings freely. This has been most exciting, and has led me to a whole new view of what administration can be. But I cannot expand on that here.

There is another very important learning which has come to me in my counseling work. I can voice this learning very briefly. *I have found it highly rewarding when I can accept another person.*

I have found that truly to accept another person and his feelings is by no means an easy thing, any more than is understanding. Can I really permit another person to feel hostile toward me? Can I accept his anger as a real and legitimate part of himself? Can I accept him when he views life and its problems in a way quite different from mine? Can I accept him when he feels very positively toward me, admiring me and wanting to model himself after me? All this is involved in acceptance, and it does not come easy. I believe that it is an increasingly common pattern in our culture for each one of us to believe, "Every other person must feel and think and believe the same as I do." We find it very hard to permit our children or our parents or our spouses to feel differently than we do about particular issues or problems. We cannot permit our clients or our students to differ from us or to utilize their experience in their own individual ways. On a national scale, we cannot permit another nation to think or feel differently than we do. Yet it has come to seem to me that this separateness of individuals, the right of each individual to utilize his experience in his own way and to discover his own meanings in it,—this is one of the most priceless potentialities of life. Each person is an island unto himself, in a very real sense; and he can only build bridges to other islands if he is first of all willing to be himself and permitted to be himself. So I find that when I can accept another person, which means specifically accepting the feelings and attitudes and beliefs that he has as a real and vital part of him, then I am assisting him to become a person: and there seems to me great value in this.

The next learning I want to state may be difficult to communicate. It is this. *The more I am open to the realities in me and in the other person, the less do I find myself wishing to rush in to "fix things."* As I try to listen to myself and the experiencing going on in me, and the more I try to extend that same listening attitude to another person, the more respect I feel for the complex processes of life. So I become less and less inclined to hurry in to fix things, to set goals, to mold people, to manipulate and push them in the way that I would like them to go. I am much more content simply to be myself and to let another person be himself. I know very well that this must seem like a strange, almost an Oriental point of view. What is life for if we are not going to do things to people? What is life for if we are not going to mold them to our purposes? What is life for if we are not going to teach them the things that *we* think they should learn? What is life for if we are not going to make them think and feel as we do? How can anyone hold such an inactive point of view as the one I am expressing? I am sure that attitudes such as these must be a part of the reaction of many of you.

Yet the paradoxical aspect of my experience is that the more I am simply willing to be myself, in all this complexity of life, and the more I am willing to understand and accept the realities in myself and in the other person, the more change seems to be stirred up. It is a very paradoxical thing—that to the degree that each one of us is willing to be himself, then he finds not only himself changing; but he finds that other people to whom he relates are also changing. At least this is a very vivid part of my experience, and one of the deepest things I think I have learned in my personal and professional life.

Let me turn now to some other learnings which are less concerned with relationships, and have more to do with my own actions and values. The first of these is very brief. *I can trust my experience.*

One of the basic things which I was a long time in realizing, and which I am still learning, is that when an activity *feels* as though it is valuable or worth doing, it *is* worth doing. Put another way, I have learned that my total organismic sensing of a situation is more trustworthy than my intellect.

All of my professional life I have been going in directions which others thought were foolish, and about which I have had many doubts myself. But I have never regretted moving in directions which "felt right," even though I have often felt lonely or foolish at the time.

I have found that when I have trusted some inner non-intellectual sensing, I have discovered wisdom in the move. In fact I have found that when I have followed one of these unconventional paths because it felt right or true, then in five or ten years many of my colleagues have joined me, and I no longer need to feel alone in it.

As I gradually come to trust my total reactions more deeply, I find that I can use them to guide my thinking. I have come to have more respect for those vague thoughts which occur in me from time to time, which *feel* as though they were significant. I am inclined to think that these unclear thoughts or hunches will lead me to important areas. I think of it as trusting the totality of my experience, which I have learned to suspect is wiser than my intellect. It is fallible, I am sure, but I believe it to be less fallible than my conscious mind alone. My attitude is very well expressed by Max Weber, the artist, when he says, "In carrying on my own humble creative effort, I depend greatly upon that which I do not yet know, and upon that which I have not yet done."

Very closely related to this learning is a corollary that, *evaluation by others is not a guide for me*. The judgments of others, while they are to be listened to, and taken into account for what they are, can never be a guide for me. This has been a hard thing to learn. I remember how shaken I was, in the early days, when a scholarly thoughtful man who seemed to me a much more competent and knowledgeable psychologist than I, told me what a mistake I was making by getting interested in psychotherapy. It could never lead anywhere, and as a psychologist I would not even have the opportunity to practice it.

In later years it has sometimes jolted me a bit to learn that I am, in the eyes of some others, a fraud, a person practicing medicine without a license, the author of a very superficial and damaging sort of therapy, a power seeker, a mystic, etc. And I have been equally disturbed by equally extreme praise. But I have not been too much concerned because I have come to feel that only one person (at least in my lifetime, and perhaps ever) can know whether what I am doing is honest, thorough, open, and sound, or false and defensive and unsound, and I am that person. I am happy to get all sorts of evidence regarding what I am doing and criticism (both friendly and hostile) and praise (both sincere and fawning) are a part of such evidence. But to weigh this evidence and to determine its meaning and usefulness is a task I cannot relinquish to anyone else.

In view of what I have been saying the next learning will probably not surprise you. *Experience is, for me, the highest authority*. The touchstone of validity is my own experience. No other person's ideas, and none of my own ideas, are as authoritative as my experience. It is to experience that I must return again and again, to discover a closer approximation to truth as it is in the process of becoming in me.

Neither the Bible nor the prophets—neither Freud nor research—neither the revelations of God nor man—can take precedence over my own direct experience.

My experience is the more authoritative as it becomes more primary, to use the semanticist's term. Thus the hierarchy of experience would be most authoritative at its lowest level. If I read a theory of psychotherapy, and if I formulate a theory of psychotherapy based on my work with clients, and if I also have a direct experience of psychotherapy with a client, then the degree of authority increases in the order in which I have listed these experiences.

My experience is not authoritative because it is infallible. It is the basis of authority because it can always be checked in new primary ways. In this way its frequent error or fallibility is always open to correction.

Now another personal learning. *I enjoy the discovering of order in experience*. It seems inevitable that I seek for the meaning or the orderliness or lawfulness in any large body of experience. It is this kind of curiosity, which I find it very satisfying to pursue, which has led me to each of the major formulations I have made. It led me to search for the orderliness in all the conglomeration of things clinicians did for children, and out of that came my book on *The Clinical Treatment of the Problem Child*. It led me to formulate the general principles which seemed to be operative in psychotherapy, and that has led to several books and many articles. It has led me into research to test the various types of lawfulness which I feel I have encountered in my experience. It has enticed me to construct theories to bring together the orderliness of that which has already been experienced and to project this order forward into new and unexplored realms where it may be further tested.

Thus I have come to see both scientific research and the process of theory construction as being aimed toward the inward ordering of significant experience. Research is the persistent disciplined effort to make sense and order out of the phenomena of subjective experience. It is justified because it is satisfying to perceive the world as having order, and because rewarding results often ensue when one understands the orderly relationships which appear in nature.

So I have come to recognize that the reason I devote myself to research, and to the building of theory, is to satisfy a need for perceiving order and meaning, a subjective need which exists in me. I have, at times, carried on research for other reasons—to satisfy others, to convince opponents and sceptics, to get ahead professionally, to gain prestige, and for other unsavory reasons. These errors in judgment and activity have only served to convince me more deeply that there is only one sound reason for pursuing scientific activities, and that is to satisfy a need for meaning which is in me.

Somewhere here I want to bring in a learning which has been most rewarding, because it makes me feel so deeply akin to others. I can word it this way. *What is most personal is most general.* There have been times when in talking with students or staff, or in my writing, I have expressed myself in ways so personal that I have felt I was expressing an attitude which it was probable no one else could understand, because it was so uniquely my own. Two written examples of this are the Preface to *Client-Centered Therapy* (regarded as most unsuitable by the publishers), and an article on "Persons or Science." In these instances I have almost invariably found that the very feeling which has seemed to me most private, most personal, and hence most incomprehensible by others, has turned out to be an expression for which there is a resonance in many other people. It has led me to believe that what is most personal and unique in each one of us is probably the very element which would, if it were shared or expressed, speak most deeply to others. This has helped me to understand artists and poets as people who have dared to express the unique in themselves.

There is one deep learning which is perhaps basic to all of the things I have said thus far. It has been forced upon me by more than twenty-five years of trying to be helpful to individuals in personal distress. It is simply this. *It has been my experience that persons have a basically positive direction.* In my deepest contacts with individuals in therapy, even those whose troubles are most disturbing, whose behavior has been most antidsocial, whose feelings seem most abnormal, I find this to be true. When I can sensitively understand the feelings which they are expressing, when I am able to accept them as separate persons in their own right, then I find that they tend to move in certain directions. And what are these directions in which they tend to move? The words which I believe are most truly descriptive are words such as positive, constructive, moving towards self-actualization, growing toward maturityn growing toward socialization. I have come to feel that the more fully the individual is understood and accepted, the more he tends to drop the false fronts with which he has been meeting life, and the more he tends to move in a direction which is forwardm

I would not want to be misunderstood on this. I do not have a Pollyanna view of human nature. I am quite aware that out of defensiveness and inner fear individuals can and do behave in ways which are incredibly cruel, horribly destructive, immature, regressive, anti-social, hurtful. Yet one of the most refreshing and invigorating parts of my experience is to work with such individuals and to discover the strongly positive directional tendencies which exist in them, as in all of us, at the deepest levels.

Let me bring this long list to a close with one final learning which can be stated very briefly. *Life, at its best, is a flowing, changing process in which nothing is fixed.* In my clients and in myself I find that when life is richest and most rewarding it is a flowing process. To experience this is both fascinating and a little frightening. I find I am at my best when I can let the flow of my experience carry me, in a direction which appears to be forward, toward goals of which I am but dimly aware. In thus floating with the complex stream of my experiencing, and in trying to understand its ever-changing complexity, it should be evident that there are no fixed points. When I am thus able to be in process, it is clear that there can be no closed system of beliefs, no unchanging set of principles which I hold. Life is guided by a changing understanding of and interpretation of my experience. It is always in process of becoming.

I trust it is clear now why there is no philosophy or belief or set of principles which I could encourage or persuade others to have or hold. I can only try to live by *my* interpretation of the current meaning of *my* experience, and try to give others the permission and freedom to develop their own inward freedom and thus their own meaningful interpretation of their own experience.

If there is such a thing as truth, this free individual process of search should, I believe, converge toward it. And in a limited way, this is also what I seem to have experienced.

PROBES

Rogers's learnings become most useful when you ask yourself the questions he implies. Do *you* find it best not to act as though you were something that you aren't? Can you listen acceptantly to your self? Can you permit your self to understand another person? Can you reduce the barriers between your self and others? Do you trust your experience? Can you believe that persons have a basically positive direction? Can you see how your responses to those questions directly affect your communicating?

You might want to relate what Rogers says here about acceptance and listening to the ideas about empathic listening in Chapter 8.

Rogers's convictions that he can trust his experience also seem to me to relate to what Boulding says about image in Chapter 1.

When I first began trying to be myself, I at times felt trapped by my feelings. I thought that I was stuck with the feelings I had, that I couldn't change them, and shouldn't try to even if I could. I saw many negative feelings inside me that I didn't want, and yet I felt that I must express them if I were going to be myself.

Since then I have realized that my feelings do change and that I can have a hand in changing them. They change simply by my becoming aware of them. When I acknowledge my feelings they become more positive. And they change when I express them. For example, if I tell a man I don't like him, I usually like him better.

The second thing I have realized is that my not wanting to express a negative feeling is a feeling in itself, a part of me, and if I want not to express the negative feeling more than I do, than I will be acting more like myself by not expressing it.

HUGH PRATHER

5

PERCEIVING OTHERS

When I'm critical of another person, when I see his behavior as a "fault," my attitude includes these feelings: I think of him as one thing (instead of having many parts). I dislike him. I "just can't understand" his action. He seems unjustified. And I think he "knows better." If I feel this way I am in reality seeing my own self-condemnation. "Fault" means failure to meet a standard. Whose? Mine. Another person's behavior is "bad" or "understandable" according to my experience with myself. My criticism of him amounts to: If I had said that or acted that way I would think of myself as selfish, opinionated, immature, etc. A part of me wants to act that way or thinks of myself as acting that way and condemns this. If I understood why I act like that, or want to, and had forgiven myself for it, I wouldn't be condemning this person now. I'm getting upset with him because there is something in me I don't understand and haven't yet accepted.

HUGH PRATHER

It seems to me that a recurrent barrier to interpersonal communication is our tendency to perceive people as if they were mechanisms or objects which can, as Paul Tournier says, "be confined within concepts, formulae, and definitions."

You and I depersonalize people whenever we treat them as if they could adequately be described by our stereotypes or generalizations. Tournier explains how seeing others as persons instead of as things can mean a "complete revolution" for some. Although he takes examples from his experience as a counselor and doctor, his ideas apply to your communication and to mine too. When we stop seeing only what Tournier calls "personages," or objectified others, and start seeing "persons," all kinds of changes are likely to take place. We can see teacher-student communication differently. Communication with family members can change. As Tournier puts it, "the atmosphere of office, workshop, or laboratory" can be "rapidly transformed when personal fellowship is established."

It goes without saying that we can't communicate person to person *all* of the time. Sometimes external factors—time, rigid roles, ignorance, fear—prevent it. Some situations call for idea-centered more than person-centered contacts. But, Tournier says, we should learn to "answer idea with idea but answer the person with the person." That is, we should know the difference between communicating interpersonally and noninterpersonally so we can strive for the former whenever it is possible.

THE WORLD OF THINGS AND THE WORLD OF PERSONS

Paul Tournier

There are two worlds, or ways of looking at the world, of entering into relationship with it, depending on the spirit in which we approach it. We may see in it nothing but things, mechanisms, from those of physics to those of biology and even of psychology. Art, philosophy, religion can also become things, collections of concepts, formulae, definitions. On the other hand, one can lay oneself open to the world of persons, awaken to the sense of the person. By becoming oneself a person one discovers other persons round about, and one seeks to establish a personal bond with them.

The person always eludes our grasp; it is never static. It refuses to be confined within concepts, formulae, and definitions. It is not a thing to be encompassed, but a point of attraction, a guiding force, a direction, an attitude, which demands from us a corresponding attitude, which moves us to action and commits us. The world of things does not commit us. It is neutral, and leaves us neutral. We are cold, objective, impersonal observers, watching the operation of blind and inexorable mechanisms.

I am not claiming that we must shut our eyes to things, nor that we should cut ourselves off from intellectual objectivity, from the fascinating study of the ordinances and mechanisms of things. But I ask that we should not limit ourselves to the study of things, for they are only one half of the world, the static, impassible, unfeeling half. Even the heavenly bodies, moving with their unimaginable velocities, return in their orbits to the same position; this is the universal cycle of things, eternally starting again.

It is the person that has meaning, a birth and an end. The God of the philosophers is immutable; only the personal God has a purpose for history and for each being. To the scientist, man is but an episode in the universal dance of the atoms and the electrons. As the old French song says of the marionettes, "Three little turns, and off they go!" Off they go to dance elsewhere in a purposeless round.

From infant school to university we are taught to know things, to isolate them, identify them, count them, measure them and classify them. There is no need for me to dwell on the enormous development that has taken place over the centuries in this field, so that now specialization within the narrowest limits is the order of the day. This has not been without its effect on our minds. They are becoming incapable of perceiving what is not objective.

In this depersonalized state of mind man himself becomes a thing. Anatomy and physiology study his body as a thing, and psychology his mind as a thing, a mechanism. Economics studies him as a thing, an instrument of production and consumption, while sociology studies him as an element of society. He is a pawn on the chess-board of politics, a cog in industry, a learning-machine, everywhere a fraction of the mass.

...What I want to show now is how this unilateral view of the world and of man is completely upset by the awakening of the sense of the person.... When I turned from ecclesiastical activity to spiritual ministry, from technical to humane medicine, I was discovering the world of persons; I was discovering persons everywhere. Since that time, though I have not stopped being interested in things, I am much more passionately interested in persons.

I remember a visit paid to me by one of my former colleagues on the executive authority of the Church. I had fought him tooth and nail—that is to say, I had treated him as a thing, an adversary. The only thing about him that had mattered to me was his opinions, and the weight they might carry in the balance of our arguments. Ideas by themselves, detached from the person, are but things, abstractions, counters in the give and take of discussion.

And now here he was opening his heart to me. I too opened mine to him. He had come to talk to me about his personal life and his sufferings. I was making the discovery of his person, which I had never looked for before, I was so busy combating his ideas. I was discovering his person, his secrets, his solitude, his feelings. I even discovered that his ideas were not abstractions, but that they arose out of the sort of person he was, and protected his suffering like a shield. I talked with him about my own personal experiences, and realized that this former adversary had the same needs and the same difficulties as I, the same longing to find life and fellowship again. . . .

A man may spend years in an office, seeing in his employees only their work, their good qualities and their failings, and then, when personal contact is established, suddenly discover what lies behind the façade: the secret sufferings, the sequels of unhappy childhood, disappointed hopes, struggles to remain faithful to ideals. Then, too, he may understand the profound significance of the qualities and failings he has seen, and the meaning that work can have when it is no longer a thing but the activity of a community of persons.

It is as if a light had shone on life and shown it up in new colours. "We live," wrote Saint-Exupery, "not on things, but on the meaning of things." The meaning of things is of the order of the person. When our eyes are open to the world of persons, things themselves become personal. It is just the reverse of the transformation of men into things of which we were speaking just now. Beasts, plants, and inanimate things take on the quality of persons. . . .

To become a person, to discover the world of persons, to acquire the sense of the person, to be more interested in people as persons than in their ideas, their party labels, their personage, means a complete revolution, changing the climate of our lives. Once adopted, it is an attitude which rapidly impregnates the whole of our lives. While at the Weissenstein conference I had occasion to congratulate one of my colleagues who had made an extremely good job of interpreting a talk I had given earlier in the day. "And do you know why?" he asked me. "It had been mentioned to me that one of our Scandinavian friends was finding it very troublesome following the speeches in foreign languages. So I interpreted for *him*; I never took my eyes off him, watching his face all the time to see if he had understood. And I found that through giving more attention to his person than to the ideas I was translating, I actually found it easier to express the ideas."

He had become an interpreter of the person, just as one can be a doctor of the person, or a teacher of the person, when one does not teach that impersonal thing, the class, but the persons of the pupils. In the same way, at a conference, one speaks quite differently if the audience is no longer an anonymous mass, if one seeks in it a few faces and exchanges glances with individuals, so that one's speech takes on the quality of a dialogue.

In the world of persons all one's professional relationships take on a new character. They become shot through with a joy that was absent when they were merely the fulfilling of a function. Everything becomes an occasion for personal contact, a chance to understand others and the personal factors which underlie their behavior, their reactions and opinions. It is much more interesting, as well as important, to understand why someone has a certain failing, than to be irritated by it; to understand why he maintains a certain point of view than to combat it; to listen to confidences than to judge by appearances.

The atmosphere of office, workshop, or laboratory is rapidly transformed when personal fellowship is established betweeen those who previously criticized or ignored each other. In a recent lecture Professor F. Gonseth, professor of philosophy at the Zürich Polytechnic, the pioneer of the review *Dialectia*, spoke of the "law of dialogue" which he believes must govern the university of the future. By this phrase he means personal contact between teacher and student, so that the person is committed in the intellectual dialectic. The condition of this contact and commitment is that the teacher should not be so absorbed in his subject that he forgets all about the persons to whom he wishes to transmit it.

I was with some friends one day, and they were advising me to give more lectures and write less books, for, they said, in my writings they missed the personal accent of the spoken word. As you see, I am not following their advice. However precious one's friends are, one must not become their slave. Being a person means acting according to one's personal convictions, due regard of course being given to those of others. And my friends' observation is true. The living word remains the chief instrument of personal dialogue.

This is clearly seen in the case of those patients who send me beforehand—in writing—a long account of their lives. This is useful as information. But the point is that the purpose of a life-history is not so much to furnish information as to lead toward personal contact. Given by word of mouth it may be less intelligible, less systematic, but it is a method which calls for a much deeper commitment of the person.

I have my patients who write me letters after each consultation. They put in them the things they have not dared to say to my face. This has its value; it is for them a commitment, a way of forcing themselves to become more personal at the next consultation. But it is also a means of sparing themselves the intense emotion of a verbal explanation. It attentuates the dialogue, making it less direct because it uses a thing—paper—as an intermediary.

But even the spoken word itself can become a thing if it adopts the neutral and objective tone of information or discussion. Paradoxical though it may seem, the true dialogue is by no means a discussion. This is my answer to those of my colleagues who are perhaps afraid of not knowing what to reply to a patient who puts to them some moral problem that is on his conscience. It is important here to make a distinction between intellectual argument and personal encounter. Answer ideas with ideas, but answer the person with the person. Then often the heart's true response is silence.

Engaging in the dialogue, in the sense in which we understand it here, does not mean plunging into religious or philosophical theories about life, man, or God. The people who have helped me most are not those who have answered my confessions with advice, exhortation, or doctrine, but rather those who have listened to me in silence, and then told me of their own personal life, their own difficulties and experiences. It is this give and take that makes the dialogue.

If we answer with advice, exhortation, or theories, we are putting ourselves in a position of superiority, not equality. We are concerning ourselves with ideas, and not with the person, confining ourselves to the objective world of things, instead of entering the subjective world of persons. When someone lays bare to me the burning reality of his life, I am well aware that most of my replies could easily be only those of my personage. . . .

The moment the personage reappears, with its system of thought and its claim to possess and express truth, our sincerest efforts to help others will finish by crushing and repressing them instead of liberating them. The dialogue between persons is replaced by a moralizing or proselytizing discussion. "Those who impose upon us their ready-made solutions," writes one of my patients, "those who impose upon us their science or their theology, are incapable of healing us."

You will see now how wide of the mark are those who describe the medicine of the person as "religious psychotherapy," in the belief that it consists in the indoctrination of the patient, denunciation of his failings, in moral uplift, or in exhorting him to accept his lot, and forcing him into confession and prayer. That indeed would be acting as a personage and not as a person. Then we should really be in danger of usurping the place of the minister of religion, and attempting to perform a function which is not proper to us.

The medicine of the person demands unconditional respect for the person of others. That does not mean putting one's own flag in one's pocket, but rather that we must state our convictions in a way that is truly personal, not theoretical, having at the same time a sincere regard for the convictions of others. In this way dialogue becomes possible where previously it has been shipwrecked on the rocks of religious, philosophical, political, or social prejudice. . . .

PROBES

Do you think that Tournier's view is "antiintellectual"? Is he saying, in effect, that we should feel our way into a relationship rather than think our way into it?

The author Saint Exupéry, as you may know, wrote *The Little Prince*. What does his statement, "We live, not on things, but on the meaning of things," say to you?

Would it be a revolutionary change for you to begin to look at the world as a world of persons rather than of things? How would your communication change?

What do you think of the last paragraph in this selection? Do you think that Tournier leaves sufficient room for personal opinion?

You might want to compare Dr. Tournier's attitude toward his patients' written and spoken communication with the ideas about nonverbal communication outlined in Chapter 3.

In the following chapter from a book called *Person Perception*, three social psychologists explain perception in general and then analyze how we perceive other people. They point out that perceiving isn't just a matter of coming into contact with what's "out there." As they put it, "the world is not merely revealed to us; rather, we play an active role in the creation of our experiences" by selecting, structuring, and giving meaning to what we perceive.

When we are perceiving people instead of objects, we select, structure, and give meaning in some special ways. In the first place, we tend to perceive people as *intending* to do what they're doing, as "causal agents" who plan and do in order to achieve some effect. We might believe that *we* often behave spontaneously, without planning or intent, but we don't see others that way. Our perception of people includes the assumption that they somehow "meant to do" whatever they're doing.

We also perceive people as being similar to ourselves. We evaluate them and what they do in part based on our attitudes about ourselves and our behavior.

Moreover, we are continually structuring our perceptions of people by putting them into categories, by stereotyping them. As the authors put it, "in perceiving attributes of another person, we focus not on his behavior, which is ever changing, but on more invariant characteristics, namely, his intents and purposes." We do that so that the other person will "hold still" and thus "make sense" to us.

All of these processes influence how we perceive other people and thus how we communicate with them. We usually don't mean to distort what we perceive, but it's just a fact about the human condition that we *cannot* get in direct contact with the world. What we perceive is always necessarily mediated by our senses, attitudes, expectations, etc. So the challenge is not to stop being subjective in our perceptions—we can't—but to realize what we are doing, make implicit assumptions explicit, and work to go beyond, to move through the initial, stereotyped ways we see people. That's what will help us to perceive, in the words of the preceding article, the *person* instead of just the "personage."

THE ISSUES IN PERSON PERCEPTION

Albert H. Hastorf, David J. Schneider, and Judith Polefka

THE PERCEPTUAL PROCESS

Both philosophers and psychologists have long been intrigued with the nature of the human perceptual process. One explanation for their interest is that man is naturally curious about his contact with the outside world and wonders how his experiences are caused and to what degree they reflect the world accurately. Beyond general curiosity, the reason for the interest stems from an apparent paradox, the basis of which lies in the difference between the nature of our experiences and our knowledge of how those experiences are caused.

. . . The world appears to be given to us in experience. Yet a causal analysis of these events indicates a very different state of affairs.

You have opened your eyes and you experience a blue vase about six inches high situated on a table. The vase appears to be at a certain distance, and its shape and color are equally clear. Let us remind ourselves of the causal events that are involved. Light waves of a certain wavelength are reflected off the vase. Some of them impinge on the retina of your eye, and if enough retinal cells are irritated, some visual nerves will fire and a series of electrical impulses will be carried through the sensory apparatus, including the subcortical centers, and will finally arrive at the cortex. This description paints a picture of a very indirect contact with the world: light waves to retinal events to sensory nerve events to subcortical events and finally to cortical events, from which visual experiences result. What is especially important is that this causal description reveals a very different picture than does our naive description of experience. (This causal description led a famous German physiologist to remark that "we are aware of our nerves, not of objects.") Thus we have a conflict between our everyday-life experiences of objects together with their properties and an analysis of how these experiences come to exist. How *does* the human being create a coherent perceptual world out of chaotic physical impingements?

Our world of experience has structure Let us begin with this fact of experience and explore how the structure may be achieved. First of all, we know that our experiences are ultimately dependent on our sensory apparatus, which for visual experiences would include both the retina of the eye and the sensory neurons connecting the retina to the visual areas of the cortex. This apparatus plays, in a manner of speaking, the role of translator. Light waves impinge on the eyes and we experience color. Sound waves impinge on the ear and we expe-

---

rience pitch. Without the sensory apparatus we would have no contact with the external world. There remains, however, the question of the nature of this translation.

A number of philosophers and psychologists have conceived of the translation process as an essentially passive one, completely determined by the physical properties of the stimulus and by the structure of the receptors and sensory nervous system. They conceive of our sensory apparatus as working somewhat like a high-speed translation device.... This conception has led to arguments as to how much of this dictionary is present at birth and how much is the product of our learning history. One reason for the popularity of the passive recording view of perception is the immediacy and "givenness" of our experience. Our experiences are immediate and they feel direct. These feelings led to the belief that the translation process must be automatic and built in.

The primary argument against that position stems from the fact that our experience of the world is highly selective. If we passively translated and recorded stimuli, our world would be a jumble of experiences: while you were reading a book, you would also be aware of the pressure of your clothes on your body and of all the sounds around you. Actually, from a myriad of impinging stimuli, we are aware of only certain objects and certain attributes of the objects. Anyone who has asked two different persons to describe the same scene has been struck by the fact that they often describe it very differently; each selects different events and different attributes of the events. Given this phenomenon, we must be more than passive translators. In fact, we must be active processors of information. The world is not merely revealed to us; rather, we play an active role in the creation of our experiences.

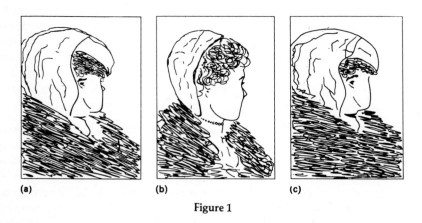

(a)   (b)   (c)

Figure 1

Let us take an example from the research of Robert W. Leeper to illustrate our point. The stimulus he used was an ambiguous picture which can be seen as either an old hag or an attractive young woman (Fig. 1). Continued inspection of the picture usually permits an observer to see first one and then the other. Leeper had the original picture redrawn so that one version emphasized the young woman (b) and another emphasized the old hag (c). Subjects who had been exposed to one or the other of these redrawings found themselves "locked in" on that view when the original ambiguous picture was presented. One hundred percent of the subjects who had had prior experience with the version emphasizing the hag saw the hag and only the hag in their first look at the ambiguous picture; ninety-five percent of the subjects who had had prior experience with the version emphasizing the young woman saw only the young woman when first looking at the same ambiguous picture. The subjects had been given a set to process the input stimuli in a certain way, and they created a structure consistent with that set. Although our experiences are both immediate and structured, extremely complex participation by the organism, including the active selection and processing of stimulus impingements, is involved in their creation.

One of the most salient features of the person's participation in structuring his experiential world can be described as a categorizing process. He extracts stimuli from the world and forces them into a set of categories. We have here a powerful example of the effects of linguistic coding on the structuring of experience. The subjects in Leeper's experiment did not see a complex pattern of light and dark nor even "a person" (a possible category); they saw an old hag or a young woman. The categories we use are derived from our past history and are dependent on our language and our cultural background. . . . Whatever the nature of the categories we use, they play an important role in the processing of information.

We have begun with the experiential fact that our perceptions are both structured and organized. This structure is immediate and appears to be given by the world of objects. . . . These structured perceptions are the outcome of the organism's engaging in active processing of information, which includes the translation of physical impingements to nerve impulses and the active selection and categorizing of the inputs.

Our world of experience has stability When we open our eyes and look at a scene, we are not overwhelmed with constant shifts in the picture as our eyes and our attention wander. There is a certain enduring aspect to our experience. We select certain facets of the situation and stick with them. Check this statement against your own experience with the ambiguous picture in Fig. 1. If it was like the experience of most people, the first organization of the picture, whether it was the old hag or the young woman, continued to demand your attention. It was hard to "find" the other one. You made various attempts to shift the focus of attention by blinking your eyes or by concentrating on a certain part of the picture, but those stratagems did not always work. Although stability in a case of this kind may frustrate us to such an extent that it deserves to be given a different and more pejorative label—rigidity—the example demonstrates that we do *not* experience a world of chaotic instability.

The most obvious example of the maintenance of stability in our experience has been termed *the constancies* in perception....Let us consider an example. You are sitting in a chair in your living room. Another person walks into the room, moves over to a table by the window, picks up a magazine, and then goes across the room to sit down and read it. What are the successive visual-stimulus events impinging on your retina and your successive experiences? Every time the person moves closer to you, the impingement, or *proximal stimulus*, gets larger; in fact, if he moves from 20 feet away to 10 feet away, the height of the image on your eye doubles in size. The opposite occurs as he moves away from you because the size of the retinal image is inversely proportional to the distance of the object from you. Furthermore, when the person moves near the window, more light is available and more light is reflected to the retina. Yet your perception does not fit this description of the stimulus events. While the person is moving about the room, you experience him as remaining relatively constant in size and brightness. In spite of dramatic alterations in the proximal stimulus, you experience a stable world. Given this discrepancy between proximal-stimulus events and experience, the organism must actively process information to produce the stability in his world of experience....

Let us think of the perceptual act as a complex form of problem-solving, the goal of which is to create a stability in which our perceptions bear some relationship to external events. We can then draw an analogy between perceptual problem-solving and scientific problem-solving. Just as the scientist attempts to reduce a complex jumble of events to a small set of variables which serve as a set of determining conditions for a particular event, so we search out the invariant aspects of a situation to produce stable perceptions. The scientist searches for invariance in order to understand and to predict the world; we as perceivers also seek to understand and to predict the world in order that we may behave in it to our advantage. In other words, the perceptual act can be said to generate a prediction that we can use as a basis for action. The goal in both cases is predictably of the environment, and the means to the goal is the specification of causal relationships.

Our world of experience is meaningful The connotation of "meaningful" here is that structured and stable events are not isolated from one another but appear to be related in some orderly fashion over time....It is so common for the world of experience to make sense to us that the most powerful way to point out the importance of the phenomenon is to suggest trying to conceive of a world that does not make sense. Events would follow each other with no apparent causal relationships. Almost every event would entail surprise. Nothing would seem familiar. The general experience would be one of chaos. Such a state of affairs is so alien to our everyday-life experience that it is extremely difficult to imagine. Our experiences usually *are* meaningful in that they are structured and they are stable; they are related in the sense that they seem familiar, but particularly in the sense that events have implications for one another. . . .

We could cite innumerable studies demonstrating the influence on perception of either the individual's past learning or his present motivational state. Leeper's experiment on the young woman–old hag picture is an example of the former. An experiment by Schafer and Murphy provides an example of the effects of motivational state on perception. They presented subjects with a simple ambiguous drawing (Fig. 2) and gave them a small monetary reward when they indicated that they saw one of the profiles but took money away when they indicated that they saw the other. The results indicated that, over time, positive consequences associated with a given perception increased the likelihood of that perception. . . .

In summary, our past experiences and purposes play an absolutely necessary role in providing us with knowledge of the world that has structure, stability, and meaning. Without them, events would not make sense. With them, our perceptions define a predictable world, an orderly stage for us to act on.

THE PERCEPTION OF PEOPLE

Let us now turn our attention more explicitly to the perception of other people. The characteristics of the world of experience in general should hold for our experiences of people, but are there special facets to our experience when we perceive other human beings? Is there not more to our experience of other people than their size, color, and shape? The answer is certainly "Yes."

As an aid in our discussion of person perception, let us consider an example of one person describing another. In *Eminent Victorians*, Lytton Strachey describes Dr. Thomas Arnold, Headmaster of Rugby School:

Such was the man who, at the age of thirty-three, became headmaster of Rugby. His outward appearance was the index of his inward character: everything about him denoted energy, earnestness, and the best intentions. His legs, perhaps, were shorter than they should have been; but the sturdy athletic frame, especially when it was swathed (as it usually was) in the flowing robes of a Doctor of Divinity, was full of an imposing vigour; and his head, set decisively upon the collar, stock, and bands of ecclesiastical tradition, clearly belonged to a person of eminence. The thick, dark clusters of his hair, his bushy eyebrows and curling whiskers, his straight nose and bulky chin, his firm and upward-curving lower lip—all these revealed a temperament of ardour and determination. His eyes were bright and large; they were also obviously honest. And yet—why was it?—Was it in the lines of the mouth or the frown on the forehead?—it was hard to say, but it was unmistakable—there was a slightly puzzled look upon the face of Dr. Arnold.[1]

First of all, this description is a special example of person perception in that it is more organized than many of our experiences in everyday-life, partly, no doubt, because the author is attempting to communicate explicitly his perceptions to others. The author also goes well beyond just providing us with a description of Dr. Arnold's physical characteristics and behavior. Many of the characteristics listed are the result of inferences by the author, and yet they are cast as if they were just as clear and as given in experience as is the individual's physical height. The leap from describing such characteristics as hair color and eyebrows to inferences about "energy" and "ardour and determination" is made with considerable agility. The author also includes statements about Dr. Arnold's intentions; he appeared, at least to Mr. Strachey, as having "the best intentions." This tendency not only to perceive others as having intentions but also to make a value judgment about the intentions is, as we shall see, apparent in our perception of others. The description also includes inferences (stated as perceptual facts) about enduring personality characteristics, such as "honesty" and "eminence." Finally, although the author cannot specify the cues, he infers that Dr. Arnold felt puzzled; he perceives the other's feelings. We can use the characteristics of this description to point out some of the special features of our perception of other people and the ways in which the perception of people differs from the perception of objects. As we noted earlier in our discussion of the constancies, the stimuli produced by objects vary as a function of the conditions under which they are perceived. This is also true of people as stimuli. Furthermore, people behave and behavior is a dynamic rather than a static thing; it is ever-changing and must be carved up into units in order that we may define the stimulus. One of the major ways we separate our ongoing behavior into distinct units is by taking into account behavioral effects. The individual does something and we observe its effect. In essence, the first level of coding in person perception consists of grouping together acts and effects to create manageable perceptual units.

Let us now turn our attention to two very crucial facets of our experience of other people. The first is that we perceive them as *causal agents*. They are potential causes of their behavior. They may intend to do certain things, such as attempting to cause certain effects; and because we see them as one source of their actions, we consider them capable of varying their behavior to achieve their intended effects....Our perception of others' intentionality leads us next to organize the behavior of other people into intent-act-effect segments which form perceptual units. We infer the intentions of another; but we go further. If we perceive a particular intent on several occasions, we are prone to perceive the other as having an enduring personality characteristic. A person who seems to intend to hurt others much of the time will be quickly labeled as hostile. Our verbal label now becomes more abstract because we are categorizing the person according to a characteristic which endures over time.

Second, we perceive other people as similar to ourselves. Hence we are pushed to infer that they possess attributes which, unlike size and behavior, we cannot observe directly but which we are aware of in ourselves. In particular, we perceive others to possess emotional states; we see them as feeling angry, happy, or sad. On some occasions these experiences are of fleeting or temporary states; however, if we perceive them often enough in a person, we code or label that person as having that state as an enduring characteristic; e.g., chronically sad people are depressed.

We can now take a brief look at how our three attributes of experience (structure, stability, and meaning) relate to the perception of people.

Our experiences of other people are structured Just as we create structure in the inanimate world by categorizing stimuli into objects and their attributes, so we create order in the world of people by categorizing them and their behavior. The number of ways that we can categorize people is overwhelmingly large: we can go well beyond any of the possible schemata for inanimate objects. The dictionary, for example, contains thousands of trait names describing ways in which we can perceive people as different. Often we use categories which have been functional in the past. The football coach will employ very different categories for perceiving members of the freshman class than will the Dean of Students or a professor of physics. You may remember that the description of Dr. Arnold by Mr. Strachey was heavily couched in "good Victorian" words like "vigour," "eminence," and "determination" rather than those we might be more likely to use today, such as "warm," "happy," or even (given Dr. Arnold's position) "intellectual."...

How you categorize and perceive me will influence how you behave toward me, and your behavior, in turn, will influence how I behave. Our point, for the moment, is to stress the role the selecting and categorizing activities of the perceiver play in *creating* his perceptions of the other and in producing structure in his world of other people.

Our experiences of other people have stability The behaviors engaged in by another person vary widely over even brief periods of time; thus the interpersonal acts of another provide as continually varying a stimulus as the size of his body provides the retina when he walks across a room. Were we to perceive as discrete all the acts of another person, our experiential world would be as rapidly changing and unstable as our experience of his size if that were dependent merely on the size of the retinal image. The stability in our experience of other people seems to be produced by processes analogous to those involved in the constancies in perception. We search to perceive the invariant properties of other people.

In perceiving attributes of another person, we focus not on his behavior, which is ever-changing, but on more invariant characteristics, namely, his intents and purposes. Since these invariant properties cannot be perceived directly, our search for invariance is centered on discovering functional relationships between behavior-effect sequences, which are observable, and intentions, which are not. For example, suppose that another person shoves you in the hall, verbally abuses you in a class, and criticizes your friends in private. The behaviors and the contexts in which they are expressed differ, but the same end is achieved: the other person hurts you. . . . Whenever we can assume that the person had the ability to produce the behaviors and hence the effects, when we can assume that he was the cause of what occurred, we tend to attribute to him the intent of producing the effect. This attribution of intent provides us with knowledge which will make our future interactions with the person more predictable.

Should we observe the same person behaving in a similar manner toward others, we go further and attribute to him the dispositional property of desiring to hurt other people; we consider him hostile or aggressive. This attribution of a dispositional property to another results again from the search for invariance. If we can classify a person according to certain traits or concepts, we can increase the predictability of our interpersonal world. An aggressive person will act to hurt not only us but others as well. We can predict his behavior in a wide variety of situations. It is also possible that such inferences about enduring dispositions will lead us into dramatic misperceptions. It is very disruptive for us to perceive as failing a person we "know" to be capable and to be trying hard. This is especially true if we have some strong loyalty to or identification with him. That our dispositional inferences can lead us astray was amusingly pointed out by the sports columnist, Red Smith:

> You see, Steve Ellis is the proprietor of Chico Vejar, who is a highly desirable tract of Stamford, Connecticut, welterweight. Steve is also a radio announcer. Ordinarily, there is no conflict between Ellis the Brain and Ellis the Voice because Steve is an uncommonly substantial lump of meat who can support both halves of a split personality and give away weight on each end without missing it.
>
> This time, though, the two Ellises met head-on, with a sickening, rending crash. Steve the Manager sat at ringside in the guise of Steve the Announcer broad-

casting a dispassionate, unbiased, objective report of Chico's adventures in the ring. . . .

Clear as mountain water, his words came through, winning big for Chico. Winning? Hell, Steve was slaughtering poor Fiore. Watching and listening, you could see what a valiant effort the reporter was making to remain cool and detached. At the same time you had an illustration of the old, established truth that when anybody with a preference watches a fight, he sees only what he prefers to see.

That is always so. That is why, after any fight that doesn't end in a clean knockout, there always are at least a few hoots when the decision is announced. A guy from, say, Billy Graham's neighborhood goes to see Billy fight and he watches Graham all the time. He sees all the punches Billy throws, and hardly any of the punches Billy catches. So it was with Steve.

"Fiore feints with a left," he would say, honestly believing that Fiore hadn't caught Chico full on the chops. "Fiore's knees buckle," he said, "and Chico backs away." Steve didn't see the hook that had driven Chico back. . . .²

Our experiences of other persons are meaningful We see other people as organized entities, and nearly always their behavior makes sense. Nonetheless, the behavior of others does confuse and puzzle us on occasion. It is probably a good guess that if a person is consistently puzzling to us, our inability to make sense of him leads us to avoid further interactions with him. No wonder the behavior of most of the people we "know" makes sense!

What are the processes by which we develop these organized perceptions of others as meaningful entities? First, as already pointed out, we organize their behavior into intent-act-effect units, and that procedure not only enables us to develop some behavioral organization but also permits and even pushes us to develop some hypotheses covering the enduring intents and dispositions or personality traits. Second, meaning derives from the fact that other people are similar to one another and to ourselves. We all share a certain number of important characteristics; we all behave, think, and feel; and some of the structured meanings we experience derive from the assumption that other people are like us. The assumption of similarity—"That's the way I would feel"—can lead to assumed relationships between both behaviors and intents. Even though the process may not be conscious, we often operate as follows: "I engage in behavior A and also in behavior B;" therefore, "if he engages in behavior A, then he must also engage in behavior B." The same operation would apply to intents and feelings. . . .

Finally, meaning derives from familiarity. When we have coded a person's behavior in a similar way a number of times and have made the same inferences about the causes of the behavior, then meaning and the feeling of understanding may result. This is especially true when we perceive that certain traits are correlated. A behavior is familiar not only in that we have seen it before but also in that it implies other behaviors. Implicit personality theories, the assumed correlations between traits which we carry around in our heads, are generalizations from behavior we may have observed in ourselves and one or two other persons. Once we have acquired these theories, we can then apply them as a general rule. The process is identical to that which produces a phenomenon usually called *group stereotypes.*

One way in which we simplify the complex world of other people is to organize them into groups. We talk of Germans, Jews, and Italians; of college students, policemen; even of little old ladies in tennis shoes; and we attribute certain characteristics to all members of each group. On reflection, we are all perfectly willing to grant that college students come in all different shapes and sizes and with very different orientations toward the world; yet we still find ourselves classifying people into groups and then imputing certain characteristics to the members of the groups. We neglect both situational pressures and disconfirming evidence in our push to categorize a person according to his group membership. . . .

Our impressions of another person are also a form of stereotype; we abstract certain aspects of his behavior, organize them around certain dispositions, and develop a picture of the person. This process permits the development of meaning in our experience of other persons. It can also restrict our awareness of some of another's behavior. Group and individual stereotypes do create stability and meaning; but they may well do it at the risk of inaccuracy.

SUMMARY

. . .We have identified certain characteristics of our world of experience, which includes the world of other people. It has structure, it has stability, and it has meaning. Furthermore, we have specified an approach to the perceptual process which assumes that perception is not the passive translation of physical energies into experience but is a process demanding active participation by the perceiver. He selects and categorizes, he interprets and infers to achieve a meaningful world in which he can act. We have also described some special features of our perception of other people. Behavior is one of the main sources of stimulation, and it is both complex and ever-changing. One of the ways we make sense out of the complexity is to make inferences that go beyond the behavioral data. We perceive other people as causal agents, we infer intentions, we infer emotional states, and we go further to infer enduring dispositions or personality traits. The social psychologist is interested in this process because it is one of the most salient outcomes of social interaction and, by the same token, one of the major determinants of the nature of interactions. One of the major variables which influence our behavior vis-à-vis another person is the sort of impression we have formed of him and the dispositions we have attributed to him. . . .

REFERENCES

1. Lytton Strachey, *Eminent Victorians* (New York: Modern Library, 1933), pp. 193–194. Quoted by permission of Harcourt, Brace and World; the Author's Literary Estate; and Chatto and Windus.
2. Red Smith, *New York Herald Tribune*, December 21, 1951.

PROBES

How does the idea that perception is an active rather than a passive process relate to what Boulding said about our images?

Are you aware of the ways in which you attribute *intent* to persons? Can you see how your perceptions of people are often your own constructions?

When are you most likely to compare people to your self? How does that affect your communicating?

Like Boulding, Barnlund, Tournier, and Rogers, these authors talk about our experiences or perceptions being "meaningful." What is it for something to be "meaningful"? How does the concept of meaningfulness relate to interpersonal communication? Do we communicate meanings? (Please say no!) Do words or gestures "have" meanings? Are meanings "in people"? Or are meanings relational; that is, does meaning happen between persons? How do you know?

These are excerpts from part of a book called *Appearances and Realities: Misunderstandings in Human Relations*. The main point of this selection moves one step beyond the main point of the previous two selections. Tournier made the general point that seeing people as persons instead of as things can drastically affect how we communicate with them. Hastorf, Schneider, and Polefka detailed specific ways our perception of people differs from our perception of objects and made some more points about how person perception affects communication. In this selection, Gustav Ichheiser points out that our perceptions of a person tend to coalesce into an "image of the other" and that our communication with that person is always greatly affected by our image of him or her, his or her image of us, and our image of ourselves. These images, Ichheiser argues, have at least as much impact on communication as do our attitudes about the person. For example, as he says, "A may envy B because, by some external reason like... gossip his image of B is distorted. What A envies is not B himself but the image of B which he has in his own mind. In this case, the image is the dynamic factor, and the attitude [envy] is only its result."

The key point is that all our communicating is continually affected by how I am seeing myself ("my me"), how I am seeing you ("my you"), how I am seeing you seeing me ("my your me"), and so on to theoretical infinity. Misunderstandings can often be traced to distorted images and often can be overcome only when those distortions are clarified.

Images don't just happen; we help create them by the ways we define ourselves—our clothes, tone of voice, facial expression, word choice, etc. Every time humans communicate, there is an incredibly complex process of image perception, image creation, and image response going on. Sometimes it makes me wonder how we can successfully communicate at all!

IMAGE OF THE OTHER
Gustav Ichheiser

Recently I read a novel which moved me profoundly. The author aroused my curiosity as a man who is alive to the perplexing and perturbing problems of our time, and a picture of his personality took shape in my mind. Then, by good fortune, I was given a chance to meet him personally. Arrangement was made by letter, but his handwriting, I found, disappointed me. In some hazily perceived way it did not fit into the picture I had formed of the man. However, giving this only momentary attention, I looked forward to the meeting with eager anticipation.

I arrived at his house punctually. I was shown into a room and asked to wait for a few minutes. As I looked around, there came again that feeling of disappointment, the more intense because now it was the second time. Just as previously the handwriting, so now the furnishing of the room failed to correspond to my preconceived image of the man. Indeed, there was actual contradiction of the picture I had formed of him in reading his novel. My perplexity was further increased by a similar lack of harmony between the handwriting and the way the room was furnished. Not only were they at variance with my expectations but each pointed in a different direction. The handwriting was empty, formal, and conventional in character; the room was furnished in poor taste, old-fashioned and overcrowded.

I was still struggling to resolve my conflicting feelings and impressions when the door opened and my host entered. Now, my confusion became actual shock. Instead of the ascetic figure I had expected, I saw a carefully dressed, rotund gentleman of advanced years who greeted me with a friendly, good-natured smile.

From Gustav Ichheiser, *Appearances and Realities* (San Francisco and London: Jossey-Bass, 1970), p. 12. Reprinted by permission.

In ill-concealed confusion we began the conversation with a few conventional phrases. Then, as we turned to more significant topics, almost imperceptibly, the picture underwent once again a metamorphosis. The man who spoke to me here, what he was saying, his manner of saying it, the tone of his voice, his shining eyes—yes, this was the man whom I had expected. True, there remained a few variant factors and certain contradictions and ambiguities of impression. Nonetheless, it was "he" himself. The handwriting which had perturbed me was forgotten; the room which troubled me disappeared; the outward appearance and the impression it had made on me were almost mysteriously transformed.

On my way home I reflected about the experience. Perhaps, so I thought, the connection between the handwriting and the personality of the man, if it exists at all, is more complicated than I had assumed in my immediate reaction. Perhaps his conventional handwriting is not a real, direct expression of himself but only a compensation for inner restlessness. Or, perhaps, there is no real connection of any kind; maybe I merely saw and interpreted a connection where actually there is none. It may be that his very careful, very bourgeois dress is only a mask, only an ironical technique for maintaining and defending the anonymity of his very unbourgeois self against unpleasant intrusion. Again, is it valid to interpret the furniture of his room as an expression of his personality? Several remarks which he made during the conversation hinted of financial difficulties. What if he himself dislikes the poor quality of his environment but is not in the position to change it? In that case, I was misinterpreting in assuming an expressive connection where in actual fact none exists. Finally, as to his physique, here, too, perhaps the relationship between the inner and the outer personality of a man is more complicated and more devious than we commonly are inclined to believe. So went my reflections.

At this point I fell to generalizing. What are the basic elements of our impressions about other people? How do the various aspects fit into the whole? By what conscious or unconscious mechanisms are elements of impression shaped into a more or less consistent image of the other man? What causes the different splits and contradictions within this image? How is this image of other people related to our attitudes toward those people? And, last but not least, how well does the image usually correspond to the other man "himself"?

The psychologically naive, unreflective person lives and acts under the silent assumption that he perceives and observes other people in a correct, factual, unbiased way. He may have his doubts as to the validity of some of his explicit interpretations and judgments about other people. He may be suspicious at times about other persons, misleading and deceiving him in word and action. However, he is unaware that certain misinterpretative mechanisms are at work within himself, distorting and falsifying his perception of other people, beginning even on the level of immediate observation. It remains concealed from him that much of what he considers as fact is permeated by, and a result of, misinterpretations functioning within his social perception and of which he is totally unaware.

PERSONALITY, IMAGE, AND ROLE

Images and Attitudes

Three aspects of human relations We can understand the structure and dynamics of human relations only if we approach them with a defined perspective. Every human relation offers three aspects. Consequently, we have always to ask three kinds of questions in analyzing interpersonal and intergroup relations. Let us assume that we are investigating the relationship between an individual A and an individual B. We have then to ask the following three sets of questions:

How does this relation look from the point of view of A? What is its significance for him? How does it reflect itself in his mind?

How does this relation look from the point of view of B? What is its significance for him? How does it present itself to his mind?

How does this relation look to an outside observer if he compares the way it looks to A with the way it looks to B? The congruence or incongruence of those two aspects has a decisive effect upon the whole dynamics of a given relation and upon its various conflicts and transformations. The following example will clarify and illustrate these facts.

Let us, then, assume that A, motivated either by his own suspicious character or by the influence of his suspicious wife, Mrs. A, believes mistakenly that his colleague B is intriguing against him in his office. Being a somewhat easygoing, timid man, he does not react with aggressiveness toward B. He prefers to solve the emerging conflict situation by avoiding so far as possible all contacts with B. On his part, B, whose inferiority feeling has been aggravated by his reading of some "helpful" articles about "how to fight inferiority feelings successfully," misinterprets the reserved attitude of A as an expression of A's looking down on him; and he, too, becomes reserved.

If, now, we approach the relation obtaining between A and B in terms of the three aspects we have identified, we may characterize this relation as follows:

The content and meaning of the relation as it looks to A is "defensive attitude on his part, including avoidance of all contacts with B, as a reaction (so it looks to him) against the intrigues of B."

The content and meaning of the same relation as it looks to B is "defensive attitude on his part, as reaction against the impudent tendency of A to look down on him (B)."

The content and meaning of the same relation in objective terms, that is, if we confront each of the aspects with the other, is "misunderstanding, arising out of mutual misinterpretations."

On the basis of this three-dimensional diagnosis, we may risk the prognosis that this relation, distorted as it is by misunderstandings, will in all probability, unless clarification of the original distortion is achieved, lead to ever increasing misinterpretations. It is an important fact of social psychology that misinterpretations and misunderstandings, once arisen, tend to multiply and to increase, unless the initial disharmony is rectified....Misinterpretations in human relations are by no means an exception. Human relations are always and essentially the result of a complicated interplay of understanding, nonunderstanding, and misunderstanding.

Attitudes and images as basic elements in human relations The concept of attitudes has attained in modern social psychology a place of great importance. This prominence may have come about because social psychologists, mainly concerned with the problems of the socialization of the individual, on the one hand, and with different forms of collective behavior, on the other, tend often to neglect the dynamics of interpersonal relations.

Yet, to approach and to analyze interpersonal (intergroup) relations only in terms of attitudes means to misunderstand their very nature. This, too, may be an obvious fact; but again one which seems never to have been grasped in its far-reaching implications. Witness the many isolated attitudes tests made and being made in studying majority-minority relations in our society.

To define the attitudes which two individuals (or two groups) take with regard to each other is meaningless if we do not define simultaneously the images which they have in their minds about each other. To state, for instance, that A and B hate or admire each other may be in itself very significant as far as the psychology of the personality of A, on the one hand, and of B, on the other hand, is concerned. But if the subject matter of our analysis is the interpersonal relation *between* A and B, then such statement remains empty, or even misleading, as long as we have not determined what kind of images they have in their minds about each other. The interpersonal significance of an attitude always depends on the content of the image about the other person to which it refers. Thus, if we wish to understand realistically the dynamics of interpersonal (and intergroup) relations, we have always to take both attitudes and images into account.

Between attitudes and images in human relations there exists a very complicated interdependence. For instance, A may have a distorted image of B, because his attitude toward B is dominated by envy. In this case it is the attitude which determines the content of the image. However, the opposite may also be true. A may envy B because, by some external reason like, for instance, gossip, his image about B is distorted. What A envies is not B himself but the image of B which he has in his own mind. In this case, the image is the dynamic factor, and the attitude is only its result.

The situation here under discussion is still more complicated by different types of rationalizations and self-deceptions which are operative in this field. So, for instance, the enemy must be conceived as a bad man. Otherwise, we could not have a good conscience in trying to destroy him. However, as will be shown below, we should be cautious not to succumb to the fallacy of interpreting all such behavior in terms of rationalization. By doing so, we would badly underestimate the amount of other types of illusions and errors of judgment which permeate the field of human relations.

Thus, again, if we wish to understand structure and dynamics of interpersonal relations and intergroup relations, we have always to know both the attitudes and the images which are involved on both sides. Unfortunately, social psychology sins heavily at present against this principle. This, in turn, leads to various, often most fundamental, misinterpretations of the relevant facts. So, for instance, many conflicts in interpersonal (and intergroup) relations are not, as it is often supposed, the result of hostile ("aggressive") attitudes with reference to each other. Rather they are the result of distorted images which the individuals or the groups have about each other. Each believes that he only defends himself and that it is the other who is the aggressor. Certainly, very often distorted images and misinterpretations are the consequence of conscious and unconscious hostilities. But also the opposite is often true: many hostilities are not the cause but the consequence of distorted images and misinterpretations. It is worth while to note at this place that, even though this may be shocking and disturbing, we have to realize that very frequently, if not always, people who are persecuting others are not aware that they are persecuting, for, in the light of the images which they have in their minds, it looks to them that they are fighting for a worthy cause or are liberating the world from an evil thing. . . .

Framework of images in human relations It is not enough to realize that always both attitudes and images constitute essential elements in all interpersonal (and intergroup) relations and that it is futile to characterize the attitudes involved without characterizing simultaneously the images to which they refer. We have, furthermore, to realize that there exists always a whole framework of images and that each image (or each group of images) has a definite place and function in this framework.

The following tabulation will be helpful in clarifying this complex of images. It should, however, not be taken too rigidly. The tabulation contains six parallel questions which one should always ask in analyzing the framework of images underlying any interhuman relation.

Individual (or group) A	Individual (or group) B
1. *Image a '* How does A see himself with reference to his relation to B?	1. *Image b '* How does B see himself with reference to his relation to A?
2. *Image a "* How does A believe himself to be seen by B?	2. *Image b "* How does B believe himself to be seen by A?
3. *Image a" '* How does A see B or some facts related to B?	3. *Image b" '* How does B see A or some facts related to A?

The functioning of a given interpersonal relation depends on how these different images are attuned to one another and to the facts to which they refer. Various discrepancies between the images themselves, or the images and the facts to which they refer, tend to produce different kinds of tensions and disturbances in the given relation. Thus, for instance, the relation between A and B may be disturbed either because A (or B) does not see himself as he really is; or because A (B) does not see himself as he is seen by B (A); or because A(B) is not aware that he is not seen by B (A) as he sees himself; or because A (B), or both, have a distorted image about each other; and so on.

It is a grave misconception to assume that tensions in interpersonal relations which arise as a result of distorted images in the minds of the interacting individuals are being normally readjusted through a rectification of those distorted images. Sometimes, of course, this may happen. But very often the process of readjustment is achieved by entirely different mechanisms: not the images are rectified according to the facts to which they refer but rather the persons concerned adapt themselves to the distorted images—either to the image in the mind of the other person or to the image which they have in their own minds. . . .

PROBES

Can you see the images operating in your communicating? What is your image of your best friend? Your worst enemy? Do you see the relationship between this idea and the point I made in the first chapter about defining our selves and others?

What is your image of me? How do you see me seeing you? How is my image of how you see me affecting my communication with you?

Who's responsible for your image of another person? The other or you?

How does image perception affect your communicating when you're in conflict with someone?

I don't want to argue any more about how he "is." You see him one way, I see him another way, he sees himself a third way. Now if you want to talk about what how we see him indicates about us . . .

HUGH PRATHER

In these two excerpts from his book *Knots*, R.D. Laing captures the essence of how person perception affects interpersonal communication. He graphically illustrates how complex and convoluted the whole processes of image creation, perception, and response can get. He also shows how communication based on distorted images can start to spiral, i.e., to fall into repetitive circles, each of which is intensified by the one before it.

Laing is convinced that the kind of communication he sketches here can—and often does—drive people crazy. I suspect that he is right. But the key to escaping the spiral is being aware of what you're doing. Reading Laing's examples and relating them to your own experience can help.

KNOTS

R.D. Laing

I.

He can't be happy
    when there is so much suffering in the world
She can't be happy
    if he is unhappy

She wants to be happy
He does not feel entitled to be happy

She wants him to be happy
and he wants her to be happy

He feels guilty if he is happy
and guilty if she is not happy

She wants both to be happy

He wants her to be happy

So they are both unhappy

He accuses her of being selfish
   because she is trying to get him to be happy
   so that she can be happy

She accuses him of being selfish
   because he is only thinking of himself

He thinks he is thinking of the whole cosmos

She thinks she is mainly thinking of him
because she loves him

She has turned to drink
   as a way to cope
   that makes her less able to cope

the more she drinks
the more frightened she is of becoming a drunkard

the more drunk
the less frightened of being drunk

the more frightened of being drunk when not drunk
   the more not frightened drunk
   the more frightened not drunk

the more she destroys herself
the more frightened of being destroyed by him

the more frightened of destroying him
the more she destroys herself

II.

Jack is afraid of Jill
Jill is afraid of Jack

Jack is more afraid of Jill   Jill is more afraid of Jack
   if Jack thinks   if Jill thinks
      that Jill thinks   that Jack thinks
that Jack is afraid of Jill   that Jill is afraid of Jack

Since Jack is afraid
    that Jill will think that
        Jack is afraid
    Jack pretends that
        Jack is not afraid of Jill
so that Jill will be more afraid of Jack

and since Jill is afraid
    that Jack will think that
        Jill is afraid
    Jill pretends that
        Jill is not afraid of Jack

Thus
    Jack tries to make Jill afraid
        by not being afraid of Jill
    and Jill tries to make Jack afraid
        by not being afraid of Jack

The more Jack is afraid of Jill
    the more frightened is Jack that
        Jill will think
            that Jack is afraid

the more Jill is afraid of Jack
    the more frightened is Jill that
        Jack will think
            that Jill is afraid

the more afraid Jack is of Jill
    the more frightened Jack is
not to be frightened of Jill
because it is very dangerous not to be afraid when
faced with one so dangerous

Jack is frightened because Jill is dangerous
Jill appears dangerous because Jack is frightened

the more afraid Jill is of Jack
    the more frightened Jill is
not to be frightened of Jack

The more Jack is frightened not to be frightened
the more frightened he is to appear frightened

the more frightened Jill is
        not to be frightened
the more frightened Jill is
    to appear to be frightened

the more frightened each is,

the less frightened each appears to be
Jack is frightened
   not to be frightened at Jill
and to appear to be frightened at Jill
and that Jill be not frightened at Jack

   Jill is frightened
   not to be frightened at Jack
   and to appear to be frightened at Jack
and that Jack be not frightened at Jill

Jack therefore tries to frighten Jill
by appearing not to be frightened
   that she appears not to be frightened

and Jill tries to frighten Jack
   by appearing not to be frightened
      that he appears not to be frightened

The more Jack tries to appear not to be frightened
   the more frightened he is that
      he is not frightened
   that he appears to be frightened
   that Jill is not frightened

the more Jill tries to appear not to be frightened
   the more frightened she is that
      she is not frightened
   that she appears to be frightened
   that Jack is not frightened

The more this is so
   the more Jack frightens Jill
   by appearing not to be frightened
and the more Jill frightens Jack
   by appearing not to be frightened

Can each become frightened of being
   frightened and of frightening
instead of being frightened
   not to be frightened
   and not to frighten?

Can Jack and Jill
   terrified that each and the other are not terrified
become
   terrified that each and other are terrified, and
   eventually,
   not terrified that each and other not be terrified?

PROBES

Have you ever felt tied in "knots" as you tried to listen to and be understood by others?

Can you identify in your own experience a spiral that's like the "drinking-to-cope-fearing-drunkenness-and-drinking-to-escape-fear" one Laing captures? How can you escape that kind of spiral?

What elements of your strongest love relationship are similar to the relationship between Jack and Jill?

How would you respond to the question Laing asks at the end of the Jack and Jill selection?

III

SHARING SELF
AND OTHERS

6

SELF-DISCLOSURE

In order to see I have to be willing to be seen.

If a man takes off his sunglasses I can hear him better.

HUGH PRATHER

I think/feel that it's important, before you read about how self-disclosure works, to be sure that you and I agree on what we're talking about. Self-disclosure is *not* interpersonal exhibitionism; it's *not* the communication equivalent of jumping onto the nearest desk or table and ripping your clothes off. People who fear the process or who want to attack the whole idea of communicating interpersonally often treat disclosure as if it were.

Self-disclosure is the act of verbally and nonverbally sharing with another some aspects of what makes you a person, aspects the other individual wouldn't be likely to recognize or understand without your help. In other words, self-disclosure is verbally and nonverbally making available information about your uniqueness, your choice-making, and/or the unmeasurable parts of you—for example, your feelings.

It's really important, I think, to remember that self-disclosure is a process that can improve a *transaction*, that can positively affect what's happening *between* persons. Disclosure is not meant to meet just one person's needs, but rather to enhance the *relationship*. Consequently, effective self-disclosure is disclosure that's *appropriate*, appropriate to the situation and appropriate to the relationship between the persons communicating. A crowded theater or a football game is not the place to discuss a profound religious experience even with your closest friend. Intimate sexual fantasies are usually not appropriate topics for a teacher to discuss with a student or for an employer to discuss with an employee. In short, you don't disclose just to make *you* feel better, but to facilitate the relationship. In other words, some disclosures are appropriate and some are not.

Self-disclosure is also not necessarily negative and not necessarily profound. You can help another know you as a person by sharing your joy, your excitement, your anticipation, or enthusiasm, and it doesn't have to be about the most weighty topic in your life. Small joys, small compliments, small successes, or even small disappointments can help others know who you are.

You might look at my comments in the introduction to this book as an example of what I'm talking about. I do want you to know more about me than just that I'm "author" or "teacher." I do want you to see some of my personness. But I'm convinced that you would probably be bored, offended, or both by a detailed account of every heavy happening I've experienced in the past four years. So I want to tell you something, but not everything, of what distinguishes me from other persons, something of the choices I've made and the changes I've experienced recently, something of my feelings about what I'm doing. Since you're not here to respond in person, I'm not sure that what I've said is appropriate to the relationship between you and me, but I am working to make it that. I chose to disclose some of my self to you because I want our relationship to be more than just "writer-reader," but I also chose *what* to disclose because I know that our relationship cannot be intimate or long-term. I would encourage you to treat self-disclosure in the same way: choose to do it because it will help others know you as a person, but base your choices on a clear understanding of what's desirable and what's possible for the *relationship*.

One more thing. Sometime people fear self-disclosure because they feel that their self is their most precious possession and that if they give much of it to others, they are liable to run out, to end up without any self left. This fear is based on the assumption that selves are like money or the hours in a day—there is only so much and when it's gone, it's gone. But the assumption simply isn't accurate. Selves aren't governed by the economic law of scarcity. Since each of us is continually growing and changing—becoming—the more we share, the more there is to share. To put it another way, when I give you something of myself, I don't give it "up"; I still "have" it, but as a result of my disclosure, now you "have" it too. As many couples who have enjoyed a long-term intimate relationship have learned, you can never succeed in disclosing everything about yourself. Similarly, the more you know about the other, the more clearly you realize how much more there is to know. Self-disclosure doesn't eliminate what Jourard calls the "mystery" of the other person; it can enhance it. In short, the fear that if you disclose you risk giving up all of your self is groundless.

It *is* true, though, that disclosure is risky. When I share something of my personness with you, I take the risk that you might reject it. That kind of rejection could hurt. But I take the risk because I know that if I don't, we cannot meet as persons. Although disclosing is risky, the relationship that can come with appropriate disclosure makes the risk, for me, worth it.

Sidney Jourard discusses several of these points in the essay that follows. Jourard has probably studied self-disclosure more and written more about it than any other person. Although this article is short, it includes many of the insights he has discovered about this aspect of interpersonal communication.

He admits that honest openness is still unusual enough in some places to arouse suspicion. But he also outlines the benefits of appropriate self-disclosure, which include the capacity to love and be loved and the ability to know your self better.

Jourard discusses the risk involved in self-disclosure and points out that when one of us is willing to take that risk, the other needs to be a person of "good will." In that way he reemphasizes the relationship between the two directions of movement focused on in Part III of this book—what you give to others (Chapters 6 and 7) and what you take from them (Chapter 8). What's required is not only open, honest giving, but also supportive, empathic listening.

SELF-DISCLOSURE AND THE MYSTERY
OF THE OTHER MAN

Sidney M. Jourard

If I look naively at my fellow man, I see him doing all manner of things, and I have no way of predicting or understanding why he does what he does. In fact, I may fear him, as I fear anything which acts with caprice. I may impute motives like mine to him, as primitive man imputed human motives to animals, the sea, plants, and the weather. I may engage in magic, ritual, or other superstitious practices, as primitive men did, in order to get others to help me or leave me alone.

But when man learned the conditions which were responsible for the behavior of the weather, the sea, plants, and animals, he feared them less and became more able to enlist their collaboration for the pursuit of his ends. He no longer imputed characteristics to these things which they did not possess, but strove, rather, to ascertain their real characteristics and to understand the forces which moved them. Man's fear changed then to respect.

With his fellow, however, man continues to behave much as he did in earlier times with plants, animals, and elements. His concepts and beliefs about the other man are usually based on insufficient or emotionally distorted evidence, and they are thus often false. Consequently, a man may find himself living in a world of strangers whose actions are either misunderstood or misinterpreted. And he becomes afraid.

The other man is a mystery. He is opaque. We cannot know in advance what he will do. We do not know his past, and we do not know what is "going on inside him." Consequently, we remain on guard when we are in his presence. Naive observation will show that the other man behaves predictably some of the time in the ritual of social living. He clothes himself, goes to work, tips his hat to ladies, utters polite conversation, and in short, seems "normal"—unless he is a foreigner, a psychotic, or a child. In the latter instances, we may be frank in admitting we don't know what he is thinking, and even if he tells us, we may not understand because we don't know his language. Or, erroneously, we may assume that we know his motives, thoughts, and reactions. But even with "normal" people, most of us feel rather uneasy, because we do not always know what they are thinking. In fact, if "normal" people tell us what they are thinking, what they feel, believe, or day-dream about, many of us feel, with a certain un-ease, that we are being "snowed"—the man isn't leveling with us. He is telling us what he thinks we want to hear. Often, he is doing just that. Because he may mislead us in telling us what he is like, we become shocked when we read that Mr. Jones, without warning, took a hatchet and butchered his family, whom he seemed to love so well.

> "Things are seldom what they seem,
> Skim milk masquerades as cream."
> "Externals don't portray insides,
> Jekylls may be masking Hydes."

Let me apologize for such atrocious verse and then point up an empirical fact. Man, perhaps alone of all living forms, is capable of *being* one thing and *seeming* from his actions and talk to be something else. Not even those animals and insects and fishes which Nature expertly camouflages can do this "seeming" at will; they do it reflexly.

Now, let me mention another truism. If Mr. Jones, the one who butchered his family, had *frankly* disclosed his inner thoughts, feelings, and plans to you, the news of his butchery would have come to you as no surprise. You would have understood it. Perhaps you could have predicted it and then interfered, thus saving the lives of his "loved ones."

It is a simple, patent fact that when a man discloses his self, his inner experience to another, fully, spontaneously, and honestly, then the mystery that he was decreases enormously. When a man discloses himself to me, I find all my preconceptions and beliefs about him becoming altered, one after the other, by the facts as they come forth—unless, of course, I have a vested interest in continuing to believe untruths about him.

In the general scheme of things, what consequences follow when men disclose their real selves one to the other? Here are some of the more obvious outcomes:

They learn the extent to which they are similar one to the other, and the extent to which they differ from one another in thoughts, feelings, hopes, reactions to the past, etc.

They learn of the other man's needs, enabling them to help him meet them or else to ensure that they will not be met.

They learn the extent to which this man accords with or deviates from moral and ethical standards for being and behaving. Here we may have a reason why people are reluctant to disclose themselves: they dread the moral judgment of their friends, family, minister, or the law.

I don't want to belabor the point, but I think it is almost self-evident that you cannot love another person, that is, behave toward him so as to foster his happiness and growth, unless you know what he needs. And you cannot know what he needs unless he tells you.

You cannot collaborate with another person toward some common end unless you know him. How can you know him, and he you, unless you have engaged in enough mutual disclosure of self to be able to anticipate how he will react and what part he will play?

Why do we disclose ourselves, and why do we not? Answers to this question are of enormous importance, since ignorance between man and man seems to be partly at the root of just about all current world problems. We do not know the Russians, for example, though I suspect we have disclosed ourselves much more to them than vice-versa; furthermore, through an effective spy service, they have learned much about us that we would not freely disclose. Possibly, the Russian leaders want to prevent us from disclosing ourselves fully to the Russian people because they fear that such disclosure will show the

Russian man-in-the-street that we have much in common with him regarding life's goals. But we have often tried to block teachers' disclosures of what they know and think about Russian life, political system, etc., because we *want* young people to have prejudiced concepts of "the Russian."

Researches that I have been undertaking point strongly to the likelihood that a person will disclose himself, permit himself to be known, only when he believes that his audience is a man of good will. To put this another way, self-disclosure follows an attitude of love and trust. If I love someone, not only do I strive to know him, so that I can devote myself more effectively to his well-being; *I also display my love by letting him know me.* At the same time, by so doing, I permit him to love me.

But loving is a scary business because when you permit yourself to be known you expose yourself, not only to a lover's balm, but also to a hater's bombs! When he knows you, he knows just where to plant them for maximum effect.

In a poker game, no man discloses the content of his hand to the other players. Instead, he tries to dissemble and bluff. If he holds four aces, he tries to get the others to believe his hand is empty, until it is time for the showdown. If he holds nothing, he tries to seem as if he holds four aces in order to get something for nothing. In a society which pits man against man, as in a poker game, people do keep a poker face; they wear a mask and let no one know what they are up to. In a society where man is *for* man, then the psychological iron curtain is dropped.

But now a paradox, turned up through research. Surely within the family, where love is expected to prevail, and people will *be* themselves, we find much evidence for dissembling, for the lack of mutual disclosure. Children do not know their parents; fathers do not know what their children think, or what they are doing. Husbands and wives often are strangers one to the other to an incredible degree.

We are said to be a society dedicated, among other things, to the pursuit of truth. Yet, disclosure of the truth, the truth of one's being, is often penalized. Impossible concepts of how man ought to be—which, sadly enough are often handed down from the pulpit—make man so ashamed of his true being that he feels obliged to seem different, if for no other reason than to protect his job. Probably the "tyranny of the should" is a factor which keeps man from making himself known as he is. Yet, when a man does not acknowledge to himself who, what, and how he is, he is out of touch with reality, and he will sicken and die; and no one can help him without access to the facts. And it seems to be another empirical fact that *no man can come to know himself except as an outcome of disclosing himself to another person.* This is the lesson we have learned in the field of psychotherapy. When a person has been able to disclose himself utterly to another person, he learns how to increase his contact with his real self, and he may then be better able to direct his destiny on the basis of knowledge of his real self.

But outside the clinic, disclosure of man to man, honest, direct, uncontrived, is the necessary condition for reducing the mystery that one man is for another. It is the empirical index of an I-Thou relationship, which I, agreeing with Buber, see as the index of man functioning at his highest and truly *human* level rather than at the level of a thing or animal. It is the means by which people become able to collaborate or else to learn that in reality they are far too different one from the other to collaborate in this particular enterprise. Disclosure of man to man appears to be the most direct means by which we can all learn wherein we are identical with our fellow man and wherein we differ. Such knowledge, suitably evaluated, then provides us with the basis for action which can either destroy man or meet his needs for more abundant and human living. Self-disclosure, my communication of my private world to you, in language which you clearly understand, is truly an important bit of behavior for us to learn something about. You can know me truly only if I let you, only if I *want* you to know me. Your misunderstanding of me is only partly your fault. If I want you to know me, I shall find a means of communicating myself to you. If you want me to reveal myself, just demonstrate your good will—your will to employ your powers for my good, and not for my destruction.

PROBES

How is your disclosing affected by the way you perceive your self? Is what you disclose affected by your body image? How so?

How is your disclosure affected by the way you perceive the other person(s)?

Do you disclosure primarily verbally or primarily nonverbally?

Do you agree with Jourard that humans are perhaps the only organisms capable of being one thing and seeming from their actions to be something else?

Do you agree that you cannot love another person unless you know his or her needs and that you can't know the person's needs unless he or she tells you?

What can you do when the other does not seem to be a person of "good will"? Have you experienced the results of self-disclosure that Jourard discusses?

I want to say something to this person but the fear
comes: "I'd better not" (he may misunderstand, he may
be in a hurry, ad infinitum). These fears are not based
on the present situation, they are based on the past, and
I don't have to be governed by what once went wrong.
The two of us are standing here in the present. What is
the situation now?

HUGH PRATHER

This is a section from John Powell's book *Why Am I Afraid To Tell You Who I Am?*
As the title suggests, the book is about self-disclosure and interpersonal communication.

Many people in my classes indicate that Powell's description of "the five
levels of communication" is one of the most useful things we discuss. Powell suggests that the *kinds*—not necessarily the amount—of information people disclose
will determine the "level" or "depth" or their relationship, and his ideas seem to
apply in most communication situations.

Powell's analysis of the relationship between judgment and emotions is also
helpful. He distinguishes between sharing a feeling—sadness, excitement, frustration, or whatever—and evaluating the other. It's the difference between "Damn it,
I'm mad!" and "You idiot! You make me so mad!" Powell also encourages us to
develop a related skill that applies to almost all communication—reporting judgments at the time we experience them.

INTERPERSONAL ENCOUNTER AND THE FIVE LEVELS OF COMMUNICATION

John Powell, S.J.

Someone has aptly distinguished five levels of communication on which persons can relate to one another. Perhaps it will help our understanding of these levels to visualize a person locked inside of a prison. It is the human being, urged by an inner insistence to go out to others and yet afraid to do so. The five levels of communication, which will be described a little later, represent five degrees of willingness to go outside of himself, to communicate himself to others.

The man in the prison—and he is Everyman—has been there for years, although ironically the grated iron doors are not locked. He can go out of his prison, but in his long detention he has learned to fear the possible dangers that he might encounter. He has come to feel some sort of safety and protection behind the walls of his prison, where he is a voluntary captive. The darkness of his prison even shields him from a clear view of himself, and he is not sure what he would look like in broad daylight. Above all, he is not sure how the world, which he sees from behind his bars, and the people whom he sees moving about in that world, would receive him. He is fragmented by an almost desperate need for that world and for those people, and, at the same time, by an almost desperate fear of the risks of rejection he would be taking if he ended his isolation.

This prisoner is reminiscent of what Viktor Frankl writes in his book, *Man's Search for Meaning*, about his fellow prisoners in the Nazi concentration camp at Dachau. Some of these prisoners, who yearned so desperately for their freedom, had been held captive so long that, when they were eventually released, they walked out into the sunlight, blinked nervously and then silently walked back into the familiar darkness of the prisons, to which they had been accustomed for such a long time.

This is the visualized, if somewhat dramatic, dilemma that all of us experience at some time in our lives and in the process of becoming persons. Most of us make only a weak response to the invitation of encounter with others and our world because we feel uncomfortable in exposing our nakedness as persons. Some of us are willing only to pretend this exodus, while others somehow find the courage to go all the way out to freedom. There are various stages in between. These stages are described below, under the headings of the five levels of communication. The fifth level, to be considered first, represents the least willingness to communicate ourselves to others. The successive, descending levels indicate greater and greater success in the adventure.

Level Five: Cliché Conversation

This level represents the weakest response to the human dilemma and the lowest level of self-communication. In fact, there is no communication here at all, unless by accident. On this level, we talk in clichés, such as: "How are you?...How is your family?...Where have you been?" We say things like: "I like your dress very much." "I hope we can get together again real soon." "It's really good to see you." In fact, we really mean almost nothing of what we are asking or saying. If the other party were to begin answering our question, "How are you?" in detail, we would be astounded. Usually and fortunately the other party senses the superficiality and conventionality of our concern and question, and obliges by simply giving the standard answer, "Just fine, thank you."

This is the conversation, the noncommunication, of the cocktail party, the club meeting, the neighborhood laundromat, etc. There is no sharing of persons at all. Everyone remains safely in the isolation of his pretense, sham, sophistication. The whole group seems to gather to be lonely together. It is well summarized in the lyrics of Paul Simon in *Sounds of Silence* used so effectively in the movie, *The Graduate:*

> "And in the naked night I saw
> Ten thousand people, maybe more,
> People talking without speaking,
> People hearing without listening,
> People writing songs that voices
>   never shared.
> No one dared
> Disturb the sounds of silence."

Level Four: Reporting the Facts about Others

On this fourth level, we do not step very far outside the prison of our loneliness into real communication because we expose almost nothing of ourselves. We remain contented to tell others what so-and-so has said or done. We offer no personal, self-revelatory commentary on these facts, but simply report them. Just as most of us, at times, hide behind clichés, so we also seek shelter in gossip items, conversation pieces, and little narrations about others. We give nothing of ourselves and invite nothing from others in return.

Level Three: My Ideas and Judgments

On this level, there is some communication of my person. I am willing to take this step out of my solitary confinement. I will take the risk of telling you some of my ideas and reveal some of my judgments and decisions. My communication usually remains under a strict censorship, however. As I communicate my ideas, etc., I will be watching you carefully. I want to test the temperature of the water before I leap in. I want to be sure that you will accept me with my ideas, judgments, and decisions. If you raise your eyebrow or narrow your eyes, if you yawn or look at your watch, I will probably retreat to safer ground. I will run for the cover of silence, or change the subject of conversation, or worse, I will start to say things I suspect that you want me to say. I will try to be what pleases you.

Someday, perhaps, when I develop the courage and the intensity of desire to grow as a person, I will spill all of the contents of my mind and heart before you. It will be my moment of truth. It may even be that I have already done so, but still you can know only a little about my person, unless I am willing to advance to the next depth-level of self-communication.

Level Two: My Feelings (Emotions). "Gut Level"

It might not occur to many of us that, once we have revealed our ideas, judgments, and decisions, there is really much more of our persons to share. Actually, the things that most clearly differentiate and individuate me from others, that make the communication of my person a unique knowledge, are my *feelings* or *emotions*.

If I really want you to know who I am, I must tell you about my stomach (gut-level) as well as my head. My ideas, judgments, and decisions are quite conventional. If I am a Republican or Democrat by persuasion, I have a lot of company. If I am for or against space exploration, there will be others who will support me in my conviction. But the *feelings* that lie under my ideas, judgments, and convictions are uniquely mine. No one supports a political party, or has a religious conviction, or is committed to a cause with my exact feelings of fervor or apathy. No one experiences my precise sense of frustration, labors under my fears, feels my passions. Nobody opposes war with my particular indignation or supports partiotism with my unique sense of loyalty.

It is these feelings, on this level of communication, which I must share with you, if I am to tell you who I really am. To illustrate this, I would like to put in the left-hand column a judgment, and in the right-hand column some of the possible emotional reactions to this judgment. If I tell you only the contents of my mind, I will be withholding a great deal about myself, especially in those areas where I am uniquely personal, most individual, most deeply myself.

Judgment	Some possible emotional reactions
I think that you are intelligent.	. . .and I am jealous.
	. . .and I feel frustrated.
	. . .and I feel proud to be your friend.
	. . .and it makes me ill at ease with you.
	. . .and I feel suspicious of you.

> ...and I feel inferior to you.
> ...and I feel impelled to imitate you.
> ...and I feel like running away from you.
> ...and I feel the desire to humiliate you.

Most of us feel that others will not tolerate such emotional honesty in communication. We would rather defend our dishonesty on the grounds that it might hurt others, and, having rationalized our phoniness into nobility, we settle for superficial relationships. This occurs not only in the case of casual acquaintances, but even with members of our own families; it destroys authentic communion within marriages. Consequently, we ourselves do not grow, nor do we help anyone else to grow. Meanwhile we have to live with repressed emotions—a dangerous and self-destructive path to follow. Any relationship, which is to have the nature of true personal encounter, must be based on this honest, open, gut-level communication. The alternative is to remain in my prison, to endure inch-by-inch death as a person.

We will say more of this level of communication, after describing the first and deepest level of communication between persons.

Level One: Peak Communication

All deep and authentic friendships, and especially the union of those who are married, must be based on absolute openness and honesty. At times, gut-level communication will be most difficult, but it is at these precise times that it is most necessary. Among close friends or between partners in marriage there will come from time to time a complete emotional and personal communion.

In our human condition this can never be a permanent experience. There should and will be, however, moments when encounter attains perfect communication. At these times the two persons will feel an almost perfect and mutual empathy. I know that my own reactions are shared completely by my friend; my happiness or my grief is perfectly reduplicated in him. We are like two musical instruments playing exactly the same note, filled with and giving forth precisely the same sound. This is what is meant by level one, peak communication.

"RULES" FOR GUT-LEVEL COMMUNICATION

If friendship and human love are to mature between any two persons, there must be absolute and honest mutual revelation; this kind of self-revelation can be achieved only through what we have called "gut-level" communication.

There is no other way, and all the reasons which we adduce to rationalize our cover-ups and dishonesty must be seen as delusions. It would be much better for me to tell you how I really feel about you than to enter into the stickiness and discomfort of a phony relationship.

Dishonesty always has a way of coming back to haunt and trouble us. Even if I should have to tell you that I do not admire or love you emotionally, it would be much better than trying to deceive you and having to pay the ultimate price of all such deception, your greater hurt and mine. And you will have to tell me things, at times, that will be difficult for you to share. But really you have no choice, and, if I want your friendship, I must be ready to accept you as you are. If either of us comes to the relationship without this determination of mutual honesty and openness, there can be no friendship, no growth; rather there can be only a subject-object kind of thing that is typified by adolescent bickering, pouting, jealousy, anger and accusations.

The classic temptation in this matter, and it would seem to be the most destructive of all delusions in this area of human relations, is this: we are tempted to think that communication of an unfavorable emotional reaction will tend to be divisive. If I tell you that it bothers me when you do something you are accustomed to do, I may be tempted to believe that it would be better not to mention it. Our relationship will be more peaceful. You wouldn't understand, anyway.

So I keep it inside myself, and each time you do your thing my stomach keeps score 2...3...4...5...6...7...8...until one day you do the same thing that you have always done and all hell breaks loose. All the while you were annoying me, I was keeping it inside and somewhere, secretly, learning to hate you. My good thoughts were turning to gall.

When it finally erupted in one great emotional avalanche, you didn't understand. You thought that this kind of reaction was totally uncalled for. The bonds of our love seemed fragile and about to break. And it all started when I said: "I don't like what she's doing, but it would be better not to say anything. The relationship will be more peaceful." That was all a delusion, and I should have told you in the beginning. Now there has been an emotional divorce, all because I wanted to keep the peace between us.

Rule one: Gut-level communication (emotional openness and honesty) must never imply a judgment of the other. I am simply not mature enough to enter into true friendship unless I realize that I cannot judge the intention or motivation of another. I must be humble and sane enough to bow before the complexity and mystery of a human being. If I judge you, I have only revealed my own immaturity and ineptness for friendship.

Emotional candor does not ever imply a judgment of you. In fact, it even abstains from any judgment of myself. For example, if I were to say to you, "I am ill at ease with you," I have been emotionally honest and at the same time have not implied in the least that it is your fault that I am ill at ease with you. Perhaps it is my own inferiority complex or my exaggerated concept of your intelligence. I am not saying it is anyone's fault, but simply giving a report of my emotional reaction to you at this time.

If I were to say to you that I feel angry or hurt by something you have done or said, it remains the same. I have not judged you. Perhaps it is my own self-love that has made me so sensitive, or my inclination to paranoia (a persecution complex). I am not sure, and, in most cases, I can never be sure. To be sure would imply a judgment. I can only say for sure that this has been and is my emotional reaction.

If I were to tell you that something you do annoys me, again I would not be so arrogant as to think that your action would annoy anyone. I do not even mean that your action is in any way wrong or offensive. I simply mean that here and now I experience annoyance. Perhaps it is my headache or my digestion or the fact that I did not get much sleep last night. I really do not know. All that I know is this, that I am trying to tell you that I am experiencing annoyance at this moment.

It would probably be most helpful in most cases to preface our gut-level communication with some kind of a disclaimer to assure the other that there is no judgment implied. I might begin by saying, "I don't know why this bothers me, but it does...I guess that I am just hypersensitive, and I really don't mean to imply that it is your fault, but I do feel hurt by what you are saying."

Of course, the main thing is that there is *in fact* no judgment. If I am in the habit of judging the intentions or motivation of another, I should try very hard to outgrow this adolescent habit. I simply will not be able to disguise my judgments, no matter how many disclaimers I make.

On the other hand, if I am really mature enough to refrain from such judgments, this too will eventually be apparent. If I really want to know the intention or motivation or reaction of another, there is only one way to find out: *I must ask him.* (Don't pass this by lightly. You don't have x-ray eyes either!)

Rule two: Emotions are not moral (good or bad). Theoretically, most of us would accept the fact that emotions are neither meritorious nor sinful. Feeling frustrated, or being annoyed, or experiencing fears and anger do not make one a good or a bad person. Practically, however, most of us do not accept in our day-to-day living what we would accept in theory. We exercise a rather strict censorship of our emotions. If our censoring consciences do not approve certain emotions, we repress these emotions into our subconscious mind. Experts in psychosomatic medicine say that the most common cause of fatigue and actual sickness is the repression of emotions. The fact is that there are emotions to which we do not want to admit. We are ashamed of our fears, or we feel guilty because of our anger or emotional-physical desires.

Before anyone can be liberated enough to practice "gut-level communication," in which he will be emotionally open and honest, he must feel convinced that emotions are *not moral* but simply *factual*. My jealousies, my anger, my sexual desires, my fears, etc., do not make me a good or bad person. Of course, these emotional reactions must be integrated by my mind and will, but before they can be integrated, before I can decide whether I want to act on them or not, I must allow them to arise and I must clearly hear what they are saying to me. I must be able to say, without any sense of moral reprehension, that I am afraid or angry or sexually aroused.

Before I will be free enough to do this, however, I must be convinced that emotions are not moral, neither good nor bad in themselves. I must be convinced, too, that the experience of the whole gamut of emotions is a part of the human condition, the inheritance of every man.

Rule three: Feelings (emotions) must be integrated with the intellect and will. It is extremely important to understand this next point. The non-repression of our emotions means that we must experience, recognize, and accept our emotions fully. It does not in any way imply that we will always *act on* those emotions. This would be tragic and the worst form of immaturity, if a person were to allow his feelings or emotions to control his life. It is one thing to feel and to admit to myself and to others that I am afraid, but it is another thing to allow this fear to overwhelm me. It is one thing for me to feel and to admit that I am angry and another to punch you in the nose.

. . . For example, I may feel a strong fear of telling you the truth in some given matter. The fact is, and it is neither good nor bad in itself, that I am experiencing fear. I allow myself to feel this fear, to recognize it. My mind makes the judgment that I should not act on this fear, but in spite of it, and to tell you the truth. The will consequently carries out the judgment of the mind. I tell you the truth.

However, if I am seeking a real and authentic relationship with you, and wish to practice "gut-level" communication, I must tell you something like this: "I really don't know why . . . maybe it's my streak of cowardice . . . but I feel afraid to tell you something, and yet I know that I must be honest with you . . . This is the truth as I see it . . . ."

. . . It should be obvious that, in the integrated person, emotions are neither repressed nor do they assume control of the whole person. They are recognized (What is it that I am feeling?) and integrated (Do I want to act on this feeling or not?).

Rule four: In "gut-level" communication, emotions must be "reported." If I am to tell you who I really am, I must tell you about my feelings, whether I will act upon them or not. I may tell you that I am angry, explaining the fact of my anger without inferring any judgment of you, and not intending to act upon this anger. I may tell you that I am afraid, explaining the fact of my fear without accusing you of being its cause, and at the same time not succumbing to the fear. But I must, if I am to open myself to you, allow you to experience (encounter) my person and tell you about my anger and my fear.

It has been truly said that we either *speak out* (report) our feelings or we will *act them out*. Feelings are like steam that is gathering inside of a kettle. Kept inside and gathering strength, they can blow the human lid off, just as the steam inside the kettle will blow off the lid of the kettle.

We have already referred to the verdict of psychosomatic medicine that repressed emotions are the most common cause of fatigue and actual sickness. This is part of the "acting out" process. Repressed emotions may find their outlet in the "acting out" of headaches, skinrashes, allergies, asthma, common colds, aching backs or limbs, but they can also be acted out in the tension of tightened muscles, the slamming of doors, the clenching of fists, the rise of blood pressure, the grinding of teeth, tears, temper tantrums, acts of violence. We do not bury our emotions *dead*; they remain *alive* in our subconscious minds and intestines, to hurt and trouble us. It is not only much more conducive to an authentic relationship to report our true feelings, but it is equally essential to our integrity and health.

The most common reason for not reporting our emotions is that we do not want to admit to them for one reason or another. We fear that others might not think well of us, or actually reject us, or punish us in some way for our emotional candor. We have been somehow "programmed" not to accept certain emotions as part of us. We are ashamed of them. Now we can rationalize and say that we cannot report these emotions because they would not be understood, or that reporting them would disturb a peaceful relationship, or evoke an emotionally stormy reaction from the other; but all of our reasons are essentially fraudulent, and our silence can produce only fraudulent relationships. Anyone who builds a relationship on less than openness and honesty is building on sand. Such a relationship will never stand the test of time, and neither party to the relationship will draw from it any noticeable benefits.

Rule five: With rare exceptions, emotions must be reported at the time that they are being experienced. It is much easier for most of us to report an emotion that is a matter of history. It is almost like talking about another person when I can talk about myself a year or two years ago, and admit that I was very fearful or very angry at that time. Because they were transient emotions and are now gone, it is easy to dissociate these feelings from my person here and now. It is difficult, however, to recapture a feeling once it has passed into my personal history. We are very often puzzled by such previous emotions. "I don't know why I ever got so excited." The time to report emotions is the time when they are being experienced. Even temporary deferral of this report of emotions is unwise and unhealthy.

All communication must obviously respect not only the transmitter of the communication but also the receiver who is to accept the communication.

Consequently, it could occur that, in the integration of my emotions, my judgment may dictate that this is not the opportune moment to report my emotional reaction. If the receiver is so emotionally disturbed himself that he could hardly be in a receptive mood, and my report would only be distorted somehow by his turbulent emotional state, it may be that I will have to defer this report.

But, if the matter is serious enough and the emotions strong enough, this period of deferment cannot be too long nor can I be frightened or bullied into complete repression of emotions. Note that this period of deferment should never be a long one, and it would seem that in most cases it would be a rare thing.

Also, it would seem to be a valid exception to this rule to defer or eliminate this report in the case of a passing incident with a chance acquaintance. The gruff manner of a bus driver may irk me, without this being the occasion for me to stand nose to nose with him and tell him about my emotional reactions to him. In the case of two people, however, who must work or live together or who want to relate deeply, this emotional reporting at the time of the emotions is vitally important.

THE BENEFITS OF "GUT-LEVEL" COMMUNICATION

The obvious and primary benefit of "gut-level" communication will be a real and authentic relationship and what we have called a true "encounter" of persons. Not only will there be mutual communication of persons and the consequent sharing and experiencing of personhood, but it will result in a more and more clearly defined sense of self-identity for each of the parties in the relationship.

Today, many of us are asking: "Who am I?" It has come to be a socially fashionable question. The implication is that I do not really know my own self as a person. We have said that my person is what I think, judge, feel, etc. If I have communicated these things freely and openly, as clearly as I can and as honestly as I can, I will find a noticeable growth in my own sense of identity as well as a deeper and more authentic knowledge of the other. It has come to be a psychological truism that I will understand only as much of myself as I have been willing to communicate to another.

The second and very important result of such communication is that, having understood myself because I have communicated myself, I will find the patterns of immaturity changing into patterns of maturity. I will change! Anyone who sees the *patterns* of his reactions, and is willing to examine them, may come to the realization that these are patterns of hypersensitivity or paranoia. At the moment the realization penetrates him, he will find the pattern changing. Notwithstanding all that we have said about emotions, we must not believe that emotional patterns are purely biological or inevitable. *I can and will change my emotional patterns*, that is, I will move from one emotion to another, if I have honestly let my emotions arise for recognition and, having honestly reported them, judge them to be immature and undesirable.

For example, if I consistently and honestly report the emotion of "feeling hurt" by many small and inconsequential things, it will become apparent to me in time that I am hypersensitive and that I have been indulging myself in self-pity. The moment that this becomes clear to me, really hits me, I will change.

In summary the dynamic is this: We allow our emotions to arise so that they can be identified; we observe the patterns in our emotional reactions, report and judge them. Having done these things, we instinctively and immediately make the necessary adjustments in the light of our own ideals and hopes for growth. We change. Try this and see for yourself.

If all this is true, and you have only to experience it to know its truth, it is obvious that the little phrase we have used so conveniently, "I'm sorry, but that's the way I am," is nothing more than a refuge and delusion. It is handy if you don't want to grow up; but if you do want to grow up, you try to rise above this fallacy.

The third benefit of "gut-level" communication is that it will evoke from others a responsive honesty and openness, which is necessary if the relationship is to be interpersonal, mutual. Goldbrunner, a psychiatrist, somewhat boastfully claims that he can gain instant access to the deepest parts of anyone within a matter of minutes. His technique is not to begin by probing with questions for this only makes the insecure person more defensive. The theory of this psychiatrist is that if we want another to be open with us, we must begin by opening up ourselves to him, by telling the other honestly and openly of our feelings.

Person is resonant to person, Goldbrunner insists. If I am willing to step out of the darkness of my prison, to expose the deepest part of me to another person, the result is almost automatic and immediate: The other person feels empowered to reveal himself to me. Having heard of my secret and deep feelings, he is given the courage to communicate his own. This, in the last analysis, is what we meant by "encounter."

PROBES

Is Powell saying that *you* can determine the level or depth or your communication by how much you share? If so, is his view consistent with what Barnlund says about communication being not linear but circular?

Powell says that gut-level communication must never imply a judgment of the other. Boulding says that even the things we call "facts" are actually value judgments, that there are no such things as purely objective, nonjudgmental statements. What do *you* think? Can you be nonjudgmental?

Try identifying your conversations by "level." Do you spend most of your time on level 5 or 4? If you are taking a class in interpersonal communication, what level does the class generally function at? How often have you personally experienced level 1, or "peak" communication? What condition made it happen?

Try "obeying" the five rules for level 2, gut-level communication. Like guidelines for empathic listening (see Chapter 8), these rules seem to me to be simple to understand but difficult to apply. Do they help make "peak," or "gut-level," communication happen for you?

I have seen "being real" act sometimes like a new kind of religion, a new form of self-justification, a new perfectionism, or even a perverse new snobbery. I experienced this recently when I found myself arguing against someone else's truth on the grounds that his truth professed to be universal whereas I knew all truth to be personal. I was in effect shouting down his throat: "You shouldn't be telling me what I shouldn't be."—or—"I won't accept your not believing in acceptance." I also sense that I am misusing the idea of being real whenever I discover myself anxiously weighing my words and actions, that is, whenever I am being careful to be "real." When I do this I am only playing a new role—the role of the "real person." Calculation does not enter into being real. Concern with appearance does not enter into it. Being real is more a process of letting go than it is the effort of becoming. I don't really have to become me, although at times it feels this way—I am already me. And that is both the easiest and the hardest thing for me to realize.

HUGH PRATHER

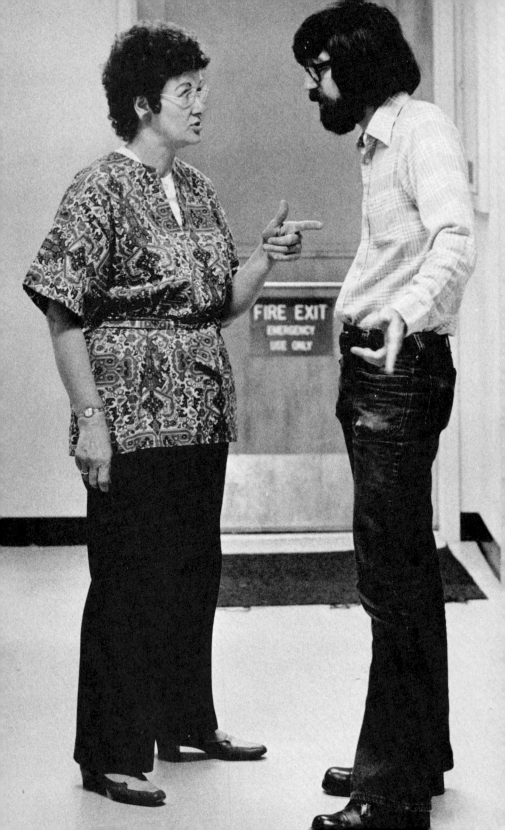

7

SELF-ASSERTION IN CONFLICT

If we do not exist as individuals then our relationship does not exist.

HUGH PRATHER

Everyone knows from first-hand experience that not all communication is sweetness and light, mutual respect, each person treating the other as a human. Objectification, conflict, and disagreements are integral parts of everybody's communication experience. As a matter of fact, there is no way to eliminate them; each person is unique and whenever two or more of those uniquenesses meet, there's a real possibility of disagreement.

Unfortunately, though, most of us tend to visualize these communication situations as miniature wars and to deal with disagreement or conflict in one of three unproductive ways: (1) We marshall all of our forces in an effort to win over the other person, show him or her who's boss, "straighten the person out," or "shut the other up." (2) If we don't feel strong enough to win the "war," we retreat, we split; we avoid contact altogether rather than risk losing the battle. (3) Our only other option, we often think, is to lose—to be overrun, crushed, ridiculed in front of people whose good opinion we care about.

The problem with the "war" point of view is that it obscures a fourth option, the only option that enables you to deal with conflict interpersonally, that is, in a way that takes into account the humanness of all the persons involved. That fourth approach is called "assertiveness," and recently it's become the subject of a variety of "assertiveness training" books, workshops, and seminars.

Assertiveness begins with a positive view of the person, with the idea that each person counts and that the individual's feeling of confidence is a vital part of his or her self-esteem. "The assertive individual is fully in charge of himself [or herself] in interpersonal relationships, feels confident and capable without cockiness or hostility, [and] is basically spontaneous in the expression of feeling and emotions. . . ."[1]

Assertiveness is emphatically *not* the same as aggressiveness. The assertive person "does not malign others or deny their rights, running roughshod over people. The assertive person is open and flexible, genuinely concerned with the rights of others, yet at the same time able to establish very well his [or her] own rights."[2]

Frequently, it's much easier to be nonassertive rather than to be assertive, to avoid a conflict even if it means saying "yes" when you want to say "no." At other times it's simpler to be aggressive, to win the argument in a way that forces the other person to lose, to exert all the power you can and really rub the other person's nose in his or her defeat. But both those alternatives have destructive outcomes. When you give in, your self suffers; when you force the other to lose, his or her self suffers.

But these are not the only alternatives. The purpose of the readings in this chapter is to outline a third way, a way to deal with disagreement without either giving up or crushing the other persons involved. The first step is to identify some of the attitudes and behaviors that create hostile communication. That's the purpose of Gibb's article on "defensive communication." As Gibb points out, when you anticipate or perceive that you are threatened by a person or a situation, you will usually react defensively and so will the other persons involved. When any combination of the six "defensiveness-producing" elements are present, a spiral usually begins, a spiral that starts with a little discomfort and often escalates into all-out conflict.

But, Gibb notes, you can also start a spiral in the other direction. The more supportive you can be, the less other people are likely to read into the situation distorted reactions created by their own defensiveness. So when you can manifest any combination of the six alternative attitudes and skills, you can help reduce the defensiveness that's present. You don't have to "give up" or "give in." You just have to stop trying so hard to demean, control, and impose your hard-and-fast superiority on the others.

Most of the people in my classes find this article pretty useful. They discover that they can apply Gibb's analysis of the six characteristics of defensive and supportive communication climates to their own experience. They also find that Gibb is right when he says that most people are much more aware of being manipulated or deceived than the manipulators or deceivers think and that such awareness creates defensiveness. They are usually able to perceive quite accurately one another's communication strategy or "gimmicks." When they learn that sometimes it's their own transparently manipulative behavior that creates defensiveness in others, they get one jump closer to communicating interpersonally.

REFERENCES

1. Robert E. Alberti and Michael L. Emmons, *Your Perfect Right*, 2d ed. (San Luis Obisop, California: Impact, 1974), p. 3.

2. *Ibid.*, p. 4.

DEFENSIVE COMMUNICATION
Jack R. Gibb

One way to understand communication is to view it as a people process rather than as a language process. If one is to make fundamental improvement in communication, he must make changes in interpersonal relationships. One possible type of alteration—and the one with which this paper is concerned—is that of reducing the degree of defensiveness.

Jack R. Gibb, "Defensive Communication," *Journal of Communication* 11, 3 (September 1961): 141–148. Reprinted by permission of the *Journal of Communication* and the author.

DEFINITION AND SIGNIFICANCE

Defensive behavior is defined as that behavior which occurs when an individual perceives threat or anticipates threat in the group. The person who behaves defensively, even though he also gives some attention to the common task, devotes an appreciable portion of his energy to defending himself. Besides talking about the topic, he thinks about how he appears to others, how he may be seen more favorably, how he may win, dominate, impress, or escape punishment, and/or how he may avoid or mitigate a perceived or an anticipated attack.

Such inner feelings and outward acts tend to create similarly defensive postures in others; and, if unchecked, the ensuing circular response becomes increasingly destructive. Defensive behavior, in short, engenders defensive listening, and this in turn produces postural, facial, and verbal cues which raise the defense level of the original communicator.

Defense arousal prevents the listener from concentrating upon the message. Not only do defensive communicators send off multiple value, motive, and affect cues, but also defensive recipients distort what they receive. As a person becomes more and more defensive, he becomes less and less able to perceive accurately the motives, the values, and the emotions of the sender. The writer's analyses of tape recorded discussions revealed that increases in defensive behavior were correlated positively with losses in efficiency in communication.[1] Specifically, distortions became greater when defensive states existed in the groups.

The converse, moreover, also is true. The more "supportive" or defense reductive the climate the less the receiver reads into the communication distorted loadings which arise from projections of his own anxieties, motives, and concerns. As defenses are reduced, the receivers become better able to concentrate upon the structure, the content, and the cognitive meanings of the message.

CATEGORIES OF DEFENSIVE AND SUPPORTIVE COMMUNICATION

In working over an eight-year period with recordings of discussions occurring in varied settings, the writer developed the six pairs of defensive and supportive categories presented in Table 1. Behavior which a listener perceives as possessing any of the characteristics listed in the left-hand column arouses defensiveness, whereas that which he interprets as having any of the qualities designated as supportive reduces defensive feelings. The degree to which these reactions occur depends upon the personal level of defensiveness and upon the general climate in the group at the time.[2]

Table 1
Categories of Behavior Characteristic of Supportive and Defensive Climates in Small Groups

Defensive Climates	Supportive Climates
1. Evaluation	1. Description
2. Control	2. Problem orientation
3. Strategy	3. Spontaneity
4. Neutrality	4. Empathy
5. Superiority	5. Equality
6. Certainty	6. Provisionalism

Evaluation and Description

Speech or other behavior which appears evaluative increases defensiveness. If by expression, manner of speech, tone of voice, or verbal content the sender seems to be evaluating or judging the listener, then the receiver goes on guard. Of course, other factors may inhibit the reaction. If the listener thought that the speaker regarded him as an equal and was being open and spontaneous, for example, the evaluativeness in a message would be neutralized and perhaps not even perceived. This same principle applies equally to the other five categories of potentially defense-producing climates. The six sets are interactive.

Because our attitudes toward other persons are frequently, and often necessarily, evaluative, expressions which the defensive person will regard as nonjudgmental are hard to frame. Even the simplest question usually conveys the answer that the sender wishes or implies the response that would fit into his value system. A mother, for example, immediately following an earth tremor that shook the house, sought for her small son with the question: "Bobby, where are you?" The timid and plaintive "Mommy, I didn't do it" indicated how Bobby's chronic mild defensiveness predisposed him to react with a projection of his own guilt and in the context of his chronic assumption that questions are full of accusation.

Anyone who has attempted to train professionals to use information-seeking speech with neutral effect appreciates how difficult it is to teach a person to say even the simple "who did that?" without being seen as accusing. Speech is so frequently judgmental that there is a reality base for the defensive interpretations which are so common.

When insecure, group members are particularly likely to place blame, to see others as fitting into categories of good or bad, to make moral judgments of their colleagues, and to question the value, motive, and affect loadings of the speech which they hear. Since value loadings imply a judgment of others, a belief that the standards of the speaker differ from his own causes the listener to become defensive.

Descriptive speech, in contrast to that which is evaluative, tends to arouse a minimum of uneasiness. Speech acts which the listener perceives as genuine requests for information or as material with neutral loadings is descriptive. Specifically, presentations of feelings, events, perceptions, or processes which do not ask or imply that the receiver change behavior or attitude are minimally defense producing. The difficulty in avoiding overtone is illustrated by the problems of news reporters in writing stories about unions, communists, Negroes, and religious activities without tipping off the "party" line of the newspaper. One can often tell from the opening words in a news article which side the newspaper's editorial policy favors.

Control and Problem Orientation

Speech which is used to control the listener evokes resistance. In most of our social intercourse someone is trying to do something to someone else—to change an attitude, to influence behavior, or to restrict the field of activity. The degree to which attempts to control produce defensiveness depends upon the openness of the effort, for a suspicion that hidden motives exist heightens resistance. For this reason attempts of nondirective therapists and progressive educators to refrain from imposing a set of values, a point of view, or a problem solution upon the receivers meet with many barriers. Since the norm is control, noncontrollers must earn the perceptions that their efforts have no hidden motives. A bombardment of persuasive "messages" in the fields of politics, education, special causes, advertising, religion, medicine, industrial relations, and guidance has bred cynical and paranoidal responses in listeners.

Implicit in all attempts to alter another person is the assumption by the change agent that the person to be altered is inadequate. That the speaker secretly views the listener as ignorant, unable to make his own decisions, uninformed, immature, unwise, or possessed of wrong or inadequate attitudes is a subconscious perception which gives the latter a valid base for defensive reactions.

Methods of control are many and varied. Legalistic insistence on detail, restrictive regulations and policies, conformity norms, and all laws are among the methods. Gestures, facial expressions, other forms of nonverbal communication, and even such simple acts as holding a door open in a particular manner are means of imposing one's will upon another and hence are potential sources of resistance.

Problem orientation, on the other hand, is the antithesis of persuasion. When the sender communicates a desire to collaborate in defining a mutual problem and in seeking its solution, he tends to create the same problem orientation in the listener; and, of greater importance, he implies that he has no predetermined solution, attitude, or method to impose. Such behavior is permissive in that it allows the receiver to set his own goals, make his own decisions, and evaluate his own progress—or to share with the sender in doing so. The exact methods of attaining permissiveness are not known, but they must involve a constellation of cues and they certainly go beyond mere verbal assurances that the communicator has no hidden desires to exercise control.

Strategy and Spontaneity

When the sender is perceived as engaged in a stratagem involving ambiguous and multiple motivations, the receiver becomes defensive. No one wishes to be a guinea pig, a role player, or an impressed actor, and no one likes to be the victim of some hidden motivation. That which is concealed, also, may appear larger than it really is with the degree of defensiveness of the listener determining the perceived size of the suppressed element. The intense reaction of the reading audience to the material in the *Hidden Persuaders* indicates the prevalence of defensive reactions to multiple motivations behind strategy. Group members who are seen as "taking a role," as feigning emotion, as toying with their colleagues, as withholding information, or as having special sources of data are especially resented. One participant once complained that another was "using a listening technique" on him!

A large part of the adverse reaction to much of the so-called human relations training is a feeling against what are perceived as gimmicks and tricks to fool or to "involve" people, to make a person think he is making his own decision, or to make the listener feel that the sender is genuinely interested in him as a person. Particularly violent reactions occur when it appears that someone is trying to make a stratagem appear spontaneous. One person has reported a boss who incurred resentment by habitually using the gimmick of "spontaneously" looking at his watch and saying, "My gosh, look at the time—I must run to an appointment." The belief was that the boss would create less irritation by honestly asking to be excused.

Similarly, the deliberate assumption of guilelessness and natural simplicity is especially resented. Monitoring the tapes of feedback and evaluation sessions in training groups indicates the surprising extent to which members perceive the strategies of their colleagues. This perceptual clarity may be quite shocking to the strategist, who usually feels that he had cleverly hidden the motivational aura around the "gimmick."

This aversion to deceit may account for one's resistance to politicians who are suspected of behind-the-scenes planning to get his vote, to psychologists whose listening apparently is motivated by more than the manifest or content-level interest in his behavior, or to the sophisticated, smooth, or clever person whose "oneupmanship" is marked with guile. In training groups the role-flexible person frequently is resented because his changes in behavior are perceived as strategic maneuvers.

In contrast, behavior which appears to be spontaneous and free of deception is defense reductive. If the communicator is seen as having a clean id, as having uncomplicated motivations, as being straightforward and honest, and as behaving spontaneously in response to the situation, he is likley to arouse minimal defense.

Neutrality and Empathy

When neutrality in speech appears to the listener to indicate a lack of concern for his welfare, he becomes defensive. Group members usually desire to be perceived as valued persons, as individuals of special worth, and as objects of concern and affection. The clinical, detached, person-is-an-object-of-study attitude on the part of many psychologist-trainers is resented by group members. Speech with low affect that communicates little warmth or caring is in such contrast with the affect-laden speech in social situations that it sometimes communicates rejection.

Communication that conveys empathy for the feelings and respect for the worth of the listener, however, is particularly supportive and defense reductive. Reassurance results when a message indicates that the speaker identifies himself with the listener's problems, shares his feelings, and accepts his emotional reactions at face value. Abortive efforts to deny the legitimacy of the receiver's emotions by assuring the receiver that he need not feel bad, that he should not feel rejected, or that he is overly anxious, though often intended as support giving, may impress the listener as lack of acceptance. The combination of understanding and empathizing with the other person's emotions with no accompanying effort to change him apparently is supportive at a high level.

The importance of gestural behavioral cues in communicating empathy should be mentioned. Apparently spontaneous facial and bodily evidences of concern are often interpreted as especially valid evidence of deep-level acceptance.

Superiority and Equality

When a person communicates to another that he feels superior in position, power, wealth, intellectual ability, physical characteristics, or other ways, he arouses defensiveness. Here, as with the other sources of disturbance, whatever arouses feelings of inadequacy causes the listener to center upon the affect loading of the statement rather than upon the cognitive elements. The receiver then reacts by not hearing the message, by forgetting it, by competing with the sender, or by becoming jealous of him.

The person who is perceived as feeling superior communicates that he is not willing to enter into a shared problem-solving relationship, that he probably does not desire feedback, that he does not require help, and/or that he will be likely to try to reduce the power, the status, or the worth of the receiver.

Many ways exist for creating the atmosphere that the sender feels himself equal to the listener. Defenses are reduced when one perceives the sender as being willing to enter into participative planning with mutual trust and respect. Differences in talent, ability, worth, appearance, status, and power often exist, but the low defense communicator seems to attach little importance to these distinctions.

Certainty and Provisionalism

The effects of dogmatism in producing defensiveness are well known. Those who seem to know the answers, to require no additional data, and to regard themselves as teachers rather than as co-workers tend to put others on guard. Moreover, in the writer's experiment, listeners often perceived manifest expressions of certainty as connoting inward feelings of inferiority. They saw the dogmatic individual as needing to be right, as wanting to win an argument rather than solve a problem, and as seeing his ideas as truths to be defended. This kind of behavior often was associated with acts which others regarded as attempts to exercise control. People who were right seemed to have low tolerance for members who were "wrong"—i.e., who did not agree with the sender.

One reduces the defensiveness of the listener when he communicates that he is willing to experiment with his own behavior, attitudes, and ideas. The person who appears to be taking provisional attitudes, to be investigating issues rather than taking sides on them, to be problem solving rather than debating, and to be willing to experiment and explore tends to communicate that the listener may have some control over the shared quest or the investigation of the ideas. If a person is genuinely searching for information and data, he does not resent help or company along the way.

CONCLUSION

The implications of the above material for the parent, the teacher, the manager, the administrator, or the therapist are fairly obvious. Arousing defensiveness interferes with communication and thus makes it difficult—and sometimes impossible—for anyone to convey ideas clearly and to move effectively toward the solution of therapeutic, educational, or managerial problems.

REFERENCES

1. J.R. Gibb, "Defense Level and Influence Potential in Small Groups," in L. Petrullo and B. M. Bass (eds.), *Leadership and Interpersonal Behavior* (New York: Holt, Rinehart and Winston, 1961), pp. 66–81.

2. J. R. Gibb, "Sociopsychological Processes of Group Instruction," in N. B. Henry (ed.), *The Dynamics of Instructional Groups* (Fifty-ninth Yearbook of the National Society of the Study of Education, Part II, 1960), pp. 115–135.

PROBES

Does Gibb see defensiveness as a relational thing—something that's created *between* persons—or does he see it as something one person or group creates and forces on another person or a group?

Like Powell in the previous essay, Gibb cautions against evaluation. Is it possible to be nonevaluative? Or is that what Gibb is asking you to do?

Although most of Gibb's examples use verbal cues, each of the categories of defensiveness and supportiveness is also communicated nonverbally. Can you identify how you nonverbally communicate evaluation? Control? Strategy? Superiority? Spontaneity? Empathy? Equality?

Self-disclosing is one way to communicate spontaneity. Can you identify communication behaviors that help create the other kinds of supportive climate?

Which categories of defensive behavior are most present in your relationship with your lover or spouse? Your employer? Your parents? Which categories of supportive behavior characterized those relationships?

I have two principal ways of discovering the areas where I fail to see myself. The first is acknowledging the qualities in others which irritate me. The second is recognizing the comments that make me defensive. All I have to do to discover what rankles me in other people's behavior is to review my latest encounters, but I have more difficulty recognizing when I am being defensive. I can identify it best by the following syndrome: I answer quickly. I feel in need of talking at length, and I feel impatient when interrupted. I explain. I try to persuade. But I feel frustrated even if I appear to succeed, as if the damage has already been done. I think hurriedly, and I feel a strong resistance to pausing and considering, as if something will be lost if I do this. My face feels fixed and serious. I usually avoid eye contact immediately after hearing the comment. I am incapable of taking the comment any way but seriously; the words never seem light or funny to me. When my reaction becomes apparent to the people present they often take the situation lightly. I feel somewhat misunderstood and misused.

HUGH PRATHER

As I said in the introduction to Gibb's article, the first step toward handling conflict assertively is to recognize the factors that create defensiveness and the factors that can help diminish it. The second step is to learn what I've found to be one of the most difficult and the most helpful of all communication skills—*owning your feelings.*

In my classes and in my own life, owning feelings has taken time to teach and learn. It also takes a great deal of effort, because it requires you to publicly take on some responsibilities that most of us are very used to shoving off onto others. But when two or more persons are able to practice this skill, it has an amazing effect on their communicating. The skill is especially useful in dealing with conflict. It does more than any other single thing to promote genuine assertiveness, to enable each party in the conflict to make his or her own position clear without stomping on the other persons involved.

In order to own your feelings, you need to start with two "truths" that sometimes *feel* like "lies." The first is that feelings are not "involuntary"; they do *not* "just happen" to you regardless of what you do. Have you ever watched someone do this—or done it yourself? While you're in the middle of a heated argument with someone, the phone rings. One of you picks up the phone and says pleasantly, "Hello. Yes, this is _____. Oh fine, how are you? Good. Next week? That would be great; we'd like to come. Thanks for calling. Goodbye." Then the person hangs up and resumes the argument at its original intensity. If feelings were really involuntary, that *couldn't* happen![1]

When you say, "I'm mad and I just can't help it!" you're really saying that you feel/think that you have a right to be angry under those circumstances and that you think/feel that anyone in the same situation would respond the same way. But you have chosen the space you are in. Feelings did not *force* you there.

As children we probably picked up from adults around us the idea that we were *supposed* to feel or even that we *had to* feel a certain way. Maybe your mom or dad responded to a loud thunderstorm with something like, "Are you afraid of the big noise?" Or maybe you "caught" a fear of bears or a love of cats from a parent or older sister or brother whom you depended on and who always strongly reacted that way. Whatever the case, although some "automatic" feeling reaction might have a strong hold on you, you can break it, and the first step is to recognize that feelings are *not* involuntary. It's a matter of learning that "I *decide* how to behave in any situation as I have learned to do. If I am to change how I behave, therefore, I have to learn some new options."[2]

The second "truth" is that feelings come from inside us; they are *not* caused by something outside. Every time we say, "You make me so mad!" or "She's really boring," we're forgetting this truth. In the first instance we are actually saying something like this: "I feel anger and it's your fault. Change what you're doing so I won't have to be angry anymore." Obviously this "truth" is related to the first one.

My anger is just that—*mine*. I might have learned over the years to feel anger every time someone disagrees with me or every time a same-sex friend beats me at a game of skill, or every time a teacher grades a paper I've written with something lower than a B. But what I've learned is my property and my responsibility. You can't give me my anger—or take it away. It's mine, and I am the only person it can have a real effect on.

I'm not saying that we always have control over everything. There are some actions that can prevent us from doing something or force us to do something else—actions of a law-enforcement agency, an employer, a school or other institution. But how we *feel* is still up to us. It's part of the choice-making power we have that makes us human.

The more I can integrate this second "truth" into my communicating, the freer I feel. The day I realized that I didn't *have* to feel defensive and hurt when someone criticized my teaching was a red-letter day for me! Since I care about my teaching, I still listen to those comments and try to respond appropriately to them. But I don't feel like the *target* of the comment now, and consequently I don't feel so defensive. It's still really difficult for me to own a strong feeling of rejection or hurt, but I'm getting there. And what a difference it makes when I succeed!

In these excerpts from a chapter of his book *Caring Enough to Confront*, David Augsburger talks about the skill of owning your anger. He emphasizes the importance of seeing anger as one part of a whole person, not something evil or antisocial. He also explains how anger frequently is a thinly concealed demand—a demand that you recognize my worth or stop trying to control me. But the demand usually arises from fear of some sort. It's really helpful for me to remember that; fear is behind most anger, and when I can get in touch with the fear, it's much easier to handle the anger constructively. Finally, Augsburger suggests how anger can help, not hinder, a relationship. Listen especially to what he says at the end of this essay. The points he makes are fairly simple, but they can make a real difference in your communicating.

REFERENCES

1. I am indebted for this example to John Narciso and David Burkett; see Chapter 4 of their book *Declare Yourself* (Englewood Cliffs, N.J.: Prentice-Hall, 1975).

2. *Ibid.,* pp. 36–37.

OWNING ANGER: LET BOTH YOUR FACES SHOW
David Augsburger

You're standing in the living room, looking out the window at your son's back. You're replaying the last moment's conversation. "How stupid can you get?" you'd said. "You blew it again like a no-good kid. That's what you are, and you better shape up or you're shipping out."

There he goes, anger and rejection showing in the slump of his shoulders. "He blew it?" you ask yourself. "Well, I blew it even worse. I get angry, I attack him personally, I put him down, I chop away at his self-esteem. I'm getting nowhere. What else can we do? If I could just deal with what he's doing without attacking him. Maybe that would make a difference. I could try it."

When angry, are you likely to attack the other person, depreciating his personality, intelligence, skill, or worth? It doesn't get you what you want either, I'll bet.

Next time, try focusing your anger on the person's behavior. Express appreciation for the other as a person, even as you explain your anger at his or her way of behaving. It lets you stay in touch while getting at what you are angry about. . . .

Do you feel comfortable with the suggestion that anger is acceptable, that it can be openly owned, that anger is a normal, natural human emotion?

Dr. Ernest Bruder, an outstanding chaplain and counselor, writes, "Growing angry is a quite normal (though very bothersome) response in human relations, but it does cut the individual off from those who are important to him. For some this is so intolerable that the anger is never admitted to awareness and the individual tries to deny those feelings which are a part of his connection with the rest of humanity."[1]

Anger is not the essence of badness.

Hate is sin	Love is virtue
Anger is evil	Affection is good
Confronting is brutal	Caring is wonderful
Openness is questionable	Diplomacy is wise

Do you find yourself thinking in such clearly defined categories? Rejecting hate, anger, honest awareness, and expression of your true feelings and perspectives and clear confrontation with others? To cut off one-half of your emotional spectrum and reject all negative feelings is to refuse to be a whole person. To deny and repress everything on the negative side is to also stifle and crush the full expression of your positive side.

There is danger in abusing and misusing others with our positive emotions and actions—love, kindness, gentleness, tolerance, sweetness—just as there is the threat of cutting and destroying others with our negative responses—anger, harshness, criticism, irritation. To be engulfed and incorporated by a smothering love, all sweet gentleness, and I'm-only-trying-to-help-you-it's-for-your-own-good kindness is more treacherous than harsh, crisp frankness. You can at least reject it without fighting an affectionate, sticky mass of divinity-candy love.

I want to be a whole person in my relationships with you. I want to be in touch with both sides of you. Give me both your cold pricklies (honest anger) and your warm fuzzies (affirming love). Let both your faces show.

There are two sides in everyone. Both sides are important. Both are acceptable. Both are precious. Both can be loved.

Your wife made a cutting remark two days ago, and still no apology. Your daughter didn't thank you for the little gift you bought her. Your son forgot to put the tools back in their place in your shop. And you're feeling angry at all of them, at everything!

Anger is a demand. Like, "I demand an apology from you—an apology that suits me." "I demand you show appreciation for my gifts—in a way that pleases me." "I demand that you return my tools—perfectly—just the way I keep them." That's the real thrust of anger. A demand that also demands others meet your demands.

Even though you seldom put the demands into words, they are there inside your feelings. And you are resentful. "What if I said what I feel, if I really made my demands clear?" you ask yourself. "Then I could either stick to them, or laugh at them and forget them. . . ."

⁄Get in touch with the demands you make of others. Recognize them. Start admitting them out loud. Then you have a choice: (1) you can negotiate the demands that matter, or (2) you can cancel the ones that don't.

Love is being honest and open about your demands. Love is canceling unfair demands. Love is freeing others to live and grow.

Underneath my feelings of anger . . .
. . . there are concealed expectations.
(I may not yet be aware of them myself.)
Inside my angry statements . . .
. . . there are hidden demands.
(I may not yet be able to put them into words.)

Recognized or unrecognized, the demands are there. Anger is a demand. It may be a demand that you hear me. Or that you recognize my worth. Or that you see me as precious and worthy to be loved. Or that you respect me. Or let go of my arm. Or quit trying to take control of my life.

The demands emerge whenever I see you as rejecting me, or foresee you as about to reject me as a person of worth.

Anger is a demand "that you recognize my worth." When I feel that another person is about to engulf or incorporate me (assuming ownership of me, taking me for granted, using me, absorbing me into his or her life-program), I feel angry.

Actually, I first feel anxious. "Anxiety is a sign that one's self-esteem, one's self-regard is endangered,"[2] as Harry Stack Sullivan expressed it. When my freedom to be me is threatened, I become anxious, tense, ready for some action. Escape? Anger? Or work out an agreement?

Escape may be neither possible nor practical. Agreement seems far away since I see you as ignoring my freedom, devaluing my worth, and attempting to use me. Anger is the most available option.

Anger is "the curse of interpersonal relations," Sullivan well said. A curse, because it is so instantly effective as a way of relieving anxiety. When a person flashes to anger, the anger clouds his recall of what just happened to spark the anger, confuses his awareness of what he is really demanding, and restricts his ability to work toward a new agreement.

But we chose—consciously or unconsciously—to become angry because:

"Anger is much more pleasant to experience than anxiety. The brute facts are that it is much more comfortable to feel angry than anxious. Admitting that neither is too delightful, there is everything in favor of anger. Anger often leaves one sort of worn out...and very often makes things worse in the long run, but there is a curious feeling of power when one is angry."[3]

Check the pattern: (1) I feel keen frustration· in my relationship with another. (2) I see the other person as rejecting me—my worth, my needs, my freedom, my request. (3) I become suddenly and intensely anxious. (4) I blow away my anxiety with anger which confuses things even further. (5) I may then feel guilty for my behavior and resentful of the other's part in the painful experience.

Anger is a positive emotion, a self-affirming emotion which responds reflexively to the threat of rejection or devaluation with the messages (1) I am a person, a precious person and (2) I demand that you recognize and respect me.

The energies of anger can flow in self-affirming ways when directed by love—the awareness of the other person's equal preciousness.

Anger energies become a creative force when they are employed (1) to change my own behavior which ignored the other's preciousness and (2) to confront the other with his or her need to change unloving behavior. Anger energy can be directed at the cause of the anger, to get at the demands I am making, to own them, and then either correct my demanding self by canceling the demand, or call on the other to hear my demand and respond to how I see our relationship and what I want.

When I am on the receiving end of another's anger, I want to hear the anger-messages the other gives to me, and check out what I am picking up as a demand. Careful listening can discern what the other is demanding, clarify it in clear statements, and lead to clean confrontation. Then I have the choice of saying yes to the other's demands, or saying no. I may feel angry in return, but I want to experience my anger with honest "I statements," not with explosive "you statements."

Explosive anger is "the curse of interpersonal relations." Vented anger may ventilate feelings and provide instant, though temporary, release for tortured emotions, but it does little for relationships.

Clearly expressed anger is something different. Clear statements of anger feelings and angry demands can slice through emotional barriers or communications tangles and establish contact.

When angry, I want to give clear, simple "I messages." "You messages" are most often attacks, criticisms, devaluations of the other person, labels, or ways of fixing blame.

"I messages" are honest, clear, confessional. "I messages" own my anger, my responsibility, my demands without placing blame. Note the contrast between honest confession and distorted rejection.

I messages	*You messages*
I am angry.	You make me angry.
I feel rejected.	You're judging and rejecting me.
I don't like the wall between us.	You're building a wall between us.
I don't like blaming or being blamed.	You're blaming everything on me.
I want the freedom to say yes or no.	You're trying to run my life.
I want respectful friendship with you again.	You've got to respect me or you're not my friend.

"I just can't help it. It makes me angry."

"It just gets to me and touches off my temper."

"It's like something comes over me, and I can't do a thing about it."

"It's other people, that's what it is. They know I've got a quick temper and they're out to get me."

"It" is the problem. "It" causes untold irritation, anger, frustration, embarrassment, pain, guilt, and misery. "It's" not me. "It's" this something, or someone, or some situations.

When you find yourself using "it" as an explanation or as a scapegoat, stop. Listen to yourself. Recognize what you're doing. Avoiding responsibility. Sidestepping the real problem. Denying ownership of your feelings, responses, and actions.

Release comes not from denying, but from owning who—what—and where I am in my relationships.

I want to own what goes on in me and accept total responsibility for it.

I discover that as I own it, accepting full responsibility, I am then able to respond in new ways. I become response-able?

A great freedom comes as I own my thoughts, feelings, words, and emotions. (1) I become free to choose my actions. (2) I become free to choose my reactions.

My actions are mine. Your actions are yours. I am responsible for my behavior. You are responsible for yours.

I also accept responsibility for my actions.

"You make me angry," I used to say.

Untrue. No one can make another angry. If I become angry at you, I am responsible for that reaction. (I am not saying that anger is wrong. It may well be the most appropriate and loving response that I am aware of at that moment.)

But you do not make me angry. I make me angry at you. It is not the only behavior open to me.

There is no situation in which anger is the only possible response. If I become angry (and I may, it's acceptable) it's because I choose to respond with anger. I might have chosen kindness, irritation, humor, or many other alternatives (if I had been aware of these choices). There is no situation which commands us absolutely. For example, I have the choice to respond to another's threat with blind obedience, with silent passivity, with vocal refusal, with firm resistance, or with anger, if that seem appropriate.

When childhood experiences are limited, a person may mature with a limited set of behaviors open to him or her. Some have only two ways of coping with another's attack—anger or submission. If these are the only ways modeled by the parents or the family, they may be the only aware-choices in the person's behavioral repertoire.

If I have grown enough in life so that more than one pattern of behavior is available to me, then I can freely select the responses which seem most appropriate to the situation.

I want to be aware of a wealth of responses, and to have them available to me. Anger or patience. Toughness or gentleness. Clear confrontation or warm, caring support. I want to be able-to-respond in any of these.

I am responsible for choosing my responses to you.

I am responsible for the way I react to you.

I am responsible for how I see you. And from the way I see you—as either friendly or hostile; accepting or rejecting; welcoming or threatening—emerge my feelings. Feelings are the energies that power the way I choose to see you, or to perceive you.

I am responsible for how I see you—and from that for the way I feel about you.

You cannot make me angry. Unless I choose to be angry.

You cannot make me discouraged, or disgusted, or depressed. These are choices.

You cannot make me hate. I must choose to hate.

You cannot make me jealous. I must choose envy.

I experience all these and more on all too many occasions, but I am responsible for those actions or reactions. I make the choice.

I love me.	I also love you.
I love my freedom	I respect your freedom
to be who I am.	to be who you are.
I love my drive	I admire your drive
to be all I can be.	to be all you can be.

I love my right
   to be different from you.
I love my need
   to be related to you.

The thoughts I think,
The words I speak,
The actions I take,
The emotions I feel—
   They are mine, for them
   I am fully responsible.

I am free
to accept or to refuse
   your wants
   your requests
   your expectations
   your demands.
I can say yes.
I can say no.
I am not in this world
   to live as you prescribe.

I am not responsible
   for you.
I will not be
   responsible *to* you.
I want to be
   responsible *with* you.
I want to be your brother.

I recognize your right
   to be different from me.
I appreciate your need
   to be related to me.

The thoughts you think,
The words you speak,
The actions you take,
The emotions you feel—
   They are yours, for them
   I am in no way responsible.

You are free
to accept or to refuse
   my wants
   my requests
   my expectations
   my demands.
You can say yes.
You can say no.
You are not in this world
   to live as I prescribe.

You are not responsible
   for me.
You need not be
   responsible *to* me.
You can be
   responsible *with* me.
You may be a brother
   with me.

REFERENCES

1. Ernest Bruder, *Ministering to Deeply Troubled People* (Englewood Cliffs, N.J.: Prentice-Hall, 1963), pp. 30–31.

2. Harry Stack Sullivan, *The Psychiatric Interview* (New York: Norton, 1954), pp. 218–219.

3. *Ibid.*, p. 109.

PROBES

Is Augsburger's view of anger consistent with the relational view of communication presented in Chapter 1? How so?

Note how much owning your feelings depends on verbal cues. You start with a nonverbal attitude, but there is a world of *verbal* difference between what Augsburger calls "I" messages and "you" messages. When you use "I" messages, how are your words functioning? To reduce uncertainty? Bring people together? Evoke emotion? Refer or stand for? Affect perception?

Augsburger says that "my actions are mine. Your actions are yours. I am responsible for my behavior. You are responsible for yours." If this is true, why should we ever communicate with one another?

If it's true that "you cannot make me angry unless I choose to be angry," is it also true that you cannot make me defensive unless I choose that? Would Gibb (see the previous essay) agree with Augsburger on this point?

There is an important difference between expressing my antagonism and being critical. When I criticize I say in effect "You are wrong," and I leave unspoken the part I am playing in the condemnation. Criticism is thus "safer" than stating my feelings as mine because the other person will usually respond to the words and not to me. If, however, I say, "This is what goes off in me when you do such-and-such," I am admitting that all criticism requires a criticizer.

HUGH PRATHER

Expressing anger is a very intimate act. And so, of course, it is very risky. It at once opens me up to a closer relationship, or to a verbal kick in the groin. I was irritated at Hank's denouncing every comment that anyone made at the meeting, but instead of telling him that, I argued against his logic. That was not expressing my irritation, it was reacting to it. Later, when I expressed it directly and told him how mad I was at his attitude, he made a very personal confession of how stupid he felt around all of us. He could have come back with a rebuff that would have hurt me.

Again and again I am surprised at how often people appreciate my going to them with my negative feelings. I am afraid that my words will hurt our friendship, but it has turned out that they usually strengthen it.

HUGH PRATHER

This section from the book *Declare Yourself* outlines a self-assertive way of communicating. This way of communicating, or "language," is a practical application of Gibb's and Augsburger's ideas about defensiveness and owning your feelings. Since this section is a fairly small part of a larger whole, I think it would help if I explained the context it fits in.

The authors of *Declare Yourself* develop the basic idea that we all have a limited number of ways of communicating in a stressful or threatening situation. Everybody experiences some stress or threat almost every day, and most people respond most of the time with communication behavior that makes things worse instead of better. In fact, it's been estimated that over 95 percent of us respond to threat or stress with some kind of destructive communication pattern.[1]

You can best identify the destructive communication patterns—and the constructive one—by thinking of each communication event as having four parts.

you
the other person(s)
the topic
the context or situation.

A family discussion might consist, for example, of you and one of your parents trying to agree about where to celebrate Christmas or Hannukah, after just finishing
Thanksgiving dinner. The participants in that situation are obviously the two of
you; the topic is where to spend the holiday, and the situation or context could be
the kitchen, dining room, or a living room full of family members in various stages
of relaxation.

If you experience threat or stress in that situation—or in any other—you'll
tend to respond with communication that cancels out one or more of the four elements that are involved. For example, you might cancel out yourself:

~~you~~
the other person(s)
the topic
the context or situation.

When you choose that pattern, you communicate in verbal and nonverbal ways
that say, "Whatever you want is fine with me. You decide; I'll go along. I'm just
here to make you happy." When you're canceling out yourself, you usually talk in
an ingratiating way, apologize, and try to please the others. Your voice is often
whiny and squeaky, and your body is in some kind of begging, uncomfortably off-
balance position. In this situation you're interested primarily in being sure that
nothing you do interferes in any way with what your parent wants, even though his
or her plans may be radically different from what you'd prefer to do. Virginia Satir
calls this choice "placating," and the authors of *Declare Yourself* call it "deferring."

On the other hand, you might respond to the threat or stress by canceling out
the other person and by communicating in ways that Satir calls "blaming" and the
authors of *Declare Yourself* call "demanding":

you
the ~~other~~ person(s)
the topic
the context or situation.

This kind of communicating is characterized by nonstop disagreeing, fault-finding,
acting superior, and being bossy. Verbally and nonverbally, you say, "It's your
fault. If it weren't for you, everything would be all right." Blaming or demanding
sentences often start with, "You never do this" or "You always do that" or "Why
don't you ever. . .?" Usually when you're communicating this way, your eyes glare,
your throat muscles tighten, and your face is screwed up into a snarl. My description may be a little extreme, but I suspect that you can recognize at least some
part of it. Blaming or demanding is a second way we often communicate in a
threatening situation.

A third way is to cancel out both yourself and the other and to focus entirely
on the situation and the topic.

~~you~~
the ~~other~~(s)
the topic
the context or situation.
You can tell when you're communicating this way by your insistence on "being objective" and "keeping personalities out of this." Satir calls this response to threat or stress "computing." She notes that when you're computing, you're very correct, cool, dissociated, not sharing any feeling—like a computer. When people compute, they also tend to use the longest and most abstract words possible. Body position is often stiff and unmoving and the voice is dead—a dry monotone.

A fourth response to stress or threat is to cancel out, as much as you can, all four parts of the communication event:

~~you~~
the ~~other~~(s)
the ~~topic~~
the ~~context~~ or situation.
Satir calls this "distracting" and the authors of Declare Yourself call it "defecting." If you don't get your way in a conversation and you feel threatened, you might defect by stomping out of the room, bursting into tears, or making threats or promises sufficiently extreme to change the point at issue entirely: "I'm walking out of here, and I never want to see you again!" Distracting or defecting communication, in other words, is irrelevant to what everybody else is saying or doing. In a group situation you can communicate this way by making off-the-topic comments, ignoring others' questions, changing the subject, and popping up and down for refreshments. When you're communicating this way, your voice, as Satir puts it, "can be singsong, often out of tune with the words, and can go up and down without reason because it is focused nowhere."[2]

To summarize, here are four of the five possible responses to threat or stress and an example of what a person communicating in each of these ways might say to apologize to someone whose arm he or she had just bumped:

Canceling	Names	Example[3]
~~you~~	Placating	"Please forgive me. I'm just a clumsy
other(s)	Deferring	oaf. I'm really sorry. I'm always
topic		stumbling into people."
context		
you	Blaming	"Ye gods, why's your arm poked out
~~other~~(s)	Demanding	there?!" Keep it in next time, will ya?"
topic		
context		
~~you~~	Computing	"I wish to render an apology. I
~~other~~(s)		inadvertently struck your arm in
topic		passing. It was certainly not my
context		intent to disturb you in any way."

~~You~~
~~Other(s)~~
~~Topic~~
~~Context~~

Distracting	"Gee, some guy's mad. Must've got
Defecting	bumped. Oh, hi, Cliff! You look
	great!"

There is a fifth way to communicate, one that doesn't cancel any of the elements involved. Satir calls it "leveling" and the authors of *Declare Yourself* call it "declaring." It is a form of what is more generally called assertive communication. As the next selection says, "In declaring I am simply saying what I want to happen rather than demanding that it happen, or deferring to the wants of the other person. And I invite my dyad partner to declare his [or her] wishes too." When our wishes differ we *negotiate* the outcome. Negotiation doesn't mean giving up or giving in, and it also doesn't mean compromising. It means. . . ." Well, they put it quite clearly, so I'll let you get it directly from them.

As you might guess, the attitudes and skills outlined here are not simple either to understand clearly or to do well, but they are tremendously useful. Assertiveness cannot only greatly improve much of your communicating, but it can also help you feel good about yourself. It takes work to develop the skills outlined here, but the effort is well worth it.

REFERENCES

1. The estimate comes from Virginia Satir, who made it after spending years helping hundreds of families improve their communicating. This section is based on the ideas in her book *Peoplemaking* (Palo Alto: Science and Behavior Books, 1972).

2. *Ibid.,* p. 70.

3. Examples adapted from Satir, p. 75.

THE NEW "LANGUAGE"
John Narciso and David Burkett

I am convinced that most of the problems people experience in interpersonal relationships are the result of restricted options. My suggestion, then, is, . . . that these people are not "ill" and requiring therapy, but rather that they need to learn a new alternative or "language."

Consider in analogy a man who had learned to speak English, French, and German. Suppose he were to find himself in a Russian village. Since he spoke no

From John Narciso and David Burkett, *Declare Yourself: Discovering the Me in Relationships,* © 1975, pp. 66–68, 72–74, 75–76. Reprinted by permission of Prentice-Hall, Inc., Englewood Cliffs, New Jersey.

Russian, he would have difficulty conducting business with the natives. He couldn't converse with them nor could he likely establish any significant relationships. This man could be termed maladjusted, but he was not ill. He did not need therapy; he wasn't sick. He simply needed to learn the Russian language.

So it is with [this] option in relationships, a new language of conducting interpersonal processes with other people in dyads.

The new option is one I call *declaring*. No one in the dyad—not ME, not YOU—is canceled, entirely.

Declaring Behavior   ME/YOU

When I am declaring, I am speaking in the first person singular. I am making declarative statements about what I want to happen, using operational definitions. I am dealing with issues based upon data I have collected. I am willing to negotiate.

[This] language may strike you as simplistic. It certainly is simple. Nearly anyone can learn it and use it, if he decides to add it to his repertoire.

In declaring, I am simply saying what I want to happen, rather than demanding that it happen, or deferring to the wants of the other person. And I invite my dyad partner to declare his wishes too.

Once we have both made our declarations, we may negotiate any differences. "Negotiation" is a key word here, and one I want to comment on at greater length.

The traditional deferring-demanding relationship often leads to compromise conditions, whereas the declaring-declaring relationship often includes negotiation. Compromise and negotiation are not the same, although at first glance they may appear to be similar.

Operationally defined, compromise might mean something such as "If you let me win this time, I'll let you win next time." The problem with compromise is that both parties are forced to keep books on whose turn it is to win, and no one is quite as good a bookkeeper as his partner would want him to be. In negotiation, both parties deal with issues rather than with feelings, and with data collected regarding the issues. In negotiation, there is no residue, no owing anybody later, no keeping of books as to who gave in to whom and when. Instead of dealing with feelings, the person who is declaring is oriented to issues. He is responsive to the situation.

Saying this another way:

When a person is blocked, he traditionally presents feelings, asking others to be responsible for them. These are...get-my-way tools...represented here as defecting behavior.

The new language or option is to deal *not* with feelings, but with *issues* based upon data collected.

As the declaring person, I evaluate the data and then declare what I want to happen, not what I want the other person to do. I recognize that I alone am responsible for my own behavior.

I talk in first person singular about what I want, and I use operational terms. . . .

The declarer does not *have* to win. He simply declares his own wants or wishes and determines how he can best go about fulfilling those wants in his hierarchical scale. He does this by being *responsive* to the total situation, including the other person's wishes, yet not being *responsible* for the other person's feelings.

Not long ago, a friend of mine stopped by my office.

"I've got a problem," he said after a while. "I can't get my wife to be on time for anything. She's always late. No matter where we go, we get there after everything's started."

"How long has this been going on?" I asked.

"Ever since we were married, I guess. About eighteen years."

"On what basis are *you* late?" I asked him.

"It's not me. I've already told you. It's my wife who's always late."

"Yes, but what keeps *you* from being on time? You have two cars, don't you? *You* could be on time, and your wife could join you later."

He paused. "No, I couldn't do that. I couldn't go without her. She'd be upset."

"But you've been upset for eighteen years, haven't you?"

My friend, a deferring person in this transaction, had been the nice guy. He had been canceling himself, but then he would manifest defecting behavior. After each social event to which he and his wife had arrived late, a day or two of "recovery" had been necessary.

I suggested to him that he might try *declaring* his wants. By doing that, I said, neither he nor his wife would have to lose entirely. He could be on time, if he wished. His wife could be late, if she wished.

Later, he told me what happened the next time he and his wife were preparing for an evening engagement.

"Honey," he had said, "the party is at eight o'clock, and I'd like to go on time tonight. I'm planning on leaving at seven forty-five. I would like to go to the party with you. I'm available to help you in any way that will assist you in being able to leave with me."

That particular time, he reported, his wife was not ready to leave at 7:45, and so he left for the party alone. She joined him there later.

"Your wife had the prerogative to go late if she wanted to," I said.

"Yes," he replied.

"And you had the prerogative to be on time if you wanted to."

"Of course."

My friend went on to explain that recently he and his wife had been going to social events on time, together. What had happened was that his wife had decided that she would rather go *with* her husband on time than go *without* her husband late, although she had both options available to her. She changed her behavior in response to her husband changing his.

In declaring, a person states what he wishes or wants to happen. There are no expectations, no dealings with feelings. Instead, there is self-responsible behavior that directly concerns issues, the situation.

I gave a talk one afternoon to a women's group. After my speech, a woman approached me and (in a demanding transaction) said, "Well, you certainly stepped on my toes with your remarks."

If I had responded in a deferring way in this transaction, how would I have behaved?

I could have said something such as, "Oh, I'm so sorry. I apologize." To which the woman might have replied (in a demanding way): "Okay, but don't do it again."

I might have elected to reply in a demanding way. My response then might have sounded this way: "No, I didn't, and besides, the fee wasn't large enough to stand out here and take this from you." Such a remark probably would have led to an additional verbal skirmish.

Or perhaps as a defector: "I can't talk with you about it right now; I have an appointment. I must go."

But I elected a *declaring* response and said: "I'm glad you've told me what you think. I appreciate the feedback." I could have responded in numerous declaring ways.

In this instance, I neither lost nor attempted to win, nor did I run away.

And in a very few moments, in the same small group in which we had been chatting, this particular woman and I were talking and smiling again.

As you have perhaps seen, the declaring response is "disarming" rather than "defeating." That's an important distinction between declaring behavior as opposed to the more traditional ways of relating, deferring-demanding-defecting.

Again, you might take time to review some of your ongoing relationships. Plot them out and determine how they might be different if declaring behavior were used.

A last point in this chapter.

In declaring behavior, the declarer states his wishes and may negotiate. But some wishes are extremely significant and nonnegotiable. When this happens, the two people involved may decide that the cost of the relationship is too great, either on a particular issue or in total.

An example of this might concern a young couple married a few years. The husband declares that he would like to have two children in the next four years. The wife declares that she wants no children at all. The issue is drawn, and data must be collected. The husband attempts to negotiate, suggesting that if the wife is afraid of pregnancy, they might adopt children. The wife replies that she is not afraid of pregnancy, that she simply does not want any children. Eventually, they conclude that they have a nonnegotiable set of wishes.

Whether this couple has children or not, one of them loses immediately, and ultimately both will lose.

In a situation of nonnegotiable wishes, there is the likelihood that staying together may cost each of the partners much too much. They may then elect to abandon the relationship.

They agree to withdraw from one another as the most appropriate response to the situation. Neither is expecting or anticipating the other to change *his* "position" to prevent the withdrawal.

Some readers may have difficulty accepting the issue-oriented concept I am proposing in this book because our society is so highly power-structured. There are countless examples of demand situations in which "the other side" is expected to defer and often does. This happens in political and social circles, in business, and within academic relationships.

While preparing this chapter, I heard a radio commentator quoting the economist Jean Monnet. The quote seemed illustrative of the issue-oriented concept I have been recommending.

Monnet had suggested that rather than two individuals or nations confronting one another across the table, it would be preferable for the two to share the same side of the table, confronting the problem on the other side.

PROBES

I see important relationships between your perception of your self, which is discussed in Chapter 4, and your ability to communicate in "leveling" or "declaring" ways. Do you see those links? How would you describe them?

When you are "placating" or "deferring," what is usually your image of the other? What is your image of the other when you're "demanding" or "computing"? What is your image of your self when you're "defecting"?

Is the "new 'language'" Narciso and Burkett describe mainly verbal or mainly nonverbal?

What do you think would happen if you responded to your spouse or lover as the husband did in the examples described in this essay? How much do you think your communicationg with your lover or spouse is affected by your *assumptions* about how he or she would respond?

Narciso and Burkett close this section with a brief comment about irreconcible conflict. How would you paraphrase what they say using the "spiritual child" metaphor I introduced in Chapter 1?

No one is wrong. At most someone is uninformed. If I think a man is wrong, either I am unaware of something, or he is. So unless I want to play a superiority game I had best find out what he is looking at.

"You're wrong" means "I don't understand you"—I'm not seeing what you're seeing. But there is nothing wrong *with you, you are simply not me and that's not wrong.*

HUGH PRATHER

8

EMPATHIC LISTENING

I am afraid of your silence because of what it could mean. I suspect your silence of meaning you are getting bored or losing interest or making up your own mind about me without my guidance. I believe that as long as I keep you talking I can know what you are thinking.

But silence can also mean confidence. And mutual respect. Silence can mean live and let live: the appreciation that I am I and you are you. This silence is an affirmation that we are already together—as two people. Words can mean that I want to make you into a friend and silence can mean that I accept your already being one.

HUGH PRATHER

You will probably note that Charles Kelly's article was originally written for a discussion textbook. I think his advice, however, is valid for almost any interpersonal-communication situation.

In this article Kelly clearly distinguishes between empathic and deliberative listening and suggests when each is appropriate and useful. Figure 1 in the selection seems to me to illustrate graphically what it's like to become involved in another person's comments, from that person's point of view. The figure indicates that in empathic listening, understanding precedes evaluation. That doesn't mean that you should try to avoid evaluation entirely; it's impossible for a human to be completely nonevaluative. But before you try to summarize or outline what the other person has said or before you agree or disagree with his or her arguments or conclusions, it's useful to try to *experience with* the other whatever he or she is thinking and feeling. In practice this suggests that your first response to the other person should usually *not* be, "Well, *I* think. . . ." or "That doesn't make sense because. . . ." or "But you're overlooking. . . ." Instead, you might try paraphrasing part of what the other said or asking questions to clarify and check your own understanding; better yet, you might allow yourself to participate in the other person's thoughts and feelings—to try and feel what he or she is feeling and to say whatever you might say if you really felt that way yourself.

Empathic listening is one of those elements of interpersonal communication that looks easy on paper but is very seldom practiced effectively. Usually people forget about it completely as soon as they get into an interesting or threatening conversation. Or when they don't, they end up frustrating the other person with mechanical echoes of everything he or she says or nonstop "Do you mean...?" questions. A key, as Kelly suggests, is your motivation. You must really want to learn to listen empathically and actually be willing to be a participant observer in part of somebody else's world.

EMPATHIC LISTENING
Charles M. Kelly

. . . Listening is a multi-faceted activity and it can be considered from different viewpoints, but at least two ways of categorizing listening seem especially fruitful for theoretical analysis: *deliberative listening* and *empathic listening*. Most recent writers have treated listening as a unitary skill, i.e., as a rather definite and "deliberative" ability to hear information, to analyze it, to recall it at a later

This is an abridgment of an essay from *Small Group Communication: A Reader*, ed. Robert S. Cathcart and Larry A. Samovar, Dubuque, Iowa: William C. Brown Co., 1970, pp. 251–259. Reprinted by permission.

time, and to draw conclusions from it. Commercially-published listening tests and most listening training programs are based on this, the deliberative listening, viewpoint. On the other hand, empathic listening occurs when the person participates in the spirit or feeling of his environment as a communication *receiver*. This does not suggest that the listener is uncritical or always in agree-

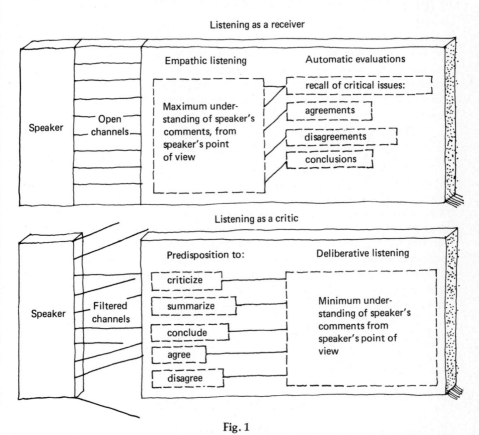

Fig. 1

The differences between empathic listening and deliberative listening are primarily motivational. Both listeners seek the same objective: accurate understanding of the communication from another. The model suggests that the motivation to receive information is superior to the motivation to use critical skills. The empathic listener lets his understanding of the speaker determine his modes of evaluation, which are automatic; the deliberative listener's understanding of the speaker is filtered through his predetermined modes of selective listening, and actually spends less time as a communication receiver. The empathic listener is more apt to be a consistent listener, and is less prone to his own or other distractions. This theory is correct only if the assumption is true that persons can and do think critically without deliberative effort—*while listening*. (Of course, if persons do not make the effort to listen *per se*, little or not understanding will occur.)

ment with what is communicated, but rather, that his primary interest is to become fully and accurately aware of what is going on. (See Figure 1.)

It should be observed that the terms "deliberative listening" and "empathic listening" are not mutually exclusive or exhaustive. Their main purpose is to differentiate between two basic ways of viewing the same listening activity. The desired result of both deliberative and empathic listening is identical: accurate understanding of oral communication. However, this understanding is achieved by different routes. The deliberative listener *first* has the desire to critically analyze what a speaker has said, and secondarily tries to understand the speaker (this can be the result of personal inclination or of training which emphasizes procedure at the expense of listening). The empathic listener has the desire to understand the speaker first, and, as a result, tries to take the appropriate action.

. . . The latter kind of listening is characteristic of the person who is able to adapt quickly to the real needs of a situation because he has a presence of mind and a greater confidence in the accuracy of his awareness—he does not handicap himself by deciding in advance that he does not have to listen to a particular person who is poorly dressed, or that he must be sure to expose all faulty reasoning if he is to demonstrate his competence.

This is not to say that various skills in critical thinking are less important than empathic listening. Without critical analysis, listening in a problem-solving discussion would be useless. The point is, however, that a person uses quite naturally whatever critical skills he has already acquired, as long as he is interested and actively listening; to the extent that he is not listening, critical skills will be of little value. Actually, a case can be made that "deliberative listening" is a self-contradiction and a misnomer—and that "empathic listening" is a redundancy. To the extent that one is deliberating (mentally criticizing, summarizing, concluding, preparing reports, etc.) he is *not listening*, but formulating his own ideas. And listening, by its very nature, *has* to be empathic; a person understands what he has heard, only to the extent that he can share in the meaning, spirit, or feeling of what the communicator has said.

There is some evidence that this line of reasoning is correct. . . .

Several studies strongly indicate that when persons know that their listening comprehension is being tested, differences between individuals are primarily matters of general mental ability; when they do not know their listening performance is being tested, differences are due to personality differences (including motivation to listen), as well as general mental ability. Of these two kinds of research situations, the latter is more representative of realistic listening events.

It is likely that most communication problems arise either because of participant inattention (poor motivation), or because of a lack of general mental ability—not because of anything that can be called "listening ability." Do teachers in a faculty meeting miss the details of registration because of a lack of listening ability, or because of a lack of motivation? Does an engineer fail to understand an explanation of a new process because he lacks listening ability, or because he simply has not yet been able to visualize unfamiliar relationships? In the rare cases when a discussion is vitally important to everyone and motivation is high (as in a listening test), there is little chance of an important point (or its significance) being missed, unless the listener simply lacked the mental ability to understand or appreciate it to begin with. But in most of the everyday discussions that deal with the nagging problems of industrial production, proposed new school construction, traffic survey, curriculum changes, etc., motivation to participate (and, hence, listen) is moderate at best and is not evenly distributed among the discussants—and with some persons, inattention seems to be habitual.

In terms of *listening* theory, it is far more important to stress empathic, rather than deliberative, listening in discussion. This observation in no way depreciates the need for education and practical experience in critical analysis, debate, general semantics—or in any of the various mental skills brought into play *while* listening. But it is a mistake to consider these skills *as* listening, since this viewpoint suggests that the listener's analysis is part of the receiving process.

The degree to which one is able to listen and to perform other mental acts at the same time is an open question; research into the exact nature of listening, as it relates to other general mental abilities, is unclear at best. However, because of the obvious difficulties that occur in discussion when listener motivation is poor or non-existent, and in view of the probability that problems in discussion are due to factors other than listening *ability* when participant motivation is high, the following suggestions seem warranted:

Remember the characteristics of the poor listener. It is easy to sit back in your chair and complain to yourself that the discussion is boring or unimportant. However, the description of the kind of person who habitually does this is not very flattering, and should serve as an incentive to better listening; research suggests that the poor listener is less intelligent, and less emotionally mature than the good listener. Obviously, there are times when a person may be just as well off *not* listening, but the poor listener tends to make this a crutch for the easy way out of difficult listening events.

Make a firm initial commitment to listen. Listening is hard work and it takes energy. If you have had difficulty listening in the past, and now decide merely to *try* to listen and to participate in the spirit of the discussion as long as you can, you will soon fall into old habits. Above all, don't make an initial decision *not* to listen; if discussions in the past have proved deficient, according to your standards, accurate listening will better enable you to correct them in the future.

Get physically and mentally ready to listen. Sit up, and get rid of distractions; put away paper you were reading, books, pencils, papers, etc., unless you plan to use them. Try to dismiss personal worries, fears, or pleasant reverie until a later time. Will these kinds of thoughts be more productive of personal gain than your participation in this discussion?

Concentrate on the other person as a communicator. View the others in a discussion as sources of ideas and information, not as personalities. If you are reacting to another as being dishonest, unethical, stupid, tedious—or as a college professor, or Republican, or student rioter, or disgruntled parent—it will be difficult for you to accurately perceive what he is trying to say. There is little to fear in such an open approach. Shoddy thinking or speaking needs no label to be recognized, and fewer good ideas will be discarded because they were never really listened to. Of course, it goes without saying that persons communicate with gestures as well as with their voices, and the listener is concerned with perceiving the total communication environment as accurately as possible.

Give the other person a full hearing. Avoid interrupting another person unless you are sure you understand him fully, and that it is necessary. If you feel that you aren't sure you understand him, a well phrased question is usually more appropriate than an attempt by you to clarify his position. Impatience with others can lead to false understanding or agreement, and eventually leads to greater difficulties.

Use analytical skills as supplements to, not instead of, listening. To the degree that successful participation in discussion requires your understanding of others, rather than your speaking contributions, it is important not to be distracted by our own note taking, mental review of main points, critical analysis, or preparation for argumentative "comeback." An especially dubious recommendation frequently found in articles on listening is that, since listeners can listen faster than speakers can talk, the extra time should be used to review main points, "read between the lines," etc. Whether this conscious effort is exerted between words, sentences, or major ideas is never made clear. However, interviews with subjects following "surprise" listening tests have indicated that one of the major causes of listener distraction was a speaker's previous point: "I suddenly realized that I didn't know what he was talking about, because I was still thinking about what he had said before.". . .

Many factors make up a discussion, and listening is only one of them; however, it is an extremely important factor, and it has been diluted in the past by a shift of its meaning from one of reception to one of critical analysis.

Empathic listening cannot of itself make a good speaker out of a poor one, a clear thinker out of a dull thinker, or a good discussion out of a bad discussion. But to the extent that problems result from a lack of participant reception and understanding of the discussion interaction, empathic listening appears to be the best answer.

PROBES

What relationships do you see between empathic listening and defensiveness?

What relationships do you see between empathic listening and self-disclosure?

Does Kelly say that empathic listening is "nonevaluative"? Does he agree or disagree with Gibb or Powell on this point? What role do *you* think evaluation plays in the kind of listening Kelly is discussing here?

How can you communicate empathy nonverbally? How can you communicate it verbally?

For more than six years, Gerard Egan has studied, participated in, and led various kinds of encounter groups. This selection, taken from the book he wrote for encounter-group participants, focuses on the kind of listening that can best facilitate interpersonal communication in the group.

Egan makes three points in this excerpt that I think are especially useful. One is that empathic listening is an active, not a passive, process, a difficult job that demands commitment and effort. You can't just sit back and soak up communication cues; you have to *work* to listen well. At the same time, listening is a *relational* thing, i.e., it demands constructive effort from both listener and speaker.

The second point is that the empathic listener listens with *all* his or her senses. I think Egan makes this point especially well in the second paragraph of the following selection.

The third point is that many obstacles can get in the way of effective listening. Egan lists eight obstacles; I see my own and others' listening being affected most by the three he calls "self consciousness," "message anxiety," and "reductive listening." As Egan admits, we cannot eliminate all obstacles, but we can minimize their impact; when we do, it becomes much easier for our communication to be interpersonal instead of objectifying.

LISTENING AS EMPATHIC SUPPORT

Gerard Egan

For our purposes, listening means becoming aware of all the cues that the other emits, and this implies an openness to the totality of the communication of the other.... Listening demands work, and the work involved is difficult enough so that the effort will not be readily expended unless the listener has a deep respect for the total communication process.

One does not listen with just his ears: he listens with his eyes and with his sense of touch, he listens by becoming aware of the feelings and emotions that arise within himself because of his contact with others (that is, his own emotional resonance is another "ear"), he listens with his mind, his heart, and his imagination. He listens to the words of others, but he also listens to the messages that are buried in the words or encoded in the cues that surround the words (the "metacommunications" of the other). He listens to the voice, the demeanor, the vocabulary, and the gestures of the other, to the context, the verbal messages, the linguistic patterns, and the bodily movements of the other. He listens to the sounds and to the silences. He listens not only to the message itself but also to the context, or in Gestalt terms, he listens to both the figure and the ground and to the way these two interact.

Some examples will help clarify this kind of active listening.

Charles: Your words say you have no problem with me, Clara, but when you talk to me there is very often an edge in your voice.

Clara: Well, some things about you do bother me, but they seem so small that I didn't want to bring them up.

Kurt: The way you are sitting back stretched out on the chair bothers me, Dan. You say that you're here, but your body tells me that you are only partially here.

Dan: Maybe I *am* only partially here. Your interaction with Sandra has been pretty long, pretty exclusive, and therefore, for me, pretty boring.

Kathy: You haven't said anything for a long while, Burt, yet I don't feel you are someplace else. I have the feeling you're very uncomfortable with what's happening here.

Burt: You and Kathy and John have been talking to one another with such care and concern. I just didn't know how to get into the conversation. I'm not used to this. My conversation is usually so superficial if not actually

---

cynical. I admire what is happening and yet I feel miserable because I can't seem to be a part of it.

Christopher: One senses an empathic understanding here that is crucial to the kinds of interaction that characterize these groups.

Bridget: Your words sound like a lecture, Chris, but I take them to mean that you're glad that I get inside you somehow and share your world. I'm glad that you share mine. You do, you know.

This kind of active listening is the basis for empathic understanding.

THE NONSELECTIVE CHARACTER OF TOTAL LISTENING

Total listening is, in a sense, nonselective: it encompasses all the cues emitted by the other, even those that the other would rather conceal and those the listener would rather not hear. For instance, the weight of an obviously overweight person is a cue to be reckoned with, for through it the other is saying something to those with whom he interacts. The message may be "I am frustrated" or "I don't care about others" or merely "I have poor self-control," but it is a message that should not be overlooked. In a group therapy session in which I was an observer, the therapist asked the wife of one of the inpatients (the patient himself refused to attend the sessions) what she thought she was trying to tell others by her obvious overweight. The therapist listened to a cue, confronted the woman in a firm, kindly, responsible way, and succeeded in instituting a dialogue that proved quite useful. Therefore, good listening demands both subjectivity—that is, engagement with the other—and objectivity—disengagement from the other—in order to pick up both positively and negatively valenced cues. The good listener is sensitive to what is and not just to what should be or to how he would like things to be.

ACTIVE LISTENING

It becomes quite apparent that the good listener is an active listener, one truly engaged in the communication process, one who goes out of himself in search of significant cues emitted by others. Listening, then, is facilitated if the listener is actively interested in others. The person who is an active listener is much less likely to stereotype others or to become guilty of univocal listening. Perhaps an analogy would make this a bit clearer. Everytime Brahms' Second Symphony (a favorite of mine) is played, the untrained ear hears only the Second Symphony; it is quite a univocal experience. The individuality of different orchestras and different conductors and the nuances of different tempos and accents are all missed. However, while there is only one Second Symphony, it can be played with quite different—and distinguishable—nuances. Similarly, John Doe is only John Doe, but John Doe, too, has different nuances of orchestration at different times, and these nuances will be missed by the untrained, passive listener who finds it more comfortable to deal with him as a stereotype in univocal terms. The active, searching listener, who is open to all the nuances of John Doe, will more likely pick up many of these cues. This openness to nuance, however, does not imply that the good listener is skilled in analyzing the other, for analysis often means reducing the other to a whole series of stereotypes, and sometimes this mistake is worse than the first.

SOME OBSTACLES TO EFFECTIVE LISTENING

A number of things can get between the one communicating himself and the listener. Awareness of them may help the listening process. *Self-consciousness*: if a person is preoccupied with himself as an interactant, he will find it difficult to catch what you are saying. *The dreamer*: such a person gets lost in his own reveries. He is thinking about what you said to him ten minutes ago and is lost to the interaction. The solution is obvious. He should share his thoughts with you as they come up instead of engaging in distancing cud-chewing. *Message anxiety*: the content of the speaker's message might be such as to arouse both the speaker's anxiety and the anxiety of those listening. This is often the case when the message is suffused with emotion. There is no simple solution to this problem. When you notice that the speaker's message is arousing his and/or your anxiety, be careful. Message distortion is just around the corner. *The long speech*: the listener tends to lose parts of longer speeches, especially the middle portion. Again the solution is obvious. Don't give long speeches or allow them to be given. The group is for dialogue, not speeches. *Reductive listening*: the listener tends to modify a new message so that it sounds like previous messages. This is quite common and quite unfair to the speaker, for it is a refusal to admit that he can change. People do change during the course of the group. If you cannot hear these changes, you can hardly accept or support them. *Hearing what one expects to hear*: this needs no comment. *You agree with me*: the listener tends to modify messages so that they are in better agreement with his own opinions and attitudes. If you are to be a good listener, you must learn how to relax your defenses a bit in order to be open and willing to explore the new. *Black-or-white listening*: we tend to evaluate messages as we hear them in terms such as "good, bad," "like, dislike," "approach, avoid," "beautiful, ugly," and the like. Such instant evaluations obviously cloud the communication process. One way of fighting this tendency is to admit to the speaker that your automatic evaluation process is getting in the way: "I didn't like what you first said and it got in the way of the rest of the message; it would help me to check your message and my feelings with the group."

It is difficult to be an unbiased listener. The pitfalls described here cannot be avoided entirely; they can only be minimized. All the blame for poor listening, however, cannot be laid at the door of the listener. Whenever a participant speaks but really says nothing, then the quality of listening in the group will go down. As a general rule, the speaker gets the kind of attention he deserves. Some participants speak vaguely and evasively because they do not want to be read by their listeners; they thrive on the haphazard listening they receive. Such tendencies should become the object of confrontation in the group.

THE EMPATHIC LISTENER: THE ONE WHO RESPONDS

The good listener, then, is the active listener, the one who is as receptive as possible to all cues and messages generated in the group, the one who is aware of and committed to combatting the variety of obstacles within himself and others to effective listening. The empathic listener, however, goes further than this; he realizes that the proof of good listening lies in the way he responds to those to whom he is listening. Accurate empathy is absolutely essential to growthful interpersonal relations. It requires you to get inside the other, to view the world through his eyes, and to *communicate* to the other your understanding of him. Accurate empathy demands, at the minimum, the ability to let the speaker know that you understand the obvious meaning of his words. A higher level of empathic understanding involves the ability to go beyond the words, the ability to put together the cues found in tone, gesture, and context and to respond to the fuller message of the speaker—the message that goes beyond his words.

> *Chester:* I feel that we're not really doing much in this group. We're not really getting in contact with one another.
>
> *Don:* You do seem to be pretty frustrated with the way things are going, Chet. You seem especially disappointed in me. In fact, I feel you are more disappointed in me than in the group or the process of the group, because you've tried to contact me several times and I haven't been very responsive.
>
> *Chester:* Well, it is you. You bother me the most.

In this example Don has listened to all the cues that Chester has emitted and he responds, accurately, not just to Chester's words but to the context of the words. He understands what is going on inside Chester and he communicates this to him. His expressed understanding, since it is caring and accurate, allows Chester to become more concrete about what is bothering him.

If you want others to involve themselves growthfully with you, you must let them know you are listening to them. The best evidence of your listening is the quality of your response to what others say both verbally and nonverbally. . . .

PROBES

How does what Egan says about listening being "nonselective" relate to what Powell says in Chapter 6 about being "nonevaluative"?

Egan makes the point that assumptions—hearing what you expect to hear—can block empathic listening. How do you see assumptions affecting other elements of interpersonal communication, e.g., self-perception, the ways you perceive others, and self-disclosure?

Which nonverbal cues most clearly tell you that your partner is listening to you? How do you nonverbally communicate that you're listening to someone else?

What relationships do you see between empathic listening and self-disclosure?

This short story is not "about" responsive listening; it describes an instance of it. I don't think it needs much introduction. But you might ask yourself if you would like to be listened to by this old man. If you would, are you willing and able to give to others what he gave to Rudolf?

THE LISTENER

John Berry

Once there was a puny Czech concert violinist named Rudolf, who lived in Sweden. Some of his friends thought he was not the best of musicians because he was restless; others thought he was restless because he was not the best of musicians.

At any rate, he hit upon a way of making a living, with no competitors. Whether by choice or necessity, he used to sail about Scandinavia in his small boat, all alone, giving concerts in little seaport towns. If he found an accompanist, well and good; if not, he played works for unaccompanied violin; and it happened once or twice that he wanted a piano so badly that he imagined one, and then he played whole sonatas for violin and piano, with no piano in sight.

One year Rudolf sailed all the way out to Iceland and began working his way around that rocky coast from one town to another. It was a hard, stubborn

John Berry, "The Listener," in Ed Rintye, *Centering a Lopsided Egg* (Boston: Allyn & Bacon, 1975), pp. 54–57. Reprinted by permission of Russell & Volkening, Inc., as agents for the author. Copyright © 1960 by John Berry.

land; but people in those difficult places do not forget the law of hospitality to the stranger—for their God may decree that they too shall become strangers on the face of the earth. The audiences were small, and even if Rudolf had been really first-rate, they would not have been very demonstrative. From ancient times their energy had gone, first of all, into earnest toil. Sometimes they were collected by the local school teacher, who reminded them of their duty to the names of Beethoven and Bach and Mozart and one or two others whose music perhaps was not much heard in those parts. Too often people sat stolidly watching the noisy little fiddler, and went home feeling gravely edified. But they paid.

As Rudolf was sailing from one town to the next along a sparsely settled shore, the northeast turned black and menacing. A storm was bearing down upon Iceland. Rudolf was rounding a bleak, dangerous cape, and his map told him that the nearest harbor was half a day's journey away. He was starting to worry when he saw, less than a mile off shore, a lighthouse on a tiny rock island. With some difficulty, in the rising seas, he put in there and moored to an iron ring that hung from the cliff. A flight of stairs, hewn out of the rock, led up to the lighthouse. On top of the cliff, outlined against the scudding clouds, stood a man.

"You are welcome!" the voice boomed over the sound of the waves that were already beginning to break over the island.

Darkness fell quickly. The lighthouse keeper led his guest up the spiral stairs to the living room on the third floor, then busied himself in preparation for the storm. Above all, he had to attend to the great lamp in the tower, that dominated the whole region. It was a continuous light, intensified by reflectors, and eclipsed by shutters at regular intervals. The duration of the light was equal to that of darkness.

The lighthouse keeper was a huge old man with a grizzled beard that came down over his chest. Slow, deliberate, bearlike, he moved without wasted motion about the limited world of which he was the master. He spoke little, as if words had not much importance compared to the other forces that compromised his life. Yet he was equable, as those elements were not.

After the supper of black bread and boiled potatoes, herring, cheese and hot tea, which they took in the kitchen above the living room, the two men sat and contemplated each other's presence. Above them was the maintenance room, and above that the great lamp spoke majestic, silent messages of light to the ships at sea. The storm hammered like a battering ram on the walls of the lighthouse. Rudolf offered tobacco, feeling suddenly immature as he did so. The old man smiled a little as he declined it by a slight movement of his head; it was as if he knew well the uses of tobacco and the need for offering it, and affirmed it all, yet—here he, too, was halfway apologetic—was self-contained and without need of anything that was not already within his power. And he sat there, gentle and reflective, his great workman hands resting on outspread thighs.

It seemed to Rudolf that the lighthouse keeper was entirely aware of all the sounds of the storm and of its violent impact upon the lighthouse, but he knew them so well that he did not have to think about them; they were like the voluntary movements of his own heart and blood. In the same way, beneath the simple courtesy that made him speak and listen to his guest in specific ways, he was already calmly and mysteriously a part of him, as surely as the mainland was connected with the little island, and all the islands with one another, so commodiously, under the ocean.

Gradually Rudolf drew forth the sparse data of the old man's life: He had been born in this very lighthouse eighty-three years before, when his father was the lighthouse keeper. His mother—the only woman he had ever known—taught him to read the Bible, and he read it daily. He had no other books.

As a musician, Rudolf had not had time to read much either—but then, he lived in cities. He reached down and took his beloved violin out of its case.

"What do you make with that, sir?" the old man asked.

For a second Rudolf thought his host might be joking; but serenity of the other's expression reassured him. There was not even curiosity about the instrument, but rather a whole interest in him, the person, that included his "work." In most circumstances Rudolf would have found it hard to believe that there could exist someone who did not know what a violin was; yet now he had no inclination to laugh. He felt small and inadequate.

"I make—music with it," he stammered in a low tone.

"Music," the old man said ponderously. "I have heard of it. But I have never seen music."

"One does not see music. One hears it."

"Ah, yes," the lighthouse keeper consented, as it were with humility. This too was in the nature of things wherein all works were wonders, and all things were known eternally and were poignant in their transiency. His wide gray eyes rested upon the little fiddler and conferred upon him all the importance of which any individual is capable.

Then something in the storm and the lighthouse and the old man exalted Rudolf, filled him with compassion, and love and a spaciousness infinitely beyond himself. He wanted to strike a work of fire and stars into being for the old man. And, with the storm as his accompanist, he stood and began to play—the Kreutzer Sonata of Beethoven.

The moments passed, moments that were days in the creation of that world of fire and stars; abysses and heights of passionate struggle, the idea of order, and the resolution of these in the greatness of the human spirit. Never before had Rudolf played with such mastery—or with such an accompanist. Waves and wind beat the tower with giant hands. Steadily above them the beacon raced in its sure cycles of darkness and light. The last note ceased and Rudolf dropped his head on his chest, breathing hard. The ocean seethed over the island with a roar as of many voices.

The old man had sat unmoving through the work, his broad gnarled hands resting on his thighs, his head bowed, listening massively. For some time he continued to sit in silence.

Then he looked up, lifted those hands calmly, judiciously, and nodded his head.

"Yes," he said. "That is true."

I can listen to someone without hearing him. Listening is fixing my attention only on the other person. Hearing requires that I listen inside me as I listen to him. Hearing is a rhythm whereby I shuttle between his words and my experience. It includes hearing his entire posture: his eyes, his lips, the tilt of his head, the movement of his fingers. It includes hearing his tone of voice and his silences. And hearing also includes attending to my reactions, such as the "sinking feeling" I get when the other person has stopped hearing me.

HUGH PRATHER

IV

APPROACHES TO
INTERPERSONAL
COMMUNICATION

9

CARL R. ROGERS'S APPROACH

Like much of Carl Rogers's work, this talk was aimed at a specific audience. If you're not a guidance counselor—or a prospective one—you might feel that he's talking to somebody else here. But I don't agree. It seems to me that regardless of his intended audience, his writings speak to all of us. Rogers suggests that the *quality* of a counselor's relationship with his or her client or "counselee" is the key to successful counseling and that the best kind of relationship happens when the participants are congruent, empathic, and regard each other positively—unconditional positively if they can.

Each of these three elements is a centrally important part of interpersonal communication. Congruence, i.e., accurately reflecting on the outside what you are experiencing on the inside, is a skill that's related to much of what is discussed in Chapter 6 of this book. Empathy is obviously what much of Chapter 8 is about. And the third element, positive regard, is the attitude that encourages you to apply just about everything in this book.

I'm not a counselor—except to the extent that we all are—and I have found that the quality of my interpersonal relationships improves to the degree that I am able to manifest the characteristics Rogers talks about. What I believe Rogers does here is successfully identify and describe in pretty concrete terms three of the hard-to-pin-down elements that separate objectified, impersonal talking *at* each other from real interpersonal communication.

THE INTERPERSONAL RELATIONSHIP:
THE CORE OF GUIDANCE

Carl R. Rogers

I would like to share with you in this paper a conclusion, a conviction, which has grown out of years of experience in dealing with individuals, a conclusion which finds some confirmation in a steadily growing body of empirical evidence. It is simply that in a wide variety of professional work involving relationships with people—whether as a psychotherapist, teacher, religious worker, guidance counselor, social worker, clinical psychologist—it is the *quality* of the interpersonal encounter with the client which is the most significant element in determining effectiveness.

Let me spell out a little more fully the basis of this statement in my personal experience. I have been primarily a counselor and psychotherapist. In the course of my professional life I have worked with troubled college students, with adults in difficulty, with "normal" individuals such as business executives, and more recently with hospitalized pyschotic persons. I have endeavored to make use of the learnings from my therapeutic experience in my interactions with classes and seminars, in the training of teachers, in the administration of staff groups, in the clinical supervision of psychologists, psychiatrists, and guidance workers as they work with their clients or patients. Some of these relationships are long-continued and intensive, as in individual psychotherapy. Some are brief, as in experiences with workshop participants or in contacts with students who come for practical advice. They cover a wide range of depth. Gradually I have come to the conclusion that one learning which applies to all of these experiences is that it is the quality of the personal relationship which matters most. With some of these individuals I am in touch only briefly, with others I have the opportunity of knowing them intimately, but in either case the quality of the personal encounter is probably, in the long run, the element which determines the extent to which this is an experience which releases or promotes development and growth. I believe the quality of my encounter is more important in the long run than is my scholarly knowledge, my professional training, my counseling orientation, the techniques I use in the interview. In keeping with this line of thought, I suspect that for a guidance worker also the relationship he forms with each student—brief or continuing—is more important than his knowledge of tests and measurements, the adequacy of his record keeping, the theories he holds, the accuracy with which he is able to predict academic success, or the school in which he received his training.

In recent years I have thought a great deal about this issue. I have tried to observe counselors and therapists whose orientations are very different from mine, in order to understand the basis of their effectiveness as well as my own. I have listened to recorded interviews from many different sources. Gradually I have developed some theoretical formulations, some hypotheses as to the basis of effectiveness in relationships. As I have asked myself how individuals sharply different in personality, orientation and procedure can all be effective in a helping relationship, can each be successful in facilitating constructive change or development, I have concluded that it is because they bring to the helping relationship certain attitudinal ingredients. It is these that I hypothesize as making for effectiveness, whether we are speaking of a guidance counselor, a clinical psychologist, or a psychiatrist.

What are these attitudinal or experiential elements in the counselor which make a relationship a growth-promoting climate? I would like to describe them as carefully and accurately as I can, though I am well aware that words rarely capture or communicate the qualities of a personal encounter.

CONGRUENCE

In the first place, I hypothesize that personal growth is facilitated when the counselor is what he *is*, when in the relationship with his client he is genuine and without "front" or facade, openly being the feelings and attitudes which at that moment are flowing in him. We have used the term "congruence" to try to describe this condition. By this we mean that the feelings the counselor is experiencing are available to him, available to his awareness, that he is able to live these feelings, be them in the relationship, and able to communicate them if appropriate. It means that he comes into a direct personal encounter with his client, meeting him on a person-to-person basis. It means that he is *being* himself, not denying himself. No one fully achieves this condition, yet the more the therapist is able to listen acceptantly to what is going on within himself, and the more he is able to *be* the complexity of his feelings without fear, the higher the degree of his congruence.

I think that we readily sense this quality in our everyday life. We could each of us name persons whom we know who always seem to be operating from behind a front, who are playing a role, who tend to say things they do not feel. They are exhibiting incongruence. We do not reveal ourselves too deeply to such people. On the other hand each of us knows individuals whom we somehow trust, because we sense that they are being what they *are*, that we are dealing with the person himself, and not with a polite or professional facade. This is the quality of which we are speaking, and it is hypothesized that the more genuine and congruent the therapist is in the relationship, the more probability there is that change in personality in the client will occur . . . .

But is it always helpful to be genuine? What about negative feelings? What about the times when the counselor's real feeling toward his client is one of annoyance, or boredom, or dislike? My tentative answer is that even with such feelings as these, which we all have from time to time, it is preferable for the counselor to be real than to put up a façade of interest and concern and liking which he does not feel.

But it is not a simple thing to achieve such reality. I am not saying that it is helpful to blurt out impulsively every passing feeling and accusation under the comfortable impression that one is being genuine. Being real involves the difficult task of being acquainted with the flow of experiencing going on within oneself, a flow marked especially by complexity and continuous change. So if I sense that I am feeling bored by my contacts with this student, and this feeling persists, I think I owe it to him and to our relationship to share his feeling with him. But here again I will want to be constantly in touch with what is going on in me. If I am, I will recognize that it is *my* feeling of being bored which I am expressing, and not some supposed fact about him as a boring person. If I voice it as *my own* reaction, it has the potentiality of leading to a deeper relationship. But this feeling exists in the context of a complex and changing flow, and this needs to be communicated too. I would like to share with him my distress at feeling bored, and the discomfort I feel in expressing this aspect of me. As I share these attitudes I find that my feeling of boredom arises from my sense of remoteness from him, and that I would like to be more in touch with him. And even as I try to express these feelings, they change. I am certainly *not* bored as I try to communicate myself to him in this way, and I am far from bored as I wait with eagerness and perhaps a bit of apprehension for his response. I also feel a new sensitivity to him, now that I have shared this feeling which has been a barrier between us. So I am very much more able to hear the surprise or perhaps the hurt in his voice as he now finds *himself* speaking more genuinely because I have dared to be real with him. I have let myself be a person—real, imperfect—in my relationship with him.

I have tried to describe this first element at some length because I regard it as highly important, perhaps the most crucial of the conditions I will describe, and because it is neither easy to grasp nor to achieve. . . .

I hope it is clear that I am talking about a realness in the counselor which is deep and true, not superficial. I have sometimes thought that the word transparency helps to describe this element of personal congruence. If everything going on in me which is relevant to the relationship can be seen by my client, if he can see "clear through me," and if I am *willing* for this realness to show through in the relationship, then I can be almost certain that this will be a meaningful encounter in which we both learn and develop.

I have sometimes wondered if this is the only quality which matters in a counseling relationship. The evidence seems to show that other qualities also make a profound difference and are perhaps easier to achieve. So I am going to describe these others. But I would stress that if, in a given moment of relationship, they are not genuinely a part of the experience of the counselor, then it is, I believe, better to be genuinely what one is, than to pretend to be feeling these other qualities.

EMPATHY

The second essential condition in the relationship, as I see it, is that the counselor is experiencing an accurate empathic understanding of his client's private world, and is able to communicate some of the significant fragments of that understanding. To sense the client's inner world of private personal meanings as if it were your own, but without ever losing the "as if" quality, this is empathy, and this seems essential to a growth-promoting relationship. To sense his confusion or his timidity or his anger or his feeling of being treated unfairly as if it were your own, yet without your own uncertainty or fear or anger or suspicion getting bound up in it, this is the condition I am endeavoring to describe. When the client's world is clear to the counselor and he can move about in it freely, then he can both communicate his understanding of what is vaguely known to the client, and he can also voice meanings in the client's experience of which the client is scarcely aware. It is this kind of highly sensitive empathy which seems important in making it possible for a person to get close to himself and to learn, to change, and develop.

I suspect that each of us has discovered that this kind of understanding is extremely rare. We neither receive it nor offer it with any great frequency. Instead we offer another type of understanding which is very different, such as "I understand what is wrong with you" or "I understand what makes you act that way." These are the types of understanding which we usually offer and receive—an evaluative understanding from the outside. It is not surprising that we shy away from true understanding. If I am truly open to the way life is experienced by another person—if I can take his world into mine—then I run the risk of seeing life in his way, of being changed myself, and we all resist change. So we tend to view this other person's world only in our terms, not in his. We analyze and evaluate it. We do not understand it. But when someone understands how it feels and seems to be me, without wanting to analyze me or judge me, then I can blossom and grow in that climate. I am sure I am not alone in that feeling. I believe that when the counselor can grasp the moment-to-moment experiencing occurring in the inner world of the client, as the client sees and feels it, without losing the separateness of his own identity in this empathic process, then change is likely to occur.

Though the accuracy of such understanding is highly important, the communication of intent to understand is also helpful. Even in dealing with the confused or inarticulate or bizarre individual, if he perceives that I am *trying* to understand his meanings, this is helpful. It communicates the value I place on him as an individual. It gets across the fact that I perceive his feelings and meanings as being *worth* understanding.

None of us steadily achieves such a complete empathy as I have been trying to describe, any more than we achieve complete congruence, but there is no doubt that individuals can develop along this line. Suitable training experiences have been utilized in the training of counselors, and also in the "sensitivity training" of industrial management personnel. Such experiences enable the person to listen more sensitively, to receive more of the subtle meanings the other person is expressing in words, gesture, and posture, to resonate more deeply and freely within himself to the significance of those expressions.

POSITIVE REGARD

Now the third condition. I hypothesize that growth and change are more likely to occur the more that the counselor is experiencing a warm, positive, acceptant attitude toward what *is* in the client. It means that he prizes his client, as a person, with somewhat the same quality of feeling that a parent feels for his child, prizing him as a person regardless of his particular behavior at the moment. It means that he cares for his client in a non-possessive way, as a person with potentialities. It involves an open willingness for the client to be whatever feelings are real in him at the moment—hostility or tenderness, rebellion or submissiveness, assurance or self-depreciation. It means a kind of love for the client as he is, providing we understand the word love as equivalent to the theologian's term *agape*, and not in its usual romantic and possessive meanings. What I am describing is a feeling which is not paternalistic, nor sentimental, nor superficially social and agreeable. It respects the other person as a separate individual, and does not possess him. It is a kind of liking which has strength, and which is not demanding. We have termed it positive regard.

UNCONDITIONALITY OF REGARD

There is one aspect of this attitude of which I am somewhat less sure. I advance tentatively the hypothesis that the relationship will be more effective the more the positive regard is unconditional. By this I mean that the counselor prizes the client in a total, rather than a conditional way. He does not accept certain feelings in the client and disapprove others. He feels an *unconditional* positive regard for this person. This is an outgoing, positive feeling without reservations and without evaluations. It means *not* making judgments. I believe that when this nonevaluative prizing is present in the encounter between the counselor and his client, constructive change and development in the client is more likely to occur.

Certainly one does not need to be a professional to experience this attitude. The best of parents show this in abundance, while others do not. A friend of mine, a therapist in private practice on the east coast, illustrates this very well in a letter in which he tells me what he is learning about parents. He says:

> I am beginning to feel that the key to the human being is the attitudes with which the parents have regarded him. If the child was lucky enough to have parents who have felt proud of him, wanted him, wanted him just as he was, exactly as he was, this child grows into adulthood with self-confidence, self-esteem; he goes forth in life feeling sure of himself, strong, able to lick what confronts him. Franklin Delano Roosevelt is an example..."my friends...." He couldn't imagine anyone thinking otherwise. He had two adoring parents. He was like the pampered dog who runs up

at you, frisking his tail, eager to love you, for this dog has never known rejection or harshness. Even if you should kick him, he'll come right back to you, his tail friskier than ever, thinking you're playing a game with him and wanting more. This animal cannot imagine anyone disapproving or disliking him. Just as unconditional regard and love was poured into him, he has it now to give out. If a child is lucky enough to grow up in this unconditionally accepting atmosphere, he emerges as strong and sure and he can approach life and its vicissitudes with courage and confidence, with zest and joy of expectation.

But the parents who like their children—if. They would like them if they were changed, altered, different; if they were smarter of if they were better, or if, if, if. The offspring of these parents have trouble because they never had the feeling of acceptance. These parents don't really like these children; they would like them if they were like someone else. When you come down to the basic fundamental, the parent feels: "I don't like *this* child, this child before me." They don't say that. I am beginning to believe that it would be better for all concerned if parents did. It wouldn't leave such horrible ravages on these unaccepted children. It's never done that crudely. "If you were a nice boy and did this, that and the other thing, then we would all love you." I am coming to believe that children brought up by parents who would like them "if" are never quite right. They grow up assuming that their parents are right and that they are wrong; that somehow or other they are at fault; and even worse, very frequently they feel they are stupid, inadequate, inferior.

This is an excellent contrast between an unconditional positive regard and a conditional regard. I believe it holds as true for counselors as for parents.

THE CLIENT'S PERCEPTION

Thus far all my hypotheses regarding the possibility of constructive growth have rested upon the experiencing of these elements by the counselor. There is, however, one condition which must exist in the client. Unless the attitudes I have been describing have been to some degree communicated to the client, and perceived by him, they do not exist in his perceptual world and thus cannot be effective. Consequently it is necessary to add one more condition to the equation which I have been building up regarding personal growth through counseling. It is that when the client perceives, to a minimal degree, the genuineness of the counselor and the acceptance and empathy which the counselor experiences for him, then development in personality and change in behavior are predicted.

This has implications for me as a counselor. I need to be sensitive not only to what is going on in me, and sensitive to the flow of feelings in my client. I must also be sensitive to the way he is receiving my communications. I have learned, especially in working with more disturbed persons, that empathy can be perceived as lack of involvement; that an unconditional regard on my part can be perceived as indifference; that warmth can be perceived as a threatening

closeness, that real feelings of mine can be perceived as false. I would like to behave in ways, and communicate in ways which have clarity for this specific person, so that what I am experiencing in relationship to him would be perceived
unambiguously by him. Like the other conditions I have proposed, the principle
is easy to grasp; the achievement of it is difficult and complex.

SOME LIMITATIONS

I would like to stress that these are hypotheses. . . . They are beginning hypotheses, not the final word. I regard it as entirely possible that there are other
conditions which I have not described, which are also essential. Recently I had
occasion to listen to some recorded interviews by a young counselor of elementary school children. She was very warm and positive in her attitude toward her
clients, yet she was definitely ineffective. She seemed to be responding warmly
only to the superficial aspects of each child and so the contacts were chatty,
social, and friendly, but it was clear she was not reaching the real person of the
child. Yet in a number of ways she rated reasonably high on each of the conditions I have described. So perhaps there are still elements missing which I have
not captured in my formulation. . . .

THE PHILOSOPHY WHICH IS IMPLICIT

It is evident that the kinds of attitudes I have described are not likely to be experienced by a counselor unless he holds a philosophy regarding people in which
such attitudes are congenial. The attitudes pictured make no sense except in a
context of great respect for the person and his potentialities. Unless the primary
element in the counselor's value system is the worth of the individual, he is not
apt to find himself experiencing a real caring, or a desire to understand, and perhaps he will not respect himself enough to be real. Certainly the professional
person who holds the view that individuals are essentially objects to be manipulated for the welfare of the state, or the good of the educational institution, or
"for their own good," or to satisfy his own need for power and control, would
not experience the attitudinal elements I have described as constituting growth-
promoting relationships. So these conditions are congenial and natural in certain philosophical contexts but not in others.

CONCLUSION

Let me conclude with a series of statements which for me follow logically one
upon the other.

The purpose of most of the helping professions, including guidance counseling, is to enhance the personal development, the psychological growth towards a socialized maturity, of its clients.

The effectiveness of any member of the profession is most adequately measured in terms of the degree to which, in his work with his clients, he achieves this goal.

Our knowledge of the elements which bring about constructive change in personal growth is in its infant stages.

Such factual knowledge as we currently possess indicates that a primary change-producing influence is the degree to which the client experiences certain qualities in his relationship with his counselor.

In a variety of clients—normal, maladjusted, and psychotic—with many different counselors and therapists, and studying the relationship from the vantage point of the client, the therapist, or the uninvolved observer, certain qualities in the relationship are quite uniformly found to be associated with personal growth and change.

These elements are not constituted of technical knowledge or ideological sophistication. They are personal human qualities—something the counselor *experiences*, not something he *knows*. Constructive personal growth is associated with the counselor's realness, with his genuine and unconditional liking for his client, with his sensitive understanding of his client's private world, and with his ability to communicate these qualities in himself to his client.

These findings have some far-reaching implications for the theory and practice of guidance counseling and psychotherapy, and for the training of workers in these fields.

And, I think Carl Rogers would agree, they also have far-reaching implications for my day-to-day interpersonal communication, and for yours. [J.S.]

PROBES

How is Rogers's concept of congruence related to Powell's "gut-level communication" (Chapter 6)?

How do Rogers's comments about being congruent about negative feelings compare to or contrast with what Augsburger says about owning your feelings (Chapter 7)?

Do you think congruence helps create a defensive climate or a supportive one (Chapter 7)?

How does Rogers's advice about empathy relate with what Tournier says about perceiving persons (Chapter 5)?

Does Rogers believe that all people are basically good?

How would you compare and contrast the philosophy implicit in Rogers's comments and Barnlund's philosophy (Chapter 1)?

10

ERICH FROMM'S APPROACH

"Love" and "interpersonal communication" are *not* synonymous. But if you describe, as Erich Fromm does here, some of the key understandings, attitudes, and behaviors that make up mature human loving, you do find that you're saying a great deal about interpersonal quality communication.

Fromm's first main point speaks to the issue of *why* humans communicate. He argues that part of what it means to be a human is to be aware of one's self. (That's similar to the point I made in Chapter 1 about humans being conscious.) Being aware of your self means being aware that you're different from and separate from others. That awareness, Fromm says, leads us to desire contact, unification, and relatedness with others. So at the most basic level, we are motivated to communicate by our awareness that we are unique, unlike all other persons and separate from them.

Fromm's second main point is that we have four ways of overcoming our separateness: indulging in orgiastic states, conforming, engaging in creative activity, or loving. The union that comes from orgiastic states—sex, alcohol or other drugs, etc.—is ultimately unsatisfactory, because it is temporary, physically debilitating, and it often produces anxiety and guilt feelings. Achieving union in conformity is not much better, because the tendency is to eliminate individual differences. Since each person is unique, a unity based on the assumption that we're the same as every other Republican, Elk, Irishman, female, American, or whatever is ultimately unsatisfactory. Separateness can also be overcome by way of creative activity, but the result of that effort is union with a thing—an art object of some sort—not with a person. So something is still missing.

Only love offers humans the opportunity to overcome our natural feelings of separateness in a satisfactory and lasting way. But, and this is Fromm's main point, you've got to realize that love is not a kind of "symbiotic union" based on two people *needing* each other. "Love," he writes, "is union under the condition of preserving one's integrity, one's individuality." That is a crucial point, I think. One of the most difficult and important things I've had to learn is how to encourage and participate in a relationship that is based on two independent persons choosing to grow together rather than on one person—or both—"needing" the other.

Fromm's final main point is that each lover exerts his or her individual power in a loving relationship by giving, not by receiving, and that there are four attitude/actions each must learn to give effectively: care, responsibility, respect, and knowledge. Again, Fromm doesn't always discuss specific interpersonal-communication variables. But he is obviously talking about interpersonal relationships, and in a way that complements, and to a degree completes, much of what's in the other readings in Parts I, II, and III.

THE THEORY OF LOVE
Erich Fromm

Any theory of love must begin with a theory of man, of human existence. While we find love, or rather, the equivalent of love, in animals, their attachments are mainly a part of their instinctual equipment; only remnants of this instinctual equipment can be seen operating in man. What is essential in the existence of man is the fact that he has emerged from the animal kingdom, from instinctive adaptation, that he has transcended nature—although he never leaves it; he is a part of it—and yet once torn away from nature, he cannot return to it; once thrown out of paradise—a state of original oneness with nature—cherubim with flaming swords block his way, if he should try to return. Man can only go forward by developing his reason, by finding a new harmony, a human one, instead of the prehuman harmony which is irretrievably lost.

When man is born, the human race as well as the individual, he is thrown out of a situation which was definite, as definite as the instinct, into a situation which is indefinite, uncertain, and open. There is certainty only about the past—and about the future only as far as that it is death.

Man is gifted with reason; he is *life being aware of itself*; he has awareness of himself, of his fellow man, of his past, and of the possibilities of his future. This awareness of himself as a separate entity, the awareness of his own short life span, of the fact that without his will he is born and against his will he dies, that he will die before those whom he loves, or they before him, the awareness of his aloneness and separateness, of his helplessness before the forces of nature and of society, all this makes his separate, disunited existence an unbearable prison. He would become insane could he not liberate himself from this prison and reach out, unite himself in some form or other with men, with the world outside.

The experience of separateness arouses anxiety; it is, indeed, the source of all anxiety. Being separate means being cut off, without any capacity to use my human powers. Hence to be separate means to be helpless, unable to grasp the world—things and people—actively; it means that the world can invade me without my ability to react. Thus, separateness is the source of intense anxiety. Beyond that, it arouses shame and the feeling of guilt. This experience of guilt and shame in separateness is expressed in the Biblical story of Adam and Eve. After Adam and Eve have eaten of the "tree of knowledge of good and evil," after they have disobeyed (there is no good and evil unless there is freedom to disobey), after they have become human by having emancipated themselves

---

from the original animal harmony with nature, i.e., after their birth as human beings—they saw "that they were naked—and they were ashamed." Should we assume that a myth as old and elementary as this has the prudish morals of the nineteenth-century outlook, and that the important point the story wants to convey to us is the embarrassment that their genitals were visible? This can hardly be so, and by understanding the story in a Victorian spirit, we miss the main point, which seems to be the following: after man and woman have become aware of themselves and of each other, they are aware of their separateness, and of their difference, inasmuch as they belong to different sexes. But while recognizing their separateness they remain strangers, because they have not yet learned to love each other (as is also made very clear by the fact that Adam defends himself by blaming Eve, rather than by trying to defend her). *The awareness of human separation, without reunion by love—is the source of shame. It is at the same time the source of guilt and anxiety.*

The deepest need of man, then, is the need to overcome his separateness, to leave the prison of his aloneness. The *absolute* failure to achieve this aim means insanity, because the panic of complete isolation can be overcome only by such a radical withdrawal from the world outside that the feeling of separation disappears—because the world outside, from which one is separated, has disappeared.

Man—of all ages and cultures—is confronted with the solution of one and the same question: the question of how to overcome separateness, how to achieve union, how to transcend one's own individual life and find at-onement. The question is the same for primitive man living in caves, for nomadic man taking care of his flocks, for the peasant in Egypt, the Phoenician trader, the Roman soldier, the medieval monk, the Japanese samurai, the modern clerk and factory hand. The question is the same, for it springs from the same ground: the human situation, the conditions of human existence. The answer varies. The question can be answered by animal worship, by human sacrifice or military conquest, by indulgence in luxury, by ascetic renunciation, by obsessional work, by artistic creation, by the love of God, and by the love of Man. While there are many answers—the record of which is human history—they are nevertheless not innumerable. On the contrary, as soon as one ignores smaller differences which belong more to the periphery than to the center, one discovers that there is only a limited number of answers which have been given, and only could have been given by man in the various cultures in which he has lived. The history of religion and philosophy is the history of these answers, of their diversity, as well as of their limitation in number.

The answers depend, to some extent, on the degree of individuation which an individual has reached. In the infant I-ness has developed but little yet; he still feels one with mother, has no feeling of separateness as long as mother is present. Its sense of aloneness is cured by the physical presence of the mother,

her breasts, her skin. Only to the degree that the child develops his sense of separateness and individuality is the physical presence of the mother not sufficient any more, and does the need to overcome separateness in other ways arise.

Similarly, the human race in its infancy still feels one with nature. The soil, the animals, the plants are still man's world. He identifies himself with animals, and this is expressed by the wearing of animal masks, by the worshiping of a totem animal or animal gods. But the more the human race emerges from these primary bonds, the more it separates itself from the natural world, the more intense becomes the need to find new ways of escaping separateness.

One way of achieving this aim lies in all kinds of *orgiastic states*. These may have the form of an auto-induced trance, sometimes with the help of drugs. Many rituals of primitive tribes offer a vivid picture of this type of solution. In a transitory state of exaltation the world outside disappears, and with it the feeling of separateness from it. Inasmuch as these rituals are practiced in common, an experience of fusion with the group is added which makes this solution all the more effective. Closely related to, and often blended with this orgiastic solution, is the sexual experience. The sexual orgasm can produce a state similar to the one produced by a trance, or to the effects of certain drugs. Rites of communal sexual orgies were a part of many primitive rituals. It seems that after the orgiastic experience, man can go on for a time without suffering too much from his separateness. Slowly the tension of anxiety mounts, and then is reduced again by the repeated performance of the ritual.

As long as these orgiastic states are a matter of common practice in a tribe, they do not produce anxiety or guilt. To act in this way is right, and even virtuous, because it is a way shared by all, approved and demanded by the medicine men or priests; hence there is no reason to feel guilty or ashamed. It is quite different when the same solution is chosen by an individual in a culture which has left behind these common practices. Alcoholism and drug addiction are the forms which the individual chooses in a non-orgiastic culture. In contrast to those participating in the socially patterned solution, such individuals suffer from guilt feelings and remorse. While they try to escape from separateness by taking refuge in alcohol or drugs, they feel all the more separate after the orgiastic experience is over, and thus are driven to take recourse to it with increasing frequency and intensity. Slightly different from this is the recourse to a sexual orgiastic solution. To some extent it is a natural and normal form of overcoming separateness, and a partial answer to the problem of isolation. But in many individuals in whom separateness is not relieved in other ways, the search for the sexual orgasm assumes a function which makes it not very different from alcoholism and drug addiction. It becomes a desperate attempt to escape the anxiety engendered by separateness, and it results in an ever-increasing sense of separateness, since the sexual act without love never bridges the gap between two human beings, except momentarily.

All forms of orgiastic union have three characteristics: they are intense, even violent; they occur in the total personality, mind *and* body; they are transitory and periodical. Exactly the opposite holds true for that form of union which is by far the most frequent solution chosen by man in the past and in the present: the union based on *conformity* with the group, its customs, practices, and beliefs. Here again we find a considerable development.

In a primitive society the group is small; it consists of those with whom one shares blood and soil. With the growing development of culture, the group enlarges; it becomes the citizenry of a *polis*, the citizenry of a large state, the members of a church. Even the poor Roman felt pride because he could say *"civis romanus sum"*; Rome and the Empire were his family, his home, his world. Also in contemporary Western society the union with the group is the prevalent way of overcoming separateness. It is a union in which the individual self disappears to a large extent, and where the aim is to belong to the herd. If I am like everybody else, if I have no feelings or thoughts which make me different, if I conform in custom, dress, ideas, to the pattern of the group, I am saved; saved from the frightening experience of aloneness. The dictatorial systems use threats and terror to induce this conformity; the democratic countries, suggestion and propaganda. There is, indeed, one great difference between the two systems. In the democracies non-conformity is possible and, in fact, by no means entirely absent; in the totalitarian systems, only a few unusual heroes and martyrs can be expected to refuse obedience. But in spite of this difference the democratic societies show an overwhelming degree of conformity. The reason lies in the fact that there *has* to be an answer to the quest for union, and if there is no other or better way, then the union of herd conformity becomes the predominant one. One can only understand the power of the fear to be different, the fear to be only a few steps away from the herd, if one understands the depths of the need not to be separated. Sometimes this fear of non-conformity is rationalized as fear of practical dangers which could threaten the nonconformist. But actually, people *want* to conform to a much higher degree than they are *forced* to conform, at least in the Western democracies.

Most people are not even aware of their need to conform. They live under the illusion that they follow their own ideas and inclinations, that they are individualists, that they have arrived at their opinions as the result of their own thinking—and that it just happens that their ideas are the same as those of the majority. The consensus of all serves as a proof for the correctness of "their" ideas. Since there is still a need to feel some individuality, such need is satisfied with regard to minor differences; the initials on the handbag or the sweater, the name plate of the bank teller, the belonging to the Democratic as against the Republican party, to the Elks instead of to the Shriners become the expression of individual differences. The advertising slogan of "it is different" shows up this pathetic need for difference, when in reality there is hardly any left.

This increasing tendency for the elimination of differences is closely related to the concept and the experience of equality, as it is developing in the most advanced industrial societies. Equality had meant, in a religious context, that we are all God's children, that we all share in the same human-divine substance, that we are all one. It meant also that the very differences between individuals must be respected, that while it is true that we are all one, it is also true that each one of us is a unique entity, is a cosmos by itself. Such conviction of the uniqueness of the individual is expressed for instance in the Talmudic statement: "Whosoever saves a single life is as if he had saved the whole world; whosoever destroys a single life is as if he had destroyed the whole world." Equality as a condition for the development of individuality was also the meaning of the concept in the philosophy of the Western Enlightenment. It meant (most clearly formulated by Kant) that no man must be the means for the ends of another man. That all men are equal inasmuch as they are ends, and only ends, and never means to each other. Following the ideas of the Enlightenment, Socialist thinkers of various schools defined equality as abolition of exploitation, of the use of man by man, regardless of whether this use were cruel or "human."

In contemporary capitalistic society the meaning of equality has been transformed. By equality one refers to the equality of automatons; of men who have lost their individuality. *Equality today means "sameness," rather than "oneness."* It is the sameness of abstractions, of the men who work in the same jobs, who have the same amusements, who read the same newspapers, who have the same feelings and the same ideas. In this respect one must also look with some skepticism at some achievements which are usually praised as signs of our progress, such as the equality of women. Needless to say I am not speaking against the equality of women; but the positive aspects of this tendency for equality must not deceive one. It is part of the trend toward the elimination of differences. Equality is bought at this very price: women are equal because they are not different any more. The proposition of Enlightenment philosophy, *l'âme n'a pas de sexe*, the soul has no sex, has become the general practice. The polarity of the sexes is disappearing, and with it erotic love, which is based on this polarity. Men and women become the *same*, not *equals* as opposite poles. Contemporary society preaches this ideal of unindividualized equality because it needs human atoms, each one the same, to make them function in a mass aggregation, smoothly, without friction; all obeying the same commands, yet everybody being convinced that he is following his own desires. Just as modern mass production requires the standardization of commodities, so the social process requires standardization of man, and this standardization is called "equality."

Union by conformity is not intense and violent; it is calm, dictated by routine, and for this very reason often is insufficient to pacify the anxiety of separateness. The incidence of alcoholism, drug addiction, compulsive sexualism, and suicide in contemporary Western society are symptoms of this relative failure of herd conformity. Furthermore, this solution concerns mainly the mind and not the body, and for this reason too is lacking in comparison with the orgiastic solutions. Herd conformity has only one advantage: it is permanent, and not spasmodic. The individual is introduced into the conformity pattern at the age of three or four, and subsequently never loses his contact with the herd. Even his funeral, which he anticipates as his last great social affair, is in strict conformance with the pattern. . . .

A third way of attaining union lies in *creative activity*, be it that of the artist or of the artisan. In any kind of creative work the creating person unites himself with his material, which represents the world outside of himself. Whether a carpenter makes a table, or a goldsmith a piéce of jewelry, whether the peasant grows his corn or the painter paints a picture, in all types of creative work the worker and his object become one, man unites himself with the world in the process of creation. This, however, holds true only for productive work, for work in which *I* plan, produce, see the result of my work. In the modern work process of a clerk, the worker on the endless belt, little is left of this uniting quality of work. The worker becomes an appendix to the machine or to the bureaucratic organization. He has ceased to be he—hence no union takes place beyond that of conformity.

The unity achieved in productive work is not interpersonal; the unity achieved in orgiastic fusion is transitory; the unity achieved by conformity is only pseudo-unity. Hence, they are only partial answers to the problem of existence. The full answer lies in the achievement of interpersonal union, of fusion with another person, in *love*.

This desire for interpersonal fusion is the most powerful striving in man. It is the most fundamental passion, it is the force which keeps the human race together, the clan, the family, society. The failure to achieve it means insanity or destruction—self-destruction or destruction of others. Without love, humanity could not exist for a day. Yet, if we call the achievement of interpersonal union "love," we find ourselves in a serious difficulty. Fusion can be achieved in different ways—and the differences are not less significant than what is common to the various forms of love. Should they all be called love? Or should we reserve the word "love" only for a specific kind of union, one which has been the ideal virtue in all great humanistic religions and philosophical systems of the last four thousand years of Western and Eastern history?

As with all semantic difficulties, the answer can only be arbitrary. What matters is that we know what kind of union we are talking about when we speak of love. Do we refer to love as the mature answer to the problem of existence, or do we speak of those immature forms of love which may be called *symbiotic union*? In the following pages I shall call love only the former. I shall begin the discussion of "love" with the latter.

Symbiotic union has its biological pattern in the relationship between the pregnant mother and the foetus. They are two, and yet one. They live "together" (*symbiosis*), they need each other. The foetus is a part of the mother, it receives everything it needs from her; mother is its world, as it were; she feeds it, she protects it, but also her own life is enhanced by it. In the *psychic* symbiotic union, the two bodies are independent, but the same kind of attachment exists psychologically.

The *passive* form of the symbiotic union is that of submission, or if we use a clinical term, of *masochism*. The masochistic person escapes from the unbearable feeling of isolation and separateness by making himself part and parcel of another person who directs him, guides him, protects him; who is his life and his oxygen, as it were. The power of the one to whom one submits is inflated, may he be a person or a god; he is everything, I am nothing, except inasmuch as I am part of him. As a part, I am part of greatness, of power, of certainty. The masochistic person does not have to make decisions, does not have to take any risks; he is never alone—but he is not independent; he has no integrity; he is not yet fully born. In a religious context the object of worship is called an idol; in a secular context of a masochistic love relationship the essential mechanism, that of idolatry, is the same. The masochistic relationship can be blended with physical, sexual desire; in this case it is not only a submission in which one's mind participates, but also one's whole body. There can be masochistic submission to fate, to sickness, to rhythmic music, to the orgiastic state produced by drugs or under hypnotic trance—in all these instances the person renounces his integrity, makes himself the instrument of somebody or something outside of himself; he need not solve the problem of living by productive activity.

The *active* form of symbiotic fusion is domination or, to use the psychological term corresponding to masochism, *sadism*. The sadistic person wants to escape from his aloneness and his sense of imprisonment by making another person part and parcel of himself. He inflates and enhances himself by incorporating another person, who worships him.

The sadistic person is as dependent on the submissive person as the latter is on the former; neither can live without the other. The difference is only that the sadistic person commands, exploits, hurts, humiliates, and that the masochistic person is commanded, exploited, hurt, humiliated. This is a considerable difference in a realistic sense; in a deeper emotional sense, the difference is not so great as that which they both have in common: fusion without integrity. If one understands this, it is also not surprising to find that usually a person reacts in both the sadistic and the masochistic manner, usually toward different objects. Hitler reacted primarily in a sadistic fashion toward people, but masochistically toward fate, history, the "higher power" of nature. His end—suicide among general destruction—is as characteristic as was his dream of success—total domination.

In contrast to symbiotic union, mature *love is union under the condition of preserving one's integrity*, one's individuality. *Love is an active power in man*; a power which breaks through the walls which separate man from his fellow men, which unites him with others; love makes him overcome the sense of isolation and separateness, yet it permits him to be himself, to retain his integrity. In love the paradox occurs that two beings become one and yet remain two.

If we say love is an activity, we face a difficulty which lies in the ambiguous meaning of the word "activity." By "activity," in the modern usage of the word, is usually meant an action which brings about a change in an existing situation by means of an expenditure of energy. Thus a man is considered active if he does business, studies medicine, works on an endless belt, builds a table, or is engaged in sports. Common to all these activities is that they are directed toward an outside goal to be achieved. What is *not* taken into account is the *motivation* of activity. Take for instance a man driven to incessant work by a sense of deep insecurity and loneliness; or another one driven by ambition, or greed for money. In all these cases the person is the slave of a passion, and his activity is in reality a "passivity" because he is driven; he is the sufferer, not the "actor." On the other hand, a man sitting quiet and contemplating, with no purpose or aim except that of experiencing himself and his oneness with the world, is considered to be "passive," because he is not "doing" anything. In reality, this attitude of concentrated meditation is the highest activity there is, an activity of the soul, which is possible only under the condition of inner freedom and independence. One concept of activity, the modern one, refers to the use of energy for the achievement of external aims; the other concept of activity refers to the use of man's inherent powers, regardless of whether any external change is brought about. . . . Envy, jealousy, ambition, any kind of greed are passions; love is an action, the practice of a human power, which can be practiced only in freedom and never as the result of a compulsion.

Love is an activity, not a passive affect; it is a "standing in," not a "falling for." In the most general way, the active character of love can be described by stating that love is primarily *giving*, not receiving.

What is giving? Simple as the answer to this question seems to be, it is actually full of ambiguities and complexities. The most widespread misunderstanding is that which assumes that giving is "giving up" something, being deprived of, sacrificing. The person whose character has not developed beyond the stage of the receptive, exploitative, or hoarding orientation, experiences the act of giving in this way. The marketing character is willing to give, but only in exchange for receiving; giving without receiving for him is being cheated. People whose main orientation is a nonproductive one feel giving as an impoverishment. Most individuals of this type therefore refuse to give. Some make a virtue out of giving in the sense of a sacrifice. They feel that just because it is painful to give, one *should* give; the virtue of giving to them lies in the very act of acceptance of the sacrifice. For them, the norm that it is better to give than to receive means that it is better to suffer deprivation than to experience joy.

For the productive character, giving has an entirely different meaning. Giving is the highest expression of potency. In the very act of giving, I experience my strength, my wealth, my power. This experience of heightened vitality and potency fills me with joy. I experience myself as overflowing, spending, alive, hence as joyous. Giving is more joyous than receiving, not because it is a deprivation, but because in the act of giving lies the expression of my aliveness.

It is not difficult to recognize the validity of this principle by applying it to various specific phenomena. The most elementary example lies in the sphere of sex. The culmination of the male sexual function lies in the act of giving; the man gives himself, his sexual organ, to the woman. At the moment of orgasm he gives his semen to her. He cannot help giving it if he is potent. If he cannot give, he is impotent. For the woman the process is not different, although somewhat more complex. She gives herself too; she opens the gates to her feminine center; in the act of receiving, she gives. If she is incapable of this act of giving, if she can only receive, she is frigid. With her the act of giving occurs again, not in her function as a lover, but in that as a mother. She gives of herself to the growing child within her, she gives her milk to the infant, she gives her bodily warmth. Not to give would be painful.

In the sphere of material things giving means being rich. Not he who *has* much is rich, but he who *gives* much. The hoarder who is anxiously worried about losing something is, psychologically speaking, the poor, impoverished man, regardless of how much he has. Whoever is capable of giving of himself is rich. He experiences himself as one who can confer of himself to others. Only one who is deprived of all that goes beyond the barest necessities for subsistence would be incapable of enjoying the act of giving material things. But daily experience shows that what a person considers the minimal necessities depends as much on his character as it depends on his actual possessions. It is well known that the poor are more willing to give than the rich. Nevertheless, poverty beyond a certain point may make it impossible to give, and is so degrading, not only because of the suffering it causes directly, but because of the fact that it deprives the poor of the joy of giving.

The most important sphere of giving, however, is not that of material things, but lies in the specifically human realm. What does one person give to another? He gives of himself, of the most precious he has, he gives of his life. This does not necessarily mean that he sacrifices his life for the other—but that he gives him of that which is alive in him; he gives him of his joy, of his interest, of his understanding, of his knowledge, of his humor, of his sadness—of all expressions and manifestations of that which is alive in him. In thus giving of his life, he enriches the other person, he enhances his own sense of aliveness. He does not give in order to receive; giving is in itself exquisite joy. But in giving he cannot help bringing something to life in the other person, and this which is brought to life reflects back to him; in truly giving, he cannot help receiving that which is given back to him. Giving implies to make the other person a giver also and they both share in the joy of what they have brought to life. In the act of giving something is born, and both persons involved are grateful for the life that is born for both of them. Specifically with regard to love this means: love is a power which produces love; impotence is the inability to produce love. This thought has been beautifully expressed by Marx: "Assume," he says, "*man* as *man*, and his relation to the world as a human one, and you can exchange love only for love, confidence for confidence, etc. If you wish to enjoy art, you must be an artistically trained person; if you wish to have influence on other people, you must be a person who has a really stimulating and furthering influence on other people. Every one of your relationships to man and to nature must be a definite expression of your *real, individual* life corresponding to the object of your will. If you love without calling forth love, that is, if your love as such does not produce love, if by means of an *expression of life* as a loving person you do not make of yourself a *loved person*, then your love is impotent, a misfortune."[1] But not only in love does giving mean receiving. The teacher is taught by his students, the actor is stimulated by his audience, the psychoanalyst is cured by his patient—provided they do not treat each other as objects, but are related to each other genuinely and productively.

It is hardly necessary to stress the fact that the ability to love as an act of giving depends on the character development of the person. It presupposes the attainment of a predominantly productive orientation; in this orientation the person has overcome dependency, narcissistic omnipotence, the wish to exploit others, or to hoard, and has acquired faith in his own human powers, courage to rely on his powers in the attainment of his goals. To the degree that these qualities are lacking, he is afraid of giving himself—hence of loving.

Beyond the element of giving, the active character of love becomes evident in the fact that it always implies certain basic elements, common to all forms of love. These are *care, responsibility, respect* and *knowledge*.

That love implies *care* is most evident in a mother's love for her child. No assurance of her love would strike us as sincere if we saw her lacking in care for the infant, if she neglected to feed it, to bathe it, to give it physical comfort; and we are impressed by her love if we see her caring for the child. It is not different even with the love for animals or flowers. If a woman told us that she loved flowers, and we saw that she forgot to water them, we would not believe in her "love" for flowers. *Love is the active concern for the life and the growth of that which we love.* Where this active concern is lacking, there is no love. This element of love has been beautifully described in the book of Jonah. God has told Jonah to go to Nineveh to warn its inhabitants that they will be punished unless they mend their evil ways. Jonah runs away from his mission because he is afraid that the people of Nineveh will repent and that God will forgive them. He is a man with a strong sense of order and law, but without love. However, in his attempt to escape, he finds himself in the belly of a whale, symbolizing the state of isolation and imprisonment which his lack of love and solidarity has brought upon him. God saves him, and Jonah goes to Nineveh. He preaches to the inhabitants as God had told him, and the very thing he was afraid of happens. The men of Nineveh repent their sins, mend their ways, and God forgives them and decides not to destroy the city. Jonah is intensely angry and disappointed; he wanted "justice" to be done, not mercy. At last he finds some comfort in the shade of a tree which God has made to grow for him to protect him from the sun. But when God makes the tree wilt, Jonah is depressed and angrily complains to God. God answers: "Thou hast had pity on the gourd for the which thou has not labored neither madest it grow; which came up in a night, and perished in a night. And should I not spare Nineveh, that great city, wherein are more than sixscore thousand people that cannot discern between their right hand and their left hand; and also much cattle?" God's answer to Jonah is to be understood symbolically. God explains to Jonah that the essence of love is to "labor" for something and "to make something grow," that love and labor are inseparable. One loves that for which one labors, and one labors for that which one loves.

Care and concern imply another aspect of love; that of *responsibility*. Today responsibility is often meant to denote duty, something imposed upon one from the outside. But responsibility, in its true sense, is an entirely voluntary act; it is my response to the needs, expressed or unexpressed, of another human being. To be "responsible" means to be able and ready to "respond." Jonah did not feel responsible to the inhabitants of Nineveh. He, like Cain, could ask: "Am I my brother's keeper?" The loving person responds. The life of his brother is not his brother's business alone, but his own. He feels responsible for his fellow men, as he feels responsible for himself. This responsibility, in the case of the mother and her infant, refers mainly to the care of physical needs. In the love between adults it refers mainly to the psychic needs of the other person.

Responsibility could deteriorate into domination and possessiveness, were it not for a third component of love, *respect*. Respect is not fear and awe; it denotes, in accordance with the root of the word (*respicere* = to look at), the ability to see a person as he is, to be aware of his unique individuality. Respect means the concern that the other person should grow and unfold as he is. Respect, thus, implies the absence of exploitation. I want the loved person to grow and unfold for his own sake, and in his own ways, and not for the purpose of serving me. If I love the other person, I feel one with him or her, but with him *as he is*, not as I need him to be as an object for my use. It is clear that respect is possible only if *I* have achieved independence; if I can stand and walk without needing crutches, without having to dominate and exploit anyone else. Respect exists only on the basis of freedom: "L'amour est l'enfant de la liberté" as an old French song says; love is the child of freedom, never that of domination.

To respect a person is not possible without *knowing* him; care and responsibility would be blind if they were not guided by knowledge. Knowledge would be empty if it were not motivated by concern. There are many layers of knowledge; the knowledge which is an aspect of love is one which does not stay at the periphery, but penetrates to the core. It is possible only when I can transcend the concern for myself and see the other person in his own terms. I may know, for instance, that a person is angry, even if he does not show it overtly; but I may know him more deeply than that; then I know that he is anxious, and worried; that he feels lonely, that he feels guilty. Then I know that his anger is only the manifestation of something deeper, and I see him as anxious and embarrassed, that is, as the suffering person, rather than as the angry one.

Knowledge has one more, and a more fundamental, relation to the problem of love. The basic need to fuse with another person so as to transcend the prison of one's separateness is closely related to another specifically human desire, that to know the "secret of man." While life in its merely biological aspects is a miracle and a secret, man in his human aspects is an unfathomable secret to himself—and to his fellow man. We know ourselves, and yet even with all the efforts we may make, we do not know ourselves. We know our fellow man, and yet we do not know him, because we are not a thing and our fellow man is not a thing. The further we reach into the depth of our being, or someone else's being, the more the goal of knowledge eludes us. Yet we cannot help desiring to penetrate into the secret of man's soul, into the innermost nucleus which is "he."

There is one way, a desperate one, to know the secret: it is that of complete power over another person; the power which makes him do what we want, feel what we want, think what we want; which transforms him into a thing, our thing, our possession. The ultimate degree of this attempt to know lies in the extremes of sadism, the desire and ability to make a human being suffer; to torture him, to force him to betray his secret in his suffering. In this craving for penetrating man's secret, his and hence our own, lies an essential motivation for the depth and intensity of cruelty and destructiveness. In a very succinct way this idea has been expressed by Isaac Babel. He quotes a fellow officer in the Russian civil war, who has just stamped his former master to death, as saying: "With shooting—I'll put it this way—with shooting you only get rid of a chap. . . . With shooting you'll never get at the soul, to where it is in a fellow and how it shows itself. But I don't spare myself, and I've more than once trampled an enemy for over an hour. You see, I want to get to know what life really is, what life's like down our way."[2]

In children we often see this path to knowledge quite overtly. The child takes something apart, breaks it up in order to know it; or it takes an animal apart; cruelly tears off the wings of a butterfly in order to know it, to force its secret. The cruelty itself is motivated by something deeper: the wish to know the secret of things and of life.

The other path to knowing "the secret" is love. Love is active penetration of the other person, in which my desire to know is stilled by union. In the act of fusion I know you, I know myself, I know everybody—and I "know" nothing. I know in the only way knowledge of that which is alive is possible for man—by experience of union—not by any knowledge our thought can give. Sadism is motivated by the wish to know the secret, yet I remain as ignorant as I was before. I have torn the other being apart limb from limb, yet all I have done is to destroy him. Love is the only way of knowledge, which in the act of union answers my quest. In the act of loving, of giving myself, in the act of penetrating the other person, I find myself, I discover myself, I discover us both, I discover man. . . .

REFERENCES

1. "Nationalökonomie und Philosophie," 1844, published in Karl Marx's *Die Frühschriften*, Alfred Kröner Verlag, Stuttgart, 1953, pp. 300, 301. (My translation, E. F.)

2. I. Babel, *The Collected Stories* (New York: Criterion Books, 1955).

PROBES

Do you agree with Fromm that each human has a basic need to overcome separateness? Or do you think that it's possible to live a fully human life as a hermit?

How do Fromm's comments about achieving union in an orgiastic state relate to the discussion of body image and communication in Chapter 4?

What are some of the ways you achieve union via conformity? How do you nonverbally communicate your conformity?

How do Fromm's comments about male and female equality relate to the discussion in Chapter 2 about sexism and the English language?

What's the difference, in Fromm's view, between *needing* to be in relationship with another person and *wanting* to?

What does Fromm mean when he says that "love is an activity, not a passive affect; it is a 'standing in,' not a 'falling for'"?

How might your communication behavior change when you view "responsibility" as "ability to respond"?

How would you paraphrase the final sentence in this selection?

11

ROLLO MAY'S APPROACH

I think that Rollo May, better than almost any other writer, is able to clarify how a mature interpersonal relationship requires both strength and surrender, power and passivity, love and will. In the process he exposes the unfair and even dangerously simplistic naivete of the "everything is sweetness and light," "let's just hold hands and smile at the sunset" view of interpersonal communication.

As May clarifies, a mature, lasting interpersonal relationship requires both love and will. Each can block the other. Will can block love when one person is determined to "take care of" without "caring *for*" his or her lover, or when he or she is determined to be an "unconquerable soul" and is unwilling to listen with and give in to the other.

Love can also block will. This happens with the "I just love everybody" point of view. As May points out, generalized love is nice in theory, but it can't respond very effectively to the actual, concrete, specific other person. Since each person is unique, and since generalized love doesn't discriminate or identify unique others, indiscriminate love is ultimately *im*personal.

Like Fromm, May argues that we need love in order to overcome our feelings of separateness, feelings that come as we develop a sense of self. As May points out, our self-will initially emerges in our saying "no"—first as infants and later even more significantly as adolescents. Each of us needs to say "no," to assert our will over our parents, their values, and other aspects of our history. But when we've established that foundation of will, we can go beyond it and move through it to a relationship based on love *and* will.

I hope that May's words will suggest a context in which you can apply the communication attitudes and skills discussed in this book. His view is especially consistent with what's said about self-assertion in Chapter 4. I also hope that May's words will constantly remind you that communicating interpersonally is not based on a hearts-and-flowers, rose-colored view of the world. Persons perform good *and* bad acts, are happy *and* sad, angry *and* pleased, selfish *and* generous, loving *and* cruel. Communicating interpersonally means communicating, as much as possible, with all that the person is.

THE RELATION OF LOVE AND WILL
Rollo May

Both love and will are conjunctive forms of experience. That is, both describe a person reaching out, moving toward the other, seeking to affect him or her or it—and opening himself so that he may be affected by the other. Both love and

Reprinted from *Love and Will* by Rollo May, pp. 276–279, 283–286, by permission of W.W. Norton & Company, Inc., and Souvenir Press Ltd. Copyright © 1969 by W.W. Norton & Company, Inc.

will are ways of molding, forming, relating to the world and trying to elicit a response from it through the persons whose interest or love we covet. Love and will are interpersonal experiences which bring to bear power to influence others significantly and to be influenced by them.

LOVE AND WILL BLOCKING EACH OTHER

The interrelation of love and will is shown, furthermore, by the fact that each loses its efficacy when it is not kept in right relation to the other; each can block the other. Will can block love. This can be seen particularly in the "will power" of the inner-directed type of man, as he appears in [David] Riesman's studies. This was the man who was often the powerful captain of industry and finance in the early decades of this century and was our link to the great emphasis that was placed on individual will power which characterized the end of the Victorian Age. This was the period in which a man could talk of his "unconquerable soul" and could proclaim, "I am the captain of my fate." But if my soul is really unconquerable, I shall never fully love; for it is the nature of love to conquer all fortresses. And if I must cling to being the master of my fate, I shall never be able to let myself go in passion; for passionate love always has tragic possibilities. Eors, we have seen in an earlier chapter, "breaks the limbs' strength," and "overpowers the intelligence in all its shrewd planning."

An example of will blocking love can be seen in the father of a young student-patient of mine, who was the treasurer of a large corporation. He telephoned me to talk about "maximizing the effectiveness of his son's treatment" exactly as though we were at his company board meetings. When the son became sick with a minor illness in college the father immediately flew to the scene to take charge; the same father became furious when his son held hands and kissed his girl friend on the front lawn of their resort home. At dinner, the father told how he had entered into negotiation to buy the company of a friend of the son's but, having become irritated over the slowness of the negotiations, had called up the would-be partners and told them to "forget the whole thing." He showed no awareness that he was sending another company into bankruptcy with the snap of his fingers. This father was a public-spirited citizen, the chairman of several committees for civic betterment; and he could not understand why, when he had been treasurer of an international corporation, his subordinates secretly referred to him as the "hardest S.O.B. in Europe." The strong "will power" which the father thought solved all *his* problems, actually served at the same time to block his sensitivity, to cut off his capacity to *hear* other persons, even, or perhaps *especially*, his own son. It is not surprising that this exceedingly gifted son failed in his college work for several years, went through a beatnick period, and ultimately had a tortuous time permitting himself to succeed in his own profession.

Typical of the inner-directed genre, the father of my patient could always take care *of* others without caring *for* them, could give them his money but not his heart, could *direct* them but could not *listen* to them. This kind of "will power" was a transfer into interpersonal relationships of the same kind of power that had become so effective in maniulating railroad cars, stock transactions, coal mines, and other aspects of the industrial world. The man of will power, manipulating himself, did not permit himself to see why he could not manipulate others in the same way. This identifying of *will with personal manipulation* is the error that sets will in opposition to love.

It is a sound hypothesis, based on a good deal of evidence in psychotherapeutic work, that the unconscious guilt which parents like this carry because they manipulate their children leads them to be overprotective and overpermissive toward the same. These are the children who are given motor cars but not moral values, who pick up sensuality but are not taught sensitivity in life. The parents seem vaguely aware that the values on which their will power was based are no longer efficacious. But they can neither find new values nor give up the manipulative will. And the fathers often seem to act on the assumption that their will therefore has to do for the whole family.

This overemphasis on will, which blocks love, leads sooner or later to a reaction to the opposite error, *love which blocks will*. This is typically seen in the generation made up of the children of parents like the father we described above. The love proposed in our day by the hippie movement seems to be the clearest illustration of this error. "Hippie love is indiscriminate," is a common principle within the movement. Hippie love emphasizes immediacy, spontaneity, and the emotional honesty of the temporary moment. These aspects of hippie love are not only entirely understandable reactions against the manipulative will of the previous generation, but are values in their own right. The immediacy, spontaneity, and honesty of the relationship experienced in the vital *now* are sound and telling criticisms of contemporary bourgeois love and sex. The hippies' revolt helps destroy the manipulative will power which undermines human personality.

But love also requires enduringness. Love grows in depth by virtue of the lovers experiencing encounter with each other, conflict and growth, all over a period of time. These cannot be omitted from any lasting and viable experience of love. They involve choice and will under whatever names you use. Generalized love, to be sure, is adequate for generalized, group situations; but I am not honored by being loved simply because I belong to the genus "man." The love which is separated from will, or the love which obviates will, is characterized by a passivity which does not incorporate and grow with its own passion; such love tends, therefore, toward dissociation. It ends in something which is not fully personal because it does not fully discriminate. Such distinctions involve willing and choosing, and to choose someone means not to choose someone else. This is overlooked among the hippies; the *immediacy* of love in the hippie development seems to end in a love that is fugitive and ephemeral.

Now spontaneity is a tremendous relief after the assembly-line, sex-on-Saturday-night artificiality of bourgeois love against which the hippies are rebelling. But what of fidelity and the lasting qualities of love? Erotic passion not only requires the capacity to give one's self over to, to let one's self be stimulated by, the power of the immediate experience. But it also requires that one take this event into one's own center, to mold and form one's self and the relationship on the new plane of consciousness which emerges out of the experience. This requires the element of will. Victorian will power lacked the sensitivity and flexibility which goes with love; in the hippie movement in contrast, there is love without the staying power which goes with will. Here we see another important illustration of the fact that love and will are inseparable from each other.

A final indication that the problems of love and will belong together is the similarity in their "solutions." Neither can be adequately dealt with in our day simply by new techniques, patching up the old values, restating old habits in more palatable form, or any other such device. We cannot content ourselves by painting the old building a new color; it is the foundations which are destroyed, and the "resolutions," by whatever name we may call them, require new ones.

What is necessary for "resolutions" is a new consciousness in which the depth and meaning of personal relationship will occupy a central place. Such an embracing consciousness is always required in an age of radical transition. Lacking external guides, we shift our morality inward; there is a new demand upon the individual of personal responsibility. We are required to discover on a deeper level what it means to be human.

UNION OF LOVE AND WILL

Man's task is to unite love and will. They are not united by automatic biological growth but must be part of our conscious development.

In society, will tends to be set against love. For this there is an important genetic history. We have a memory, a "reminiscence" in Plato's sense, of a time when there was a union of ourselves with our mothers in the early experience of nursing at mother's breast. Then we were also at union with the universe, were wedded to it and had the experience of "union with being." This union yielded a satisfaction, calm happiness, self-acceptance, and elation. This is what is relived in meditation of the Zen or Hindu variety and in some drug experiences; it is a union with the universe which is shown in mysticism and produces a mild ecstasy, a blissful feeling that I am completely accepted by the universe. This is the backdrop of human existence implied in every myth of the Garden of Eden, every story of paradise, every "Golden Age"—a perfection which is deeply embedded in man's collective memory. Our needs are met without self-concious effort on our part, as, biologically, in the early condition of nursing at the mother's breast. This is the "first freedom," the first "yes."

But this first freedom always breaks down. And it does so because of the development of human consciousness. We experience our difference from and conflict with our environment and the fact that we are subjects in a world of objects—and even mother can then become an object. This is the separation between self and world, the split between existence and essence. Mythologically, it is the time when each child re-enacts the "fall" of Adam. This first freedom is inadequate because one cannot remain in it if we are to develop as a human being. And though we experience our separation from it as guilt . . . we must nevertheless go through with it. But it remains the source of all perfection, the backdrop of all utopias, the perpetual feelings that there ought to be a paradise someplace, and the efforts—forever creative but forever doomed to disappointment—that make us try to recreate a perfect state like the early one in our mother's arms. We cannot—not because of something God does, or some chance accident, or some happenstance that might have been different. We cannot because of the simple development of human consciousness. But nevertheless, we still always seek, as when we write a good paragraph or do a good work of art. We "fall" anew, but we remain ready to arise and pit ourselves anew against our fate.

This is why human will, in its specific form, always begins in a "no." We must stand against the environment, be able to give a negative; this inheres in consciousness. Arieti points out that all will has its source in the capacity to say "no"—a "no" not against the parents (although it shows itself in coming out against them, representatives of the personal authoritative universe as they are). The "no" is a protest against a world we never made, and it is also an assertion of one's self in the endeavor to remold and reform the world. Willing, in this sense, always begins *against* something—which generally can be seen as specifically against the first union with mother. Small wonder that this is done with guilt and anxiety, as in the Garden of Eden, or with conflict, as in normal development. But the child has to go through with it, for it is the unfolding of his own consciousness which prods him. And small wonder that, though he affirms it on one level, on another he regrets it. . . . During a re-experiencing of this period, one patient dreamt of a "tiger" which he was wont to interpret as his mother. But the therapist, with a wisdom which comes from having a view of the whole, continuously remarked "The tiger is in *you*." He was by this means able to give up fighting it and assimilate it, take it in as part of his own strength, and, as a result, become more affirmative as a person.

Will begins in opposition, begins in a "no" since the "yes" is already there. The danger is that this stage of development will be interpreted negatively by the parents, as shown in their excessive anger or interpretation of the child's original "no" as personally against them; and thus they may be seen by the child as opposing his development and autonomy. And he may, getting recriminations against choices, be tempted (and, to some extent, even give in to this temptation) to give it up, go back to the "bliss" (which now is now a bliss only in quotation marks). This is the hankering, nostalgic and self-defeating, which we see in adult neurotics, to go back to the first union again. But the past cannot be resurrected or ever made real again.

This is why the reuniting of will and love is such an important task and achievement for man. Will must come in to destroy the bliss, to make possible a new level of experience with other persons and the world; to make possible autonomy, freedom in the mature sense, and consequent responsibility. Will comes in to lay the groundwork which makes a relatively mature love possible. No longer seeking to re-establish a state of infancy, the human being, like Orestes, now freely takes responsibility for his choices. Will destroys the first freedom, the original union, not in order to fight the universe forever—even though some of us do stop at that stage. With the first bliss of *physical* union broken, man's task is now the *psychological* one of achieving new relationships which will be characterized by the choice of which woman to love, which groups to devote himself to, and by the conscious building of those affections.

Hence, I speak of the relating of love and will not as a state given us automatically, but as a task; and to the extent it is gained, it is an achievement. It points toward maturity, integration, wholeness. None of these is ever achieved without relation to its opposite; human progress is never one dimensional. But they become touchstones and criteria of our response to life's possibilities.

PROBES

Is May's perspective on interpersonal communication more like Powell's perspective (Chapter 6) or Augsburger's point of view (Chapter 7)?

Which is a greater problem in your experience—love blocking will, or will blocking love?

Do you agree that generalized love is ultimately *im*personal?

How does May's view of spontaneity compare and contrast with Gibb's view of spontaneity (Chapter 7)?

If will begins, as May suggests, with saying "no," how can will be a part of loving?

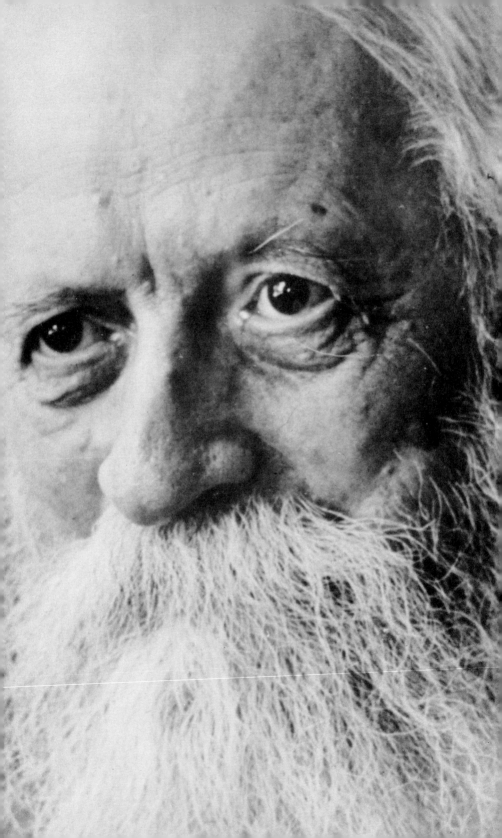

12
MARTIN BUBER'S APPROACH

Martin Buber, a Jewish philosopher, teacher, and theologian, was born and raised in what is now part of the Soviet Union and died in 1965 in Israel. Throughout his life, Buber was both a "scholar" or "intellectual" and an intensely practical person interested in everyday life experiences. As an intellectual, he was hungry to learn and to write all he could about how humans relate with one another. As a practical person, he was determined to keep all of his theorizing and scholarship firmly based in and applicable to the concrete events he experienced every day. Because he was raised by his grandparents in Europe during the late nineteenth and early twentieth centuries (Buber's parents were separated), lived through both world wars, was active in several political movements, and was a well-known, even famous, citizen of Israel, his life experiences are different in many ways from yours and mine. But for me, Buber's peculiar genius is that he can sense that part of his experience which is universal and can project that universal knowledge about human meetings through his European heritage and his "foreign" native language in such a way that he talks to me directly. In other words, even though he is in many ways very different from me, he says, "this is my experience; reflect on it a little and you might find that it's your experience too." Sometimes I stumble a little over Buber's language, the way he puts things. But when I listen to him and do what he asks, I discover that he's right. It *is* my experience, only now I understand it better than I ever did before.

I don't know whether this one excerpt from Buber's writing will work that way for you. But the possibility is there if you will open yourself to hear him.* That's one thing about Buber's writings. Although he's a philosopher, he has been criticized because he doesn't state philosophical propositions and then try to verify and validate them with "proof." Instead, Buber insists that his reader try to meet him in a *conversation*, a dialogue. The main thing is for the reader to see whether his or her life experiences resonate with Buber's. This resonance is the only "proof" of the validity of Buber's ideas that the reader will receive. So far, millions of persons have experienced that resonance. Books by and about Buber, especially his *I and Thou*, have been translated into several languages and are read around the world.

In almost all his writing, Buber begins by observing that each of us lives a twofold reality. To be an *individual*, we need only to interact with other objects —human and otherwise—in the world. To function effectively as an individual, we merely need to develop and maintain our ability to be "objective," to explain ourselves and the world with accurate theories and valid cause-and-effect formulations. But we become fully human *persons* only in genuine relationships with

---

*You might also be interested in other things written by or about Buber. For starters I recommend Aubrey Hodes, *Martin Buber: An Intimate Portrait* (New York: Viking, 1971); or Hilary Evans Bender, *Monarch Notes: The Philosophy of Martin Buber* (New York: Monarch, 1974). Buber's most important and influential book is *I and Thou*, trans. Walter Kaufmann (New York: Scribner, 1970).

others, only when we meet another and "make the other present as a whole and as a unique being, as the person that he is."

This genuine relationship Buber talks about is the "highest form" of what I've been calling interpersonal communication. You've probably heard of Buber's term for it—an "*I-Thou* relationship."* According to Buber, the individual lives always in the world of *I-It*; the *person* can enter the world of *I-Thou*. Both worlds are necessary. You can't expect to communicate interpersonally with everyone in every situation. But you can become a fully human person only by sharing genuine interpersonal relationships with others. As Buber puts it, ". . . without *It* man cannot live. But he who lives with *It* alone is not a man."

This article is taken from a talk Buber gave when he visited the United States in 1957. It's especially useful because it is a kind of summary of much of what he had written in the first 79 years of his life (he died when he was 87).

I've outlined the article to simplify it some and to show how clearly organized it actually is. As you can see from the outline, Buber's subject is interpersonal relationships, which he calls "man's personal dealings with one another," or "the interhuman." Like the rest of this book, Buber's article doesn't deal with some mystical spirit world in which we all become one. Rather, he's writing about communication between today's teachers and students, politicians and voters, preachers and parishioners, and between you and me. First, he explains some attitudes and actions that keep people from achieving "genuine dialogue." Then he describes the characteristics of this dialogue, or *I-Thou* relationships. In the outline I've paraphrased each point that he makes.

When you read the essay, you'll probably be able to see where several of the other writers in this book got some of their ideas. For example, compare Carl Rogers' explanation of "congruence" with what Buber says about "being and seeming." Or note Buber's way of talking about the six "persons" in a one-to-one conversation—my me, your you, etc.—which were also identified by Dean Barnlund in Chapter 1.

Whether or not you note that kind of thing, however, read this article as thoughtfully as you can. It sums up everything in this book. And I know from the experience I have lived that it's worth understanding.

OUTLINE OF MARTIN BUBER'S "ELEMENTS OF THE INTERHUMAN"

I.   Interhuman relationships are not the same as "Social Relationships."

    A. Social relationships can be very close, but no *existential* or person-to-person relation is necessarily involved.

---

*Buber's translators always point out that this "thou" is not the Shakespearian or religious term of formal address. It is a translation of the German *Du*, the familiar form of the pronoun "you." As Walter Kaufmann, one of Buber's translators, explains, "German lovers say *Du* to one another and so do friends. *Du* is spontaneous and unpretentious, remote from formality, pomp, and dignity."

B. That's because the collective or social suppresses individual persons.

C. But in the interhuman, person meets person. In other words, "the only thing that matters is that for each of the two men the other happens as the particular other, that each becomes aware of the other and is thus related to him in such a way that he does not regard and use him as his object, but as his partner in a living event, even if it is no more than a boxing match."

D. In short, "the sphere of the interhuman is one in which a person is confronted by the other. We [i.e., Buber] call its unfolding the dialogical."

II. There are three problems which get in the way of dialogue.

A. The first problem is the duality of *being* and *seeming*. Dialogue won't happen if the people involved are only "seeming." They need to "be."

  1. "Seeming" in a relationship involves being concerned with your image or front—with how you wish to appear.

  2. "Being" involves the spontaneous and unreserved presentation of what you really are in your personal dealings with the other.

  3. These two are generally found mixed together. The most we can do is to distinguish between persons in whose essential attitude one or the other (being or seeming) predominates.

  4. When seeming reigns, real interpersonal communication is impossible: "Whatever the meaning of the word 'truth' may be in other realms, in the interhuman realm it means that men communicate themselves to one another as what they are."

  5. The tendency toward seeming, however, is understandable.

    a. We *essentially* need personal confirmation, i.e., we can't live without being confirmed by other people.

    b. Seeming often appears to help us get the confirmation we need.

    c. Consequently, "to yield to seeming is man's essential cowardice, to resist it is his essential courage."

  6. This view indicates that there is no such thing as "bad being," but rather people who are habitually content to "seem" and afraid to "be." "I have never known a young person who seemed to be irretrievably bad."

B. The second problem involves the way we perceive others.

  1. Many modern fatalists, such as Jean-Paul Sartre, believe that we can ultimately know *only* ourselves, that "man has directly to do only with himself and his own affairs."

  2. But the main prerequisite for dialogue is that you get in direct touch with the other, "that each person should regard his partner as the very one he is."

    a. This means becoming aware of the other person as an essentially unique being. "To be aware of a man...means in particular to perceive his wholeness as a person determined by the spirit; it means to perceive the dynamic centre which stamps his every utterance, action, and attitude with the recognizable sign of uniqueness."

    b. But this kind of awareness is impossible so long as I objectify the other.

3. Perceiving the other in this way is contrary to everything in our world that is analytic or reductive.

    a. This is not to say that the sciences are wrong, only that they are severely limited.

    b. What's dangerous is the extension of the scientific, analytic method to all of life, because it is very difficult for science to remain aware of the essential uniqueness of persons.

4. This kind of perception is called "personal making present." What enables us to do it is our capacity for "imagining the real" of the other.

    a. Imagining the real "is not a looking at the other but a bold swinging—demanding the most intensive stirring of one's being—into the life of the other."

    b. When I *imagine* what the other person is *really* thinking and feeling, I can make direct contact with him or her.

C. The third problem which impedes the growth of dialogue is the tendency toward imposition instead of unfolding.

1. One way to affect a person is to impose yourself on him or her.

2. Another way is to "find and further in the soul of the other the disposition toward" that which you have recognized in yourself as right.

    a. Unfolding is not simply "teaching," but rather *meeting*.

    b. It requires believing in the other person.

    c. It means working as a helper of the growth processes already going on in the other.

3. The propagandist is the typical "imposer"; the teacher can be the correspondingly typical "unfolder."

4. The ethic implied here is similar to Immanuel Kant's, i.e., persons should never be treated as means to an end, but only as ends in themselves.

    a. The only difference is that Buber stresses that persons exist not in isolation but in the interhuman, and

    b. for the interhuman to occur, there must be:

        (1) as little seeming as possible,

        (2) genuine perceiving ("personal making present") of the other, and

        (3) as little imposing as possible.

III. Summary of the characteristics of genuine dialogue:

A. Each person must turn toward and be open to the other, a "turning of the being."

B. Each must make present the other by imagining the real.

C. Each confirms the other's being; however, confirmation does not necessarily mean approval.

D. Each must be authentically himself or herself.

    1. Each must say whatever she or he "has to say."

    2. Each cannot be ruled by thoughts of his or her own effect or effectiveness as a speaker.

E. Where dialogue becomes genuine, "there is brought into being a memorable common fruitfulness which is to be found nowhere else."

F. Speaking is not always essential; silence can be very important.

G. Finally, all participants must be committed to dialogue; otherwise, it will fail.

Again, Buber's language sometimes can get in the way of understanding him. But if you can listen empathically, I think you will be able to resonate with at least some of what he says.

ELEMENTS OF THE INTERHUMAN
Martin Buber

THE SOCIAL AND THE INTERHUMAN

It is usual to ascribe what takes place between men to the social realm, thereby blurring a basically important line of division between two essentially different areas of human life. I myself, when I began nearly fifty years ago to find my own bearings in the knowledge of society, making use of the then unknown concept of the interhuman, made the same error. From that time it became increasingly clear to me that we have to do here with a separate category of our existence, even a separate dimension, to use a mathematical term, and one with which we are so familiar that its peculiarity has hitherto almost escaped us. Yet insight into its peculiarity is extremely important not only for our thinking but also for our living.

We may speak of social phenomena wherever the life of a number of men, lived with one another, bound up together, brings in its train shared experiences and reactions. But to be thus bound up together means only that each individual existence is enclosed and contained in a group existence. It does not mean that between one member and another of the group there exists any kind of personal

"Elements of the Interhuman," translated by Ronald Gregor Smith, in *The Knowledge of Man* by Martin Buber, edited by Maurice Friedman, translated by Maurice Friedman and Ronald Gregor Smith. Copyright © 1965 by Martin Buber and Maurice Friedman. Reprinted by permission of Harper & Row, Publishers, Inc., and George Allen & Unwin Ltd.

relation. They do feel that they belong together in a way that is, so to speak, fundamentally different from every possible belonging together with someone outside the group. And there do arise, especially in the life of smaller groups, contacts which frequently favour the birth of individual relations, but, on the other hand, frequently make it more difficult. In no case, however, does membership in a group necessarily involve an existential relation between one member and another. It is true that there have been groups in history which included highly sensitive and intimate relations between two of their members—as, for instance, in the homosexual relations among the Japanese samurai or among Doric warriors—and these were countenanced for the sake of the stricter cohesion of the group. But in general it must be said that the leading elements in groups, especially in the later course of human history, have rather been inclined to suppress the personal relation in favour of the purely collective element. Where this latter element reigns alone or is predominant, men feel themselves to be carried by the collectivity, which lifts them out of loneliness and fear of the world and lostness. When this happens—and for modern man it is an essential happening—the life between person and person seems to retreat more and more before the advance of the collective. The collective aims at holding in check the inclination to personal life. It is as though those who are bound together in groups should in the main be concerned only with the work of the group and should turn to the personal partners, who are tolerated by the group, only in secondary meetings.

The difference between the two realms became very palpable to me on one occasion when I had joined the procession through a large town of a movement to which I did not belong. I did it out of sympathy for the tragic development which I sensed was at hand in the destiny of a friend who was one of the leaders of the movement. While the procession was forming, I conversed with him and with another, a good-hearted "wild man," who also had the mark of death upon him. At that moment I still felt that the two men really were there, over against me, each of them a man near to me, near even in what was most remote from me; so different from me that my soul continually suffered from this difference, yet by virtue of this very difference confronting me with authentic being. Then the formations started off, and after a short time I was lifted out of all confrontation, drawn into the procession, falling in with its aimless step; and it was obviously the very same for the two with whom I had just exchanged human words. After a while we passed a cafe where I had been sitting the previous day with a musician whom I knew only slightly. The very moment we passed it the door opened, the musician stood on the threshold, saw me, apparently saw me alone, and waved to me. Straightway it seemed to me as though I were taken out of the procession and of the presence of my marching friends, and set there, confronting the musician. I forgot that I was walking along with the same step; I felt that I was standing over there by the man who had called out to me, and without a word, with a smile of understanding, was answering him. When consciousness of the facts returned to me, the procession, with my companions and myself at its head, had left the cafe behind.

The realm of the interhuman goes far beyond that of sympathy. Such simple happenings can be part of it as, for instance, when two strangers exchange glances in a crowded streetcar, at once to sink back again into the convenient state of wishing to know nothing about each other. But also every casual encounter between opponents belong to this realm, when it affects the opponent's attitude—that is, when something, however imperceptible, happens between the two, no matter whether it is marked at the time by any feeling or not. The only thing that matters is that for each of the two men the other happens as the particular other, that each becomes aware of the other and is thus related to him in such a way that he does not regard and use him as his object, but as his partner in a living event, even if it is no more than a boxing match. It is well known that some existentialists assert that the basic factor between men is that one is an object for the other. But so far as this is actually the case, the special reality of the interhuman, the fact of the contact, has been largely eliminated. It cannot indeed be entirely eliminated. As a crude example, take two men who are observing one another. The essential thing is not that the one makes the other his object, but the fact that he is not fully able to do so and the reason for his failure. We have in common with all existing beings that we can be made objects of observation. But it is my privilege as man that by the hidden activity of my being I can establish an impassable barrier to objectification. Only in partnership can my being be perceived as an existing whole.

The sociologist may object to any separation of the social and the interhuman on the ground that society is actually built upon human relations, and the theory of these relations is therefore to be regarded as the very foundation of sociology. But here an ambiguity in the concept "relation" becomes evident. We speak, for instance, of a comradely relation between two men in their work, and do not merely mean what happens between them as comrades, but also a lasting disposition which is actualized in those happenings and which even includes purely psychological events such as the recollection of the absent comrade. But by the sphere of the interhuman I mean solely actual happenings between men, whether wholly mutual or tending to grow into mutual relations. For the participation of both partners is in principle indispensable. The sphere of the interhuman is one in which a person is confronted by the other. We call its unfolding the dialogical.

In accordance with this, it is basically erroneous to try to understand the interhuman phenomena as psychological. When two men converse together, the psychological is certainly an important part of the situation, as each listens and each prepares to speak. Yet this is only the hidden accompaniment to the conversation itself, the phonetic event fraught with meaning, whose meaning is to be found neither in one of the two partners nor in both together, but only in their dialogue itself, in this "between" which they live together.

BEING AND SEEMING

The essential problem of the sphere of the interhuman is the duality of being and seeming. Although it is a familiar fact that men are often troubled about the impression they make on others, this has been much more discussed in moral philosophy than in anthropology. Yet this is one of the most important subjects for anthropological study.

We may distinguish between two different types of human existence. The one proceeds from what one really is, the other from what one wishes to seem. In general, the two are found mixed together. There have probably been few men who were entirely independent of the impression they made on others, while there has scarcely existed one who was exclusively determined by the impression made by him. We must be content to distinguish between men in whose essential attitude the one or the other predominates.

This distinction is most powerfully at work, as its nature indicates, in the interhuman realm—that is, in men's personal dealings with one another.

Take as the simplest and yet quite clear example the situation in which two persons look at one another—the first belonging to the first type, the second to the second. The one who lives from his being looks at the other just as one looks at someone with whom he has personal dealings. His look is "spontaneous," "without reserve"; of course he is not uninfluenced by the desire to make himself understood by the other, but he is uninfluenced by any thought of the idea of himself which he can or should awaken in the person whom he is looking at. His opposite is different. Since he is concerned with the image which his appearance, and especially his look or glance, produces in the other, he "makes" this look. With the help of the capacity, in greater or lesser degree peculiar to man, to make a definite element of his being appear in his look, he produces a look which is meant to have, and often enough does have, the effect of a spontaneous utterance—not only the utterance of a physical event supposed to be taking place at that very moment, but also, as it were, the reflection of a personal life of such-and-such a kind.

This must, however, be carefully distinguished from another area of seeming whose ontological legitimacy cannot be doubted. I mean the realm of "genuine seeming," where a lad, for instance, imitates his heroic model and while he is doing so is seized by the actuality of heroism, or a man plays the part of a destiny and conjures up authentic destiny. In this situation there is nothing false;

the imitation is genuine imitation and the part played is genuine; the mask, too, is a mask and no deceit. But where the semblance originates from the lie and is permeated by it, the interhuman is threatened in its very existence. It is not that someone utters a lie, falsifies some account. The lie I mean does not take place in relation to particular facts, but in relation to existence itself, and it attacks interhuman existence as such. There are times when a man, to satisfy some stale conceit, forfeits the great chance of a true happening between I and Thou.

Let us now imagine two men, whose life is dominated by appearance, sitting and talking together. Call them Peter and Paul. Let us list the different configurations which are involved. First, there is Peter as he wishes to appear to Paul, and Paul as he wishes to appear to Peter. Then there is Peter as he really appears to Paul, that is, Paul's image of Peter, which in general does not in the least coincide with what Peter wishes Paul to see; and similarly there is the reverse situation. Further, there is Peter as he appears to himself, and Paul as he appears to himself. Lastly, there are the bodily Peter and the bodily Paul. Two living beings and six ghostly appearances, which mingle in many ways in the conversation between the two. Where is there room for any genuine interhuman life?

Whatever the meaning of the word "truth" may be in other realms, in the interhuman realm it means that men communicate themselves to one another as what they are. It does not depend on one saying to the other everything that occurs to him, but only on his letting no seeming creep in between himself and the other. It does not depend on one letting himself go before another, but on his granting to the man to whom he communicates himself a share in his being. This is a question of the authenticity of the interhuman, and where this is not to be found, neither is the human element itself authentic.

Therefore, as we begin to recognize the crisis of man as the crisis of what is between man and man, we must free the concept of uprightness from the thin moralistic tones which cling to it, and let it take its tone from the concept of bodily uprightness. If a presupposition of human life in primeval times is given in man's walking upright, the fulfillment of human life can only come through the soul's walking upright, through the great uprightness which is not tempted by any seeming because it has conquered all semblance.

But, one may ask, what if a man by his nature makes his life subservient to the images which he produces in others? Can he, in such a case, still become a man living from his being, can he escape from his nature?

The widespread tendency to live from the recurrent impression one makes instead of from the steadiness of one's being is not a "nature." It originates, in fact, on the other side of interhuman life itself, in men's dependence upon one another. It is no light thing to be confirmed in one's being by others, and seeming deceptively offers itself as a help in this. To yield to seeming is man's essential cowardice, to resist it is his essential courage. But this is not an inexorable state of affairs which is as it is and must so remain. One can struggle to come to oneself—that is, to come to confidence in being. One struggles, now more successfully, now less, but never in vain, even when one thinks he is defeated. One must at times pay dearly for life lived from the being; but it is never too dear. Yet is there not bad being, do weeds not grow everywhere? I have never known a young person who seemed to me irretrievably bad. Later indeed it becomes more and more difficult to penetrate the increasingly tough layer which has settled down on a man's being. Thus there arises the false perspective of the seemingly fixed "nature" which cannot be overcome. It is false; the foreground is deceitful; man as man can be redeemed.

Again we see Peter and Paul before us surrounded by the ghosts of the semblances. A ghost can be exorcized. Let us imagine that these two find it more and more repellent to be represented by ghosts. In each of them the will is stirred and strengthened to be confirmed in their being as what they really are and nothing else. We see the forces of real life at work as they drive out the ghosts, till the semblance vanishes and the depths of personal life call to one another.

PERSONAL MAKING PRESENT

By far the greater part of what is today called conversation among men would be more properly and precisely described as speechifying. In general, people do not really speak to one another, but each, although turned to the other, really speaks to a fictitious court of appeal whose life consists of nothing but listening to him. Chekhov has given poetic expression to this state of affairs in *The Cherry Orchard*, where the only use the members of a family make of their being together is to talk past one another. But it is Sartre who has raised to a principle of existence what in Chekhov still appears as the deficiency of a person who is shut up in himself. Sartre regards the walls between the partners in a conversation as simply impassable. For him it is inevitable human destiny that a man has directly to do only with himself and his own affairs. The inner existence of the other is his own concern, not mine; there is no direct relation with the other, nor can there be. This is perhaps the clearest expression of the wretched fatalism of modern man, which regards degeneration as the unchangeable nature of *Homo sapiens* and the misfortune of having run into a blind alley as his primal fate, and which brands every thought of a breakthrough as reactionary romanticism. He who really knows how far our generation has lost the way of true freedom, of free giving between I and Thou, must himself, by virtue of the demand implicit in every great knowledge of this kind, practice directness—even if he were the only man on earth who did it—and not depart from it until scoffers are struck with fear and hear in his voice the voice of their own suppressed longing.

The chief presupposition for the rise of genuine dialogue is that each should regard his partner as the very one he is. I become aware of him, aware that he is different, essentially different from myself, in the definite, unique way which is peculiar to him, and I accept whom I thus see, so that in full earnestness I can direct what I say to him as the person he is. Perhaps from time to time I must offer strict opposition to his view about the subject of our conversation. But I accept this person, the personal bearer of a conviction, in his definite being out of which his conviction has grown—even though I must try to show, bit by bit, the wrongness of this very conviction. I affirm the person I struggle with: I struggle with him as his partner, I confirm him as creature and as creation, I confirm him who is opposed to me as him who is over against me. It is true that it now depends on the other whether genuine dialogue, mutuality in speech arises between us. But if I thus give to the other who confronts me his legitimate standing as a man with whom I am ready to enter into dialogue, then I may trust him and suppose him to be also ready to deal with me as his partner.

But what does it mean to be "aware" of a man in the exact sense in which I use the word? To be aware of a thing or a being means, in quite general terms, to experience it as a whole and yet at the same time without reduction or abstraction, in all its concreteness. But a man, although he exists as a living being among living beings and even as a thing among things, is nevertheless something categorically different from all things and all beings. A man cannot really be grasped except on the basis of the gift of the spirit which belongs to man alone among all things, the spirit as sharing decisively in the personal life of the living man, that is, the spirit which determines the person. To be aware of a man, therefore, means in particular to perceive his wholeness as a person determined by the spirit; it means to perceive the dynamic centre which stamps his every utterance, action, and attitude with the recognizable sign of uniqueness. Such an awareness is impossible, however, if and so long as the other is the separated object of my contemplation or even observation, for this wholeness and its centre do not let themselves be known to contemplation or observation. It is only possible when I step into an elemental relation with the other, that is, when he becomes present to me. Hence I designate awareness in this special sense as "personal making present."

The perception of one's fellow man as a whole, as a unity, and as unique—even if his wholeness, unity, and uniqueness are only partly developed, as is usually the case—is opposed in our time by almost everything that is commonly understood as specifically modern. In our time there predominates an analytical, reductive, and deriving look between man and man. This look is analytical, or rather pseudo analytical, since it treats the whole being as put together and therefore able to be taken apart—not only the so-called unconscious which is accessible to relative objectification, but also the psychic stream itself, which can never, in fact, be grasped as an object. This look is a reductive one because it tries to contract the manifold person, who is nourished by the microcosmic richness of the possible, to some schematically surveyable and recurrent structures. And this look is a deriving one because it supposes it can grasp what a man has become, or even is becoming, in genetic formulae, and it thinks that even the dynamic central principle of the individual in this becoming can be represented by a general concept. An effort is being made today radically to destroy the mystery between man and man. The personal life, the ever-near mystery, once the source of the stillest enthusiasms, is levelled down.

What I have just said is not an attack on the analytical method of the human sciences, a method which is indispensable wherever it furthers knowledge of a phenomenon without impairing the essentially different knowledge of its uniqueness that transcends the valid circle of the method. The science of man that makes use of the analytical method must accordingly always keep in view the boundary of such a contemplation, which stretches like a horizon around it. This duty makes the transposition of the method into life dubious; for it is excessively difficult to see where the boundary is in life.

If we want to do today's work and prepare tomorrow's with clear sight, then we must develop in ourselves and in the next generation a gift which lives in man's inwardness as a Cinderella, one day to be a princess. Some call it intuition, but that is not a wholly unambiguous concept. I prefer the name "imagining the real," for in its essential being this gift is not a looking at the other, but a bold swinging—demanding the most intensive stirring of one's being—into the life of the other. This is the nature of all genuine imagining, only that here the realm of my action is not the all-possible, but the particular real person who confronts me, whom I can attempt to make present to myself just in this way, and not otherwise, in his wholeness, unity, and uniqueness, and with his dynamic centre which realizes all these things ever anew.

Let it be said again that all this can only take place in a living partnership, that is, when I stand in a common situation with the other and expose myself vitally to his share in the situation as really his share. It is true that my basic attitude can remain unanswered, and the dialogue can die in seed. But if mutuality stirs, then the interhuman blossoms into genuine dialogue.

IMPOSITION AND UNFOLDING

I have referred to two things which impede the growth of life between men: the invasion of seeming, and the inadequacy of perception. We are now faced with a third, plainer than the others, and in this critical hour more powerful and more dangerous than ever.

There are two basic ways of affecting men in their views and their attitude to life. In the first a man tries to impose himself, his opinion and his attitude, on the other in such a way that the latter feels the psychical result of the action to be his own insight, which has only been freed by the influence. In the second basic way of affecting others, a man wishes to find and to further in the soul of the other the disposition toward what he has recognized in himself as the right. Because it is the right, it must also be alive in the microcosm of the other, as one possibility. The other need only be opened out in this potentiality of his; moreover, this opening out takes place not essentially by teaching, but by meeting, by existential communication between someone that is in actual being and someone that is in a process of becoming. The first way has been most powerfully developed in the realm of propaganda, the second in that of education.

The propagandist I have in mind, who imposes himself, is not in the least concerned with the person whom he desires to influence, as a person; various individual qualities are of importance only in so far as he can exploit them to win the other and must get to know them for this purpose. In his indifference to everything personal the propagandist goes a substantial distance beyond the party for which he works. For the party, persons in their difference are of significance because each can be used according to his special qualities in a particular function. It is true that the personal is considered only in respect of the specific use to which it can be put, but within these limits it is recognized in practice. To propaganda as such, on the other hand, individual qualities are rather looked on as a burden, for propaganda is concerned simply with *more*—more members, more adherents, an increasing extent of support. Political methods, where they rule in an extreme form, as here, simply mean winning power over the other by depersonalizing him. This kind of propaganda enters upon different relations with force; it supplements it or replaces it, according to the need or the prospects, but it is in the last analysis nothing but sublimated violence, which has become imperceptible as such. It places men's souls under a pressure which allows the illusion of autonomy. Political methods at their height mean the effective abolition of the human factor.

The educator whom I have in mind lives in a world of individuals, a certain number of whom are always at any one time committed to his care. He sees each of these individuals as in a position to become a unique, single person, and thus the bearer of a special task of existence which can be fulfilled through him and through him alone. He sees every personal life as engaged in such a process of actualization, and he knows from his own experience that the forces making for actualization are all the time involved in a microcosmic struggle with counterforces. He has come to see himself as a helper of the actualizing forces. He knows these forces; they have shaped and they still shape him. Now he puts this person shaped by them at their disposal for a new struggle and a new work. He cannot wish to impose himself, for he believes in the effect of the actualizing forces, that is, he believes that in every man what is right is established in a single and uniquely personal way. No other way may be imposed on a man, but another way, that of the educator, may and must unfold what is right, as in this case it struggles for achievement, and help it to develop.

The propagandist, who imposes himself, does not really believe even in his own cause, for he does not trust it to attain its effect of its own power without his special methods, whose symbols are the loudspeaker and the television advertisement. The educator who unfolds what is there believes in the primal power which has scattered itself, and still scatters itself, in all human beings in order that it may grow up in each man in the special form of that man. He is confident that this growth needs at each moment only that help which is given in meeting and that he is called to supply that help.

I have illustrated the character of the two basic attitudes and their relation to one another by means of two extremely antithetical examples. But wherever men have dealings with one another, one or the other attitude is to be found in more or less degree.

These two principles of imposing oneself on someone and helping someone to unfold should not be confused with concepts such as arrogance and humility. A man can be arrogant without wishing to impose himself on others, and it is not enough to be humble in order to help another unfold. Arrogance and humility are dispositions of the soul, psychological fact with a moral accent, while imposition and helping to unfold are events between men, anthropological facts which point to an ontology, the ontology of the interhuman.

In the moral realm Kant expressed the essential principle that one's fellow man must never be thought of and treated merely as a means, but always at the same time as an independent end. The principle is expressed as an "ought" which is sustained by the idea of human dignity. My point of view, which is near to Kant's in its essential features, has another source and goal. It is concerned with the presuppositions of the interhuman. Man exists anthropologically not in his isolation, but in the completeness of the relation between man and man; what humanity is can be properly grasped only in vital reciprocity. For the proper existence of the interhuman it is necessary, as I have shown, that the semblance does not intervene to spoil the relation of personal being to personal being. It is further necessary, as I have also shown, that each one means and makes present the other in his personal being. That neither should wish to impose himself on the other is the third basic presupposition of the interhuman. These presuppositions do not include the demand that one should influence the other in his unfolding; that is, however, an element that is suited to lead to a higher stage of the interhuman.

That there resides in every man the possibility of attaining authentic human existence in the special way peculiar to him can be grasped in the Aristotelian image of entelechy, innate self-realization; but one must note that it is an entelechy of the work of creation. It would be mistaken to speak here of individuation alone. Individuation is only the indispensable personal stamp of all realization of human existence. The self as such is not ultimately the essential, but the meaning of human existence given in creation again and again fulfills itself as self. The help that men give each other in becoming a self leads the life between men to its height. The dynamic glory of the being of man is first bodily present in the relation between two men each of whom in meaning the other also means the highest to which this person is called, and serves the self-realization of this human life as one true to creation without wishing to impose on the other anything of his own realization.

GENUINE DIALOGUE

We must now summarize and clarify the marks of genuine dialogue.

In genuine dialogue the turning to the partner takes place in all truth, that is, it is a turning of the being. Every speaker "means" the partner or partners to whom he turns as this personal existence. To "mean" someone in this connection is at the same time to exercise that degree of making present which is possible to the speaker at that moment. The experiencing senses and the imagining of the real which completes the findings of the senses work together to make the other present as a whole and as a unique being, as the person that he is. But the speaker does not merely perceive the one who is present to him in this way; he receives him as his partner, and that means that he confirms this other being, so far as it is for him to confirm. The true turning of his person to the other includes this confirmation, this acceptance. Of course, such a confirmation does not mean approval; but no matter in what I am against the other, by accepting him as my partner in genuine dialogue I have affirmed him as a person.

Further, if genuine dialogue is to arise, everyone who takes part in it must bring himself into it. And that also means that he must be willing on each occasion to say what is really in his mind about the subject of the conversation. And that means further that on each occasion he makes the contribution of his spirit without reduction and without shifting his ground. Even men of great integrity are under the illusion that they are not bound to say everything "they have to say." But in the great faithfulness which is the climate of genuine dialogue, what I have to say at any one time already has in me the character of something that wishes to be uttered, and I must not keep it back, keep it in myself. It bears for me the unmistakable sign which indicates that it belongs to the common life of the word. Where the dialogical word genuinely exists, it must be given its right by keeping nothing back. To keep nothing back is the exact opposite of unreserved speech. Everything depends on the legitimacy of "what I have to say." And of course I must also be intent to raise into an inner word and then into a spoken word what I have to say at this moment but do not yet possess as speech. To speak is both nature and work, something that grows and something that is made, and where it appears dialogically, in the climate of great faithfulness, it has to fulfill ever anew the unity of the two.

Associated with this is that overcoming of semblance to which I have referred. In the atmosphere of genuine dialogue, he who is ruled by the thought of his own effect as the speaker of what he has to speak has a destructive effect. If, instead of what has to be said, I try to bring attention to my *I*, I have irrevocably miscarried what I had to say; it enters the dialogue as a failure and the dialogue is a failure. Because genuine dialogue is an ontological sphere which is constituted by the authenticity of being, every invasion of semblance must damage it.

But where the dialogue is fulfilled in its being, between partners who have turned to one another in truth, who express themselves without reserve and are free of the desire for semblance, there is brought into being a memorable common fruitfulness which is to be found nowhere else. At such times, at each such time, the word arises in a substantial way between men who have been seized in their depths and opened out by the dynamic of an elemental togetherness. The interhuman opens out what otherwise remains unopened.

This phenomenon is indeed well known in dialogue between two persons; but I have also sometimes experienced it in a dialogue in which several have taken part.

About Easter of 1914 there met a group consisting of representatives of several European nations for a three-day discussion that was intended to be preliminary to further talks. We wanted to discuss together how the catastrophe, which we all believed was imminent, could be avoided. Without our having agreed beforehand on any sort of modalities for our talk, all the presuppositions of genuine dialogue were fulfilled. From the first hour immediacy reigned between all of us, some of whom had just got to know one another; everyone spoke with an unheard-of unreserve, and clearly not a single one of the participants was in bondage to semblance. In respect of its purpose the meeting must be described as a failure (though even now in my heart it is still not a certainty that it had to be a failure); the irony of the situation was that we arranged the final discussion for the middle of August, and in the course of events the group was soon broken up. Nevertheless, in the time that followed, not one of the participants doubted that he shared in a triumph of the interhuman.

One more point must be noted. Of course it is not necessary for all who are joined in a genuine dialogue actually to speak; those who keep silent can on occasion be especially important. But each must be determined not to withdraw when the course of the conversation makes it proper for him to say what he has to say. No one, of course, can know in advance what it is that he has to say; genuine dialogue cannot be arranged beforehand. It has indeed its basic order in itself from the beginning, but nothing can be determined, the course is of the spirit, and some discover what they have to say only when they catch the call of the spirit.

But it is also a matter of course that all the participants, without exception, must be of such nature that they are capable of satisfying the presuppositions of genuine dialogue and are ready to do so. The genuineness of the dialogue is called in question as soon as even a small number of those present are felt by themselves and by the others as not being expected to take any active part. Such a state of affairs can lead to very serious problems.

I had a friend whom I account one of the most considerable men of our age. He was a master of conversation, and he loved it: his genuineness as a speaker was evident. But once it happened that he was sitting with two friends and with the three wives, and a conversation arose in which by its nature the women were clearly not joining, although their presence in fact had a great influence. The conversation among the men soon developed into a duel between two of them (I was the third). The other "duelist," also a friend of mine, was of a noble nature; he too was a man of true conversation, but given more to objective fairness than to the play of the intellect, and a stranger to any controversy. The friend whom I have called a master of conversation did not speak with his usual composure and strength, but he scintillated, he fought, he triumphed. The dialogue was destroyed.

PROBES

What does it mean to you when Buber says that social contacts don't involve an *existential* relation, but that interhuman contacts do?

How is Buber's discussion of "being" and "seeming" similar to and different from Rogers's discussion of "congruence" (Chapter 9)?

For Buber, does "being" mean total honesty? Is "seeming" lying?

What circumstances make it difficult for you to "be"? How can you best help others to "be" instead of "seem"?

How do Buber's comments about the way we perceive others relate to the discussion of person perception in Chapter 5?

It sounds as if Buber is saying that science *cannot* be used to study human life. Is he saying that? Do you agree with him? Why or why not?

How is Buber's discussion of "imagining the real" related to what Kelly (Chapter 8) and Rogers (Chapter 9) say about empathy?

Which teacher that you've had has functioned most as an "imposer"? Which teacher has been most consistently an "unfolder"?

What does "personal making present" mean to you? What do you need to do in order to perceive someone that way?

Have you ever experienced a silent "dialogue" of the kind Buber mentions here? What happened?

*Ideas are clean. They soar in the serene supernal. I can
take them out and look at them, they fit in books, they
lead me down that narrow way. And in the morning
they are there. Ideas are straight—*

  *But the world is round, and a
  messy mortal is my friend.*

Come walk with me in the mud. . . . .

HUGH PRATHER

INDEX

PT 194
790